LAN Party

Hosting the Ultimate Frag Fest

LAN Party

Hosting the Ultimate Frag Fest

William "The Ferrett" Steinmetz

Wiley Publishing, Inc.

LAN Party
Hosting the Ultimate Frag Fest

Published by
Wiley Publishing, Inc.
10475 Crosspoint Boulevard
Indianapolis, IN 46256
www.wiley.com

Library of Congress Control Number: 2004101792

ISBN: 0-7645-5895-1

Manufactured in the United States of America

10 9 8 7 6 5 4 3 2 1

1B/TR/QT/QU/IN

Published by Wiley Publishing, Inc., Indianapolis, Indiana

Published simultaneously in Canada

WILEY

About the Author

The Ferrett's uncle gave him way too many quarters as a child, inspiring a lifelong love of videogames and gaming in general. The current editor-in-chief and Webmaster of `StarCityGames.com`, the Web's largest and best independent *Magic: the Gathering* site, he has also co-authored *Paint Shop Pro 8 For Dummies* and *Internet: The Complete Reference*. He writes computer book reviews for Amazon.com and Techsoc.com and currently has one of the largest LiveJournal followings around, under his handle "theferrett." He finishes about 15 video games a year, and if he blows a deadline, it's because he's just *one level away from finishing*. He lives in Cleveland and is geeky.

Credits

Vice President and Executive Group Publisher
Richard Swadley

Vice President and Executive Publisher
Bob Ipsen

Vice President and Publisher
Joseph B. Wikert

Executive Editorial Director
Mary Bednarek

Executive Editor
Chris Webb

Editorial Manager
Kathryn A. Malm

Senior Production Editor
Fred Bernardi

Development Editor
Scott Amerman

Production Editor
William A. Barton

Copy Editor
Luann Rouff

Media Development Specialist
Travis Silvers

Permissions Editor
Laura Moss

Cover Designer
Anthony Bunyan

Text Design and Composition
Wiley Composition Services

Project Coordinator
Erin Smith

Graphic and Layout Technicians
Jennifer Heleine
Lynsey Osborn

Quality Control Technician
Brian H. Walls

Proofreading and Indexing Services
Publication Services

Introduction

LAN parties are at an interesting crossroads right now; they're big enough that most gamers *know* about them, but are complex enough that many people are afraid to *hold* one. Sure, your average gearhead has been holding parties for a year now. But thousands of casual gamers still play online and love it but are intimidated by the thought of setting up their own network. They'd love to play *Counter-Strike* with a few pals in their own apartment, but they don't know a thing about IP addressing.

Conversely, some sophisticated gamers think that because you need technical skills to hold a LAN party, technical skills are the *only* thing you need to hold a LAN party. People think that if you know routing protocols, you know how to host a first-class party, but that's not true. A lot of gearheads could wire an excellent network, but have *no* ability to make their party guests feel at home and relaxed.

In other words, one must consider both parts of the equation: the LAN *and* the party. You can have a great LAN and a pretty lousy party; sure, the network has zero ping time, but everyone's crammed into uncomfortable seats, they're hungry, and the power keeps going out.

This book joins both halves, giving you all the information you need to enjoy an excellent LAN *and* a kick-butt party.

On the LAN side, if you're confused about home networks, don't be. Yes, there are a lot of details in networking, but they're fairly simple, and I can walk you through them. Throwing LAN parties is easy. And better yet, I can show you how to hold a LAN party on the cheap.

Want to improve an existing LAN party? Well, I've interviewed 25 die-hard LAN partiers to find out the difference between "okay" and "totally in-your-face gaming *mania*." I've scoured the land for the most enjoyable LAN side events, such as the LAN party drinking game, the Nerf real-life first-person shooter, how to custom-mod a soft DDR pad for arcade-like fun, and whacko tips such as hiring a techno DJ to add an edgy atmosphere to your party.

LAN parties are, as the saying goes, like pizza (or other adult activities, if you get my drift). There's no such thing as *bad* pizza. Likewise, there's no such thing as a bad LAN party. However, the difference between a LAN party where people play and a LAN party where people *can't wait to do it again, can we do it next week, please?* is in giving people exactly what they want.

I'll show you how to hold a party that people will be talking about for *weeks*. All you have to do is buy the book.

Who This Book Is For

Although this book by necessity deals with technology, I look at a LAN party as a method to a goal.

When I'm playing, I don't care about *how* the packets are shuffled around a network; I care about grabbing the rocket launcher without having to worry about some server glitch misregistering my movements. I don't care what a router is, I just want to play some *Star Wars: Galaxies* on the side. And I don't care about the power, except that I want it *on* — all the time.

As such, this book is geared for people who look at a LAN party as an organic whole, and view technology as a means to an end. Yes, about half of this book is devoted to learning networking and troubleshooting, and I do discuss the latest home networking trends, but if you're reading this to find out some obscure TCP/IP hacks, you're looking in the wrong place.

If what you want to do is get your friends onto a *Counter-Strike* server ASAP and start blowing AI terrorists away, then you're at home, my friend. I can help you.

How This Book Is Organized

This book starts with the nascent beginnings of a LAN party, ramps up to the technological underpinnings you need to know in the middle of the book, and finishes up with advanced concepts that you aren't required to know in order to run a LAN party, but are certainly nice techniques to have in your pocket.

Not all chapters are meant for all users; many smaller LAN parties (10 people and under) don't need the level of preparation that larger LAN parties do. In many chapters, I've divided LAN parties into three separate categories:

- You and a few friends (10 people or fewer)
- The neighborhood party (10 to 30 people)
- The megaparty (30 people or more)

I often take some time at the beginning of a chapter to tell you how the topic of the chapter applies to each level of LAN party. In addition, I generally tell you at the beginning of the chapter how relevant the subject matter is to your situation; if a chapter is superfluous to hosting a small (or large) party, I'll be honest so that you don't waste your time.

If you are planning a small LAN party, only two chapters are of questionable use. Chapter 3 deals with choosing an external site for your party when your group of gamers has outgrown your house (but even then, it discusses a common alternative to apartment/home parties that works quite well for smaller parties). Chapter 13 covers what a large party's normal schedule looks like, but smaller parties can play it by ear.

The rest of the chapters are chock-full of useful information for small parties. I only mention the preceding two so you know what you're paying for.

The chapters contain the following material:

Chapter 1, "The Elements of a Good LAN Party," clears up some common misconceptions about LAN parties (unlike what the media frequently says, most players are nice and safe people), and discusses the kinds of social groups that usually hold LAN parties.

Chapter 2, "Setting Your Party's Parameters," discusses all of the questions you need to answer before you plan your LAN party: How many people will be attending? Do you want to allow headphones? How about allowing minors? What about Internet access? Chapter 2 covers everything you need to think about before you hold a LAN party so that when the times arrives, you've considered every aspect and anticipated nearly every need.

Chapter 3, "Choosing a Site for Your Party," describes the pros and cons of the various places you can hold a party, and discusses the best methods for finding and renting a place once you've outgrown your house or apartment.

Chapter 4, "The Complete Preparty Timeline," lists everything you need to do before the party, breaking it down into "A Couple of Months Before," "A Week Before," and "The Night Before."

Chapter 5, "Saving Money on Your LAN Party," is one of the most invaluable chapters for any LAN partier. It discusses the various time-tested ways of saving money on your LAN party: how to leverage your friends for equipment, how to arrange sponsorships to get free stuff (or stuff at substantially reduced prices), and what's involved in going pro and charging admission.

Chapter 6, "Avoiding Power Failures," shows you how to power map a room to avoid blown fuses. I also cover basic electrical safety issues.

Chapter 7, "The Least You Need to Know about Networking," is the big chapter for all of you technophobes. Using many real-life examples, I describe the various parts of home networks and show you how they work. I've tested this chapter on my own wife, who is smart but not a techie, and she said she understood it, so I feel safe saying that it's probably useful for even the most inexperienced users.

Chapter 8, "Networking for Large Groups and the Internet," discusses advanced networking concepts such as firewalls, routers, and Network Address Translation. If you want to add Internet access to your LAN party—and most of you do!—then you should probably scan this as well.

Chapter 9, "Sample LAN Party Layouts," elaborates on a lot of the material found in Chapter 3 and Chapter 7, and shows you what happens when you mix network layouts and real-space layouts. I show you three sample party layouts to give you an idea of how you might want to lay out a party in your home.

Chapter 10, "The Least You Need to Know about Configuring Your Computer," goes over the most common things you need to do at a LAN party with the most commonly used operating systems.

Chapter 11, "Staffing Issues and Common LAN Party Roles," describes the kinds of things that need to be done at almost any LAN party, and talks about who should do them. Even if it's just you doing all the work, understanding what sorts of jobs people do at larger LAN parties can show you how to hold a good small party.

Chapter 12, "Setting up a Dedicated Game Server," shows you how to set up a computer that's exclusively devoted to giving you the best game play.

Chapter 13, "The Complete Day-of-the-Party Timeline," shows you what to expect on the day of a large LAN party, going over it from start to finish to prepare you—and your guests—for the day's events.

Chapter 14, "Legal and Safety Issues," talks about the unthinkable: What if someone gets hurt (or loses some equipment) at your party and decides to sue? There's not much you can do if someone decides to sue you, but you *can* "lawyer-proof" your party, taking a few steps to make it highly unlikely that anyone *would* sue you, and ensuring that any case brought against you would be so weak that any competent lawyer wouldn't take the case. Need I say more?

Chapter 15, "Something Just Went Wrong! Fixing Party Problems," talks about troubleshooting. Whether your network goes down, or someone can't log on, or — God forbid — someone's acting like a big jerk and refuses to leave, I will tell you how to handle each problem.

Chapter 16, "Cool Things to Do at Your LAN Party," is the dessert. You've been going through a bunch of chapters about planning, about setup, about work — here are all the goony things you can do at your LAN party to make it fun for everyone!

And lastly, to help you plan your party, we've included an appendix with two checklists of common tasks that must be finished and questions that must be answered before your LAN party goes online.

What You Need To Use This Book

First of all, it's a very good idea to have played games online at some point. I'm not talking about exclusively online games such as *EverQuest* — I mean a normal game that has an Internet component, such as playing *Medal of Honor* online with other people on an Internet server, or hooking up for a game of *Warcraft III* on Battle.net. Most games these days have built-in connections so you can connect to a remote server right from the menu, but this book will be a lot easier if you understand basic concepts such as ping time and lag.

(Note that this book doesn't provide tutorials on individual games. There are far too many games out there, with new ones arriving all the time, and a book that detailed every game that could be used at a LAN party would be heavy enough to break your legs when you put it on your lap.)

The most important thing you'll need is a computer that's fast enough to run the game you want to play, and a couple of friends to get together with (although if you don't have any pals yet, Chapter 1 offers a couple of suggestions for where to find them). There is other equipment you'll need in order to run a LAN party, of course, but you'll learn just what that equipment is and how to get it in the course of the book.

The Companion Web Site

The companion Web site for this book can be found at www.wiley.com/compbooks/extremetech.

Acknowledgments

First, profuse thanks go to the following:

- Tim Martin of www.spoklan.net in Spokane, Washington
- Ralph Evans of www.hatlan.no-ip.info in Buena Park, California
- Eli Hodapp of www.langasm.com in Aurora, Illinois
- "iNsAnE" Rick at www.asylumlan.com in Evansville, Indiana

Each of these guys consented to 90-minute interviews as I double-checked my facts and probed them extensively about their opinions on how to hold a proper LAN party; they generously gave me answers — many answers — and their enthusiasm for the format is infectious. If you're in their area, stop by and attend one of their parties. They'll do ya right.

Also, many thanks go to Mark Terhune, a fine electrician (and family friend) who discussed electrical wiring with me. If you live in Fairbanks, Alaska, he's the best electrician you'll find (and, yes, wise guy, there are other electricians in Fairbanks).

Shorter interview thanks go to LAN party gurus Rick Cisco (of Digital Demise), Olivier Adam (of LANparty.com), Tim Welford (of Moongames), Pat "the Paradox" (who is not at all like Pat the Bunny and is affiliated with The Hopeless Valley LAN), Kayomani (of Planet Annihilation), Les "Punishing1" (of Detroit LPB), Ryan Masanz (of MultiMayhem), Greg Roland (of PCALAN), Myles Wakeham (of LAN Party Heads), Jeff Lundberg (of MPCon), Paul Tyropolis (of LanPFC), Cory Gibbs (of Lan-I-Am, which wins the "Coolest LAN Party Name" prize hands-down), Michael Fredrickson (of Fusion LAN Gaming), Jared Richards (of Realms of Chaos), Peter Maryan (of Beat2K), Dale White, Austin Gabel, and James Horsfall (of TuxLAN), all of whom I asked for the coolest LAN party ideas they had.

They were all pleasant, and willing to talk to a total stranger asking prying questions. This alone is worth thanks, especially when the stranger is me.

My boss, Peter "Darth Junior" Hoefling, turned out to be an unexpected source of wisdom when I was looking for information on the best ways to rent sites. I had forgotten that even if he doesn't hold LAN parties, he *does* rent halls on a monthly basis to hold large Magic tournaments, and that he has been doing it for years. His advice steered me down the right path, and reminded me that everything can (and should) be negotiated. If you buy Magic cards at all, you darn well better buy 'em from www.starcitygames.com.

Lastly, thanks go to my buds Rich "Moocowrich" Kasper and Axel "Monkeycid" Ljungkvist for double-checking my facts and telling me that, no, nondedicated servers are *not* the work of the devil. However, the finest techno-feedback came courtesy of Jacob, a.k.a. "marleyboy," an upstanding member of www.gamingorgy.com, Winnipeg's dominant LAN party group; Jacob's preliminary read caught a couple of embarrassing goofs in the networking chapters, and set me on the right path. This book would be much worse without his feedback. All three of them have accounts on LiveJournal, so if you're reading LJ, you could do worse than to add 'em to your friends list.

Of course, you just don't get away with finishing a book without thanking your wife. Hey, Gini? I love you. A lot. Thanks for letting me be obsessed. By the way, Gini would like you all to know that she took some of the photos in this book, and so is now an officially published photographer—a fact that amuses her to no end.

Contents at a Glance

Contents

The Elements of a Good LAN Party

You know the worst part about gibbing someone with a rocket launcher when you're playing *Quake III* online?

You can't see the look on the other person's face.

Oh sure, you've racked up your score, but you're still alone in your room. There's the explosion onscreen, and the little line that says "Frobozz is nuked." But look away from the screen and ignore your surround-sound speakers, and you will hear no cheers of congratulations for taking down the best player on the server. You won't see the grin on your opponent's face as he or she vows a bloody revenge.

And when you finally disconnect, there you are at the computer. Alone.

Maybe you can go to the kitchen and eat cold pizza by yourself.

But you can change that! What if I told you that you could have a bunch of people in your house, laughing and screaming whenever you pulled off some insane multiperson kill? What if people cheered whenever you pulled victory out of the jaws of defeat, and sat behind you to give you play advice when you'd lost for the eighth time in a row and didn't know why you were losing? What if when you went to the kitchen, two players were debating the best tactics to use in *Warcraft III*, and asked you what you thought?

You can have all that. You can turn that solitary, lonely experience into a raucously fun time.

There are a lot of good technical reasons to hold LAN parties, not the least of which is insanely low ping times that can't be matched. But the *real* fun of LAN parties is that they are social events where like-minded gamers get together to have a good time in that scary world called *real life*. In a LAN party, all the computers are in the same house, so all of your opponents are within walking distance. And when you're tired of blowing people to shreds, you can go share a Mountain Dew and compare video cards with someone else who really cares about vertex shading.

The accent's on the *party*, not the LAN.

Cross-Reference If you are new enough to online computer gaming that you don't know what a *ping time* is, you will need to read Chapter 7, "The Least You Need to Know about Networking" (which explains networks and ping time).

LAN Party Basics and Some Common Misconceptions

A LAN is a small network in which all of the computers are connected directly to each other. Because your computer doesn't have to send information to a central server that's miles away, the response times are *amazing*. You will be playing with practically no lag. Say goodbye to the days of missing someone you had dead in your sights just because the server couldn't keep up with you!

You can play pretty much any game at a LAN party that you could online (except for massively multiplayer online role-playing games such as *EverQuest* and *Star Wars: Galaxies*, but even with these you can log on and play if the party has an Internet connection). That's a big list: *Counterstrike*, *Warcraft III*, *Battlefield 1942*, every flavor of *Quake*, every flavor of *Unreal Tournament*, *Return to Castle Wolfenstein*, *Medal of Honor*, *Command and Conquer*, every flavor of *Diablo*, the yet-to-be-released-as-I-write-this *Doom III* and *Half-Life 2*, and pretty much every other game with online support.

However, many misconceptions floating around make people loathe to hold LAN parties. But none of them should stop you from holding one. The most common untruths are shown in the following sidebar.

Let's examine each one of these misconceptions in detail.

Not knowing enough about computers to hold a LAN party

Thinking that you need to be a computer whiz to hold a LAN party is nonsense! Networking companies have been working overtime to make networking PCs as painless as possible. Setting up many LAN parties involves little more than running cables from your computer to a broadband router and booting up.

Common Misconceptions about LAN Parties

- I don't know enough about computers to hold a LAN party.
- If I know how to set up a LAN, I know how to hold a LAN party.
- LAN parties attract dangerous, Columbine-style antisocial people.
- I'll be embarrassed at a LAN party 'cause I don't know how to play the games well.

It's true that a LAN party involves *some* technical know-how; otherwise, I wouldn't have had to write a book on it. But I have written this book so that it contains the *absolute minimum* amount of information that you need to know in order to hold a LAN party. I figure that if you know how to set up a LAN, you're going to skip the technical stuff anyway—and if you don't know, then why swamp you with needless details?

A LAN party at its core is pretty much plugging wires. You plug one end into your network card and the other into a hub or switch. If you can plug things in, you can run a LAN party.

Knowing how to set up a LAN is the same as knowing how to hold a LAN party

Knowing how to set up a LAN is not quite the same thing as knowing how to hold a LAN party. There are all sorts of other details involved, from setting ground rules to making sure you don't blow the power when everyone boots up. LAN parties involve people, and in the course of this book I have interviewed no less than 10 experienced LAN hosts in order to distill their collective wisdom.

The technical stuff is the glue that holds everyone together, but it's not the party in and of itself. When someone is crammed into a corner that you thought was big enough to hold him, is going deaf because the player next to him likes to play loudly and you didn't tell people to bring headphones, and is starving because nobody wants to go in on a pizza—well, suffice it to say that your knowledge of routing protocols is *not* going to ensure a good time.

LAN parties attract dangerous, Columbine-style antisocial people

You'd be surprised how often this misconception comes up, even among die-hard gamers.

The shadow of the Internet troll and incoherent AOL l33tsp34k3rz looms large over many potential LAN parties. People think, "Hey, if I invite these people into my house (or my game), I'll be stuck with a bunch of fat, smelly guys who can't make eye contact and may be dangerous. *I'm* fine, but I don't know about the other *Counterstrike* players."

But the interesting thing is this: In the course of interviewing people for this book, the one thing that I heard over and over again was, "Tell everyone how wonderful these get-togethers are. Tell them how LAN parties bring people together, inspire friendships, and make entire social circles come alive." Almost every person I talked to wanted the world to know that LAN parties are just good, clean fun between good friends.

Some gamers are shy, sure—but LAN parties bring out the best in people. You meet new people who share your interests. Most of them are normal people, just like you and me.

Alas, people frequently confuse the violence simulated in the game with what happens in real life. Capping someone in *UT* does not equate with having an urge to kill real people. The skillsets are two entirely different things; clicking a mouse and keeping a three-pound gun steady through a 30-pound recoil have nothing in common.

Most people who play computer games are friendly, wonderful people just like you. Keep that in mind.

FIGURE 1-1: Is this man dangerous?

I'd be embarrassed at a LAN party because I don't play the games well

You cannot possibly be worse at playing than I am. I am a *terrible* player.

And yet I have a good time.

Most LAN party participants understand. There is trash-talking, of course, and there are some places where people go for blood. But most LAN parties have a few top-tier players who dominate, a few who are pathetic, and the majority somewhere in the middle.

You can expect to take some good-natured ribbing, but that's par for the course. And if you really want to improve your skills, what better way is there than to have the best player at the party watching over your shoulder and giving you suggestions?

What You Need to Hold a LAN Party

Like I said, LAN parties are pretty easy to throw together (well, at least the smaller ones are). But you need to possess certain things to throw one. Following are the most important elements:

- Friends
- Networking hardware
- A place to play with enough tables
- Prep time
- Technical know-how
- Time and effort

Let's check out each of these.

Friends

Having friends to play with is critical. Holding a one-person LAN party is distinctly unsatisfying.

My editor tells me that I must have more than a one-paragraph entry here, so let me elaborate. Usually, if you're looking to hold a LAN party, it's for one of three reasons:

- You haven't held (or attended) a LAN party, but you know enough gamers in town that you decide it's a good idea to play together, as opposed to logging onto online servers via the Internet. Usually, it's an incremental thing, glommed together from various sources — you know one local guy who plays *CounterStrike*, and he knows two local guys, and one of them wants to bring a friend.

- You usually don't know all of these people well when you agree to hold the LAN party. Sometimes it's *scary* having strangers to your house. ("What if they don't like me?" "What if they're creepy?")

  The good news is that LAN parties are usually good bonding experiences. You get to know people at LAN parties, strange as it sounds, and you come away with a solid acquaintanceship that can easily deepen into friendship. And LAN parties are like potato chips; hardly anyone ever wants to play at just one. Chances are good that assuming you've read this book and done your prep work, you'll be asked to hold one again.

- You've attended LAN parties in the area before, but for whatever reason (the organizer moved away, you no longer work at that computer lab), the party died. This makes it a lot easier, as you have an idea of how LAN parties work, and you can just shoot off a couple of e-mails to the old gang and re-ignite the party.

  In this case, this book is actually more important than you might think; yes, you may know how to hook up a small network, but LAN parties are organic and require more people-handling than you dreamed. If you want your LAN party to go well (and to have a longer half-life than the old LAN parties you used to attend), then you definitely want to check out the information in this book.

If you had regular LAN parties in the past but moved to an area where there are none now, first do a search on www.lanparty.com and www.bluesnews.com to make sure there are none in your area. LAN parties are a lot easier to attend than to host!

However, if nothing is available locally, you might want to use the bulletin boards on these sites (as well as any local user groups or gaming stores) to see if you can gather a group of new people to your lair to play a little face-to-face fragging.

In general, LAN parties are a good way to make new friends if you're looking for them — assuming, of course, that you're even moderately socially adept. (If you never shower and hold every conversation at a hundred decibels, you can get people over to your house, but they probably won't stay for espresso afterwards.) With very little effort, you can usually spin a LAN party into other social events, like attending the premiere of geek-themed movies or test-driving new games the day they come out. ("Dude! *Half-Life 2* is out! Wanna come over and see how it plays? These graphics are *awesome!*")

That's the beauty of LAN parties. They start with hardware, but they always end with people.

Networking hardware (and friends)

The bad news is that, yes, you will need equipment in order to network PCs together — stuff such as switches, network cables, and extension cords.

You can find out what equipment you'll need and what each of these things is in Chapter 7, "The Least You Need to Know about Networking."

The good news is that if you have friends who game, one of them is likely to have at least some of the equipment you'll need. If you have multiple friends, chances are excellent that all of them put together will have all of the equipment you need.

I'll repeat it again later in Chapter 5, "Saving Money on Your LAN Party," but memorize the LAN Party Host's Creed now.

A place to play with enough tables

For most people, the place to hold the LAN party is going to be their house. But keep in mind that if your party becomes popular, eventually you'll have to move the party out of the house to an external location such as a cybercafe, a church, or a VA hall.

The LAN Party Host's Creed

Beg before you buy.

Also, each computer takes up about a square yard of space — and people hate playing on the floor. You'll need to make sure that you have enough sturdy tables to support all this hardware.

Cross-Reference For the ins and outs of location, see Chapter 3, "Choosing a Site for Your Party."

Prep time

The key to a good LAN party is preparation. It might be okay for small parties of six or less to just show up and start fraggin'. But even then, there are issues you might miss, such as seating, power supply issues, and people breaking house rules that you really didn't think of as house rules. (Most rules are created because some people do things that really irritate everyone else at the party, and defend themselves by saying, "Well, nobody said anything to *me* about it!" You'd be surprised how many unofficial house rules you already have — you just don't think of them as "rules" because nobody's broken them. Yet.)

A good LAN party host spends some time thinking about things in advance. It saves valuable time later.

Cross-Reference For more on the ground rules for planning, see Chapter 4, "The Complete Preparty Timeline." House rules are covered in Chapter 2, "Setting Your Party's Parameters."

Some technical know-how

You don't need to be Bill Gates or John Romero to know how to set up a network, but you should at least have an understanding of basic networking principles in case anything goes wrong. LAN parties won't usually come to a crashing halt if something is misconfigured, but you do need to be able to troubleshoot to help individual people out.

Cross-Reference A baseline technical understanding can be gleaned in Chapter 7, "The Least You Need to Know about Networking." Troubleshooting methodologies are covered in Chapter 15, "Something Just Went Wrong! Fixing Party Problems."

Time and effort

LAN parties are very rewarding, but they can be exhausting, too. If you're the host, you'll still get your frag-time in — just not as much as some of the other players. On the other hand, you get to be the leader of a new community, and it's surprising how grateful people can be when you offer to host. And the feeling of satisfaction you get when your weekend-long LAN party comes to a close?

Priceless.

Summary

LAN parties are a lot of fun, and they're really for everyone who enjoys playing online games of any sort. Yeah, you can play by yourself, but having a bunch of like-minded addicts around multiplies the entertainment.

The next chapter discusses a very important topic: What kind of party do you want to have? There are many variants on LAN parties and a lot of things to consider, and the next chapter should help you narrow down your options.

Setting Your Party's Parameters

Going through a big checklist before you host a LAN party might seem like a pain, particularly if you're just looking to invite a few friends over for the afternoon. Why should you ask so many questions about the number of participants, the setup, the food, and all that jazz?

You need to consider these questions each time for the following two main reasons:

➤ They come up at every LAN party, from a three-person *Diablo II* session to a thousand-person professional event.

➤ They affect how much fun everyone has.

Some questions are more critical than others, of course; ordering a pizza if you didn't plan a dinner break is no problem, but an extra four people showing up when you only have a six-port hub to work with is game-breaking. Answering these questions before the party starts enables you to smooth out issues in advance and prevents last-minute problems from marring the fun you're going to have.

Moreover, the best part is that it doesn't take that long. At the end of this chapter, I'll give you a checklist. Assuming you've read the relevant sections in this book (and I'll tell you which sections are critical), it'll take you no more than 20 minutes to figure out exactly what kind of LAN party you're going to have.

So let's get this party started!

The Biggest Question: How Many People?

"How many people will be at the LAN party?" is the question that drives every other question you'll need to answer. More people means more planning, more networking equipment, and more space.

LAN parties can generally be broken down into three categories, each with its own special planning needs:

- You and a few friends (10 people or fewer).
- The neighborhood party (10 to 30 people).
- The megaparty (30 people or more).

Note   Megaparties can scale to really impressive heights—more than 1,500 people attend QuakeCon every year. However, 30 people is about the breaking point when an informal LAN party turns into a professional large-scale party.

But before you can resolve *that* issue, you need to ask yourself an even more critical question: Who gets invited, and how?

Is this party open, closed, or capped?

It's actually more important to figure out how many people are showing up at a small LAN party than it is for a large one. The reasoning is that smaller parties usually don't have surplus networking hardware available; when all you have is an eight-port switch, all you can have are eight players.

As such, laying down the ground rules for who's invited is important. There are three approaches to LAN party invitations: *open, closed,* and *capped.* There are mixes and half-breeds of these three approaches, but most LAN parties fall into these basic categories.

The open party

An *open party* means that you make room for anyone who shows up. This is the default mode for a lot of casual parties, as in, "Hey, my pal Skullscorch wants to play tomorrow, is that okay?"

The advantages of an open party are that it's a lot friendlier ("Sure she can play! The more, the merrier!") and your parties can become very popular very quickly. After all, if Skullscorch has a good time, she's going to invite her pals along to your next party—and they'll tell two friends, and they'll tell two friends, and so on.

The disadvantages are that unless you're careful, you can wind up with more people than you have space, power, or networking hardware for. Also, if you're *too* casual, open invitations lead to people showing up at the last minute—and then you'll be holding everyone up while you try to find the space to cram in two more people.

The closed party

A *closed party* means that it's invitation-only; nobody shows up without your say-so, and everyone knows it. Anyone who wants to bring a friend along has to ask you first. The advantage of this type of party is that it's very easy to plan for; after all, you're in total control!

The disadvantage is that it's hard to host a closed party without looking like a total jerk. If Skullscorch wants to show up and you tell her no, chances are good she's going to think you're some sort of LAN party fascist. Also, with a closed party, the growth is a lot slower—which may actually be an advantage if you want a friends-only club.

Getting Nervous Nellies to Attend Your Capped Party

If you're worried about stifling attendance at a capped LAN party, let people know what your average attendance is. If you have a 32-player cap but only 20 people normally show up, *say so*. It's a good way of telling potential participants that 32 players is a "just in case" figure.

The capped party

A *capped party* is a common compromise between open and closed parties, and is usually used when you have a set limit of slots available thanks to a fixed amount of networking hardware. In a capped party, anyone can show, but only a limited number of slots are available; if you tell everyone in advance that you have space for eight people, the ninth person to show up is out of luck. The advantage is that it's hard to go wrong; you lay out your networking hardware in advance, and just slot people in as they arrive.

The disadvantages are almost all on the players' side; it's infuriating to haul your computer all the way across town, only to find that you arrived 10 minutes too late. As a result, capped parties can sometimes result in lower attendance as people figure, "Why chance it?"

So what's the best solution?

For most parties, capping it is the way to go. Map out your space and see how many people you can hold, and then set that as your limit. In order to map out your space, you'll need to consider your power supply (as described in Chapter 6, "Avoiding Power Failures"), how much physical space you have, and how many hubs, switches, and cables you have available.

Cross-Reference If you want more networking equipment, go to Chapter 5, "Saving Money on Your LAN Party," where you can find out about the best and cheapest method for getting free hubs and switches; if you don't even know what networking equipment *is*, flip ahead to Chapter 7, "The Least You Need to Know about Networking," where I'll give you the rundown.

A cap enables you to have a moderate amount of growth, but it prevents the growing pains that often ensue when popular parties become overloaded. If you wind up turning people away because you don't have enough slots, get more switches for the next time.

The three types of parties

The number of people who will show up at your party drastically affects how you have to plan for it—your location, your hardware, the amount of planning you have to do. Keep in mind that each party has a different feel, depending on the mix of people, and that feel becomes more impersonal as you add more people.

Reserving Seats

Capped parties can sometimes be a hassle at smaller parties when strangers show up before your friends do, locking your best friend out of a seat. (Okay, they're not strangers *per se* — they're friends of your other friends — but you don't know them that well.) If you're worried about a horde of friends-of-a-friend swarming your scene, a good compromise is to reserve seats in advance. That way, you can make sure that your pal is always number 1 on the list.

Be warned, however, that players are notoriously flighty when it comes to reservations; everyone says that they'll show up, but you'd be surprised how many people will have forgotten all about the event come the big day. If you're holding a for-profit event for which getting your entry fee is important, Chapter 13, "The Complete Day-of-the-Party Timeline," describes the tricks of converting promises into cold hard cash.

You and a few friends (10 people or fewer)

Good news! The small party of you and a few friends is the easiest, lowest-hassle sort of party, and it can be a blast. You need minimal networking equipment and minimal planning; with six people or fewer, all you need is a lot of cable and a switch to plug everyone into, and you're good to go.

However, there is one drawback to this: you're most likely playing in someone's house, and as such you have to do some pre-planning to clear a space among the usual nerdy household clutter (like piles of books and CDs) for the computers. Also, you'll need to map your power circuits to ensure that you don't overload them and blow a fuse; unlike dedicated venues, your electrical outlets will be supporting your DVD players, your PS2s, and your fridge in addition to your computers.

For this size party, your most important issue is choosing the game to play.

The neighborhood party (10 to 30 people)

The neighborhood party is a mid-level party. Unless you have a really big house or a customized garage, you're going to need an external site. Add the cost of rental onto the increasing amount of networking hardware and planning you're putting in, and your biggest issue becomes how to minimize the expenses. Many neighborhood parties charge admission in order to defray costs.

Cross-Reference Fortunately, this book has an entire chapter devoted to reducing the strain on your wallet; for details, check out Chapter 5, "Saving Money on Your LAN Party."

Furthermore, this is where you have to start planning your event professionally, even if it's just for your friends. With a smaller party, you can tell everyone just to plug in wherever — but when you have 15 people, you pretty much *have* to do the tedious advance work of mapping out tables, balancing power supplies, and figuring out where cables go. Otherwise, you'll have blown fuses, people tripping over wires, and fights over space.

The Best Advice: Start Small

When I interviewed LAN party hosts across America, I heard the same two words repeatedly:

Start small.

Build your knowledge incrementally. If you start with a four-person LAN party, it's relatively easy to learn things as you go, and there's little pressure to get it right. But many people figure, "What the hell! I want all of my friends there!" and invite 25 people to their first fragfest, at which they promise Internet access, five different game servers, a DHCP server, dial-in servers, and a nanotechnology machine that serves up free diamonds and strippers to anyone who asks.

The cardinal rule of LAN parties is that *things will go wrong*. A good rule of thumb is to try one new thing per LAN party. Start off by just holding a LAN party (that's a new thing by itself if you haven't done it before), then add another switch to hold additional players at your next party, then add global Internet access, and so on. That way, if the one new thing doesn't work out, it's not a huge failure.

Taking on too much can mean the collapse of your entire party. Baby steps, my friend; take baby steps.

If you're going pro, you also have to contend with the various issues that come with dealing with strangers; and in particular, the legal issues that arise when teenagers attend.

For this size party, your most important issue is not losing your shirt.

The megaparty (30 people or more)

At this point, you're almost certainly expanding because your party's so popular that you just can't stop the love. You're probably an experienced network admin by now, and your biggest challenges revolve around adding new things to keep it fresh. Internet access? Damn straight. New games? Yep. Ladder tournaments and crazy case-modding contests? Yep.

You may also have to expand outward into larger venues to hold you, which means that you're going to spend a lot of time hunting down the right place, negotiating prices, and planning where everything goes.

At this point, you're almost certainly investing enough time and effort into this game that you've gone pro. As such, your most important issues are most likely making money (which is why keeping it fresh is important — repeat customers are your most important asset) and reducing your workload.

Cross-Reference If you're trying to build a megaparty from nothing other than the enthusiasm you hear from other people when you talk about holding a LAN party, first look at the sidebar entitled "The Best Advice: Start Small," earlier in this chapter. Then see Chapter 5, on lowering expenses. In particular, read the section that discusses how easy it is to go broke hosting these events, and how most larger parties often have a lot of people promising to attend, but few people actually showing up.

If the information about starting small hasn't convinced you not to shoot for the moon your first time out, go ahead. I can't stop you. While you're at it, why don't you play Russian roulette and film your own *Jackass* videos?

Other Questions You Must Answer

Because almost none of the issues discussed in the following paragraphs will prevent a LAN party from happening, the temptation may be strong to ignore them and just forge ahead. After all, there's always the chance that everyone wants the same things from a LAN party that you do.

But all of these assumptions have one thing in common: *If they're wrong, it can seriously limit everyone's fun.*

It's not a backbreaker to have, say, speakers as opposed to headphones (unless it shorts out your power). But when you're all sitting in the same room, with most of you turning your volume to 11 in an attempt to be heard over Joe Subwoofer in the corner, feeling your eardrums vibrate like a flag whipping in the wind, chances are good you're not enjoying yourself as much as you could be.

So answer the questions. Get everyone on the same page.

This approach is safer.

Hardcore or casual?

People usually approach gaming in one of two distinct ways:

- **It's just entertainment.** If you have to put as much effort into your hobby as you do at your job, then it's no fun. The whole point of getting together for a LAN party is to goof around and blow off steam.

- **It's about the win.** You should approach games the way you approach life: to break the system. Hobbies are only entertaining when you throw yourself into them full tilt, honing your skills to the max, and treating it as seriously as you would any other challenge.

Needless to say, there can be conflict between the hardcore players and the casual ones.

Note

This applies only to smaller parties, of course. As one friend said on reviewing this book, "Can you imagine walking into QuakeCon, one of the world's largest LAN parties, and seeing a sign that says, 'No Railgun Spawn Camping'?"

The good news is that at most LAN parties, you're inviting your friends, and you know what *they're* like. Most likely, you share the same attitude about computer games. The conflict comes when some newbie — the proverbial "friend of a friend" — is invited in and begins kicking butt or whining because everyone's using cheesy tactics.

The two groups can co-exist, of course, but you have to set some very clear guidelines in order to harmonize them.

Decide what tactics are cheesy

What consitutes "cheesy" varies from game to game. But it helps to think hard about what game maneuvers you consider to be just *too* easy to pull off—the ones that generate cheap wins. Do you hate snipers? Does the "early rush" tactic ruin your day? Is there some ridiculously overpowered weapon that's off-limits?

The easiest solution for all of these is to play only on game maps that discourage the "good" tactics. If you hate snipers, pick a map that has no sniper's nests. (Or, better yet, pick a map that has precisely *one* sniper's nest, and everyone knows where it is.) If you despise the BFG 3000 and think it's an overpowered cannon of destruction, use a map that doesn't have it.

If you can't find an appropriate map, or if the game itself has a strategy that's too optimal, declare it off-limits beforehand. Put it on your Web site and fliers, and in the e-mail invitations.

After you've outlined what tactics are no-gos, you'll then have to handle two sorts of people, and you need to do so firmly:

- **Hardcore:** "Why should I handicap myself by not playing with something that wins?" *Answer:* "That's just the way this party is; we're pretty casual here. If you can't deal with it, here's the door."
- **Casual:** "That tactic's so cheesy!" *Answer:* "Sorry, friend, nobody else here has a problem with what he's doing. You're going to have to adjust."

Another solution that can work at larger parties is to have separate servers—one for the hardcore crowd and one for the casual crowd. Users can connect to either, of course, but the casual players will know that the "M4XX0R H4XX0R" server is where anything goes. (In some cases, they may go there *because* they appreciate the challenge.)

Discovering a Cheesy Tactic on the Spot

Sometimes, the newbie will surprise everyone with an approach that nobody else considered and dominate the field with it. That's normal. Generally, within an hour or so, people will either assimilate the tactic into their own arsenal or come up with a foil for it.

But what happens if three hours pass and nobody's learned how to defend themselves?

The trick is to appeal to the ego. Walk up to the newbie and say quietly, "Dude, you've dominated us all for the past three hours. We acknowledge that this works really well. Will you teach us how to do it, and then cut it out for a while so we can have fun? Just assume you would have kicked our butt for the rest of the day."

Most gamers love to show off, especially when you're acknowledging their mad skills, and they'll cheerfully acquiesce. If they refuse to stop despite kind requests, then they're jerks and you shouldn't feel too bad about giving 'em the ol' +b.

The only problem with this scenario is that sometimes the hardcore players will stop by the casual servers just to pick on the fishies. Generally, you can get them back where they need to be by rampant humiliation.

Prize offers

To bring out the strongest competitiveness in people, you have the option of offering big prizes to the winner. A goofy prize like a block of cheese is fine, but putting a video card up for grabs will make people play at their top level, no matter what you do.

For more on the option of offering prizes, check out the discussion in Chapter 5, "Saving Money on Your LAN Party."

If you don't like harsh competition, don't offer prizes. If you do, there's no better way to get some.

Watch the trash talking

A certain level of smack talk is par for the course. Some may frown when you scream "PER-FECT KILL! BOOYAH!" after a perfectly placed bazooka shot, but I smile upon you beatifi-cally. Part of the fun of LAN parties is doing the little monkey dance right where your freshly gibbed opponent can see you.

But sometimes the trash talk turns dark and veins start throbbing in people's necks and fore-heads. That's when you need to invoke the default rule of any LAN party:

Trash talking's fine until someone's feelings are hurt.

It doesn't matter how sensitive someone is; if that person is upset by someone's comments, the other person has to either dial it down or cut it out. (Later, you may want to consider whether you want to invite Mister or Ms. Sensitive to your *next* party, but while that person is there, you respect his or her emotions.)

The Three Types of Dangerous Smack Talk

Three categories of smack talk tend to draw blood on a regular basis, and it's in your best inter-est to pay attention to these conversations (and calm these people down) before their language crosses the line.

- **The Losing Streak.** Whether it's Joe Casual getting huffy because he's not as good as some-one who spends 30 hours a week playing *Doom III*, or Frederica Hardcore getting vexed because she's on an 0–7 losing streak to her number-one rival, the trash talk usually starts to draw blood when someone's a little too confident in his or her winnings.

Therefore, watch what the leader in the standings says, particularly if they're on a winning streak. It doesn't matter if they're saying the exact same things they said an hour ago; now that they're winning, even an innocent comment can set someone off.

- **The Strategy.** Some people talk smack as a way of rattling their opponents, spicing up their triumphal shouts with personal insults that get the blood boiling. These folks tend to come out of the woodwork when you take the gloves off and go for all-out competition.

  You have to tell these folks that it's completely unacceptable to smack talk just to get people angry. You'll probably have to tell them more than once; they usually stop for a while after a good talking-to, but revert to old habits the next time they're losing.

- **The Insecurity Complex.** Alternatively, a mediocre-to-bad player can smack talk the entire room to make up for his or her lack of skills. We call people like that "big whopping jerks" if they're upsetting everyone else — and if they won't shut up, we advise you to boot 'em as soon as possible.

What games will you be playing?

Most people don't want to play the same game all day. Unless you're really die-hard, people like to play another game, even if it's for a short while — think of it as the sherbet that cleanses the palate between courses.

Therefore, figure out what games you'll have available, and tell people in advance so they can bring their CDs and other items. Nothing's worse than showing up and finding out that you're the only one who won't be playing *Diablo II*.

Mix Up the Genres!

Wow. You mean we can play both *CounterStrike* and *Quake III, and Unreal Tournament 2003* to boot? Be still, my beating heart!

When I say "switch games," I mean find different *kinds* of games. Mix up real-time strategy games with first-person shooters. If the biggest difference is the bitmapping on your gun, you've failed.

It's also a good idea to have some completely brainless, noncompetitive games hanging around, generally console games such as *Grand Theft Auto III*, *Mario Party*, and *Dance Dance Revolution*. All of that fragging is hard work, and taking a break to go play something fun can shake up the ol' neurons!

Also, even if you're playing the same game, you'll want to mix up the formats to keep some variety. Following are some of the more common formats — and forgive me if this is old hat to you:

- **Deathmatch.** Hello? You bought this book and you don't understand the free-for-all? /me no understand.

- **Single-Elimination Deathmatch.** Each person gets one life, and everyone heads into the arena of your choice. The last person standing wins. These are usually fast and brutal, and best played on maps that don't feature overwhelmingly powerful weapons such as rocket launchers or BFGs.

- **Capture the Flag.** A team game, and one of the most popular. Each team has a base at which one or more flags reside; your job is to infiltrate the other team's headquarters for a set period of time, or to bring their flag back to your base. This requires tight cooperation between players, and is a supreme test of skill and group tactics.

  Many games, such as *Counterstrike* and *Battlefield 1942*, have very elaborate Capture the Flag-style variants whereby you can choose from a variety of support roles, such as medic, mechanic, and sniper.

- **Cooperative Play.** Instead of going head-to-head, why not try teaming up against the AI? In cooperative play, you play the single-player game, but with more people on your side. This isn't very popular, as no artificial intelligence is as smart as a human being, but it can be a fun way to crack open a brand-new game.

  Alternatively, many map designers *love* cooperative play maps. Continually designing maps for a person can be stifling; sometimes, it's great to let loose and create overwhelmingly tough situations in which only tight squadrons of teammates working together can survive.

- **Alternate-Win Matches.** Generally, winning these matches involves pulling off some ridiculously difficult thing repeatedly — the player with the most head shots wins, for example, or the player who gets the most frags with the twitchiest weapon. These are great for clearing the palate after some long, drawn-out match.

- **Severe Handicapping.** Every player gets the same weapon, and it's the sucky "knife"-style, no-range weapon that most first-person shooters come with. Needless to say, the map doesn't have anything better than a knife on it (unless you're very cruel and put a single rocket launcher in a very hard-to-reach location.).

- **Psychotic Locales.** Places with low (or no) gravity, small islands of turf amidst lava pits, all-warren mazes in which sniper rifles are useless, a big football field filled with rocket launchers — the possibilities are endless for single-time "fun" maps that become boring quickly but are a great change of pace in the middle of a long day.

- **Ladder Tournaments.** Each person gets one life and goes head-to-head with someone else. The winner advances. The loser is out of the tournament. Eventually, two of the best players face off, and the last person standing wins. These are usually fast and brutal.

  In one variant of the preceding, each person is allowed to play one timed game, and the person who racks up the most frags before the timer runs out advances. In either case, you match people up according to a chart that looks like the one shown in Figure 2-1 — hence, the "Ladder" tournament:

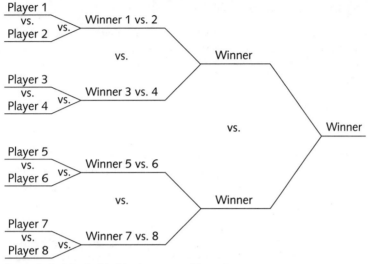

FIGURE 2-1: A typical ladder tournament layout

Several other variants are possible, many of which are amusing for a game or two. Be sure to have one or two planned in order to keep people from getting bored; however, don't go Richard Simmons-style spastic, either, switching games every half an hour. Changing pace every two or three hours is about right.

Do you want speakers? (Hint: No!)

Speakers have two major drawbacks:

- **They turn the room into a cacophony.** I don't care how well-behaved your guests are, the phenomenon of speaker creep is unavoidable: One person can't hear something in the game, so they turn their speaker up *just* a notch. Then the next person does it. Pretty soon, the entire room is blaring like a bunch of tortured parrots, everyone cranked to the max.

  You yell at them all to turn it down. They do. An hour later, everyone's crept back up to 10 again.

- **They use more power.** Tiny speakers are generally harmless, but nobody ever wants the itty-bitty speakers. No, they want their massive, television-sized subwoofers so they can hear the windows shake when someone sets up the bomb. Speakers make it more diffi-cult to plan power needs — and as you'll examine in Chapter 6, you need to consider your power requirements in order to avoid sudden blackouts. Meanwhile, headphones use absolutely no detectable power at all.

Keep in mind that large speakers may also take up more room than you've allotted. Unless you have a circumstance for which you want everyone to have speakers (for example, when one of your sponsors is an earplug manufacturer), I advise you to just check the "no" column and move on.

Do you want Internet access?

For many die-hard fans, Internet access is a constitutionally mandated right; were he alive today, Thomas Jefferson would demand life, liberty, happiness, and a hot ADSL connection. But adding World Wide Web access to your LAN party comes with advantages and drawbacks. Let's examine each in turn.

The pros of Internet access

Let's go over the good stuff first:

- **People expect it.** If you're holding a for-profit party, many guests will be surprised if you *don't* have it. If you're holding a small party, your party may have too few players to have fun playing team-based games like *Counterstrike*; many games and game formats assume that you will have eight players or more. You may need an outside connection for some games to achieve critical mass.

Note

Many groups consider Internet access a must-have for all LAN parties, and will be surprised when I suggest that a "dark" LAN party is a valid option. But if you can't imagine a fragfest without an IRC chat, check out the negatives; there is a case to be made for not allowing net access.

- **It enables better downtime.** Internet access gives your guests more options; if they don't want to play the DDR machine in the corner and everyone else is into the latest fragfest, they can hop online and AIM it up, or even work on buffing their level 37 Druid on *Everquest*. People are a lot happier when they have other stuff to do.

- **Easier patch access/easier map access.** You don't have to have a file server if you have the Internet; people can get the latest 1.x patch from the official Web site, as opposed to you having it locally. (It'll take a lot longer than a local server, and it may temporarily choke your Internet bandwidth, but it's still less work for you.)

- **It makes for better PR.** If people have Internet access, chances are good they'll be chatting to other people at some point, or posting to their favorite online forum. Internet access helps to get the word out in a very dynamic way that closed parties just can't match.

- **Better technical support.** Have you ever tried to troubleshoot faulty software without being able to download patches or get online tech support? If you haven't, I'll sum up in two words: *It bites.*

The drawbacks of Internet access

Having Internet access sounds pretty good, doesn't it? Well, consider these factors:

- **It can be a pain to set up.** Often, setting up is as simple as plugging a router into an external Internet connection. But other times (and particularly if the next bulleted point is an issue), getting your Network Address Translation software working properly can cause you to tear your hair out.

- **People will download illegal software.** Many people use LAN parties as an excuse to download copyrighted files, and groups such as the RIAA and the MPAA are suing large numbers of people for downloading music and movies. You can be sued if someone downloads the latest *Matrix* movie on your watch.

  Also, the ISPs are the first to be sued if someone breaks a law. Many ISPs have started watching the network traffic at LAN parties to see whether anyone is downloading illegal files, and they may well shut you down mid-party if someone's breaking the law.

For a more complete discussion of warez and your legal liabilities, check out Chapter 14, "Legal and Safety Issues."

- **People will overload the connection.** *Oh,* someone thinks, *I have an Internet connection! Why don't I download all eight seasons of the X-Files while I'm here?* The next thing you know, file sharing and huge downloads will eat up every last kilobyte of the shared bandwidth. You *can* block the appropriate ports, if you need to (as outlined in Chapter 8), but that leads to more technical setup issues.

- **It provides greater security issues.** If someone downloads a virus, everyone else will have it within seconds. Furthermore, people who know about your party and are maliciously inclined now have an access point to hack in.

- **It can be harmful to minors.** Okay, I know *you* don't care if Little Jimmy Peterson, age 12, decides to go browsing around SplatteredBust.com. But Jimmy's mom will. And if she discovers that her little guy was downloading porn on your watch, you could get in serious trouble. We're talking "corruption of a minor" lawsuit-style trouble, if she's particularly zealous. Unless you're willing to monitor content in some manner, open Internet access is a huge liability issue hanging over your head.

- **It can be disruptive.** Particularly if people are downloading porn — and people do — you can wind up with clusters of people grouped around someone's screen, watching the latest movie trailer. Sometimes it takes a concerted effort to get people back to, well, *gaming.*

Of all the ominous preceding factors, the technical setup and liability issues are the biggest problems — with liability holding a distinct lead. All it's going to take is one newspaper headline saying "Minors Caught Downloading Porn at Local Sex-and-PC Party!" to ensure that your real-time fragging days are over.

The choice is up to you, and what you feel comfortable with. Among the LAN party hosts I interviewed, there was a *slight* preference for having no Internet access at parties, but not enough to make it definitive.

What should your guests bring to the party?

Defining what everyone is responsible for bringing to the party now avoids miscommunications later ("How was *I* supposed to know I needed a power strip?"). You can ask your guests to bring several things, but the following items (see Figure 2-2) are core essentials:

FIGURE 2-2: Things to bring to a party

- **A PC with a NIC card.**

- **Keyboard, mouse, and (if necessary) mouse pad.** For the record, optical mice are *far* superior to mechanical mice, as you usually don't have to worry about slippage.

- **A power strip.** Said strip should also be a surge suppressor to protect against wayward electrical fluctuations.

- **A monitor.** Depending on your space, you may also want to restrict the maximum size of the monitor; those 27-inch billboard-sized jobbies are beautiful, but do you have a place to put it?

- **Headphones.** Or a speaker, I suppose. But didn't I tell you that you don't *want* speakers?

- **Software.** Most games require a valid copy of the disc to play; leave it at home and you can look forward to playing very intense games of Solitaire all day. Also, it's not a bad idea to have a copy of your current operating system and device drivers, should anything go wrong.

- **Category 5 cable.** While many professional parties have cable pre-laid out for you, most smaller parties require you to bring your own cable. Make sure you ask your guests to bring at least a 20-foot length in case you need to stretch to reach the switch.

"I'll Just Burn You a Copy"

There is a tendency in the LAN party world to be, how shall we say it, *casual* with the issue of copyright infringement. People burn off copies of game discs all the time, with $50 games changing hands for free like it ain't no thang.

This is bad. Stop it.

Yes, you can make all of the arguments about how software is overpriced and run by Big Evil Fatcats. But as someone who used to work in the industry on the bean counter side, I can tell you that it's not true. It's not like these guys are skimming a $30 profit off of each $50 box; if they're lucky, after costs and expenses, they make $2 or $3. At most.

Considering how much a video game costs to produce, that amount isn't much.

I could trot out the usual old-school warnings about how "piracy is wrong," and all of that jazz. But, frankly, if you're stealing software on a regular basis, you're probably beyond any discussions of morality, so instead I will ask you to consider this: *Every time you steal someone's game, the less likely the game's creator is to keep making them.*

Want a sequel to your favorite game? Reward the people who made it for you. If you're playing a copied game on a regular basis, pony up the money you owe so that the creators will make more and better games. Don't just take the entertainment; pay for it.

It's only fair.

(Of course, then the question becomes, "What if I steal a game and I don't like it?" Well, my answer is, "Hey, look—*Elvis! Right behind you!*" as I scurry off.)

Do you need to serve food and drink?

At smaller parties, you can tell people to bring their own food—which works great if they all remember. In my experience, one person *always* forgets to bring a favorite soda, and never wants to make a supermarket run alone, so the next thing you know, you're missing three or four players. Therefore, the answer to the question of whether you need to serve anything is, in most cases, yes.

Even if you're ordering out for pizza, it's a good idea to have some munchies around the house and a variety of sodas that people like. You can collect a food fund beforehand; the other option is to have people strip your fridge bare.

If you're holding an off-site event, you absolutely should offer food or drink, as you can sell it on-site to help pay for your rental costs. The markup on food and drink is phenomenal; you can charge a buck a can for soda, and even at 50 cents you still make good money. Generally, you should shoot for a sales markup of about 100 percent, or twice what you paid for it.

Cross-Reference You'll learn how to buy food cheaply and sell it for profit in Chapter 5, "Saving Money on Your LAN Party."

The only downside to the whole "food-selling" thing is that generally you need to keep someone on guard by the food 24/7 to make sure that nobody makes off with your money or the food.

Will you require a viral scan before logging on?

In the hothouse environment of a LAN party, computer viruses can spread terrifyingly fast. We've heard nightmare stories of LAN parties that were completely blitzed by the latest virus; somebody downloaded it in an e-mail or a file and it spread, frying everyone's PCs.

Many LAN party hosts, legitimately paranoid about the new boatloads of viruses out there, require that you scan your computer with the freeware viral program of their choice before you log on. If you're convinced all of your friends are responsible citizens who *always* scan their PCs once a week and floss before bedtime, then you can consider skipping this step. But if you are inviting people you don't know that well, or have Internet access, I strongly suggest you do the scanning thing.

The Logistics of Pizza

While doing the research for this book, I was surprised to find that many LAN hosts put more effort into their pizza orders than their network setups. On second thought, that shouldn't be surprising; greasy piles of bread and cheese are staples at every LAN party. As long as I gathered all of this information, I thought I'd share a few pizza statistics:

- Your average medium pizza contains 8 slices; your average large pizza contains 12. (Your industry-standard small pizza has 6, but why bother?)

- As a general guideline, each person will consume 2.5 pizza slices. Strangely enough, this number seems to be true regardless of the size of the pizza — but remember, large pizzas have more slices to work with.

- When you're ordering for a large group and don't want to take specific requests, go with a meatball pizza (or "ground hamburger," in some areas) if you're only ordering one. If you order two, make one the vegetable special and the other the meatball pizza. The third pizza, if you must, is the meat lover's special.

- Mushrooms and anchovies are highly volatile ingredients and may lead to knife fights.

- If you have large groups of eight or more and they're relatively homogenous in their tastes, get a "party pizza" — a pizza so big that you have to tilt it to get it through the door. They run about $20, and can save a lot of money in the long run.

- The average tip for the delivery person should be about $2 per pizza — less if the pizzas are cold. Remember: considering that pizza is the foundation of any LAN party, you want to inspire loyalty in your delivery guys.

Tip

Many LAN parties burn a Welcome CD for each attendee; it contains a freeware virus scanner and all the latest patches and maps you'll be using that day. (See Chapter 13, "The Complete Day of the Party Timeline," for further details.) You would be well-advised to have one handy for each guest.

Will you allow drinking?

If it's going to be a small party, this isn't an issue. If someone has a beer at your house (assuming they're of legal age, of course), nobody's going to break in and ask you for ID. However, at larger events — and particularly external ones — you run into many legal issues, including the following:

- Does this place have a liquor license?

- How will you check ID? What happens if a minor drinks?

- What's considered a "public place" if someone gets rowdy?

- What happens if someone gets drunk, drives home, and injures himself — or worse yet, others?

Alcohol's a risk, and even though it can be a lot of fun getting blasted with your pals (we even suggest a LAN-related drinking game in the last chapter), you can get sued — or worse yet, you can kill someone. As such, I'll answer all of these questions in some detail in Chapter 14, "Legal and Safety Issues." I *strongly* recommend you head straight to Chapter 14 and read the section on the legal liabilities of drinking before you check "yes" on this one. *You have been warned.*

Cross-Reference

The legal liabilities for drinking are discussed in Chapter 14, "Legal and Safety Issues." Please check them out before you even *think* of opening an alcoholic beverage.

Will you allow smoking?

A lot of cities now prohibit smoking in public areas, and a lot of people are either allergic to cigarette smoke or just totally repulsed by it. I advise that you disallow smoking at your LAN parties (you can always go out on the porch for a cigarette), but the choice is yours. Just check with your rental space if you're hosting an external party.

Will you allow minors?

Children under the age of 18 present very real legal issues for any LAN party. If they're unaccompanied by their parents, you can be held legally responsible for whatever happens to them while they're at your party. And, unfortunately, teenagers are the sort of people who tend to get into trouble. You may want to bar minors from your party because of this, or you may want to require that their parents sign a disclaimer form.

Cross-Reference

Once again, this is more of a legal issue, so see Chapter 14 for details.

Will you allow nonparticipants?

A LAN party can sometimes attract a lot of people who don't play—but they like to talk. Sometimes, this makes it more of a community event, as nonplaying spouses and significant others get together and play cards. Other times, it can be highly disruptive, as you wind up with nonparticipants bugging players in the middle of games, hogging Internet connections on vacant computers, playing roughhouse games in the aisles, and reducing the number of players on game servers.

Furthermore, there's a serious theft risk. If you have people you don't know hanging around, Lord knows what they're up to. My recommendation is that you disallow nonparticipants, but make exceptions for well-behaved players for whom *you*—not others—can vouch for.

Should you charge an admission fee?

This is a no-brainer for small parties, which are generally at someone's house. The answer? Of course not! However, if the party is taking place off-site, you may want to consider charging a fee in order to recover the rental cost.

For the pros and cons of charging admission, check out the last part of Chapter 5, specifically, "Charging Admission and Going Pro."

What side events will you hold?

Many LAN parties aren't just about networking—they have weirdo side events such as case-modding contests, office chair Olympics, squirt-gun maze chases, and DDR face-offs. You need to consider whether you want to have these and how attractive they would make your party to others.

If you'd like some ideas about side events, turn to Chapter 16, "Cool Things to Do at your LAN Party," for the best ideas culled from LAN parties around the nation!

Will you need a lost and found?

Leaving something behind is no big deal if you're playing at someone's house, but if you drop your *Fountains of Wayne* CD at the Shriner's Hall, you're not going to get it back. Having a catch-all location for the detritus that accumulates at any LAN party is a necessary step for any semi-pro get-together.

Fortunately, it's as simple as getting a cardboard box ready, telling everyone where it is, and putting it in a secure place.

Setting Ground Rules

Having rules of conduct posted for all to see is very important for one reason: *It stops arguments.*

If you catch someone being a complete jackass and begin to lecture them for their abysmal behavior, the first thing you'll usually hear is a sullen, "Well, *I* didn't know!" Whether this is true or not is debatable — although generally, the things these guests do are so rude that it's hard to believe they *didn't* realize it would offend someone.

But if you have your rules of conduct written in advance and posted where everyone can see them, you can simply point to them and say, "The rules were right there."

Suddenly, they can't argue. You had the rules up all along. They just chose to ignore them.

Now, keep in mind that most people aren't jerks. Yes, you will encounter occasional behavior problems at your party, but most of those problems will stem from one of two things:

- Ignorance or laziness, or both, on the part of your guests ("I just plugged into the first outlet I saw, dude.")
- Excitement ("I'm sorry, I didn't mean to yell, but I just BFG'd five guys at once!")

While nothing really helps to tone down the excitement problems (and it could be argued that it's better to calm down overly enthusiastic guests than it is to have a boring party), ground rules help to stem some of the ignorance and laziness issues. The rules tell your guests precisely what is expected of them, and it makes it extremely clear that any ignorance is *their* fault, not yours.

In this section, I'll give you a bunch of good, tried-and-tested ground rules, and let you select the ones that fit your party best. But first, let's take a look at the most important thing about ground rules: Making them work.

Making your ground rules effective

Without enforcement, your ground rules are simply words on paper. Without publicity, nobody will know that your rules exist. Therefore, before you start, you have to ask yourself two important questions:

- Am I willing to go out of my way to tell people what these rules are?
- Am I willing to kick someone out of my party?

If you're not, save yourself the time. Nobody's going to pay attention to you anyway.

If you are, then read on.

Getting the word out

The first thing you want to do with your ground rules is post them on your Web site (or in your initial announcement e-mail) well in advance, so that everyone knows what they are.

Then, on the day of the party, make sure that you have the rules posted in a prominent place. For smaller parties, that can be as simple as tacking a printed copy to the bulletin board; for larger parties, we suggest photocopying the rules onto a large poster board at a professional copy shop so that everyone can clearly see them.

Then, at the beginning of the event as most of the people are there and checking in, we suggest having "the introductory talk." This is where you congratulate any staff and thank people for lending you equipment. But more importantly, this is when you read the rules aloud so that everyone hears them. Smaller parties can get by with an informal, "Okay, um, don't drink outside and plug in where I tell you to," but at larger parties, you should probably read the rules off the wall, exactly as written, as it sounds more official.

Cross-Reference You'll examine the acknowledgments and posting of the rules in more detail in Chapter 13, "The Complete Day of the Party Timeline."

You'll feel kind of foolish the first time you stand up and tell people what they're supposed to do, but you'd be surprised how few people actually read the rules of their own volition. Reading them in a loud, clear voice makes it impossible for anyone to deny that you *told* them.

Rules without enforcement = nothing

Realize that unless you're actually willing to kick someone out of your party, your rules mean nothing. Giving someone the boot should always be your *last* resort, but it needs to be done when someone steps way out of line. If you're unwilling to follow up on your rules with something other than vague threats, your rules are meaningless. The more serious infractions, such as bullying, illegal drug use, and cheat programs, may warrant lifetime bannings (as in, this person will never attend another party that you host).

Your rules are as good as your follow-up. If you post rules, be prepared to tell renegades that they have to go. As for how to handle shirkers and scofflaws, you'll find out more about kicking people out in Chapter 13.

A reasonably complete selection of sample rules

The paragraphs that follow provide a laundry list of ground rules; you can select the ones you want to use. All of them are pretty good ideas.

These rules are divided into two sections: a set of rules that I strongly suggest should be instituted at every party, and a set of optional rules that can be tweaked to your satisfaction. The optional rules often contradict each other, but that's okay because you should pick *only* the rules that you want to institute at your LAN party. There are several suggested methods for handling alcohol usage; if you want an alcohol-free party, just choose the rule that says "No drinking" and you can safely ignore the rest of the booze-related ones.

I've written these rules so that you can literally copy and paste them onto your Web site, thus assembling a full list of ground rules in seconds. Feel free both to use any portion of the rules you wish and to reprint them for your party.

The core guidelines that every party should follow

- **The LAN party hosts are not responsible for anything that might happen to you or your equipment.** You are.

- **The LAN party hosts have final say about everything that happens at this event.** We can, and will, remove jerks to make things more enjoyable for everyone else. Hopefully, you're not a jerk; if you aren't, you're going to have a great time today.

- **You are responsible for having all appropriate hardware and software.** Unless you're renting a computer from us, you are expected to bring a working computer with a network card and legal copies of all relevant game software already installed. Please do not bring a broken computer and ask us to fix it; please do not ask us to wait for 20 minutes while you install the game and all the latest patches.

- **Plug in only where you are told.** Doing otherwise may lead to power outages. In particular, do not plug into someone else's power strip. If you're not sure where to plug in, ask a staff member.

- **Keep your station clean.** You are responsible for leaving your area as clean as you found it. If your area accumulates too many bottles and candy wrappers during the day, we may ask you to clean it up immediately; please do not give us flak about this.

- **Do not touch other people's stuff without permission.** The difference between "borrowing" and "theft" can become very difficult to prove, and we don't intend to try. Also, you might break something.

- **No stealing.** If you are caught, we will not only ensure that your weaselly little butt never plays a game in this town again, but we will call the police to ensure that charges are pressed against you.

- **No horseplay, no running around, no throwing things.** This room is filled with thousands of dollars of fragile equipment. You can damage something very easily. Therefore, no wrestling matches, no affectionate tussles, no tossing disks or foosballs around. Obviously, violence of any sort will lead to instant ejection and a permanent ban.

- **No speakers.** Speakers create an incredible racket and drain excessive power. Headphones only, please.

- **No cheating.** This includes bots, hacks, or anything else that isn't strictly aboveboard. Remember, this LAN party is not the American justice system; it is an enlightened tyranny. If we think that whatever you're doing is sufficiently shady, you will get booted.

- **You may be ejected from the LAN party for breaking any of these rules or at the discretion of the LAN party hosts.** You are not entitled to a refund if you are ejected for any reason.

- **Have fun!** We're sorry to have to start out with such an ominous set of rules, but it's necessary to ensure that the event runs smoothly. The whole point of these rules is to make sure that everyone has the best time that they possibly can — *so get out there and start fraggin'!*

Optional ground rules for your party

- **No one will be allowed to play without signing a liability waiver.** While we'll take reasonable precautions to make sure this is a safe party, you are ultimately responsible for everything that happens to you here. You must acknowledge that legally before you can set up.

- **Virus scans must be run on every computer before you plug in.** We have provided the appropriate viral software for you; you are expected to do a complete scan before you place your computer onto our network.

- **No one under the age of 18 will be admitted.** We're sorry, but there are legal issues with minors.

- **No one under the age of 18 will be admitted without a signed parental permission slip.** We're sorry, but there are legal issues with minors and we have to ensure that the parents are aware of all potential hazards at this party.

- **No one under the age of 18 will be admitted without their parents or a legal guardian present.** We're sorry, but there are legal issues with minors.

- **No one under the age of 13 will be allowed under any circumstances.** There is a lot of fragile equipment here, and kids running around might break something.

- **No spectators.** If you aren't here to play, you're distracting other people.

- **No smoking.** It's unhealthy, and it irritates many of our players. If you want to smoke, take it outside.

- **No drinking.** We have a firm no-alcohol policy, as we believe you can have more fun without booze than you can with it. Anyone caught drunk on the premises will be kicked out.

- **No drugs or alcohol are allowed inside the LAN room.** Anything you choose to do offsite is your business (and your responsibility), but no drugs or alcohol are allowed inside the room.

- **No alcohol is allowed outside the LAN room.** We have a liquor license, and anyone caught drinking away from the gaming area may lead to police action. Please keep all drinks inside the LAN gaming area.

- **No alcohol is allowed outside the house.** This is a private residence, and you're not allowed to be drunk in public. Please keep all drinks inside the LAN gaming area.

- **No alcohol will be given to minors.** We let you have your booze, but no sneaking drinks to anyone who's not of legal age themselves. Anyone caught doing this will be expelled, as will the underage drinker.

- **You are responsible for bringing your own food to the party.** If enough people agree, we may run for pizza later in the evening, but no food or drinks are on the premises.

- **Outside food and drink are not permitted.** Only food and drink that are purchased on the premises may be consumed here.

- **Outside food and drink are not permitted until after the food concession is closed.** Any food and drink consumed on the premises must be purchased from the concession while it is open. After it closes, feel free to bring in your own stuff.

- **No loud noises.** We are in an enclosed area with neighbors who get very upset about loud noises. We don't want the cops called on us, so keep it down.

- **Keep the noise level to a minimum.** Occasional shouts of glee are fine when you cap someone, but repeatedly shouting how great you are will not be tolerated. Keep it down.

- **No vulgarities.** We all know what the F-word and the S-word are. We don't want to hear them from you.

- **No insults.** Good-natured ribbing is fine, but the moment someone gets upset, you stop *immediately*. Repeated violators will be ejected.

- **No inappropriate material.** No pornography or any other offensive images should be on anyone's screens today. That includes screensavers and backgrounds. Minors may be present, and showing minors pornographic images is illegal. We do not want to be sued by angry parents.

- **No trading of copyrighted material.** Anyone caught exchanging or downloading warez, MP3s by RIAA-backed musicians, or any other copyrighted files will be booted. We don't need the hassle of getting sued.

- **No bandwidth hogging.** We have a limited Internet connection. Downloading six 300 MB files simultaneously will choke everyone else's connection. If you need to download something big, like a patch, let everyone know in advance.

- **No monitors over 21 inches.** If you arrive with a larger monitor, you will not be allowed to play.

- **Private games and FTP servers are not allowed.** We have only so much bandwidth to go around, and we need to ensure that it's not siphoned away by unauthorized servers. If you'd like your own server, ask in advance.

Summary

That's a fair amount of prep work to do, but every house needs a solid foundation, and this is the foundation of your LAN party. By now, you know that you need to consider a lot of issues when planning your party; hopefully, this chapter has answered them all!

In the next chapter, you'll consider where to hold your party. Most people are going to hold it at their house, but other places are good for a small party, and if you ever need to rent a hall, you may need to know the intimate details of property rental!

Choosing a Site for Your Party

I'll be honest: For most parties, the location is going to be your house. Your house (or apartment or dorm) is available any time you want it, it's infinitely customizable, and it's free. If you're holding a small party (or have a large house), you can probably skip this chapter altogether.

(However, don't be too quick to flip by, my homebound friend; there's one other option for you here. You may want to look into *cybercafes*.)

But for the rest of you, this chapter's all about space — comparing the various places you can rent for a LAN party, snagging the best price for *any* location, and knowing your way around a rental contract. It's easier than you'd think; with a little moxy and elbow grease, you can find an excellent space when the LAN party overflows your home.

Locations by Party Size

As we said earlier, most parties can be split into three sizes — and the biggest concern as you add more people is, not surprisingly, space. Wiring 15 computers together so they can all talk to each isn't nearly as complicated as finding the space to put them all in! So let's go over the various options available to you at each party breakpoint, and find out the advantages and disadvantages of each.

You and a few friends (up to 10 people)

When you're dealing with small crowds, the default place to play is someone's home. In fact, it may not have occurred to you that there's another option! But there is one other place you might want to check out if you're willing to pay a little extra for a lot of convenience: the local coffee shop (preferably a wired one, also known as a *cybercafe*). The cafe offers a good space with some pretty nice conveniences.

Inviting the whole neighborhood (10 to 30 people)

The neighborhood parties tend to get a little raucous, and you have a choice between three separate locations. First, you can take someone's house — not an apartment, an actual house — and rewire the entire thing so that the garage is set up to handle the extra people. (You'll probably need to drop in a couple of extra power circuits.) Second, you can find a local cybercafe and campaign for them to expand, as most cafes will handle only about six to 12 players at a time.

Third, you can sigh and resign yourself to finding a church basement, VA hall, or similar public meeting place and set up. It's a pain, but I'll walk you through it.

The megaparty (30+ people)

At this point, you have to go with a meeting hall. Your big question is, do you go with the old, familiar, and comparatively cheap Shriners Hall, or do you pay extra for the pizzazz of the up-to-date, technosavvy convention center with an attached hotel?

Both have advantages. But to be honest, the larger your LAN party becomes, the more likely it is that you're going to have to opt for the convention center.

The Most Common LAN Party Locations

Five basic spots can be used to hold LAN parties, and each of them has its own advantages and disadvantages:

- Your house or a friend's house
- Coffee shops or cybercafes
- Existing networks
- Churches or Shriners or Veterans Administration halls
- Convention centers

The following sections examine each of these options in turn.

Your house (or a friend's house)

Most home LAN parties are held there because they're cheap — so in a way, it's redundant to list the advantages and disadvantages. For a lot of people, you'll be playing at someone's house whether you want to or not!

That said, given that about 75 percent of you will be holding your fragging in your living room, you'll be pleased to know that a home or apartment is a *fine* place to hold a party when you're just starting out. It's where most of us take our baby steps.

But let's list the ups and downs of fragging where you live, because one other spot is pre-made for small groups of gamers: the cybercafe. You may want to think about trying that out, too.

The advantages of using your house

- **It's free.** I know this is an amazing concept, but you've *already* paid the rent on your house or apartment. The space is yours to use at no additional cost. (I suppose you could charge yourself admission if you really wanted to, but that would just be silly.)

- **No advance scheduling is needed.** Most places need at least a week's notice, but not you. You're the wind, baby. Call your pals up at 7:00, you're fragging by 8:00.

- **No time limits.** Many rental places require you to vacate the premises at a specified time unless you've made prior arrangements. Your home closes when you say it does. The all-night fragfest is totally under your control.

- **You have absolute control.** Since you own everything, you can move whatever you like around without worrying about annoying the man who holds your security deposit. If you own a home, you can even install your own power circuits and drill holes in the walls to drop wires through! Be messy! Scrub your kitchen floor with pizza if you like! It's yours, yours, *yours*!

- **You don't have to move.** You're in your favorite chair, at your favorite desk, with your favorite setup, and your favorite CDs are on the shelf. All you do is hook up to the LAN. You're so good to go.

The disadvantages of using your house

- **Neighbors.** Especially if you live in an apartment, it's likely that eventually you'll have to deal with people who aren't quite thrilled with hearing you all yell, "YEAH! TAKE THAT! COMPLETE DENOGGITATION!" at three o'clock in the morning. That means your parties will either be periodically interrupted by angry knocks on the door (sometimes from the police), or you'll have to keep your noise levels to a minimum. (That, or you have to find some *really* cool neighbors.)

- **Cohabitants.** If your roommate or girlfriend or boyfriend likes computer games, you're in the clear. But quite often, you're sharing a space with someone who doesn't like to play, and you're essentially taking over their living space for a day or so. Unless you give them a lot of sweet talk and consideration, they're going to cause a scene. And who wants to be considerate?

  Also, if you're still living at home, do not forget your parents. They may be tolerant, but a bunch of loud teenagers running amuck combined with a lot of weirdo wires is enough to try any dad's patience!

- **Cramped space.** It's not a convention hall, and most houses don't have rooms big enough for multiple computers in one place. You'll be cramming people into the dining room and the hallway sometimes, and it's highly unlikely that you can fit more than six or eight people into your average living space comfortably. LAN parties aren't quite as much fun when you can't see everyone.

Park Your Party Out Back

When your home is just about out of space, don't forget your garage! Many houses have garages that can be converted into impromptu LAN party locations to hold groups of ten or more, and three-car garages can hold twenty or thirty people easily.

Not every garage can work for this, though; for one thing, many garages (particularly garages that aren't connected to the house) are messy and may require a lot of cleaning to get them into shape. Also, many garages have minor drips and leaks, which are very bad when you have electricity. They may not be heated, making them unsuitable for use in the winter months. And last, most garages have only one or two power circuits, and they are almost never wired for Internet access.

That said, if you have a clean and dry garage, you can run cables and electrical cords out to the garage to take up the slack—or, for a more permanent solution, you could call an electrician to install another couple of power circuits.

- **Limited Furniture.** You usually have only one or two tables in your house that are large enough to hold a computer. You will probably need to borrow some, which can be an annoyance.

- **It's just you, baby.** You have no janitorial staff to make sure the house is pristine before you get there, and certainly nobody but you will sweep the floor after everyone is gone. The entire house is yours, and keeping it up to par is entirely your responsibility. Everyone wants to attend the LAN party, but nobody ever wants to help clean up.

Cybercafes: The quickest route

Let's clear something up: The cafes don't necessarily have to be cyber. Generally, a good coffee shop has both the space to accommodate a small group of people and enough tables to sit them all down. If you work out the details in advance with the manager, sometimes you can set up a switch right at the coffee shop, and just bring all of your computers down to the cafe!

Plus, you have immediate access to two of the three gamer food groups: sugar and caffeine. (The third food group, incidentally, is "grease.")

But if the local coffee shop is good, a cybercafe is even better. They have computers already set up, and the networking equipment's usually right in place. For convenience, it's hard to beat the cafe.

The advantages of using the coffee shop

- **(Cybercafes only) Everything is set up for you.** The computers are already in place, the networking has been thoroughly tested, and you know they have Internet access. The only downside is that they might not have your game installed on their machines, but most shops are amenable to trying out a new game or two.

- **(Cybercafes only) Nobody has to bring a computer.** As just mentioned, they have PCs right there. You bring yourself and a credit card. That's not bad.

- **Inexpensive compared to other out-of-home options.** That Shriners Hall is going to set you back $300 easily. The cybercafe? Well, it depends on their hourly rate — but even accounting for iced mochas, it's still a lot cheaper than the hall. And many noncybercafes will allow you to play for free, as long as you agree to buy food.

- **Other customers may show up.** If you're an inclusive bunch of folks, the idea that anyone could wander in and start playing with you is a checkmark on the "positive" side.

- **A clean, professional environment.** It's likely a big space and, unlike in your house, in the coffee shop chances are good that you'll all be in the same room. The staff cleans up after you're done. Just leave a big tip for them.

- **Food and drink are right at hand.** Hey, want that triple-latte espresso shot? You got it. Want a biscotti? You got it. That's what they do.

- **Potentially great service.** For many shops, a regular crowd of four people can make an evening profitable. Therefore, you can frequently work with the manager in order to get things done the way you like them.

- **Cute staff to flirt with.** I'm not being sexist here; I've seen the women smile at the cute men behind the counter just about as often as the men chat up the women serving the drinks. It's always nice to have someone else to talk to when you're tired of nerding out, and often it's a nice change of pace to talk to someone who doesn't care about computers.

The disadvantages of using the coffee shop

- **More expensive than a home.** Though they're the cheapest for-pay option, coffee shops still cost money — unlike a house. If you're looking to play on no budget, you're out of luck when it comes to coffee shoppage.

- **Busiest on weekend nights.** And that's usually when you want to play, right? In your spare time, when classes are over?

- **Limited hours.** You're not playing at a coffee shop until 3:30 in the morning unless you have a *very* good rapport with the staff. When the doors close, party's over.

- **Limited seating.** Unless you arrange a special time for you and your pals in advance, quite frequently you're at the mercy of the crowd that shows up. And you might even get bumped, if you show up late and someone's occupying one of the seats you wanted. It's not *that* hard to work out reservations in advance, but it usually involves extra moolah. Plus, many cybercafes don't have that many seats available; usually, it's four to six. If your group grows, you could be in trouble.

- **Forced decorum.** With other customers there, you generally can't swear, burp, or shout. Not that I recommend yelling and screaming all the time, of course, but sometimes you really wanna let loose.

- **Limited food options.** Many cafes are understandably upset if you decide to order pizza, or bring your own food in. Therefore, sometimes you're stuck eating biscotti when you really want a hoagie.

- **Other customers may show up.** If you're an insular group that doesn't want to have to deal with newbies or idiots, you may be out of luck. The cybercafe wants money. Anyone who's willing to put cash on the barrelhead can play.

- **(Cybercafes only) Nobody has to bring a computer.** If you're a bunch of hardware snobs, the rigs at most cybercafes aren't top of the line, and you don't get to show off your new 3D video card. Boo.

Existing networks

Let's be honest, here: *existing networks* is a nice way of saying "hijacking your work or school network to play silly videogames." And I say, "*hell*, yah!" If you can take over the office after-hours and play *Duke Nukem* until dawn, then go for it. The problem, however, is not getting booted.

Advantages of using existing networks

- **They're fully set up.** You mean, everything's all in one place? With routers and really high-speed connections? *Yee haw*!

- **They generally have a large number of seats.** Considering that you generally don't set up an office or classroom LAN for less than eight people — and it's usually sixteen or more — pre-existing networks are ideal for large-scale get-togethers.

- **They're where everyone hangs out anyway.** You spend your day filling out spreadsheets and crunching numbers. Then, when five o'clock rolls around, you just start up a different program. You don't even have to move.

 Tip

College networks are absolutely great for this. Most campuses don't care if you play on their network, making college campuses absolutely wonderful for LAN parties. In most cases, you need neither permission nor stealth.

Disadvantages of using existing networks

- **You need permission, or you need stealth.** If The Powers That Be are okay with your after-hours LAN parties, that's great. But many administrators aren't cool with "play" on "work" computers. They may try to ban gaming traffic from their network altogether, at which point you have to hack the system in order to play.

    If you have a cool boss and a network admin who likes to do the gaming thing, you're in clover. Otherwise, you don't have a party.

- **Slower computers.** Those of you who are big on games may have squinched up your face at the mention of *Duke Nukem* in the introductory paragraph. "Who in blue blazes plays *Duke Nukem* these days?"

    Well, it might be you. Most office machines are designed to handle spreadsheets and word documents, not polygons and trilinear bitmaps. Unless you're a high-end programmer or a graphic designer, your rig may not be able to handle the latest hi-tech monstrogame.

Should You Hack Your Office LAN to Set Up a Party?

Duh. *No.*

For the record, I do not condone breaking into an office LAN in order to play videogames. The whole point of this book is that it's *easy* to hold LAN parties; do you really want to risk your job or school career just to save yourself the effort of stringing a few wires together? If you get yourself fired or kicked out for your trouble, don't say I didn't warn you. Take your game elsewhere.

Before you do, of course, ask your boss or network admin if they want to play at your LAN party. I have heard a couple of stories about network admins who absolutely refused to hold gaming traffic on their watch, until the office discovered the NA's weakness for real-time strategy games.

- **Limited hours.** Many businesses shut down after 10:00 or so, and there's really no negotiation. The security guards may chase you out if you haven't gotten prior permission.

- **Painful setup issues.** Many networks are firewalled, so that only very specific types of network traffic are allowed. Strangely enough, *Medal of Honor Allied Assault* packets are not usually considered business-critical information. You may have to tinker with routers and firewalls to get everything to work right — and unless you're already a system administrator, you might not have the access codes or the experience to do it.

Churches, Shriners Halls, and Veterans' Administration Halls

These are small-time outlets — the little spaces that are rented out for bingo, church socials, and really cheesy weddings. Generally, the rooms are fairly small (at least compared to the big-time convention services, discussed in the next section), and the atmosphere's like a lunchroom cafeteria. But if you need to get 20 or 30 people in one place, you can't beat the price.

These places go by many different names. We'll show you how to track them down in the next section.

The advantages of using churches, Shriners Halls, and Veterans Administration Halls

- **The cheapest way to hold a large-scale event.** Coffee shops and homes are nice, but if you're looking to move out of the basement, the local Moose Hall is the most inexpensive method to do it.

- **Family ties can help.** If you have a grandfather or an uncle who's a member — or if you're a member yourself — you can sometimes get these places for free, or at a vastly reduced cost.

- **Late-night mayhem.** Very few people hang around a church basement or a VA hall late at night, so if you can get permission to lock the doors behind you, you're pretty much on your own. As long as nobody calls the cops on you, you can yell and scream and hoot to your heart's content.

- **Many halls have kitchens.** Oh, it's very sweet to have a stove, a fridge, and a counter from which to serve foodstuffs. It makes things *so* much more convenient, and the soda's always cold.

The disadvantages of using churches, Shriners Halls, and Veterans Administration Halls

- **Scheduling.** You usually have to schedule at least six weeks in advance. And that's assuming that they don't have something else planned. These sorts of halls tend to run their own events for their members, and rent out space only when they have nothing better to do themselves. As such, scheduling a time can sometimes be tricky.

- **Local wariness.** Most of the people who run these establishments tend to be on the older side, and may be downright nervous about allowing a bunch of young people to come in and play violent videogames. They've read about the effects that these blood-spattered FPS shooters have on people. As such, you sometimes have to do a lot more convincing and reassuring than you might otherwise with other venues. And you definitely have to be on your best behavior.

- **Still fairly expensive.** You can figure $200 minimum — and that's *rock* bottom — to rent a hall for a day, plus a security deposit if they don't like your looks. It's not as bad as a full-fledged convention center, but it's still a big drain on the wallet.

- **Technological constraints.** Needless to say, most (but not all) churches and VA Halls aren't wired for Internet access. You may not even have easily accessible phone lines for dialup! Their power loads also can be a little bit shaky. Remember, these places were designed for a bunch of people to hold a ceremony and then have coffee and cake, not to host 17 cutting-edge PCs. You get what you pay for, and the cost of a cheap rental space may well be 1950s technology.

- **Not the best section of town.** Many local clubs were located in the best parts of the city back when, but the neighborhood has often crumbled around them. (There's a reason they go for cheap.) You may have to consider security issues in a whole new way.

Tip If you rent a hall, ask about tables. Most places will have tables they can lend you, but if they don't, you'll need to rent some. Also, be sure to look at the tables (some of the ones you'll find at Shriners halls are pretty beat-up) and make sure that they're sturdy enough to hold the weight of a monitor without collapsing.

Convention centers

These are the top-of-the-line places — hotels and business centers that specifically cater to upscale clientele. If you want to share a T1 line, you've got it. If you want a techie to come out and help you pack, you got it.

The downside is, of course, that you pay for it. But sometimes, it's worth it if you need consummate professionalism. The following sections outline the advantages and disadvantages of going this route.

The advantages of using convention centers

- **Technologically up-to-date.** Generally, these folks do have an Internet connection, and are used to having people share it. They may even have a service technician who'll come in and troubleshoot your connection for you. If you'd like to rent projectors or borrow an Ethernet cable, chances are good that you can do it.

- **Usually available when you need them.** Unlike a Shriners Hall, the only conflicts you have to worry about are with other paid customers. That means there's a much better chance you'll be able to snag the date you want.

- **Used to gatherings of nerds.** Many of these places host tech conventions and training courses. They're not used to people yelling and screaming, of course, but they do understand the dynamics of computer groups and will be okay with it.

- **Tables and chairs are usually included.** Because they're continually using said tables for various gatherings, you rarely have to worry about having enough.

- **Hungry for business.** Because renting out space is their primary business, convention centers will go to great lengths to keep you as a repeat customer (assuming, of course, that you're courteous and professional in return). This allows you room to negotiate contracts, reduced costs for multiple bookings, and so forth.

- **Discounts available for room bookings.** Many hotels offer discounts on their convention centers if a certain number of people rent rooms. If you're having friends fly in from out of town for a large gathering, often you can shave 10 or 20 percent off the bill.

The disadvantages of using convention centers

- **Way pricey.** Of all the options presented so far, convention centers are, hands down, the most expensive. You can negotiate better prices, of course, and sometimes you actually save more money by not having to put up with inferior equipment, but don't start here if you're running something on the cheap.

- **Hands off the equipment.** Many hotels and convention centers are reluctant to give you access to the fuse box or the Internet connection themselves, so they'll try to get a handyman to fix it for you. That's fine if it happens at three o'clock on a Saturday afternoon, but what if it's three o'clock in the morning?

- **Lots of drop-ins.** You may be sharing your convention center with another business gathering, or even a hotel where guests just drop in. As you'll see in Chapter 9, "Sample LAN Party Layouts," drop-ins tend to be more trouble than regular LAN party guests. And even if they're no trouble at all, you wind up spending a lot of time explaining things to them.

- **Early closing time.** Most convention centers are designed for businesses and conventions, which close no later than 10:00 P.M. In fact, they may not understand that you want to play all night. If that's the case, you have to read the contract very carefully and arrange a late-night session in advance.

Going Outside the Home: How to Rent without Getting Ripped Off

You may have noticed that in all of the discussions on renting places thus far, you haven't seen any price ranges to work with outside of general comparisons. That's because I can't give you exact prices. They vary dramatically from city to city, from weekend to weekend, from location to location, and, most importantly, from deal to deal.

The average cost of rental is *so* mercurial, in fact, that I couldn't even tell you what an "average" price would be in Cleveland—and I *live* in Cleveland. Two identical hotels in the same neighborhood can have a $300 difference between quoted prices, even if the convention centers are the same size and they're a part of the same chain.

There is one thing that all of these rental places have in common: The owners are motivated to rent their location *every weekend*. Every day that they're not renting their property, they're losing money to property taxes and heating bills and whatnot.

If you walk away and they can't find anyone else, they lose money.

In other words, even if they make *no money at all* by renting to you, it can still be better than paying their property taxes and janitorial staff expenses out-of-pocket. Of course, the rental locations are going to do their best to make a profit off of your event—that's only natural—but the "rent it or eat it" nature of their business means that they're far more willing to cut a deal than most services you're used to.

This brings us to the first rule of renting:

Rule Number 1: Everything is negotiable.

And I mean *everything*. The price. The deposit. The cost of chairs and tables. Hooking in an Internet connection for your use. The time you need to book it in advance. Discounted rooms at the local hotel. Custom wiring. It can all be negotiated. Negotiating can be slightly harder at larger chains (but only slightly) because they're more impersonal, but you have to realize that the *first* quoted price is never the *last* quoted price.

At least not if you're smart.

Why Do Prices Vary?

Who knows why prices vary from location to location? Some of the factors that affect this maddening variety in prices include the hotel's property taxes, their regular business clients, the local economy, their business plan, and the business savvy of the guy who takes the reservations.

In the end, it doesn't matter. Just know that prices vary wildly, and assume that you can do better than their first offer.

Pay Attention to the News

It's a sad fact of life, but local tragedies do impact your rental options. For example, for about six months after September 11, 2001, people were afraid to fly, and most conventions were cancelled. As a result, you could get just about any convention space dirt-cheap . . . If you felt like playing.

As I write this, there has been a horrific fire in California, and hundreds of people are out of their homes. Getting a convention center there would be difficult, since a lot of people will be staying in hotels and many emergency services are renting those convention centers to provide free food and bedrolls.

Don't exploit tragedy, of course, but be aware of any upcoming events or local disasters that might impact your LAN party's location.

So when you're looking around, be bold and keep asking for more than you think you can get. You might not get it all, but you'll be surprised at how much you *do* get.

In addition, be creative. Point out, for example, that if they go to the expense of hooking in an Internet connection for your LAN party, they will be able to charge more to their *other* customers who want Internet access. If you're really tech-savvy, you might be able to convince them that, in fact, *you're* the man who can install the DSL line for them (for the cost of a free weekend's rental, of course).

Remember that. Get them to come to you and give you the best deal possible, because *they're* the ones under the gun — not you.

Can that freedom be intimidating? Yep. It's just like shopping for cars, and the flexibility in price is not for everyone — nobody likes wondering whether they got ripped off! But there's only one way to make sure you're getting the best deal, and that is to comparison shop. Don't just get a quote from one place; get a quote from three or four rental locations, and then choose the best one.

The second rule of renting?

Rule Number 2: Shop around. A lot.

With those two important commandments out of the way, let's get to the meat of the matter — namely, how do you find a location that's right for you?

Preparing to look for a location

The first things you need to know when you're space hunting are answers to three questions: When? How much? How many? If you don't know the answers to these three questions, don't pick up the phone.

When do you plan to hold your LAN party?

Generally, you want to try to book at least a month in advance in order to guarantee a space. Like everything else, though, that's subject to negotiation; if the weekend is fast approaching and your local convention center hasn't had any other offers to rent their space, you can sometimes snag a prime location with a day's notice.

You shouldn't count on that, though.

As a general rule, the more people you have, the farther in advance you'll have to book. You can usually find a 300-square-foot location (which is teeny) with a week's notice, max. If you want a 15,000-square-foot location for a thousand-person fragathon, six months is the minimum time you need to book in advance.

In addition to the date, check the time; *you* want to play all night, but when does this place close? Many convention centers are used to early closings, well before midnight, whereas most outside LAN parties are all-nighters. You need to ask up front what time they close, and whether that time is negotiable.

How much are you willing to pay?

There's no sense looking off-site unless you have a clear figure in mind. As you will see in Chapter 5, "Saving Money on Your LAN Party," you never want to hold a LAN party that you can't afford to pay for yourself. If everybody gets sick at the last minute, you're the one who's going to be stuck with the bill.

Therefore, assuming that it's all going onto your credit card, how much are you willing to pay? Figure that out beforehand, so you know what's unacceptable.

How many square feet will you need?

Rental properties are measured in square feet. An average apartment is between 500 and 1,000 square feet, but that square footage is broken up into tiny rooms. Most rental properties offer one room, and that room can be 300 square feet (small) to 30,000 square feet and up (such as the E3 Expo in Los Angeles).

Playing Chicken with the Rental Property

If you're willing to play very fast and loose, sometimes you can get amazing deals. The closer it is to the actual date of the event, the more eager a property owner will be to cut you a magnificent deal. Of course, last-minute plans also make it more likely that someone else may step in and snap up your space at the last moment. (Or, as is more likely, the property owner will sense that you're trying to rip him off and just tell you to get lost.)

If you absolutely need to commit to a date—as in, you're holding a professional event to which people are paying admission—then plan it a minimum of a month out. If you're just looking to goof around with some friends, you can sometimes afford to wait until the last minute to see how low the price will drop.

How Many People Are Attending?

You'll probably want to flip over to Chapter 5, and specifically the section "Figuring Out How Much to Charge," which details how to accurately estimate the number of people who will really attend. In most cases, more people will promise to attend than will actually show up.

In order to figure out how much square footage you'll be using, you need to know the number of players who'll be attending your little shindig.

As a general rule, every player uses between 9 square feet (if you're assuming a 3-foot square space, or two people sharing a 6-foot table) and 25 square feet (if you're assuming a 5-foot square, or two people sharing a 10-foot table). The average seems to be about 20 to 25.

Don't forget that you have to add in space to actually move around—otherwise, you'll have all of the tables jammed up against each other—so a good rule of thumb is about 25 to 30 square feet per player, or just over a 5-foot square per player, including aisles and wiring.

Once you know those three variables, you can pretty much ask all of the relevant questions. As an added bonus, since the average computer uses about 3 amps, you can calculate your total power supply (3 × the number of users = total power needs).

Cross-Reference If you're confused about what amps and power supplies mean, go to Chapter 6, "Avoiding Power Failures" and find out all about them.

Hunting Down a Location

You can check the following three sources to find a good LAN party location:

- The yellow pages
- Friends and relatives
- The Internet

The best method is the least obvious to wireheads like us.

The Yellow Pages

"What?" you shout. "This is the age of Google and Yahoo! and Web searches! Why would I bother to haul out some antiquated pressed-wood technology when I have *the Net?*"

Well, if you're starting out, you'll want to look for the smallest, cheapest location. And those cheap locations are the ones that *don't* make their full-time living off of renting property. Places like church basements, 4-H Halls, Veterans Halls, Shriners Halls and the like all bought their buildings in order to hold their own private functions, and rent only to help defray their operating expenses.

As mentioned earlier, convention halls and hotels are very visible, very technologically up-to-date, and very expensive. If you want to pay top dollar, be my guest. The good, cheap rentals come from the Loyal Order of Moose Internationals and other fraternal organizations that *aren't* going out of their way to advertise.

Get out a phone book, look under "Fraternal Organizations," and then call them up one by one to see if they are willing to rent out their hall. Then call your local churches and see if they have space. If the church doesn't rent, talk to the pastor and see if he knows of any places that do rent to smaller organizations. Chances are good that he does know — churches hold a lot of social functions.

The following are good places to call if you're stumped or don't have a phone book handy:

- The local veterans' organization (often called "The Veterans of Foreign Wars," "The VA Hall," the "(insert ethnicity here) Legion of American Vets," and so forth
- The American Legion
- 4-H
- The Salvation Army
- The Shriners
- The Masonic Lodge
- The Loyal Order of Moose
- The Fraternal Organization of Eagles
- The Knights of Columbus
- The Elks Lodge
- The Independent Order of Odd-Fellows
- Any police officers' organizations

You can find a thousand more local chapters of various brotherhoods, but that's a place to start. You can find *some* of these places listed on the Internet, but many more aren't, and the ones that aren't in Google are going to be cheaper.

Tip Always keep in mind family discounts and Masonic connections. Remember, if your uncle is a member of the Loyal Order of Moose, you can use that to get priority reservations. Most of these places are old boys' clubs in one form or another, so if you know Uncle Phil's a Water Buffalo, use that connection. It pays off.

Friends and relatives

Actually, a lot of times, the best source of information is good ol' Mom. If she's lived in the area for a while, Mom will frequently turn up the name of a good place that held a tag sale or a bake sale a while back, so *ask her*.

Now, maybe your mom's not that active in the community. But who said we were talking about *your* mom? *Someone's* mom probably knows—or if it's not mom, it's an aunt or an uncle. Have everyone ask their relatives if they know of a good place for a small convention of computer users.

The Internet

You can do searches on the Internet—just look up "Convention Centers" in your area, or go to www.meetinglocations.com. The danger of Internet rankings, however, is that they frequently involve a kickback of some sort; usually, the search engines are weighted subtly (and sometimes invisibly) to steer you toward a more expensive option.

MeetingLocations.com in particular is very good and very thorough, giving you the square footage of each location, the largest ballroom, and the number of hotel rooms available. Note that it doesn't show you all the sites, however. It just shows you the ones that have paid to advertise on MeetingLocations.com.

As such, the Internet is a very good starting place, particularly for larger get-togethers, but be sure to do some real-life digging or you may find yourself paying more than you have to.

Dealing with the Columbine aftermath

So you've got a couple of places you want to call. Now what?

First, you'll have to deal with a rather unfortunate fact of life that all LAN parties have to deal with: the long shadow that a pair of disturbed teenagers has cast over computer gaming as a whole.

On April 20, 1999, Dylan Klebold and and Eric Harris stormed into Columbine High School in Colorado armed with guns and explosives, and decided to kill as many people as possible. They killed 12, and injured many more, before finally taking their own lives in the high school library.

Now, these were seriously disturbed youths who'd had violent fantasies for a long time. But in the rush to judgment that followed immediately after this terrible tragedy, people looked for any reason why two kids would massacre their fellow schoolmates.

Many theories abounded, some valid, others not, but one seemed to stick more than any other: *The Columbine killers had played violent videogames. That's why they killed.*

Hmm.

The *games* did it? And not two young men who had a very distorted view of reality, not to mention violent impulses? The prevailing theory seems more than a little bogus to me. Lots of people play videogames all the time, and they're as nice and friendly as can be.

But, alas, when you're going around trying to get people to rent you a space to play videogames, the first image that leaps into most people minds is the Trenchcoat Mafia, guns in hand.

You are going to have to convince them that you're *not that*.

As such, when you call a rental property, speak softly and politely. When you meet a prospective renter, dress well; put on a button-down shirt and wear clean pants. Be prepared for any nervousness — particularly from church officials or older people who don't play computer games — and reassure them that yes, while the games themselves can feature blood, clicking a mouse is nothing like firing a real gun, and everyone there knows that it's just a game. It's just a very hi-tech version of playing Cowboys and Indians.

Make it sound like a fun social activity, and stress that it's a meeting place for teenagers and adults to socialize — unlike the solitary Columbine kids, who preferred to stay by themselves. Talk up how great it is to meet people face-to-face, and mention that you have pizza and soda and other wholesome American foods.

Above all, be honest. If you're going to spend the evening shouting obscenities and downloading naughty pictures, you will eventually be caught. Be up-front about what you do, and be prepared to walk away if it's not a good fit.

Casing the location

After you call and get an initial price that you're comfortable with (you never start negotiations until you've seen the location), drive on down with a friend to take a look, and ask to tour the site with a maintenance person who has access to the circuit breakers and understands the electrical system. (Power supplies are *very* important.)

Before you go, ask the maintenance person to bring *a copy of the room's floor plan,* including outlet locations and exact physical dimensions; explain that you will need the floor plan to determine whether you can fit all of the computers into the room. If the floor plan isn't available for some reason, you'll have to make one at the site.

As for you, bring some form of pluggable device to verify that an outlet is working (a cell phone recharger or even a cheap nightlight will do just fine in the absence of professional equipment such as a tone generator) and a tape measure.

Now you are ready to drive out there and ask what's included.

Is the room big enough?

This is the big one. Square footage is a strangely mutable figure; I've lived in 750-square-foot apartments that felt larger than 1,250-square-foot homes. Walk it off, and try to determine whether you can fit in all the tables.

In addition, take a hint from *D&D* and don't split the party into two rooms unless you have to. Many places will tell you they have the total square footage that you need, but it's spaced out between two rooms. In my experience, two rooms are a lot more of a pain to administer; you have to run more cable, you have to make announcements in two rooms, you have to bring extra speakers for any music.

Keep it to one large open space, if at all possible. You'll thank yourself for it later.

Is the power supply sufficient?

Right after being too small, this is the big deal breaker — and it's why you want a maintenance person there with you. Walk through the space and map the room's power circuits, double-checking that you have enough circuits available to plug everyone in without blowing a fuse.

Outlets Are Not Circuits

I discuss this in Chapter 6, but it's worth repeating here: The number of outlets in a room has *nothing* to do with the number of computers you can plug in. What's important is how many power circuits are available in the room, a fact that can only be known after you've power-mapped the room.

In fact, power is so utterly critical to the well-being of your party that I've devoted an entire chapter to it. I suggest you read Chapter 6 before you scout out any site.

Cross-Reference For more on mapping circuits, check out Chapter 6, "Avoiding Power Failures."

Ask whether the circuits are 15-amp circuits or 20-amp circuits, and don't accept an uncertain answer. If you guess the amperage and get it wrong, your party will grind to a halt as you frantically try to shunt power from other circuits. Mark where the outlets are on the floor plans.

In addition, you want to look at the circuit breaker box to ensure that you're not actually using fuses. You want switches, which are much easier to maintain.

Are Internet connections available?

See if the space you would like to use has a DSL or T1 high-speed Internet connection, and whether it can be shared. Many pre-established LAN connections at rental properties are plug-and-play, utilizing NAT technology to share an outside connection, and feature their own DHCP service. This can be a real timesaver; all you have to do is plug a couple of switches into their main panel, and bingo! Everyone has their own IP addresses and are ready to frag.

Cross-Reference For details on NAT, check out Chapter 8, "Networking for Large Groups and the Internet."

But be sure to ask how the connection works, as some older systems may require a logon ID and password. Also ask whether there's a firewall, and whether it can be preconfigured to allow outside access, assuming that's what you want.

If the location doesn't have a high-speed Internet connection, ask if there is an outside line that you can use for dialup. In addition, ask if you have to dial 9 or something similar to get a line, and whether the line is deactivated by default. (You may have to pay a fee or ask the maintenance person to activate the line for you.)

What tables and chairs are available?

Many locations offer tables and chairs free of charge for use during the event. (Sometimes they'll first offer to rent them to you for a reasonable price, but if you negotiate you can usually get them thrown in.) Ask to see the tables, and evaluate the condition they're in. Rusted struts and cigarette-burned tabletops are no fun, but you can work with them (unless they're not able to support a pair of 20-pound monitors).

In addition, measure the tables so you can map out the space at your convenience. Remember that tables represent the space on which you'll be setting everyone up, so knowing how much space they occupy is crucial.

What's the neighborhood like?

Do you feel safe in the neighborhood, or is it in a completely run-down location? If you don't feel like you could load, oh, $20,000 worth of computer equipment into an area without being mugged, maybe you'd like to reconsider.

And is there a suitable food store nearby? Is going out for snacks going to involve a three-hour drive? When do those stores close, or are they all-night establishments?

What type of tech support is available?

If the building blows a fuse, will you be able to access the circuit panel? As you'll find out in Chapter 6, many hotels have their circuit panel locked to prevent outside tampering. Will they either give you the key (unlikely) or give you the home phone number or pager of an on-duty maintenance person who can *quickly* drop by in case of an after-hours emergency?

Making the offer

Once you've determined that the room is workable, and you've convinced the owner or manager that you're not wild-eyed psycho killers, it's time to do the tough thing.

Now you've got to dicker. It can be hard and embarassing if you're not used to it. You now have to look this person straight in the eye and say, nicely but firmly, "That's not good enough. Give me more."

Some of them may get offended. You must be polite enough to give them an opportunity to decline, by saying something like "I don't know whether I can afford that much. I like this location, though; is there any way to come down on the price?"

The sections that follow will give you an idea of the primary rules of negotiation you should follow in order to get the best deal.

1. Never give them a specific price.

2. If they won't budge on price, get them to throw in freebies.

3. If they won't budge on price or freebies, consider walking.

4. When you sign over a deposit, always get a receipt.

5. If it's not in writing, it's worthless.

Let's examine each of these in turn.

Never offer a specific price

Suppose you're trying to rent a space from a property owner. Once you offer a figure, owners know that they can go above that — whereas if you offer no guidelines at all as to what you can afford, they are going to try to lowball it as much as possible. Why offer $550 if they might be thinking $400?

Get the other person to go first. If he or she won't commit to a figure either, then suggest the absolute best price you think you could get for the room — not what you think is reasonable, but the "shoot-for-the-moon" price that would enable you to later tell all of your friends, "*I got the room for $250!*"

The property owner may say, "I can't do that," in which case, you once again try to elicit a specific number by saying something like, "So what are you comfortable with?" If you still can't get the price reduced, follow the next rule.

Get them to throw in freebies if they won't come down in price

Be creative, but get the property owner to throw in tables and chairs, or the key to the circuit panel, or free soda. See if you can get *something* for free; don't be too greedy, but try to get some spice on the deal.

Note, however, that the smaller the location, the less room you have to negotiate. That may sound silly, but remember: The primary motivation of the Shriners Hall or church basement is generally not to make a profit, but to defray costs. If you come across as too aggressive, they may just say, "To hell with you, you're too much trouble," and walk. Convention centers are terrified to lose any money.

So when you ask, be nice, and be willing to give something back in return. Negotiating isn't about getting what you want — it's about meeting in the middle, so *both* parties can walk away happy.

If, after several moments of dickering, you're not getting anywhere, follow the *next* rule.

Considering walking if they won't budge on price or freebies

Remember, you don't have to take a particular place. There are others. Go out and look for them.

If you can both reach an arrangement, the owner will generally ask for a deposit on the space, either by check or by credit card, at which point you will need to commit a certain amount of money in order to guarantee the space. (The amount of the deposit is also negotiable, and smaller establishments may not require one at all.)

When providing a deposit, always getting a receipt

You don't want to wind up in court, claiming that you gave someone a check. Whenever you hand over any money, make sure you have proof that the property owner accepted it.

Once you've handed over the deposit, you'll generally be given a boilerplate contract — a premade contract with blank spaces for typical items (such as the date, the deposit amount, and your name). Read the contract carefully, and make sure there are no strange clauses you're uncomfortable with.

Bear in mind that even the contract is negotiable; if there's a part you object to, ask to have it struck out. All you have to do is draw a firm line and an "X" through the part of the contract you don't like, and if both of you sign it then that part of the contract no longer applies.

And don't forget that you can add things to the contract, too. Did your property owner promise to have the circuit breaker key available to you the night beforehand? Write that in. Did they promise to waive the normal operating hours? Write that in. And be sure to have the owner initial all the changes to provide legal proof that everything was okayed. This part is important, particularly if you're dealing with a manager who might have given too much away and is tempted to try to take something back when the boss sees the deal.

Once you're done, sign on the dotted line, but remember Negotiating Rule Number 5:

Getting it in writing

If you have a property owner who wants to do things on a handshake, *run*. Verbal agreements can be contested in court, but they're so difficult to prosecute that they might as well be lost causes. A person who wants a verbal agreement is either hopelessly naive or hoping to cheat you.

When you have everything in writing beforehand, no one can contest what was agreed upon; it's all there. If it's not in writing, one of you can "forget" what you agreed to. *Always* keep a paper trail, or risk losing everything.

Once you've done that, take a copy of your contract (and make sure it has all of the changes you both agreed on), and you're ready to start promoting your event!

Cross-Reference

For more on promoting the event, see Chapter 5, "Saving Money on Your LAN Party."

The Hotel Room Discount and Group Rates

One of the most common deals you'll see at big convention centers is the "group rate" trick. Most large convention centers are associated with a large hotel, and the hotel wants to rent rooms as well as convention space. The group rate trick is where the hotel sets aside a block of rooms at the official hotel under your LAN party's name. Anyone who asks for those rooms specifically gets a discount. The more people who stay in those rooms, the bigger the discount you get on your convention space.

A win-win situation? It would seem so, particularly if you have a lot of people coming in from out of town. And the out-of-towners get a discount, right?

Well, not necessarily. For one thing, gamers tend to be cheap by nature, and the "discount" price you get for reserving a room isn't nearly as great as, say, booking a room in advance via Priceline.com. For another thing, gamers tend to have fewer qualms about sharing a room than most people do. Whereas business travelers will sleep two or three to a room, gamers will cram six or seven people in and let half of them sleep on the floor.

In other words, technically you can get a discount via the "group rate," but only if you can convince all of your gamers that booking the hotel room is critical to your success. Otherwise, you may wind up short.

Getting ripped off

You're not likely to get ripped off. If you follow my rules, most rentals will go quite smoothly, especially if you look at several places and choose from the best. Occasionally, things do go wrong, and sometimes you lose money. If that happens, you do have options — unless you closed the deal with a handshake.

If you didn't get anything in writing, you're pretty much out of luck. As I said, you can sue, but your evidence is a lot weaker, and who wants to spend time and money on court costs? Conversely, if the owner breaks the contract in some easily verified way (for example, not having it ready for you on the agreed-upon date), then your first avenue of recourse should be to try to get your deposit back, plus any expenses incurred. To do that, you'll need evidence. Take photos of anything that may be disputed later (and put a newspaper next to it to verify the date as best you can), such as the condition of the hall or a circuit breaker that was locked when it wasn't supposed to be. Then gather all of your paperwork and prepare to launch an informal case against the property owner.

First call and try to get through to the owner; if you can't work out a deal via the phone, then write a polite letter detailing your troubles, explaining the situation, and asking for reparations before you have to go to court.

If that accomplishes nothing, report the person to the Better Business Bureau so the establishment has a mark on its record, and then consider whether you want to take it to small-claims court.

The laws specifying what's a valid small claim vary from state to state, but generally you have to be able to prove a financial loss between $3,000 and $7,500. However, be warned that the court will *not* assist in collection; they can rule that the property owner owes you $5,000, but they cannot demand immediate payment. As such, the important question is not "How much can I get?" but "Can I collect if I win?" If the answer is no, eat your loss in dejected silence.

If you think that you can strong-arm the person — and sometimes you can stir up a fuss in the local media to force compliance — then feel free to bring them to court. Many courts require one of two options:

- **Pre-trial mediation.** This is where a neutral third party comes in to try to settle the dispute before going all the way to a judge. These mediators tend to be effective — over half of all claims are usually settled to both parties' satisfaction. You may not get everything you wanted in a successful mediation deal, but you will usually get *something*.

- **Automatic countersuing.** If the property owner feels that you have a nuisance case — one in which you're just wasting their time — they can choose to countersue, so if you lose, you'll owe *them* money. In order to prevent frivolous lawsuits, several states *mandate* that any small-claims lawsuit must be countersued; after all, you're far less likely to file a claim if there's a chance you could lose money on the outcome!

You don't need a lawyer in small-claims court, but you do need to have your evidence, and make it clear. The judge knows neither of you — so dress well to convince him or her that you're the offended party, have all of your paperwork and photographic evidence handy to prove that Logic Is On Your Side, and prepare a concise opening statement — something like the following:

Your honor, on September 5, 2003, I gave Ron Samson a $200 deposit to rent his meeting hall on October 23, 2003. Here's the deposit receipt, and here is the contract. When I arrived on the specified night, my friend Keith Krempels — who can testify today — and I discovered that the hall was locked, and that Mister Samson was not reachable at the phone number that was given to us.

Remember that the property owner is likely to have a story that is completely at odds with yours. Stick to the facts, have eyewitnesses handy to testify if need be, and bring all of the paperwork with you. If you do your homework, chances are good that you'll win.

Laying Out Your LAN Party

Earlier in this chapter I said you'll want a copy of the floor layout. Now you want to take it back home with you and start marking it up. If you've done things right, you'll have a floor plan with an accurate power map. Now you get to do the important bit: the layout.

The first step is to figure out what the scale of the floor map is, and then get out the construction paper. Thanks to earlier measurements, you know how big your tables are going to be. You will now cut out little construction paper tables that are sized to the scale of the room, as shown in Figure 3-1.

FIGURE 3-1: Using construction paper to lay out a room

This will enable you to move tables around in real time without having to redraw everything every time you want to shift a line of tables. Simply line them up in a pattern that works for you — just don't sneeze! Be sure to cut out placemarkers for any other large items you may need — things such as Playstation 2s and the televisions, projection screens, DDR machines, large sound systems, and so on. Your layout will eventually look similar to the one shown in Figure 3-2.

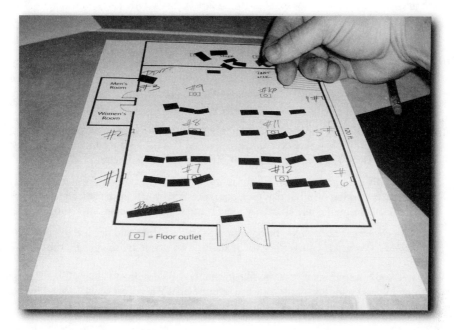

Figure 3-2: A drawing of a bigger place

Now use some colored pencils to lay out cables and wiring, so that you can erase them when necessary. Get to work!

When you lay out your LAN party, keep the following things in mind:

- **Table space.** Generally, each player requires about 3 feet worth of table, though it can be more or less if you desire. A 6-foot table holds two people, a 10-foot table holds three.

- **Power circuits.** Remember that, on average, you can hook only six computers up to a power circuit before it goes kablooey. You can run extension cords to carry power from one end of a room to the other, but you need to plan on that extension cord. When you're mapping out a room, be sure to include all power strips and extension cords neces- sary to get the electricity under the tables that need them.

- **Networking cable.** Figure out where your main switches and hubs will be, and then determine where you're going to lay the cable to the individual computers. Take into account any set limits on cable, and take careful measurements to determine how long each line is. Nothing's worse than finding out that you have 5-foot cables and 6-foot distances.

Bundle your cables! Try to run extension cords and networking cable side by side, preferably along the sides of (or underneath) tables. A messy LAN party with spaghetti-style wiring almost inevitably involves someone tripping.

- **Aisles of access.** First-time LAN partiers often assume that computers will just magically appear on the day of the event. They don't. Unless you strategically arrange for 5-foot-wide corridors to enable people to lug heavy monitors to their assigned locations, you're likely to bruise the backs of people's heads as newcomers clumsily strong-arm 20-pound pieces of equipment down 2-foot-wide corridors.

- **Line of sight.** Remember that you're going to be making announcements all day; try to put your head table where everyone can see you. You don't want to force people to stand up to see where you are. Is a raised platform available? Even better.

- **Air conditioning/heat vents.** If your rental space has them, try to keep people away. If the AC is working on a hot day, fine, but more often you'll force someone to endure a continual stream of chilly air all day long. Naturally, most people don't bring sweaters.

- **Dark corners.** Nobody likes being crammed into a corner, and particularly one that's all shadows. People keep forgetting you're there. It's nasty, so try to keep that to a minimum.

When you've got everything where you like it, simply use a dollop of Elmer's Glue™ to get everything in place, and then photocopy the layout. Voilà! You've just accomplished the easiest, most customizable way of laying out your party!

Summary

In this chapter, you've considered the pros and cons of each kind of place, and learned how to get the best prices. (Ask for the stars, and don't be ashamed to ask for a little more.) You've also reviewed the guidelines you need to follow in order to create a LAN party layout, though I'll go into more detail on physical layouts in Chapter 9.

Now that you've decided what kind of party you want to have and know where you're going to hold it, it's time to move on to the next topic: planning the party in advance.

The Complete Preparty Timeline

L AN parties can be as simple as calling two friends on Friday afternoon for a Friday Night Frag, or as complex as a thousand-person party that needs to be reserved eight months out. Most parties, however, fall somewhere in the middle; they need to have some of the details planned in advance, and it can be very easy to drop the ball. Therefore, just to help you out, this chapter presents a handy little schedule to help you know when your deadlines are due.

One to Six Months Before: Establishing the Guidelines

This is the advanced planning stage, though the exact amount of time you need changes depending on how many people will be attending. This can be condensed to as little as two weeks out if you're holding a smaller LAN party of seven or eight people. Conversely, larger 500-person LAN parties usually start planning six months to a year before the event. However, the further out you plan, the more likely it is that you can get the equipment you need, and that everyone will be able to attend.

Setting your parameters

As mentioned in Chapter 2, you want to figure out the basics: a rough estimate of how many people will be attending, what floor rules you want to have, and what games you'll be playing.

Finding a place to play

If it's at your house, make sure any roommates or live-in partners are cool with the date. More than one LAN party has been scotched because someone scheduled a big LAN party during a roommate's finals week or on a partner's anniversary date.

If your party's going to be too big for your house, reserve the venue right now and lock in the date. I showed you how to do all of that in Chapter 3. But just for you lovely people skimming through, note that six weeks to two months is about the time you want to start thinking about reserving an outside venue for a medium-sized party. You can get better prices if you're willing to wait until closer to the date, as rental halls get desperate when facing empty spaces, but you also risk having last-minute plans backfire and being left without a place to play. For more information, refer to Chapter 3, "Choosing a Site for Your Party."

Setting the date

Obviously, if you're running a small-time party, you may not have to go to great lengths to set the date. You might just be able to say, "Hey, what's everyone doing next Friday?" In my experience, the best LAN parties tend to be mini-events, and the further out you set them, the more it feels like Somewhere To Be. If you hold your in-house LAN parties once a month and set a regular date (say, the first Saturday of the month), you'll generally have more people show and they'll be more jazzed about being there.

Requesting the equipment

As you'll learn in Chapter 5, "Saving Money on Your LAN Party," your friends are your best resource when it comes to snagging enough networking equipment to get your LAN party up and running. In that chapter, I suggest that you make a list of everything you could possibly need for the party, and then send it out to everyone who's attending to ask if you can borrow anything.

The time to do this is *now*.

Stating the Obvious

One horrible thing about being a computer book author is that you must occasionally state things that are *painfully* obvious to most people on the off chance that someone is so catastrophically deprived that he or she cannot figure this out on his or her own. One of these facts is this:

If you want specific people to be there, make sure those people can attend on the day you'll be holding the party.

In other words, before you set a date, make sure that everyone you really want at your party can be there and doesn't have, say, a play rehearsal or a hot date scheduled. If you're a college student, don't plan a big party during finals month.

Figuring out who's on your staff

I go over the rules of staffing in Chapter 11, "Staffing Issues and Common LAN Party Roles," where I explain what common roles staffers play, guidelines for getting people to work for you, and who you should choose to help out.

Choosing your best friend as a staff member may not be your wisest move.

Now is when you ask people whether they'll be willing to help you out, and tell them what you'd like them to do.

Looking for sponsorship

If your plan is to hand out any sorts of free trinkets, such as keychains or mouse pads, letting the companies that provide those items know far in advance is a Real Good Idea. Some companies send stuff out the day you ask for it, but others have this vast bureaucratic process that takes weeks. Unless you know what kind of company you're dealing with (or have an excellent contact within that company), get your requests in early.

If you're looking for any *good* stuff, such as a video card or a hard drive, definitely ask as far in advance as you can. Obviously, these items usually take longer to ship than a free box of demo disks, and it will probably take you some extra time to convince the company that it's in the company's best interest to donate something valuable.

If you'd like to know how to get a company to give you free stuff, that dirt can be dug up in Chapter 5, "Saving Money on Your LAN Party."

Starting the publicity

If you're going to hold a party for profit, you'll probably want to advertise. Now's about the time you want to update your Web site (or create one), e-mail notices to appropriate people (including any mailing lists), post the event on LANParty.com and BluesNews.com, and initiate any other contact with the public you'd care to make.

One thing you should *not* do yet is post fliers. Post a flier a month in advance and chances are good it'll be taken down long before the party starts. Hold off.

Drawing up the party map

You learned about the guidelines for laying out a party at the end of Chapter 3, "Choosing a Site for Your Party," and several sample layouts are provided in Chapter 9. You should take the time now to wander around whatever space you'll be using and map it out (including power circuits), plotting out where everyone will set up their computers and where they will plug in.

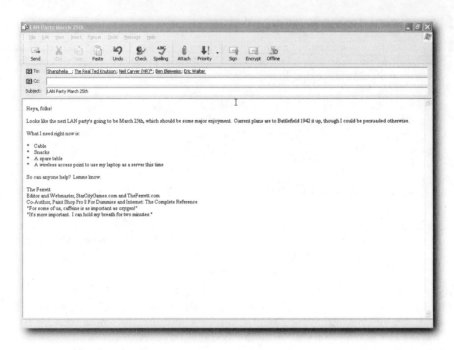

FIGURE 4-1: Publicity mailing

You especially need to carefully map out configurations in smaller spaces such as apartments, where you don't have much room for error. (Of course, if it's your house, you're probably not planning a month in advance.) Considering that you'll probably have to shift bookcases and the like in order to make room for everyone, and maybe borrow a table or two, you *definitely* want to figure out where everyone is sitting. Nothing is worse than showing up for a LAN party, only to find that you're the person who has to sit in the beanbag chair.

The Week Before: Notifying Participants and Preparing Materials

You're getting closer to the date now. This is when you do your reminders and get your grunt work done in advance.

Reminding your lenders and setting a pick-up time

As already mentioned, the most efficiently run LAN parties tend to run on borrowed equipment. If you're borrowing someone's hardware, this is when you phone them (don't e-mail them) and say, "Hey, don't forget, you promised to lend us your 36-port router this Saturday. When can we come get it?"

Doing so will help you ensure that you'll have everything you need. Chapter 5 notes several danger signs of people who will mysteriously disappear the day before the LAN party; you might want to brush up on that, just on the off chance your lender's a flake.

Posting fliers

Seven to ten days prior to your event, people are beginning to plan their next weekend. That's when your fliers (see Figure 4-2) will be effective; people can remember that a big LAN party's coming up next weekend, but they usually won't remember that one's planned for two months from now.

As for where to actually *put* your fliers, well, I'll tell you that in Chapter 5.

Burning the appropriate CDs and creating welcome materials

As I suggest in Chapter 13, "The Complete Day-of-the-Party Timeline," it's usually a pretty good idea to burn a welcome CD for everyone. A good welcome CD contains a free virus scanner, the latest game patches, your customized maps, and any other software (such as game clients) that you think your guests will need. In addition, you can burn some pretty great tunes on there while you're at it.

FIGURE 4-2: Posting an invitational flier

Since it can take a while to burn multiple CDs, and it's kind of a pain to sit there swapping out discs, I advise doing this well in advance to free up time on the night before the party. You'll be spending your time laying out cable and troubleshooting the night before, and if something goes wrong, you'll be glad you did this already.

In addition, if you have anything else you want to hand to people as they walk in through the door — fliers for supporters, a copy of the floor rules, an "orientation sheet" with lists of all the local restaurants and nightspots — then do it now.

Making and testing cables

If you're going to be making cables — and you probably should be at larger parties — then spend some time crimping and capping them tonight (see Figure 4-3), making sure you have the right lengths, and verifying that they can carry an actual signal. Cable-making is one of those activities that always seems to take more time than you think it will, so allot a large space on your schedule for this.

Cross-Reference If you don't already know, you can learn how to make cables in Chapter 8, "Networking for Large Groups and the Internet."

Figure 4-3: Crimping cables before the big event

The Night Before: Setting Up and Testing

You are now approaching zero hour. Tonight is the night you want to have everything laid out and ready to go, so that you have plenty of time to fix things should they go wrong. Ideally, you set everything up so that you can wake up in the morning and just start the party.

Note — Extremely large parties require a lot more setup time. If you're creating a 300-person LAN, don't expect to lay it all out in one night — you may need to start a week or more in advance.

Picking up the equipment

You've already asked people if you could borrow stuff, and you've reminded them of their promise earlier in the week. Now go walkabout and get all of your loaned goodies.

Caution — You can pick up the equipment on the morning of the event, of course, but that means if Joe Lender isn't there, you're going to have less time to scramble. I always advise at least a previous-night pickup, and maybe two or three days earlier, depending on how reliable — or unreliable — your source is.

While you're at it, get all the food, freebies, and any other things you need. This is your last chance.

Checking into off-site locations

If you're playing at an external location, now is when you go to your rental property owner and pick up the key. Before the owner leaves, you will want to do the following:

1. Get the name and phone number of the maintenance person. Double-check that the maintenance person will be available on the night of the party and that he knows you may need his services. (Remind the owner, gently, that you won't pay full rental fees if you spend three hours in the dark.)

   If the owner seems reluctant to provide this information, why not ask one last time if you can have the key to the circuit box and save him the trouble?

2. Walk around to double-check that there aren't any major problems with the rental space on the day that it's handed off to you. In particular, look for dirty areas or broken property that might result in lawsuits later if the owner decides to claim that you're the one who broke it. If there are any questionable areas, ask the owner to sign and date a piece of paper acknowledging that the rental property was presented to you with some major flaw. (Obviously, mention what that flaw is on the slip of paper.)

3. If the room has Internet access, double-check the connectivity.

Say Cheese!

It's not a bad idea to take Polaroid photos of the place when you first check in, just in case there's a legal dispute later about the condition in which you returned it. Photos will show the initial condition of your rental space; just be sure to write the date and time on the back of the photo.

(Incidentally, digital photos aren't as convincing as Polaroids, because everyone knows that you can alter digital photos. Stupid? Maybe, but the idea is to convince a judge.)

---

4. Check all keys that you are given, verifying that they are the proper keys and that the locks work.

5. If you have negotiated extra hours for an all-night or late-night event, remind the owner of these special hours and make sure that any overnight or closing-shift staff are aware of this. (This is usually an issue only at convention centers, but it may well be a problem if they have a janitor who cleans at midnight.)

Setting up your LAN

Naturally, you will have created a paper plan well in advance, and will have brought a large copy that you can tape to a wall.

Tip If you're running a big event, you'll also want to print smaller copies of the plan that your setup folks can carry in their back pockets.

Following are the usual steps for setting up a LAN:

1. Set up the furniture.

2. Lay out the LAN.

3. Lay out the power.

4. Test the equipment.

5. Clean up.

Each of these is discussed in the following sections.

Setting up furniture

Because people are going to be putting computers on tables, now is when you move all of your tables, chairs, speakers, and any other hard-to-move equipment into position.

Ideally, you will have laid out the furniture placements in advance with a map so you'll know exactly where each table, chair, and server needs to be. Thus there's not a lot to say here.

Is There *Anything* Duct Tape Can't Do?

Some people are very retentive in how they lay out their tables, using rolls of duct tape to lay out a "grid" to show everyone *precisely* where the tables should be placed. If you have a particularly large room with an empty space in the middle (or a lot of people working setup duty), this isn't a bad idea; you can use a measuring tape to make sure everything's in a straight line, and then roll the tape along it.

Laying out the LAN

Laying out the LAN involves stringing out all the cable; putting all the routers, hubs, and switches into place; and configuring any complex network hardware, such as routers.

In addition, you'll want to set up your servers now—particularly your game servers. When you get to the testing phase in a moment, you'll want to verify that you can connect to a live game server and join in a game. Repeat after me: *Pinging is not playing*. Sometimes, you can ping a server and yet still not be able to join a game on it—thanks to a misconfigured firewall or router.

Cross-Reference

If you don't know what a ping is—or even what a switch or a hub or a router is—don't worry. I explain all this networking stuff in Chapter 7, "The Least You Need to Know about Networking."

Laying out power

You can sometimes do this at the same time that you do the LAN layout, depending on the size of your party; in any case, you will need to run extension cords, put in surge suppressors, and mark *very clearly* where everyone is supposed to plug in at each station.

Testing, testing, testing

Laying out the cables is easy. Now you want to make sure that your LAN is configured properly. That's a multi-step process that usually includes the following tasks:

- **Ensuring that your DHCP server, if you have one, is working.** If you've gone with the convenience of a DHCP server, make sure that it's configured properly and hands out IP addresses the way you like. Verify that at least one computer at each switch and hub on your network can request a valid IP address.

- **Verifying that every computer station can ping the relevant servers.** That's usually as simple as hauling a laptop around to each station and pinging any servers a computer there will need to talk to—game servers (particularly game servers on other switches), DHCP servers, routers, and DNS servers.

 This is also the point at which you test any shared Internet access you have.

■ **Connecting to the game server(s) and playing.** As mentioned earlier, in large-scale setups, you may have firewalls that prevent game data from passing through. These firewalls may be configured to allow pings but will block unknown network traffic, such as *Counterstrike* packets. You don't have to connect and play from every station, but you should try to connect to each server from at least one station on every switch at the party. (Generally, if one computer on a switch can connect to a game server, all of the computers on that switch can.)

Cleaning up

After you've got everything in place and you're sure it's all working, tidy it up and tape it down. Now is when you go through the entire area and bundle up those loose cables, move cables off to the sides so they're not where people are likely to walk (and then tape them down so they can't shift unexpectedly), and, in general, people-proof the room so that nobody's likely to trip or otherwise injure themselves. And don't forget to throw out the trash.

Now post your floor rules somewhere prominent — preferably where they can be seen when you walk in through the door.

When that's done, do one final walkabout — and I mean *walk*, as in "walk around the room to see everything from a first-person perspective." Not all safety hazards are obvious from a sniper's perspective. If it's safe, feel free to lock up and go to bed with the satisfaction of a job well-done.

You'll find out what you do on the day of the actual party in Chapter 13, "The Complete Day-of-the-Party Timeline."

The Simplest Troubleshooting

Eighty percent of all connection problems are caused by one of two things:

■ A dead or disconnected cable

■ A dead port on a switch, hub, or router

Therefore, if you can't connect to a server, do the following:

1. Check to determine whether all the cables between the computer and the server are firmly plugged in.

2. Determine whether all the cables between the computer and the server are able to carry data.

3. Confirm that all the ports into which any of the computers are plugged are working (generally by plugging each cable into another port).

For more information on troubleshooting procedures, see Chapter 15, "Something Just Went Wrong! Fixing Party Problems."

Summary

In this chapter, you learned everything you need to do before the day of the party. First, you set the location, the games, and the staff. Next, you get the equipment. Finally, the night before, you set up the actual LAN itself — and you're well on your way to holding your first LAN party! Some of these steps can seem a little intimidating for the first-time host, but I assure you, it's easier than it looks!

In the next chapter, you'll learn about something that's close to the heart of every LAN party host (and often the guests) — the budget. Every LAN party has some expenses, but with some careful planning and a little help from your friends, you can reduce your costs to almost nothing. So let's go!

Saving Money on Your LAN Party

Before we get started, you need to understand the unbreakable rule of every LAN party:

You will not make any money at it. You will probably, in fact, lose money.

This doesn't really matter if you're just planning on hauling five PCs over to Phil's house to spend a pleasant Saturday blasting your buddies. Yeah, you'll drop thirty bucks for chips and soda, but you'd do the same thing if you were having a George Romero film festival at your house or getting together to watch the Super Bowl. (That doesn't mean you should skip this chapter, though; I will show you ways to save money on the chips, both the potato and silicon kind.)

But a strange thing happens when a LAN party gets so big that it expands out of the house: People think they can make a profit off of it.

And why not? They're renting halls, buying cable, and going to a lot of effort for what used to be a simple task. They might as well try to skim some cream off the top, right?

Well, here's the blunt honest truth: Most "professional" LAN parties are lucky if they break even. After you factor in the help, the rental costs, and everything else that tallies up, you're looking at a huge bill — and somehow, you always wind up with fewer people than you had planned on to pay your entry fees.

Don't go nuts. The whole point of this chapter is to show you the tricks of running a LAN party on the cheap. Start small, and stay low; only add additional things when you're forced to. Be Scroogelike in your expenditures. Don't add things in an effort to draw in new people so that you can pay for the event.

If you follow the guidelines presented here, after all is said and done, hopefully the only thing you'll have invested into your LAN party will be a boatload of effort. Oh, you'll get paid for your troubles — but that payment will come in the form of a weekend's worth of unparalleled enjoyment, not in cash.

Three Ways to Lower Your LAN Party Costs

LAN Party expenses can usually be broken down into three basic categories:

- **Hardware.** You need to have switches, cables, power strips, and God knows what else to connect all these computers and keep them running.

- **Snacks.** Yes, you can tell everyone to bring their own, but that never really works out. Someone always forgets to bring their Cheesy Poofs and decides to run out to the store, but of course they want someone to go with them. And before you know it, half of your LAN party will be at the local QuickieMart and the other half will be arguing over pizza toppings. Trust me; it's best to have some basic drinks and chips in place at the party just to save time.

- **Space.** You need a place to put all of these computers. At smaller parties, this can be the various rooms in someone's house, but at bigger LAN parties you'll need to rent space. (I show you how to do that in Chapter 3.)

Of the three expenses, space and hardware are the most expensive, while the snacks are the biggest pain. (Unless you're an extremely small and homogenous group, *someone's* always going to complain about your choice of soda.) The following list describes the most common methods to defray these costs:

- **Borrowing stuff.** A reminder: You will most likely be gathering a bunch of computer geeks together to play. *Someone* has the switch, cable, or hardware that you need.

- **Sponsorship.** A common misperception that people have about sponsorship is that it's all or nothing: You get it free or you pay full price. But it's often true that if you have a regular LAN party of a fair size (ten or more), you can leverage your friends to get discounts on the things you need.

- **Charging entry fees and allowing strangers to participate.** When this happens, suddenly your party isn't just a fun get-together. Now that people will be shelling out the shekels to hop on your network, they expect professional entertainment.

The first two methods can be used at almost any LAN party; the third option is a little bit trickier, and it's not for everyone, so we'll leave that until last.

The Automatic Fourth Option

The one thing not mentioned yet is membership in a price club, such as BJ's Wholesale Club, Sam's Club, or Costco Wholesale. That's because it's pretty much mandatory for any serious fragaholic.

Price clubs require a membership fee up-front before they even let you in the door, but once you're a member, you can buy bulk foods at a heavily discounted price. (They also have deeply discounted DVDs, furniture, kitchen equipment, some computer hardware, and audiovisual equipment for sale.)

If you plan to hold LAN parties on a regular basis, you'll find the capability to buy entire pallets of soda and huge tubs of popcorn at a wholesaler's discount invaluable. If you're not a member of one already, find a local price club and spend the $40 for a membership; it'll pay for itself almost immediately.

Borrowing: Beg Before You Buy!

When you're starting any LAN party, you first figure out how many people are attending, and then create a comprehensive list of what you'll need. List every hub, switch, cable, NIC card, and game server you'll need to make this party hum.

Now make a list of all the noncomputer stuff. Write down how many tables you'll need, how many chairs you'll require, how many bags of Cheetos you'll collectively eat, and how many registered copies of the games you'll need. Go nuts. Tally up *everything* you need to make this party happen.

E-mail the list to everyone who's planning on showing up. Ask them if they have any of these items lying around that they can spare.

The amazing thing is that it doesn't matter how arcane or silly the item is — *someone almost always has it.* And if you need proof, check this testimonial from Ralph Evans at HatLan.com:

> When I rented a warehouse for a year to hold our regular LAN parties in, I realized that it would take about ten thousand dollars to get all of the hardware, tables, and equipment we needed. Instead of investing ten grand into it, I put out the call for switches and routers. Some guys had tremendously powerful routers that their bosses were tossing out; one guy brought us three servers; one guy brought us a small DHCP server. My Web server for HatLan was donated by one of the guys. A lot of the computer tables came from me, but a dozen came from another house, and six came from another house. People volunteered to do the labor, about six guys working for a week who set it up really nice — so everything came for free. Everyone put up their share, and it wound up costing me about three grand for the setup — just for the rooms, wall units, and deposit.

In other words, Ralph saved *more than 70 percent* just by asking his friends. And this was for a top-of-the-line deluxe LAN party. How much do you think you can save by asking your own friends?

Don't even think about it. Just beg!

Begging for services

Don't forget what your friends do for their day jobs, too. Any carpenters out there? Yeah, they can make good tables for cheap. Any electricians out there? Maybe they can wire another circuit or two into your house.

Never forget that holding a good LAN party is a collective effort. It's your job to collect everybody!

Working Stiffs

If someone lends you a complex piece of equipment, either ask him flat-out to configure it for you or take care of it yourself. One of the rudest things you can do is the old bait and switch, where you invite someone over to play at your party and then stick him with the gross details of router configuration. Be up-front about what you need so your lender knows what to expect.

Begging beyond your friends

The world of LAN parties is still mostly an underground phenomena. Yeah, there are a few high-profile events, but mostly it's just avid hobbyists getting together with their buddies. And if there's one thing that hobbyists love, it's other hobbyists.

If someone else in your town holds LAN parties, don't be afraid to call him or her up and ask a favor! Quite often, other people will be happy to lend you some upscale equipment as long as you have someone who can vouch for you. (And as long as they don't have their own event going on that weekend — but that goes without saying.)

Of course, if you're going to ask to borrow a thousand-dollar router from someone you barely know, be polite. Remember, they don't owe you anything; you're asking a *favor* here. In fact, it's probably a good idea to invite them to your party. The folks who hold LAN parties never get to play as much as they'd like to, and giving them free reign to frag over at someone else's place is always a nice touch.

Borrowing effectively

You want two things to happen when you borrow something: to have your borrowed items available for the party, and to be able to borrow that person's stuff again in the future. In order for this to happen, you need to do several things, which are discussed in the following paragraphs.

Asking nicely

Remember that the people loaning you stuff don't *owe* you anything. You need to be understanding about their concerns and not get bent out of shape if someone won't lend you something. Some people are retentive about the stuff they own. If they won't give with the goods, shrug and move on.

(Of course, there's nothing that says you need to invite this jerk to your *next* LAN party.)

Reminding and revising

Call your lenders two days before the event to remind them of the loan. (Don't e-mail. Nothing beats a good old-fashioned phone call for a gentle kick to the tuchis) Thank them again for offering to bring whatever it is that they're loaning you, and confirm that they remember the offer. Explain once again what time you need it there by, and ask for a number at which you can call them in case something goes wrong.

I Know You're Smarter Than This

A lot of the material that follows falls under the category of "stuff I shouldn't have to say." But you never know who's reading this. There are plenty of Internet trolls who've been raised on chat windows and not Miss Manners, so if this all seems self-evident, forgive me. If you have even the slightest semblance of common courtesy, you can probably move straight to the next section.

Be sure to have contingency plans for what happens if someone doesn't bring the desired item. If your party cannot function without it, it's not a bad idea to have someone else on call who can also lend it to you.

If you cannot reach a designated lender, or if they forget about the loan entirely — or, worst of all, they won't give you a number for getting in touch with them, claiming that "I'll remember" — *make other plans*. Immediately.

Returning equipment in good condition

Before you borrow a complex piece of equipment, ask your lender whether they want it back with the same settings. If you borrow a router and change everything in it to suit your LAN party, you might be sticking your benefactor with an hour's work restoring the default settings. If you're not sure, write down the settings on a sheet of paper and restore them before you give the item back.

If possible, you want to return anything you borrow in nicer condition than it was given to you. Tie up those loose cables! Dust it off! Give it a 409 rubdown! (And if it came in a box, *don't lose the box*!)

Most important, God forbid, if something goes wrong — your friend spills sticky cappuccino on a table someone lent you, or a router gets fried — be apologetic and prepared to pay damages. It's only fair.

Showing your appreciation

If your mom is anything like my mom, she forced you to write thank-you notes to your Gramma for your birthday presents. The difference between your Gramma and the friend who's lending you a preconfigured *Battlefield 1942* server is that your Gramma is genetically predisposed to love you and will always send you a birthday present, even if you're a total snot-nosed ingrate.

The friend with the server, however, is not required to be nice to you. As such, writing a follow-up e-mail — even one as simple as "thanks for the equipment" — the day after the party makes all the difference (and makes the lender feel good about lending you items in the future).

Of course, there are additional ways to express your gratitude. Inviting your lenders to the event is pretty much par for the course, but one of the best ways to say thank-you is to have everyone at the party stop fragging for a moment, and then make an announcement such as the following: "I'd just like to thank Karen, because without her router, this party wouldn't exist. Can I get a round of applause for Karen?"

She'll feel good, *you'll* feel good, and, more importantly, you'll be able to scam all the routers you need from Karen until the end of time.

Scratching everyone's back

Naturally, should anyone who's lent you an item ever ask you for something in return, lend it out. Don't be a miser.

Reducing Costs with Sponsorship

Sponsorship is commonly seen as a way of getting free stuff to give away. And, yes, that's one way of doing it. If you're holding a paid event, it never hurts to offer attendees a much-coveted item as a door prize to encourage them to pay the $15 entry fee. This is called *full sponsorship*.

But there is another form of sponsorship, called *partnership*, which is actually far more effective in the long run. In a partnership, you're not asking for free stuff. Instead, you're looking to buy the things you need at a deep discount. It's not as flashy, and it requires more effort, but in the end you'll find it a lot more rewarding.

Both types of sponsorship have something in common, though: You're asking people to essentially give you something for free. Whether it's a discount or a free hard drive, you're asking for a business to hand you over a slice of their profits in exchange for future profits. And that's not easy, because the golden rule of any business is that if it doesn't give them cash, it's not important.

Remember: *Businesses care about money.* That's *all* they care about! They don't care about friendship, they don't care about being nice, they don't care about how cool your party is or how you overclocked your chip. They care about putting money in their cash registers, and if you're not doing that, you're wasting their time.

(That doesn't mean that everyone who runs a business is a heartless capitalist swine, of course. Actually, "being nice" and "being fair" are excellent business tactics!)

The trick lies in convincing a potential sponsor that this is not a giveaway — it's an *investment.* They are giving something to you because *you* will deliver customers to their door — paying customers who will eventually buy product that is worth more than the freebie they just gave you.

That means you can't just start a sponsorship out of nowhere. You need two things: a track record, to convince them that the event is regular enough to be worth sponsoring, and enough people to make it worth their while.

The track record doesn't have to be stellar; generally, if you've held three or more events on a more-or-less regular basis, you've got enough of an official gathering to start trying to leverage some swank for your next fiesta.

As for people, usually you need at least 10 folks who show up on a regular basis. Ten people seems to be the critical mass point at which you can start to say, "I have 10 people who buy a lot of computer equipment (or pizza, or videogames, etc.). I think I can encourage them to buy their stuff from you."

Note Ten people is a starting point, but it's still not a lot of people from a retailer's perspective. Don't expect to get good freebies, such as video cards or DVD-ROM drives, with a 10-person group.

Who can you ask for sponsorship?

You can ask pretty much anyone for sponsorship. Although the traditional sponsorship model involves computer hardware, you can try to find a sponsor for just about any item that you use a lot of at your parties. People have successfully gotten partial sponsorships from pizza places, soda distributors, and even office supply houses (for labels and paper goods). When you're trying to reduce costs, consider *everything* that costs you money. And then make the pitch to everyone who sells those items to you.

You can go to virtually anybody for sponsorship, but two types of sponsors are more important than all the others: your local computer shop and hardware manufacturers. Let's examine each of these in turn.

Your local computer shop

The local computer shop is your best ally — *if* you can get them on your side. They're generally hungry for business, they're small enough to keep track of their customers, and they have the most room to maneuver on price. They're also very handy in emergencies, as they can usually get the latest hardware to you at a moment's notice.

However, they also tend to be tough to convince. Because they're an independent business in a very competitive market, their profits are also razor-thin — and they're loathe to spend money unless they're guaranteed an immediate profit. The good news is that if you can get them to sponsor you, even two or three new customers will often be enough to make a huge difference in their bottom line. Moreover, once they're convinced that you're worth their while, they can promote your next LAN party like nobody's business.

Local computer shops are tough to convince, but stay with them. They're worth it in the long run.

Going Straight to the Top

When you make your sponsorship pitch, always talk to the owner or manager. Be polite to everybody, however. Remember that the floor clerk, who is likely to be the first person you see, can always foul the deal by telling the head honcho what an arrogant jerk you are. Of course, waste as little time with nonmanagers as possible. Go straight to the person who's going to make the decision!

Why Not a Chain Store?

The big chains such as CompUSA generally aren't as responsive to sponsorship requests. Their hardware is bought by buyers at the corporate level, and they can't cut deals as effectively; furthermore, they have so many customers that the five or six people you can bring in often won't make a difference. In addition, they get a *lot* of requests from everyone else in town. That's not to say that you can't try to cut a deal with a nationwide computer chain, but it's often an uphill battle.

However, if you bought this book at a big computer chain, you might try them first. They've stocked this book, which is a good sign that they're open to attempts to improve their business.

Tip Considering that most people who work at computer shops are hard-core nerds, it never hurts to invite the employees and owners to the party — even if the store refuses to give you sponsorship. Their tune may change after they attend a couple of events and get to know you better!

Hardware manufacturers

The people who make all of those droolworthy video cards, hard drives, and monitors can sometimes be persuaded into a giveaway, which is well worth it if you can get it!

Be warned, however, that the big guys often require a huge number of people to attend a LAN party — 50 or more — and require a lot of tit-for-tat in terms of mandatory posters and banner ads. You also need to make sure you know what you're getting: I've heard horror stories about parties that plastered their Web site LAN party announcements with ugly, vibrating banner ads for months at a time, only to get a handful of mouse pads and lapel pins in the mail.

Making the pitch

You get one shot to get someone to give you money. If you walk into Joe's Computer Shack and say, "I want a free Radeon graphics card," Joe is going to ask you — and quite rightfully — why he should give you a $200 card for free. If you answer, "Well, uh, my LAN party's pretty cool and we have some people," Joe will think you are an idiot.

Joe does not give free graphics cards to idiots.

Therefore, before you go to any potential sponsor, you need to do your homework. The first question you must be prepared to answer is the first one they'll ask you: "Why should I give anything to you?"

That answer has five parts, and you must have each of them ready at hand:

- **The number of people at your party.** Obviously, the more people who attend your LAN parties, the better. However, Joe could advertise in a newspaper and reach thousands of people for less money. Thus, you have to emphasize the next point to convince him.

- **How often they buy the product.** A newspaper ad might put Joe's name in front of five thousand people, but how many of them buy computer parts on a regular basis? The good thing about LAN parties is that they're usually made up of die-hard geeks. You can inform Joe of your group's fascination with case-modding.

- **How much additional business this will bring in.** If most (or all) of your party members already shop at Joe's Computer Shack, you're in a bit of a bind. Joe wants to give you free video cards in order to bring in new business, but in this case he wouldn't get anything in return. Ideally, you have to present the ability to bring new people into Joe's shop.

- **How influential your party is.** Be sure to mention it if you have any people in your group who are in touch with other crowds who also buy Joe's product — like, for instance, the head of the local Linux users group or an IT tech at a large independent business.

- **Exactly what you're asking for.** Telling Joe that you want "well, I dunno, whatever you can spare" is not likely to convince him to be generous. Consider beforehand the needs of your group and what Joe can offer, and then ask for it specifically.

The "exactly what you're asking for" part is the most troublesome. You have to come up with a reasonable business plan before you approach a potential sponsor. Therefore, you need to first define what sort of terms you're trying to establish: Do you want *full sponsorship* or a *limited partnership*?

Limited partnership

The case for a limited partnership is much easier to sell, because you're not trying to get a free item from your sponsor, you're attempting to facilitate the sale of *discount* items. This means that your sponsor won't be losing any money (they might even turn a thin profit), and as such they can give bigger and better things away.

The down side, of course, is that you're still paying. You're paying a lot less, but your wallet's still being emptied. This is the best method for trying to get discounts from nontraditional sponsors such as pizza parlors and office supply stores.

The Blackmail Alternative

If everyone already buys their stuff from Joe's Computer Shack, you could just threaten to take your business over to Fred's Computer Shanty across the way. However, that's sure to anger Joe — and if Fred decides he doesn't like you, you may well have alienated every computer store in town. Where will you promote future LAN parties? Think very carefully before threatening to take your business elsewhere. It's generally not worth annihilating a working relationship for the sake of a discounted motherboard!

Wholesale? What's That?

Some businesses, especially small ones, don't sell to other businesses; thus, they don't have a wholesale price list. In that case, offer to buy the desired item at 5 percent above cost, which means that the sponsor tacks on a 5 percent profit to whatever price they paid for the item that you want. Just be careful that a 5 percent profit isn't more than they normally make!

Following are three approaches you can take:

- **Buy at cost.** This means that you offer to buy an item for whatever the sponsor paid for it. The sponsor earns absolutely no profit, but loses nothing either. Most businesses will do this once or twice, but after a while it becomes too much of a bother to do it for no money. After all, even if the *cost* to them is eliminated, they still have to fill out the paperwork to order the item(s).

- **Buy at wholesale price.** When businesses sell to other businesses, they sell at a deeply discounted price called the *wholesale price*. This is about as good a deal as you can expect to get on a regular basis, and is often your best starting point for negotiations.

- **Some other deal.** Here's where you get creative and go for something wacky: a "buy one, get one free" deal; giveaway coupons; a special sale that's accessible only to people who attend your LAN party. Anything your little brain can imagine.

As a guideline, however, remember that the average margin on computer products is about 8 percent, meaning that if you buy a hundred-dollar piece of software, the store takes home $8. (No, they really don't make a lot.) Therefore, asking for a "buy two, get one free" deal for those $100 graphics cards may sound like a great idea, but after you do the math, it's a bloodbath for the store:

- The store pays $92 for each $100 video card, for $276 investment total.

- They sell three of them for $200 total.

- They lose $76 in the deal.

Remember that you're attempting to help them make money. Be sensitive to their needs. Take a look at past sales and try to get an idea of what a good discount looks like for them, and then go about 10 to 15 percent below that. Keep in mind that they can always make a counteroffer. As long as you're polite and realistic about it, you can generally get some pretty good deals this way.

What If They Only Offer Free Stuff?

Some companies, particularly food companies, have a weird way of handling charity; their *only* method of sponsoring a local business is to give the food away free, as a donation. Otherwise, they offer no discount. If that's the case, you're very unlikely to convince them to cater your events for free every month. Instead, try to negotiate an on-again, off-again schedule so that they give you every fourth event for free, which is effectively a 25 percent discount.

Full sponsorship

Here, you're asking for people to give you products in return for exposure. This generally doesn't work at the small store level (though it can't hurt to try); this is generally what you angle for when you're speaking directly to the manufacturer of a product. In this case, they actually make the product, so their cost is almost half of what a retailer pays — and they can write off the giveaway as "promotional expense."

That said, you'll often be requested to go to greater lengths to get full sponsorship. The least you can expect to come away with is banner ads on your Web site (so you'd better have one, and a good-looking one at that), but often you'll be sent physical banners that you're expected to hang somewhere. Sometimes they'll even say that every mention of your LAN party has to include the manufacturer, such as "The Dallas Fragathon, sponsored by BAWLS Guarana."

Furthermore, as mentioned earlier, in general you need a much larger party to get full sponsorship than you do for a limited partnership.

Food Sponsorships

Getting your pizza subsidized, even partially, is a great uphill battle. The same goes with soda. After all, places that sell these items already sell a *lot* of pizza and a *lot* of soda, and it's not likely that they're going to be overly concerned about losing your business. There are plenty of others who'll replace you.

That being the case, you generally have to establish a consistent pattern of buying from them for a *much* longer period of time, and you may want to keep receipts to document exactly how much you've bought. This is one of those rare times where you might want to (gently) threaten to take your business elsewhere, saying, for example, "We've been buying $50 in pizza and anchovies every other Saturday for the past four months. That's $400 worth of business. All we're asking for is some form of discount, since we're such *regular customers* and have been *so loyal.*"

Most of the time, that's enough of a hint. They'll figure out something. Be aware, however, that if you threaten to walk, you need to have someplace else to take your business. Don't alienate the only good pizza shop in town!

On Giving Stuff Away

Because you generally only give items away as door prizes, I'll show you what to do with your cool freebie once you get it in the next section, "Charging Admission and Going Pro."

Closing the deal

A solid pitch looks something like this:

> I have a group of about 15 people who visit my house on a regular basis to play networked games, and we've been getting a lot of interest from new people in town, so we're going to be holding our next party at the Shriners Hall next month. So far, we estimate that about 20 people are going to show up. About two of the regulars at my party are heavily into case-modding, and they generally order their parts online, but I think I can get them over here if you agree to sponsor us. They're real fanatics.
>
> As for sponsoring us, ideally, it would be great if you'd offer us that shiny new video card over there for a giveaway, but if that's not an option, maybe you could help me to buy it at cost? And would you mind if I put posters up here to advertise the party?

If they agree, *your job does not end there*. You now have two other responsibilities: getting the word out and making sure that the party knows who's buying.

Getting the word out

If you get a small business to sponsor you, go all-out to promote them. Give the owner of the store an invitation to come play, and then make an announcement several times during the course of the event that "Joe's Computer Shack has generously given us this video card for our giveaway — his store is located at 245 Maple Street, it's open Monday through Saturday, and he offers a *lot* of case-modding stuff right here in town."

Sell your sponsors big and you'll be rewarded big.

Making sure everyone knows who's buying

An often overlooked aspect of sponsorship is *telling people to inform a business that they went there because of their sponsorship*. If, after six weeks of negotiation, you finally get Guiseppe's Pizza Parlor to offer you a discount, make sure that your LAN party is mentioned every time you or anyone else in your regular party group orders a pizza from there. If someone buys a replacement fan from Joe's Computer Shack, make sure Joe knows where that new business came from!

After all, it's no good increasing their business if they can't thank you for it! It *is* all about the bottom line, baby. Never forget that.

Charging Admission and Going Pro

Once you move out of the house, your expenses skyrocket. Going to a Shriners Hall is going to cost you a couple of hundred bucks for the weekend, and it's really not fair for *you* to pay for everything.

If you have good, solid friends, we suggest the *chip-in,* whereby you figure out what your expenses will be up front and ask everyone to share the load before you rent a location. The chip-in's a lot easier because there's no guesswork and very little chance of losing cash; if there's not enough money, you don't rent the hall. Furthermore, you don't have to worry about strangers (unless you like strangers, of course). It's a closed session, and if you haven't paid the cash, you don't get in. It's a lot easier to plan.

The professional LAN party — namely, one that's open to the public — is a lot harder to plan for, and runs a greater risk of losing money. That's not to say that it can't be done, of course, but there are some risks:

- **Uncertain cash flow.** Now you're trying to figure out what sort of money you'll get based on the number of strangers who might attend. If you guess wrong, you are stuck with the bill.

- **Responsibility.** A funny thing happens when people pay you; they feel like you owe them something. If the power goes out in your freebie LAN party, people will groan and shrug their shoulders. Now that everyone's paid to be there, they're not going to be as patient when waiting for you to remap the circuits.

- **Slightly more difficult planning.** You don't know what computers are going to be on your network now. Most of them are going to be PCs, of course, but some of them might have odd setups that you're not used to. You're still going to have to slot that guy in.

- **Strangers.** Introducing new people runs the risk of letting jerks in. Ninety-nine percent of all LAN party attendees are just fine, of course — I don't want to make you paranoid — but if Mr. l33T h4xx0R decides to show up and spend the day making fun of everyone, you're the one who has to deal with him.

Tip
If you should ever have to throw someone out of your party — which is a thankfully rare occasion — Chapter 15, "Something Just Went Wrong! Fixing Party Problems," will explain how to do it.

So how do you take your first steps toward moving out of the basement and becoming a public event? The following sections will walk you through everything you need to know.

Figuring out how much to charge

Charging the right admission fee is critical to making your money back. If you charge too little, you wind up sinking your own money into what's supposed to be a "fun" event; if you charge too much, people will refuse to come.

The primary rule of admissions, however, is this:

Don't ever hold an event that you can't pay for yourself.

If everything goes wrong, you're the one who is stuck with the bill. If three or four people you were counting on don't show up, the extra expense goes on your credit card. Fortunately, smaller LAN parties aren't that expensive—maybe a couple of hundred bucks—so it's not a huge loss for most people if it all hits the fan. But remember that old Vegas rule: *Never commit more than you can afford to lose.* If you're pouring in a thousand bucks on the assumption that 60 people will show up, think twice if the loss of that thousand bucks would make you miss your rent payment.

That said, you should do a little homework to determine your admission fee. Here are the five major steps:

1. Determine how many people are attending, and do a reality check.

2. Estimate expenses.

3. Calculate the entry fee.

4. Determine if there will be any giveaways.

5. Do another reality check.

Let's examine each of these in turn.

Why You Want Payment in Advance

It doesn't matter whether your players are hardcore *Counterstrike* clans or prefer playing *Super Mario Party*; there are two things that can be easily predicted about any group of gamers:

- They will all show great enthusiasm for your party, but half of them will have forgotten all about it when the day arrives.

- Those who *do* attend will all wait until the last minute to sign up.

Unfortunately, these tried-and-true gamer habits make it hell when it comes to accurately estimating how many people will show up. Therefore, you want to encourage people to pay you in advance and reserve slots for the event as far in advance as possible.

The best way to do this is to set up an *early signing discount*, whereby you offer a 10 percent or 25 percent discount on the admission fee in exchange for signing up before a cut-off date—generally a week before the event. That will force the people who *think* they'll show up to commit in advance (and if they forget, at least you have their cash in your pocket), and it will help alleviate many of the last-minute "Oh! I nearly forgot!" issues.

Event Caps

If the space in question can only hold a limited number of people—or you're simply not willing to handle more than a specified number of people—there's no shame in setting a maximum number of players. Just make sure you do it in advance and publicize the cap, so that everyone knows that there's a risk they could be locked out.

How many people are attending? Really?

The first mistake that people make when they go professional is to wildly overestimate the number of people who will attend. It's *possible* that your regular group of 12 could get an additional 20 people to show up for your first public party, but it's not likely. Most LAN parties start small and work their way up in increments.

Furthermore, consider this: *Everyone* says they'll attend a LAN party when you ask them. Why wouldn't they? It sounds like fun. But when the day actually arrives, you'll be surprised by how many people don't show.

Thus, when calculating how many people will show up, you *lowball like crazy*. Unless you have real, concrete reasons to believe that you'll be picking up massive numbers of new members—and by "concrete," I mean they've written you the check in advance or they're offering to pitch in to set up—figure that adding between two and five new people for a spanking-new LAN party is probably about right. (And that's assuming you do all the proper publicity work.)

I'm not trying to discourage you, mind you; it's entirely possible that you'll have a hugely popular event at which boatloads of people show up. Nonetheless, *start small. Build slowly.*

Where are you holding the party?

Find a site that will hold enough people for your party. (That's such a large task that it warrants its own separate chapter—see Chapter 3, "Choosing a Site for Your Party.") Figure out what it will cost you to rent a space for the event.

What are your other expenses?

As mentioned earlier in the chapter, one of the first things you want to do when planning any LAN party is to make a list of all the computer hardware, cables, food, door prize expenses, and everything else you'll need to keep the event going. Then send that list to all your friends and ask them who's willing to donate what.

Anything left over that you'll have to buy outright—and there usually won't be much—is an additional expense. Add that on to the total.

How much can you afford to charge?

Divide your total costs, including the rent and the other expenses your friends couldn't cover, by the *frighteningly low* number of people that you are estimating will attend. (Remember that you're lowballing your initial attendance; if you overestimate your total attendance, don't say I didn't warn you.)

Now add between two and five bucks to that. That's your starting entry fee.

Do you have a door prize?

If you have some sort of really good giveaway that you can raffle off, then you can generally get away with charging a couple of bucks extra. After all, if they could win a new DVD-ROM drive just for showing up, they'll pay a little more to get in. Depending on how good your swag is, you may be able to charge up to five bucks more.

Is the fee realistic?

It doesn't matter how good your swag is or how smooth your network runs; if you're charging $35 for a Saturday-only party with no Internet access, chances are good you're doomed to failure. At the time of this book's publication, most LAN parties run between $10 (the low end) and $25 (the high end) per day, averaging out at about $15 per day (or $30 for a two-day event).

If you can't charge a reasonable price and you're not prepared to lose the money you sink into it, then maybe it's time to find either another location or another way of holding the party.

Alternatively, maybe you can lower the admission and make up the difference from your own pocket. A lot of people do that, figuring that it's worth laying out a hundred bucks for the fun of watching all their friends in the same room. There's nothing wrong with that.

Publicizing your event

After you've decided where and when you're holding the event, the next big step is to get the word out so that everybody knows about it. This is called publicity, of course, and it's time to sell yourself out every place you can get. Since you've decided that you want people to show up, you might as well go all the way.

You can employ several methods to generate publicity, but there's one method that is a necessity in these days of ADSL and cable modems: using a Web site.

Creating a Web site

Let me be absolutely clear: *Every public LAN party needs a Web site* (see Figure 5-1). LAN party enthusiasts don't use the yellow pages to find things; they use Google. If you don't have a Web site that can be found with a search, you're at an almost crippling disadvantage.

Food Shortages

You can also, in some cases, make up for a low admission price by selling food at the event, as I'll discuss later in the chapter. But like all things here, you shouldn't rely on food to make up the admission. As mentioned earlier, don't spend more than you can afford to lose—and lowballing the event in anticipation of making your money back on soda and chips is just asking for trouble.

Of course, this book isn't about Web design, so I won't go over the details of HTML and reserving domains. (I will say, however, that a site with its own domain—such as www.ferrettslanparty.com—is a lot more professional than a freebie, hosted site such as geocities.com/Area51/snazzbo/LANParty.htm, and domains are reasonably easy to get.) However, be aware of certain items that every LAN party site should feature:

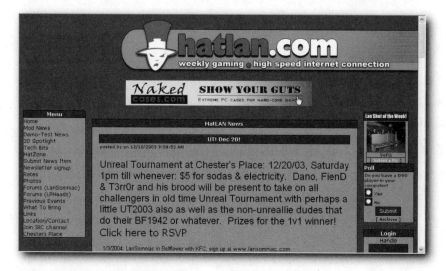

FIGURE 5-1: Web site for a LAN party

- **The event's name, location, time, the games that will be played, and admission fee.** And don't put it on some weirdo subpage, either; have all critical event information on the first page that people see.

- **The rules of the event.** You do have them, right? A list of things you expect from everyone who attends the event? If you don't, scurry on back to Chapter 2, "Setting Your Party's Parameters," and work up a list for these people!

- **A person to talk to.** Put your e-mail address on the home page, and make it prominent so that people can contact you with any questions.

- **A place to send you money.** As I said earlier, you want people to pay you in advance in order to lock them into attendance. You need a mechanism on your Web site that takes people's money automatically, even if it's just "To sign up in advance, send $20 to this e-mail account via PayPal."

- **An extremely well-written title.** For the record, this is what you put in the <TITLE> tag of your page, and it's very important because it's one of the things Google (and every other search engine) ranks very highly in determining whether your page is relevant to someone's search. You definitely want your location, your name, and the date of the party, as well as the words "LAN party" somewhere in there, as shown in the following example:

```
<TITLE>Fragorama: Sheboygan's Biggest LAN Party, July 17 -
19</TITLE>
```

- **Easily searchable <META> tags.** Google also searches by keywords encoded within the <META> tags in the header of your page. Put in these tags about 20 words that you think people might enter when searching for a LAN party in your area, as shown in the following example:

```
<meta content="LAN party, LAN parties, Sheboygan, Battlefield
1942, Half-Life 2, network, tournament, ladder tournament,
Fragorama" name="Keywords" />
```

Of course, that's just the bare minimum. Most well-designed LAN party sites have most, if not all, of the following bells and whistles:

- **Banner ads.** Hey, if you've got sponsors, don't you want to link back to them? Sure you do.

- **Forums.** Getting your players to talk to one another on the site fosters a sense of community—which is exactly what you want. If you can somehow generate a healthy amount of forum traffic whereby your LAN party attendees trash talk and exchange the latest gaming news, chances are pretty good that you'll have regularly successful events.

- **Online seating reservations.** If you've played at the same location a couple of times, chances are good that you've settled upon a standard layout that everyone's familiar with. Since you're encouraging reservations in advance, why not let the early adopters snag the best seats?

- **Mailing lists.** If you can't do the forum thing, you might want to start up a ListServ or similar software to put everyone on an e-mail list. (And www.yahoogroups.com also offers free mailing lists.)

- **Pictures of your latest event.** If you want to get people excited, show them pics of the coolest case mods, the watergun fight you had, the strangest accoutrement. Of course, nothing gets people more excited than seeing their picture on the front page!

A Prize That Costs You Nothing

Most Internet forum software enables you to assign a custom title to a forum member. Tim Martin, proprietor of SpokLAN.com, says that giving a custom forum title to the winner of the last tournament has been a *great* prize. It may seem like a small thing—but most people would be secretly, if not openly, proud to see "January SpokLAN CHAMPION!" under their name with every post. Moreover, it's a cost-free and pretty sweet way to remind everyone else of a victory.

PayPal Is Your Friend

There are a lot of ways you can take people's money over the Internet, but the easiest and quickest method is PayPal, which is as close to an Internet-standard money transfer system as you'll see. Just set up an account to which people can wire you funds, indicate your e-mail address, and you're ready to go!

You do have other options, but they aren't very good ones.

- **The latest game news.** Hey, is *Diablo 3* out? Maybe you should let everyone know!

- **Patches and custom maps.** Ideally, you'll have these available at the party via file sharing or FTP, but if you have the bandwidth to spare, why not make them available on the Net? (Be warned, however; because most patches these days weigh in at a couple of hundred megabytes, you can burn through your allotted bandwidth very quickly. Be sure to check in with your server host before you put up any big files to ensure that you won't incur any extra charges.)

Registering your site

Certain big sites, such as www.lanparty.com and www.bluesnews.com, allow you to list your event online. These sites get more traffic than your tiny site ever will, so listing your event there is a pretty fine idea.

Making and distributing fliers

After all of that Web stuff, aren't you glad to hear how low-tech and easy this next step is? Use a graphics program to print out a flier you can hang at various businesses (see Figure 5-2). Mention the time of the event, your Web site, the admission cost, and the rules. Print out 50 copies or so, and then hang them up around your local computer places. Other excellent places to try hanging your fliers are local bookstores, coffee shops (geeks love caffeine), and video stores.

Always ask the management first whether it's okay to hang up your flier! (Otherwise, it might be ripped down later that day.) Be prepared to explain what a LAN party is, and be sure to be polite. Bear in mind that some people think that all computer gamers are asocial oddballs; a pleasant smile will go a long way toward changing that attitude.

User groups

Nerds of a feather flock together. Do some Googling yourself and see if there's a local *user group*, which is a gathering of like-minded computer fans. Generally, they're Linux user groups, but you'll often find groups devoted to case-modding or programming languages.

These groups are chock-full of your target market: die-hard enthusiasts who love to play. If you can get someone to bring your flier to their local meeting, you're almost guaranteed to get a new player or two.

FIGURE 5-2: Sample Word flier for a party

Mailing lists

If you do a search on Yahoogroups, quite often you'll find local groups of potential players. (Look under your city name, the games you'll be playing at the event, and LAN Party.) Contact the list admin to find out whether it's okay to mail the list with a brief announcement — you don't want to be a filthy spammer now, do you? — and then send it out. Chances are good that someone will be happy to hear from you.

How to give away a door prize

I discussed how to get a prize in the "Reducing Costs with Sponsorship" section, but generally, you're only giving things away at paid events. A *door prize*, in case you don't know, is a desirable item given away at the event. Generally, everyone who pays admission gets a single numbered ticket when they pay their entry fee; at some point during the evening, you pull a number out of a hat, and whoever has the matching number wins the prize.

Door prizes, as noted, are a minor draw that serve a useful purpose: They enable you to bump up the price of your entry fee, and they get your players all excited. If that's the route you decide to take, the following sections outline several guidelines you should follow when giving the good stuff away.

Why Not Give the Prize to the Game Winner?

It seems like a fine idea; *award the prize to the player with the highest frag count!* However, that act has two unintended consequences—one which affects the tone of your LAN party, and the other which affects your bottom line.

First, putting a prize up is often like pouring blood into the water: All the sharks come out. If you've been having fun with a casual tournament and you put a $200 computer case on the line, suddenly everyone will be accusing each other of cheap tactics, claiming cheat programs, and pulling every cheesy trick out of their pocket to win. Now winning *means* something.

That may not bother you; some people like a hardcore game. But the *second* unintended consequence is that now the mediocre and novice players are never going to win anything. Every regular LAN party has a couple of players who dominate; if you make it so that your local stars are the only ones who take home the good swag, pretty soon the mediocre and novice players stop showing up.

By leaving it up to chance and allowing anyone to be a winner—even 11-year-old Timmy Peterson, who hasn't quite mastered the art of using the keyboard and mouse at the same time—you make it a much more enjoyable party. Stick to door prizes.

Checking your local laws

In 90 percent of all cities, it's perfectly legal to give away door prizes, whereby a ticket is given away with attendance and each attendee has an equal chance of winning. However, it is illegal (or regulated) in a few select towns, so call your local city hall and ask if there's anything you need to do first.

What *is* usually illegal (or, again, heavily regulated) are *raffles*, whereby you sell multiple tickets to a single person for cash. Most towns have strict laws in place to prevent the public from getting ripped off by some shady con artist who sells a thousand tickets but has no prize. Therefore, you can expect to fill out a few forms and provide proof of your prize if you want to raffle something off.

Raffles are sometimes good as a quick fundraiser, but you can get burned. Furthermore, they don't do a thing to increase your LAN party attendance, which is the best long-term method of making a profit. In short, I don't recommend them.

Getting a roll of tickets and determining your no-show policy

Available at your local Costco or other price club, these rolls of two-part numbered tickets enable you to keep track of who has what. You do need to consider, however, what will happen if you pull a number and nobody claims the prize.

The best solution is to let everyone know what time the prize will be awarded, and do it well in advance. (Preferably, you have that time available on your Web site and introductory fliers.)

That way, everyone knows when to be there for the big prize drawing, and if they have to clear out early, they can give the ticket to a friend. If they're not there at the specified time, pull another number and give the prize to someone who is.

Being creative when it comes to prizes

Although the focus so far has been heavily weighted toward getting computer hardware as a prize, you can award any desirable item as a prize. Some of the best prizes are off-the-wall stuff that your local group enjoys, such as nerf guns (always a favorite), DVDs of favorite movies, music CDs, custom-made maps, and weirdo animals. It's almost impossible to get sponsorship for these kinds of items, but don't forget about that Costco card to get you stuff on the cheap.

Getting a bunch of tchotchkes

Having only one door prize kind of stinks. Everyone waits for six hours, and then it's all over in six minutes. A better solution is to get a bunch of lead-up prizes — cheapie freebies like mouse pads, T-shirts, and keychains, which hardware and software manufacturers are often happy to give away. Then raffle them off every hour or so, just to break the rhythm.

Spreading the love

If you have a good door prize, *build up to it*. Don't blow your wad right at the beginning; save it for later in the day, just when everyone's getting tired and looking for a change of pace. (And, if possible, as described in the preceding section, scatter little mini-giveaways throughout the event to further establish a rhythm.)

Selling food at your event

If you go pro, an excellent way to skim some cream off the top is to sell food and drinks. Gamers are always thirsty for caffeine, and many of them snack obsessively while they're gaming.

As a general rule, you want to sell food at 100 percent markup — for example, if you paid fifty cents for that can of soda, you want to sell it for a dollar. That's a nice round number and it makes food a very profitable investment.

Where to get food

This might seem like a no-brainer: "You get food at the supermarket! Duh!" But if you buy something at supermarket prices and then double it, nobody's going to buy it from you. They'll just go to the supermarket themselves.

What you need to do is find food at obscenely low prices. Typically, you have three ways of finding cheap food:

- **A price club.** As I mentioned earlier in the chapter, membership at a price club is de rigueur when you're hosting LAN parties. You can buy entire cases of soda for less than fifty cents a can, which allows you to sell it at a reasonable price. You can also pick up entire trays of cookies, huge bundles of potato chip packets, and so forth.

- **Wholesalers.** Since you're reselling, you can try to buy from a local distributor or deli at discount prices. Usually, people will only sell you food wholesale if you can buy a large amount in one shot, though the definition of "a large amount" varies from place to place. For a distributor that sells to supermarkets and delis, a large amount might be ten cases of soda; for an independent deli that does maybe $500 in sales a day, six pre-wrapped sandwiches might be enough to seal the deal. Check with people to find out.

- **Ordering out.** Every LAN party orders out for pizza and sells it for two bucks a slice, which is a ruinous price. But people are willing to pay extra if it's delivered to their station and it's hot. (They will probably be less likely to pay extra for soda and Cheetos, which can be bought anywhere and last forever.)

What kind of food to sell

Generally, you want to provide items from each of the major food categories:

- **Cold caffeinated drinks.** Preferably in cans or small bottles, and served piping cold. You don't need a complicated setup to sell drinks: an ice chest, refilled periodically, will do.

  You generally want a mixture of normal sodas (for example, Pepsi or Coke), diet sodas (for example, Diet Pepsi or Coke), clear sodas (for example, Sprite), some form of juice (for example, Fruitopia), and some form of hypercharged caffeine drink (for example, Red Bull or Jolt).

  However, be warned that soda preferences can (and have) caused holy wars at some parties. Many people have strong preferences for drinks, and will chug endless amounts of it if it's available. (Give me a source of Diet Pepsi at a LAN party and you can get ten bucks a day out of me, easy.) Pay attention to what your guests want, and give it to them.

- **Fruit.** Many gamers are vegetarians or prefer to eat healthy. You would be surprised how much you can sell fruit for, considering how cheap it is to get. A couple of bananas and apples will sit quietly on the shelf until you sell them.

- **Chips.** You can sell just about anything salty that comes in little bags for a ridiculous markup. Of course, this won't be effective if you're in a rental location that has a vending machine around the corner, in which case you'll have to compete with either a) reasonable prices or b) larger packages (as in, you sell 11-ounce bags, rather than the machine's five-ouncers).

- **Sugar.** Pudgy dudes like me rely on that rush of sugar to get our reflexes pumped . . . and you'd better provide it! Since candy bars are available just about everywhere, your best bet is to either get some sort of baked goods from Costco or a local deli or buy larger candy bars than people can get at the vending machines.

- **Sandwiches.** You do not want to sell your own sandwiches; you'll be guilty of all sorts of health code violations if you leave a chicken sandwich at room temperature all day. However, you can often buy pre-wrapped sandwiches from a deli, which can be stored safely in the other side of the ice chest. The deli can probably tell you the temperature at which you have to keep them. (If they can't, you might not want to get your sandwiches there.)

- **Pizza and other take-out foods.** Order them in, and sell them on the spot. An advantage to this method is that you can ask for a show of hands before you order to see how many people are hungry, which will prevent you from over-ordering as you can with other foodstuffs.

Bad types of food are the ones that involve a lot of maintenance: hot dishes that cool to room temperature, food that may spoil, messy foods, and so forth.

Handling cash

There are two aspects to handling cash that you should be aware of, even at the smallest party:

- **You need change.** My friend Jim calls $20 bills "Yuppie Food Coupons" because ever since the invention of the ATM, that's all anyone ever has to offer. Make sure you stop by the bank the day before your event and get at least 20 singles, 10 five-dollar bills, and five ten-dollar bills to break up those twenties. (That's $120, in case you weren't paying attention.)

  For larger parties, the standard is 50 singles, 20 five-dollar bills, and five ten-dollar bills, and you'll definitely want a cash register. (That's $200.) Of course, if admittance to your party is in nice even denominations ($10, $15, or $20), you can probably skip getting the singles.

  If you have a party where you'll need change, the standard is four rolls of pennies, one roll of nickels, two rolls of dimes, and three rolls of quarters.

- **You need security.** I once had a friend who worked at an independent movie theater. The theater was going under because nobody wanted to watch good art films, and my friend frequently moaned about how once this theater went out of business, she wouldn't have any place to watch the latest Quentin Tarantino flick.

  To my great surprise, I discovered that she was stealing from the owner. "Why not?" she shrugged, ignoring the fact that she liked the owner personally and was putting him out of business. (Eventually, she succeeded.)

  That taught me a very valuable lesson: Anyone can steal, no matter how nice or motivated they may seem.

  If you put someone out there who takes money, make sure you trust him absolutely, and then verify the count at the end of the day. It's very easy to stuff an admission fee or two in a pocket or to let a friend in for free. Count up the total earnings, subtract any change money you had in the register at the beginning of the day, and make sure it adds up to the total number of players who should have paid during the event.

  In addition, only one person should handle the money. If something *does* go wrong, you'll want to know who's responsible, and that's impossible if seven or eight people have been doing check-in duty. Of course, I realize that it's almost impossible to keep the same person at the register for an entire LAN party, but do your best to keep it to two or maybe three people. It helps deter shifty money practices.

Getting Receipts

It's very common at LAN parties to take care of needed expenses by yanking money out of the cash register, as in "The pizza's here! Someone get a couple of twenties out of the cash drawer!" However, this can lead to problems at the end of the day when you count the drawer and find out it's $40 short. You might forget about the pizza you ordered and panic—or, even worse, accuse someone of stealing.

Therefore, whenever you tap the register for expenses, always put a receipt in the drawer to remind yourself. Even if it's just a scribbled note that says "Pizza $40," it will remind you later when you do your end-of-party tally.

Also, if this becomes a taxable business, you'll *really* need the receipts come April 15th. Be sure to save them after the party and file them away.

Summary

It's been a long haul, but by now you should have discovered the secret of saving cash at a LAN party: Ask for a discount. It won't kill you, and most of the money-saving tips involve asking around to see if someone will give you something. A little bit of chutzpah can lighten the load on your wallet considerably!

Also, when you're dealing with money, be conservative. Guard your cash closely, both by being extremely realistic when it comes to estimating expenses and by literally watching your cash to make sure that nobody pockets it.

In the next chapter, I'll discuss the lifeblood of any LAN party: electricity. If you want to avoid power outages—and I assure you that you do—then follow me to Chapter 6!

Avoiding Power Failures

I f you go to a lot of LAN parties, sooner or later you're going to encounter the much-feared *Clickaww*. The Clickaww is a sound that haunts LAN parties all over the world, and it happens in two parts:

The first part is the tiny "Click" you hear as an entire section of the room goes dark.

Then there's the heartfelt "*Awww!*" that goes up as everyone realizes that their game just ended.

Computers burn up a lot of electricity when they're tracking imaginary railguns, and a single outlet can sustain only so many PCs. Fortunately, learning how to map a house's power supply and how to properly distribute a power load is a relatively simple task. This chapter explains everything you need to know to keep your party running without interruption, even into the wee hours of the night.

Avoiding Brownouts and Blackouts

Power is the foundation of every LAN party. You don't need cables, because you can play wireless; you don't need a house, because you can play outside as long as you have a plug. But without electricity? You're reduced to playing hopscotch.

And unfortunately, if you don't know what you're doing, it's pretty easy to overload your power circuits and turn your party into a fiesta that only a Luddite could love. In order to learn how to avoid blowing a fuse, you first have to know how computers and electricity work.

How a computer gets power

When a computer is turned on, it needs to pull a steady flow of electricity from the socket in order to keep the motherboard humming. The amount of electricity a computer needs is measured in *amperes*, colloquially known as *amps*.

The reason blackouts happen is because wires can only hold so much power before they melt. If you try to shove too many amps of electricity through a wire, it will heat up, perhaps spark, and then melt, probably setting something on fire in the process. Homeowners throughout the ages have had a distinct aversion to having their houses burn down, so you need to introduce a safety feature that will cut off the power if the wire becomes overloaded.

The safety feature is known as a *fuse* or a *circuit breaker*. If too many amps are being pulled into a particular wire, the circuit breaker will trigger and shut down all power to that wire to prevent spontaneous combustion.

If, God forbid, an electrical fire should break out, *do not throw water on it.* Instead, use a fire extinguisher with a "C" rating. If you don't have one, may I suggest you purchase one before the party?

Older houses use *fuses*—one-shot metal-and-glass doodads composed of cheap wire that melts harmlessly inside the glass casing when a circuit is overloaded. They're a pain, because every time one burns out you have to replace it with a new fuse—and God help you if you run out. Circuit breakers are preferable because they have a spring-loaded switch that snaps to "off" whenever the wire gets hot. Breakers are both more convenient and a lot safer. Not only is there zero possibility of screwing in a circuit breaker wrong, but whenever it trips, you just flip the switch back into the "on" position and you're done.

Be aware of one other aspect of this wire thing. Not only is it difficult to push a load of power through one big wire (every wire has a certain amount of electrical resistance, which means that it loses power over distance), if one outlet overloads the line, the *entire house* goes dark. To make things easier, electricians split electrical loads over different *power circuits*, assigning, say, all of the outlets in the dining room to circuit breaker number 1, and the living room outlets to circuit breaker number 2.

The industrial standard for a power circuit is 16 amps of continuous load with a 20-amp circuit. That means if you hit 20 amps, you will blow a fuse and hear the infamous *Clickaww*.

Don't *Do* That!

Some people go to great lengths to avoid changing blown fuses, doing things like putting pennies in the sockets instead of UL-approved fuses. Doing this actually works at first, because the penny conducts electricity in the same way that the fuse did, except that the penny will never burn out. Instead, the penny will allow all the amperage in the world to flow freely through your circuits, and eventually your wires will melt and things will burst into flame.

Net savings on fuses: about $1.50. Net loss on house: about $150,000. But at least you don't have to deal with those annoying fuses!

Fuses are there for a reason. Unless it's a trained electrician who's doing it, don't mess with the fuses or circuit breakers.

When Power Goes Bad

Drawing too much power from too many computers can melt your wires. But the amount of power flowing through a circuit is not steady; it can fluctuate. Sometimes, *way* too much power comes charging out of that socket (after, say, a lightning strike somewhere), and if it gets to your computer, it can fry critical components inside your box like a bug on a bug zapper.

Given that that's the case, you should *never, ever* plug a piece of computer hardware directly into an electrical socket; always plug your computer into a *surge suppressor*, which prevents any sudden spikes from destroying your motherboard.

And never, ever use an adaptor to plug a computer into a two-pronged outlet, even with a surge suppressor. That third prong grounds your computer and keeps it safe. Don't stay home without it.

And let's get one thing straight: *The number of electrical outlets in a place has nothing to do with how many circuits there are, and vice versa.* I've heard of vast ballrooms with 20 electrical outlets, all of which run on *one* 20-amp circuit. (For the record, that's barely enough to run a lamp off each plug without blowing a fuse.) With this scenario, want to guess what happens when 40 computers try to boot up simultaneously?

We've also heard of small halls that have only three outlets, but each outlet is on a separate circuit. In other words, the small three-outlet hall has access to *three times* as much power as the big 20-outlet ballroom. The ballroom has a lot more plugs, to be sure, but with so little electricity available to them they are mostly decorative.

Hey! Where Are the Ohms and Volts?

I could cheerfully offer page after page describing the difference between an *amp* (the measure of electrical flow rate), the *voltage* (the electrical pressure that is flowing through a circuit), and an *ohm* (the resistance that causes power to drop over distance). Then I could trot out all the relevant formulas, explaining how the resistance necessary to produce one volt of voltage drop with one amp of current flowing is the voltage divided by the current.

And none of it would matter.

Unless you're an electrician or just really into details, all you need to know is that each circuit in a building can provide up to a certain amount of energy, known as *amps*, and if you go past that limit, you will be sitting in the dark. Any other considerations are unlikely to come up, very confusing, and mostly entirely irrelevant to the day-to-day activities of LAN parties. As such, I'm skipping the topic. If you'd like more detailed (and advanced) information, pick up a book. Wiley recommends *Audel Electrical Course for Apprentices and Journeymen, 4th edition*, by Paul Rosenberg (Wiley, 2004).

Given that there is no standard ratio of outlets to circuits, it is imperative that you find out which outlets are on which circuits and distribute your computers so that no circuit has more than 20 amps on it at a time.

Mapping power circuits

When I interviewed an electrician for this book to see whether there were any standard guidelines for determining how many outlets went on a power circuit, his response was, "Heck if *I* know." Until the National Electrical Code standardizes this and enforces it, you're going to have to check these things out for yourself—and that involves mapping the power circuits so you know which outlet is connected to which fuse.

Every power circuit in a building is controlled from one central place, known as the *circuit panel*. (Very large buildings may have two or three circuit panels, but even then you'll generally only be concerned with the one that controls power to your LAN party area.) The circuit panel holds all the fuses and circuit breakers that control the power in the building; when something overloads a circuit and causes a fuse to blow, this is where you'll go to fix it.

In most cases, you'll need access to the circuit panel in order to map the power circuits, so your first job in balancing power is to find the circuit panel. It's generally in the basement, in a closet, or in the garage—somewhere remote.

After that, the rest is just gravy. Mapping power is *easy*, my friends.

The four methods of mapping power

There are four ways to map power circuits and identify which outlets are on what circuit:

- Use trial and error
- Put labels on the circuit panel
- Contact the maintenance person
- Get a tone generator

LAN Parties at Older Buildings and Homes

Many buildings erected before 1950 or so have older electrical systems that are troublesome for LAN parties. You can generally identify these places right away because they have fuses (as opposed to circuit breakers) and two-pronged outlets. I don't advise holding LAN parties at older houses for two reasons: one, the electrical systems tend to be slightly more prone to danger if there's an overload (even with a three-prong adapter, you do *not* want to ever plug a complex piece of hardware into a two-pronged outlet), and two, a lot of older houses have circuits that can handle only 16 amps maximum before you blow a fuse.

Because these older houses are more dangerous *and* they tend to have blackouts more often, I advise just finding somewhere else to play.

Testing for Live Plugs

While people use the darndest things to check for live plugs—I've seen people carrying around table lamps—I find that a cell phone recharger (see Figure 6-1) is perfect for informal tests like this; it's small, it's portable, and chances are good you already have one. Simply connect your recharger to your cell phone, and then plug it in; most modern cell phones will light up when you plug them into a working outlet. (Just make sure that your cell phone *isn't already turned on* when you're checking, you big doof.)

The following sections describe each of these methods.

Using trial and error

The most common way of mapping power circuits is to turn things off and see what goes dark. You simply station a friend at the circuit panel, and he or she switches off one circuit at a time, either by unscrewing the fuse or switching the circuit breaker to off. Meanwhile, you walk around with some small electrical appliance that you can plug in to each outlet to check whether it's working. If the outlet's dead, you know it's on the power circuit you currently have turned off.

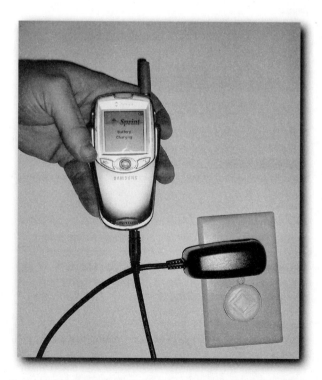

FIGURE 6-1: Using a cell phone charger to look for live outlets

Of course, if you're dealing with a big event for which power is critical, you'll probably want to double-check that each outlet has power once you turn the circuit on. It's very rare, but sometimes in large institutional halls, you'll find a dead outlet that isn't connected to *anything*.

Labeling the circuit panel

Most circuit panels will have tiny, scribbled labels next to each circuit (see Figure 6-2). Sometimes these labels are indecipherable or cryptic (what does "Sq. Mdrn" mean?), but usually they'll indicate the room that this breaker controls.

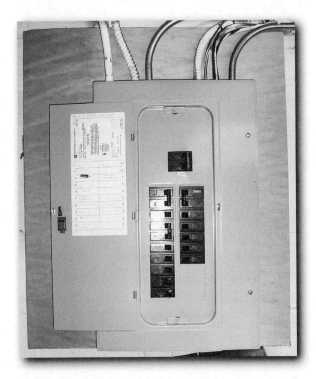

FIGURE 6-2: A typical circuit panel

If you're using someone's home, the circuit panel labels are generally good enough to map your panel. Be warned, however, that labels aren't always 100 percent accurate; sometimes there's a stray outlet in the kitchen that's secretly hooked into the living room circuit. (This is more likely to be the case when custom electrical work has been done on the house.) If you find yourself overloading and you can't figure out why, it may be time to go back to trial and error.

Contacting the maintenance person at your rental place

In hotels, VFW halls, or other rented establishments, there is generally a maintenance person whose job it is to make sure that everything is running smoothly. This person is your best friend. If you make his life easy, he can often provide you with a big pregenerated power map, showing you which outlets go where. Alternatively, if a physical map isn't available, the maintenance person can just walk you around the place and point out the right outlets for you.

Being friends with the maintenance person is important for another reason: *She or he is the person who has the key to the circuit panel.* In most places, the circuit panel is kept under lock and key, since public places don't like the idea of strangers wandering downstairs to monkey with the electrical supply. If something blows, you'll have to find the maintenance person to unlock the panel so you can reset the circuit.

Therefore, note the following two recommendations when you're dealing with a rented hall:

- **Know who the maintenance person is.** Get the maintenance person's phone number in case there's an emergency. If the power blows, you don't want to hang around for two hours while management pages Rizzo the attendant to find out where he is. Get that info right up front.

- **Angle for the key.** Particularly if you're running an all-night event, it's a lot easier to fix things quickly if you can unlock the circuit panel yourself. You generally won't be able to do this the first time you rent a place, but if you prove trustworthy, management will often give you the key at your next function. If they won't give you the key and this is an all-night event, make it clear to them that you may need to access the circuit panel at 2:00 A.M. in case someone blows a fuse — and as such, you'll need a pager number or a home phone number where you can reach them at all hours.

If you make his or her life easier, the maintenance person can make yours a dream. It's worth it to kiss up to this person.

Getting a tone generator

If you find yourself with a very large building or a very complex circuit (or both), you might want to investigate buying a *tone generator*. A tone generator costs between $60 (for a bargain cheapie) and $175 (for a top-of-the-line model), and it's a two-part device consisting of a tone generator and a *tone probe*. You hook the tone generator up to an electric socket and then you wave the probe near any other outlets you suspect may be connected to it. If the two outlets are on the same circuit, the tone probe will emit a sound.

Tone generators generally aren't necessary for power mapping, but they can come in useful in other situations. If you hook a tone generator up to *any* wire — and that includes Category 5 cable or a phone line — the tone probe will buzz whenever it's near any other wire on the same circuit. If you have a sprawling computer network with lots of wires that aren't particularly well-labeled, you can use a tone generator to "trace" a Category 5 cable back to a particular hub, or to determine whether a cable is broken or not.

Note Tone generators are also used to detect crude phone bugs. You hook the generator up to the phone and use your probe to hunt for any suspicious wires that don't lead directly back to the phone punch panel. No, this doesn't really apply to LAN parties — but, hey, it's interesting nonetheless.

Keeping track of outlets

All of this mapping work is to no avail if you can't remember what outlets are on what circuits when you're done. There are two ways of doing this, but one is slightly more ambitious:

- **Post-It™ notes.** Oh, you laugh, but putting little sticky notes over each outlet works wonderfully for smaller get-togethers. Just write "#1" to inform everyone that a particular outlet is on circuit number 1. Then tell people what outlets they're allowed to use. ("You're on the number 2 outlets, Susie.") And then you'll be good to go.

- **Actual maps.** For larger events, you need to plan where everyone's sitting. In that case, you need to make a rough map of the rooms you'll be using and the outlets that are in them, along with the power circuits those outlets are on. Figure 6-3 shows what a rough power map should look like.

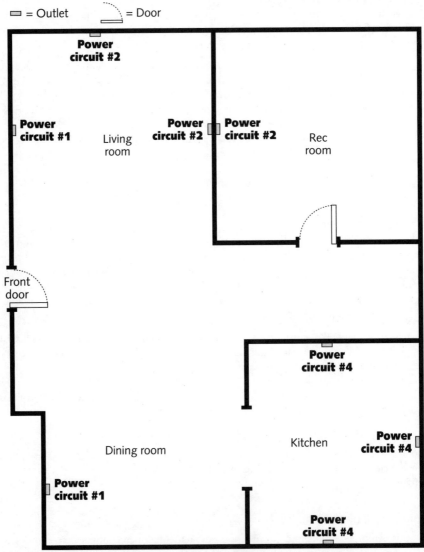

FIGURE 6-3: A house, roughly power-mapped

Not All Outlets Are Created Equal

Some circuits have a lot more than 20 amps in them, but they're mostly in offices, and are dedicated to providing power to specialty appliances—such as a trio of vending machines or a central air conditioning unit. In an emergency, you may be able to unplug whatever's in those outlets and use them to power a *lot* of computers. However, you are very likely to irritate the management if you do this, and you will also annoy everyone who wants to get something from the unplugged vending machine. I only mention it so you know that it's sometimes an option, but I advise against unplugging existing machines in all but the direst of circumstances.

Power maps can be used for more than just remembering where outlets go, though; for example, they're very handy for tracking problems when and if the power blows, and you can modify them to tell people where they're supposed to plug in. If you're holding a mid- to large-size party, I seriously advise that you whip up an actual map.

How to Measure an Outlet's Amp Output
(Although You Don't Have To)

The industry standard for a power circuit is 16 amps continuous, with a 20-amp cap—a fine rule of thumb that saves you a lot of time. But there are always those people (the same ones who need to know whether anal-retentive is spelled with a hyphen) who want to know *precisely* how many amps are in each power circuit.

You *can* find out—but it's not only overkill in most circumstances, it also creates a lot of extra work. As I'll explain later, depending on overclocking, monitors, case, and a host of other variables, a laptop can draw as little as 1 amp, whereas a fully loaded home-built case-mod can draw as many as 3 or 4. In other words, even if you've measured the maximum load a circuit can take out to three decimals, you *still* won't know exactly how many amps your collected computers will use.

The 20-amp limit is a good solid estimate. Unless you have reason to believe that a circuit might be significantly underperforming (or overperforming, as in the case of a vending machine outlet), don't bother measuring it.

Of course, if the urge seizes you and won't go away, you can use a tool called a *multimeter*, which will measure not only the DC current as expressed in amps, but also electrical resistance and voltage. Digital multimeters (which are the easiest to use) start at about a hundred bucks but can run you a half a grand, so I advise you to try to borrow one from someone you know.

Distributing power evenly

Now that you've mapped outlets to circuits, you want to know how to keep 30 PCs fueled with electricity. Well, you may have noticed that I've been dancing around one major question — and it's time to answer it.

How many amps does a PC use?

A PC uses varying amounts of amps. In theory, a PC-and-monitor combo uses about 2 amps each, meaning that you could fit 10 computers on a power circuit. However, several factors make that "10 to a circuit" rule extremely dangerous:

- **Bootup.** When you turn on a PC, it draws in a lot of power as it gets everything up and running at once, spiking to about 4 or 5 amps. If you have nine PCs on a line and someone turns on that tenth PC, you're going to blow a fuse.

- **Monitors.** Old CRT monitors use a lot more power than the newer flat-panel versions and LCDs. A row of CRTs could spell doom.

- **Speakers.** Speakers use a lot of power, particularly the surround-sound versions with sub-woofers. (This is yet another reason to mandate the use of headphones at every LAN party.)

- **Overclocking.** A PC with an overclocked processor and video card draws more power than a normal one. But gamers *never* overclock their PCs, right?

- **Printers.** A laser printer can draw up to 16 amps by itself when it boots up or when it prints. You're not likely to have multiple printers on a circuit at a LAN party, but be warned that a laser printer and a PC or two is about as much as most circuits can reasonably handle.

When theory smashes into reality, the results are ugly. To prevent such unfortunate things from happening, I suggest you run between six and eight PCs on a power circuit, depending on what sorts of computers you think people will be bringing. If you want to be *absolutely* safe, go with five — but if you opt for such a low computers-to-circuit ratio, you'll run out of power circuits very quickly.

(For the record, laptops use a lot less power than normal PCs, so you probably *could* fit 10 laptops on a circuit. Don't be afraid to throw an extra laptop or two onto a power circuit with seven PCs on it.)

How many amps do other appliances use?

Note that a power circuit can support six to eight PCs *when it has nothing else on it*. If you're using someone's home, remember that people usually have other things plugged in — televisions, CD players, lamps, stereos, electric fans, and so on. Take those into account, too; you don't want a guest to turn on the television and pop the breakers!

For reference, Table 6-1 provides a rough estimate of how many amps each common appliance draws when it's running — and only when it's running. A microwave uses 10 amps when it's actually microwaving something, but it requires next to no power just to keep the LCD on. Also, keep in mind that many appliances draw a lot more power when they're first turned on.

Again, these are *approximations*. If you want to know the exact current an appliance needs, look in the user manual.

Can You Fit More PCs onto a Circuit?

In interviewing people for this book, I've found that the "official" number of amps that a PC uses is a topic of some debate in the LAN party community: Some say a computer uses as few as 1.25 amps when booting, and others claim they use as many as 5. When I say you should put no more than six PCs on a circuit, that's an estimate based both on my personal experience and the averaged numbers from everyone I spoke to.

However, you may find that your computers use less power. If you'd like to experiment, don't think of the number six as a hard-and-fast limit; rather, think of it as a "safe limit" at which you can be absolutely certain that no fuses will be blown. Some parties put twelve computers on a circuit and have no problems. Me? I can get about seven before the lights dim.

Table 6-1   Power Usage of Major Household Appliances

Appliance	Amp Usage (approximate)
Microwave	10 amps
Refrigerator	5 amps
Toaster Oven/Hot Plate	10 amps
Coffee Maker	3 amps
Dishwasher	10 amps
Air Conditioner (Room)	8 amps
Air Conditioner (Central)	15–40 amps
Electric Fan	Negligible (1/4 amp)
Furnace Blower	7 amps
Washing Machine	3 amps
Clothes Dryer (Electric)	20–40 amps
Clothes Dryer (Gas)	3 amps
Blow Dryer	8 amps
Vacuum	4 amps
TV (25")	1 amp
Stereo (full stereo)	1 amp
Boom Box	Negligible (1/4 amp)
VCR	Negligible (1/4 amp)
100 watt light	1 amp
Garage Door Opener	3 amps

Spreading power around

Once you've got an idea of where the power circuits are, you can use extension cords to route the power to where you need it. Simply plug the cord into a free power circuit and then run it over to where the power's needed. Note two caveats, however:

- **Tape the cords down or otherwise conceal them.** The last thing you want is some clumsy yutz to trip over the extension cord and unplug seven people at once. (And to add insult to injury, he could then sue you if he hurts himself!) Lay extension cords along walls or along rows of tables whenever possible to ensure that they're out of the way. And if they are in the way, tape them down or throw carpet remnants over them.

- **Use at least 12-gauge cord if you're running power over a hundred feet.** The lower the gauge number, the thicker the wire. Thinner extension cords have more electrical resistance, which means over long distances they'll lose power and heat up — possibly to the point of burning. Most retail electrical cord is 14 or 16 gauge, which is fine for the draw of low-amp Christmas lights but not the heavy load of six fully modded PCs. If you need to run an extension cord across a big room, invest in a safe 12-gauge or 10-gauge cord.

Tip

At large-scale parties, extension cords can become cumbersome — and you may discover that there aren't enough outlets to go around. In that case, you need someone who can drop in 220-volt lines to carry power to remote sections of your party. I wouldn't advise doing it yourself if you're not an electrician, but it is a vital tool for parties held in big halls. If you're holding a big party, get someone who knows how to put in additional lines.

The number one cause of power outages in properly mapped LANs (and how to avoid it)

The thing that will kill you if you're not careful is the "plug and play" mentality. Unless you're very specific about telling your guests where they're supposed to set up and how to do it, they will just plug their power strips into the closest available socket.

Doing so will result in one of two things:

- **A blown fuse.** Everyone plugs into the same power circuit and overloads it.

- **Daisychaining.** Joey plugs his power strip into the right place on the extension cord, but Jimmy isn't paying attention and plugs his strip into Joey's power strip. Then Franny plugs her strip into Jimmy's, and one of two things happens: Either the power circuit gets overloaded and blows, or Joey goes home early and accidentally unplugs Franny and Jimmy right in the middle of the ladder tournament.

The common problem here is *poor communication*. You need to make it very clear that Joey's supposed to plug in *here*, and Franny's supposed to plug in *there*. You can avoid user foul-ups by using one of the following methods.

The Most Frequently Used Circuit in Your Home

When you're LAN partying in someone's house, *use the kitchen's power circuit last*. The kitchen generally contains a lot of appliances that use excessive amounts of power when they're turned on—things such as microwaves and electric stoves draw a *lot* of amps. If you hook a PC into a kitchen power circuit, you're just asking for a power failure.

The pre-setup talk

When everyone's setting up, call a brief time-out and explain where everyone's supposed to plug in, and what will happen if they don't. All gamers hate time-outs, so they'll generally listen when you tell them that ignoring you means half an hour's downtime.

The power map

If you have a larger group, you may want to use your power map to show everyone who's on what circuit and where they're supposed to plug in. A good power map might look similar to what is shown in Figure 6-4.

Restricting everyone to power strips

Nobody sane would show up at a LAN party without a power strip that also serves as a surge suppressor (do you *want* to fry your motherboard?), but people do it all the time, plugging their stuff directly into extension cords and outlets without a care in the world. As such, it's a good idea to disallow the use of direct plug-ins, forcing everyone to plug their hardware into a power strip.

Providing power strips for everyone

You can avoid a lot of heartache by providing a power strip for every seat; when your guests arrive, the strips are right underneath the tables and ready to go. Sure, it's more expensive, and takes more work to set up, but it leaves very little room for error about where everyone's supposed to plug in. Figure 6-5 shows what it looks like.

Alternatively, you can plug a single power strip into each socket, and tell everyone to plug into that. Figure 6-6 shows what this looks like.

Clear labeling

If you have marked each of your allotted table spaces, you may want to put large labels on the table, with smaller labels over each of the sockets. That's a pretty clear way of letting people know where they belong.

Blocking outlets

Sometimes, people will plug in to any free outlet, no matter *what* threatening signs you hang over and around them. If you have an outlet that you're reserving, a good trick is to use the plastic outlet covers that are used to babyproof houses. Use a marker or nail polish to write "NO!" on the cover, and then stick it into the socket. If they don't get the hint then, they're either completely braindead or just willful.

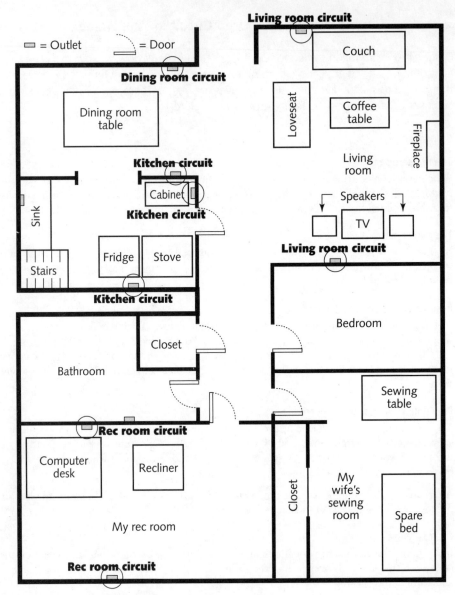

FIGURE 6-4: A good power map

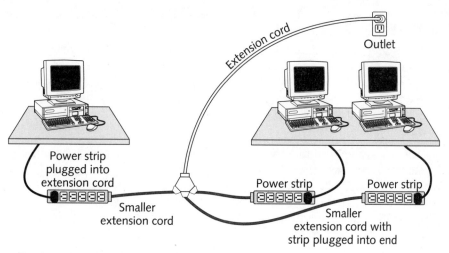

FIGURE 6-5: The "one person, one strip" method

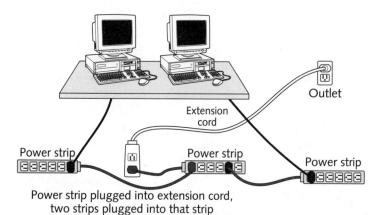

FIGURE 6-6: The "one plug, one strip" method

If you don't have enough power

Every building has a finite amount of power it can draw at one time, and it's generally written right on the circuit panel. In older houses, the sum total can be as low as 60 amps, but generally most houses run between 120 and 240 total amperage. The total power available for rental properties varies wildly, so if you're planning to hold a large-scale party, you should track down the maintenance person and/or the circuit panel and take a look.

If you tally everything up and you still don't have enough power, two options are available: You can hire an electrician to run in an extra circuit and a few outlets, or you can rent a gas generator.

Should You Have a UPS?

A UPS, which is short for *uninterruptible power supply*, is a large battery about the size of a normal computer. You plug your computer into the UPS, and the UPS into a socket; if the power fails, the UPS will sense that and automatically switch to battery power, providing continual service even in a blackout. Most UPS batteries are good for between one and three hours, assuming you've fully charged them by hooking them up to a live outlet for at least eight hours beforehand.

UPSes are fine items, and great for servers. Remember that if the circuit with a game server on it blows, then a good chunk of your LAN party will be taking a nap while you get it back up; with a UPS, even the worst blowout won't stop the fragging. Furthermore, some game servers take a while to configure properly, and it's awful when they go down and you have to spend another half hour resetting everything the way you like it. If you can beg a good UPS for your LAN party, then by all means do so.

In a pinch, you can also buy a UPS. They run from about $50 for a real cheapie to $600 for a solid mid-range model. But remember the LAN partyholder's code: *Beg before you buy.*

The electrician's really only an option for a permanent location—after all, you don't want to spend your hard-earned money renovating someone else's rental property! Depending on where your circuit panel is located, putting in an extra circuit and outlets will take between three and eight hours' worth of work, depending on how easily accessible your circuit panel and wall internals are.

The gas generator is something that you'll have to rent, but it can be a blessing at large parties where the hall you're using doesn't have the juice. You can find generators for every size of party, ranging from a tiny 20-amp generator to a high-end industrial one that puts out 1,000 amps.

The only trick is that generator power isn't normally measured in amps; it's measured in *watts*. To figure out how many amps a gas generator can supply, either ask the person you're renting it from, or divide the number of watts by 120 (which is the American standard voltage). Thus, a 2,500-watt generator *sounds* impressive, but at 20.83 amps, it's just a little more than an additional power circuit.

What to Do When the Power Goes Out

You've done all of this planning, mapping power and running cords to distribute electricity about the room. And something's gone *snap*. What do you do now?

Step 1: Stay calm

Power failures happen — and they rarely happen right at the start of a party. Generally, it takes a while for the wire to heat up and carry the current, meaning that most power failures will happen just as things are really getting interesting.

Shrug it off. You'll fix this in just a bit, but you can't do that if you're running about like a headless chicken!

Step 2: Make an announcement

Explain to the people what just happened, and that it's easily fixable. Tell them to stay calm while you get the power back up, and tell them that hopefully things will be fixed shortly. Ask them to check their own stations to make sure that they're plugged into the correct outlet, and remind them that you have these silly rules about plug-in locations for a reason.

Quite often, someone will find the mistake and point it out to you. Needless to say, this can save you a lot of time.

In addition, tell everyone in the area to set their power switches on all of their equipment to the "off" position. You don't want to switch the power back on only to have five PCs reboot simultaneously and overload the circuit all over again. Another danger is that there can be a power surge when the circuit becomes active again, frying someone's computer. I've heard tales of woe from people who've lost motherboards, so make sure that the computers are off and the surge protectors are on.

Step 3: Figure out which circuit just blew

This is a snap if you've already mapped the circuits; look at which computers are now powerless, and see what outlets they're hooked up to. If you've done the work, you'll know exactly what switch has blown without even having to venture out to the circuit panel. Generally, you'll find that it's one circuit that's blown, though occasionally multiples will fire off simultaneously.

Step 4: Confirm that everything's plugged in correctly

This is where it *really* comes in handy to have an official power map that shows you which computers have been assigned to which outlets.

First, search methodically through the affected area, looking at each of the wall outlets on that circuit to double-check that nobody's plugged into the wrong place by mistake.

For Renters Only

If you're renting a space, this is when you call the maintenance person in order to get the key for the circuit panel.

If that's not the case, the problem is probably that some idiot has disobeyed your instructions and plugged their PC into someone else's power strip. Check each of the power strips and surge suppressors attached to this circuit and verify that the only computers and electrical appliances drawing power from this circuit are the ones that are *supposed* to be there. If someone's screwed up, unplug them and put them on the correct circuit.

However, even if you find a rogue PC, don't stop there; look for any nonstandard equipment in the area that might be the cause of overload. Some of the more common power abusers are computer speakers, elaborate case-mods with light-up displays, and hot plates. You can yell at someone to unplug their hot plates and speakers, of course, but you may have to move the gamer with the big Matrix-style neon-lit case over to another circuit.

Then count the number of computers plugged into this circuit again. You didn't accidentally tell nine people to hook up their PCs here instead of eight, did you? Hey, it's not like your *guests* are always at fault.

If there is no obvious cause of the blowout, it may just be that this circuit's a little weak and can't hold the number of PCs you thought it could. You'll need to move one or two PCs onto another circuit.

Step 5: Move things around

Whether it's due to a trio of overclocked case-modders or just a weak circuit, sometimes a power circuit can't hold the number of PCs that you thought it could. In that case, you'll have to rearrange your outlet and move over to other power circuits.

Ideally, you'll have some spare extension cord handy so that you can just plug into another circuit's outlet, and then run a wire over. Be careful with that wire; yes, people are tapping their feet impatiently while you're trying to get the power back up, but there's no sense in doing a sloppy job of it. Run the cord along the walls, and tape it down if you need to.

In a worst-case scenario, you may have to ask someone to move their equipment over to another seat. Ask very, *very* nicely. This is a huge pain for someone who's just gotten set up.

Step 6: The triple-check

Go over all of the plugs one more time. Make sure everything's where it should be. The only thing worse than the *Clickaww* is telling people, "All right, folks–boot up!" and then hearing everything go dark *again*.

Step 7: Get to the circuit panel

This is pretty simple for you home folks: You go downstairs and flip the circuit breaker back to "on," or you replace the fuse. But it may be more complex for those of you who are renting halls. As I said earlier, most rental places keep their circuit panels locked; hopefully, by now you've gotten in touch with the maintenance person, who will come over and reset the power circuit for you.

Beware! *Do not let the maintenance person leave before you're sure the problem is taken care of.* Have him or her hang around for at least 20 minutes or so to confirm that the circuit is now fixed and won't blow again. Offer any maintenance people soda and a snack to make it up to them, but don't let them head out that door before you're comfortable that everything's back to normal. If they're really grumpy about having to stay (and they may well be if it's after ten o'clock at night), remind them that all you need is the key to the circuit panel and that you will take very good care of it, if they entrust it to you.

Step 8: Reboot

One by one, turn the computers on the circuit back on. (Remember, a PC's power usage can spike to 4 or 5 amps when it's booting up, so four computers rebooting at once will almost certainly cause an instant return to darkness.) When one computer has fully rebooted, wait two minutes and then reboot the next one.

Ideally, all of the computers will merrily get back online and into full frag mode. In the worst-case scenario, five of the computers will come back up without a problem, but that sixth PC will cause a relapse. If that's the case, move that computer over to another circuit and try again.

Summary

In this chapter, you learned that computers draw power through the electrical wires in a building or house — and if they try to draw too much power, those wires will heat up and set things on fire. In order to prevent houses from going up like fireworks on the Fourth of July, electricians put in circuit breakers to shut down the electricity when the current gets to be too hazardous. Your job as a LAN party host is to spread the computers out among the various power circuits so that no circuit becomes overloaded.

The next chapter is one of the longest in the book, but also the most vital — it explains what your computer does with all of that power, and how you network computers together to create a living, breathing fragfest where all of you are playing together! Let's roll out, folks, and learn the mysteries of the LANs.

The Least You Need to Know about Networking

Fragging your friends at a LAN Party is as sweet as a hot fudge sundae. There's nothing better than having a fully charged network running underneath your roof, the hum of seven or eight computers all firing at once, and the instantaneous, lagless kill time.

Networking technology is the spinach. Nobody likes it. It's a pain. But, much like eating at your mom's house, you do *not* get the dessert until you've eaten your spinach.

As the person hosting the party, you'll most likely be Johnny-on-the-spot if something goes wrong. And, computers being the twitchy technobeasts that they are, *something's* guaranteed to go down. Sure, you might be able to delegate the actual LAN part of your party to someone else, but there's no guarantee that your networking guru won't fall sick at the last moment or will be winning the latest fragfest and can't fix it for an hour.

If that's the case, shouldn't you at least know what's going on?

Where Networking and Gaming Intersect

The paragraphs that follow will walk you through the absolute basics of computer networking as it applies to a *small* LAN party with no frills. If all you want to do is to hook five or six computers together to play — no Internet access, no file sharing — then this is what you need to know. (Actually, this basic information will serve groups up to 30.)

This stuff is the heart of every LAN party. Learn it well, young Padawan.

A simple networked game

There are two types of computers in gaming: *servers* and *clients*. If you've ever played an online game, you're familiar with servers: They're the central computer that coordinates the game. When you connect to a server to play a game on it, your PC is called a *client*. Servers and clients are connected by a *medium* that they use to talk to each other, usually wire or cable of some sort.

When you play, your computer handles all of the graphics and the movements, and it sends frequent updates over that wire to the server about everything else: "Player 1 moved to the left! Player 1 just shot a rocket! Now Player 1 is jumping!"

The server receives your update — as well as the updates sent in by any other clients — and coordinates them into one big picture. It then sends its own signals back out to all the clients to update everyone on what's happened: "Player 3 just moved to the right! Player 2 has just come through the doorway! Player 6 has been splattered all over the wall!"

Your computer processes that data, updates your screen, and then sends a new update to the server about what you've just done. Then the server replies with another update about what everyone else has done. That continual back-and-forth flow of information is how the game plays out.

Sometimes your signal takes too long to get to the server, as often happens when you're sending a signal to a computer hundreds of miles away. In those situations, the server may actually process several other people's moves while it waits for yours to arrive, which is what usually causes the dreaded online *lag*. (Too many players connecting to a slow server can also cause lag; a computer can choke and stutter as it struggles to keep up with the flow of data from multiple clients, which is why your server should almost always be a very fast computer, if not your fastest.) Depending on what game you're playing, the server may do one of two things. One, it may cause your movements to stop until it receives an update (which is why you can be clicking "Fire" when you have someone in your sights and you still miss; the fire button signal was processed after the server registered the other player's movement). In other cases, it may process all of your movements at once, causing you to jump and flicker about the screen as you're teleported in an instant to where you were headed.

Note The official measure of lag is called *ping time,* and it's the number of milliseconds it takes a server to respond to a request from your computer, including the travel time that it takes for the request to get there and back. I discuss the official ping utility in Chapter 10, "The Least You Need to Know about Configuring Your Computer."

But that's why you're holding a LAN party, isn't it? To avoid lag? Yes, but the price of no lag time is setting up your own network. And, to set up a network, you're going to need more information than just this basic overview.

The five things that connect computers together

When you have only two computers, it's easy to get them to speak to each other — just string a wire between them. They can simply transmit information over that wire when the other computer isn't talking, and they know that any data they "hear" on the wire is the other PC. It's a lot like a two-way phone conversation.

Suppose, however, that you want *six* computers to be able to talk to each other. The easiest way to do this would be to hook them all up to one big wire so they can share it — much like a six-way conference call. When one computer "talks" over the wire, the other five can hear it.

It *sounds* good in theory, but as anyone who's ever held a six-way conference call in real life knows, things get messy very quickly. Everyone starts talking at once, people have trouble determining who's talking to whom, and getting everyone on the same page requires someone to organize the entire thing.

Furthermore, that conference call is more complex than you might realize. The phone company handles all the messy details of stringing cables across the country so that, for example, Phil's phone in Hoboken has a direct connection to your office phone. When you're setting up a network to host a LAN party, however, you'll have to lay that cable yourself.

That's what computer networks are for. They arrange computers so that they can all talk to each other on the same line and then organize the communications so that everyone can be heard. Every computer network has five parts that need to be in place before your computer can call up the server and tell it what it needs to know:

- Medium
- Topology
- Central connection
- Protocol
- Network Interface Card (NIC)

The sections that follow describe each of these components.

A medium

Three years ago, cable was practically the only thing that connected computers together. Nowadays, with the advent of wireless networking, connections consist of more than just cables, so now I have to describe what a *medium* is.

As any good science student knows, when we talk to each other, we're actually hearing sounds that are transmitted through the air; take away that air, and suddenly we can't hear anything. In the case of hearing, air is the *medium* through which we talk. Computers also need a medium with which to carry data back and forth, and the most common medium is still a cable, though in these newfangled days of wireless, your PCs could well be talking to each other via radio signals. Savvy?

A topology

A *topology* represents the way that your computers are all physically connected to your medium, and it defines how each computer broadcasts on it. Topologies can be complex, but for small parties, you really only have one option, a star topology, which is described further in the section "Your most likely network setup," later in this chapter.

A central connection

In order to be a network, there has to be *something* that takes all of these separate wires and hooks them together so that everyone can talk on the same line (or, in the case of wireless, a central transmission point that listens to all the broadcasts and collates them). That central connection is generally a hub, a switch, or a router, and you'll learn more about these shortly.

A protocol

Much as in real life, computers need a form of etiquette in order to talk to each other. They need to know each other's names, they need to know when to talk and when to stay quiet, and they need to be sure they're all speaking the same language. A protocol is a bunch of agreed-upon standards so everyone knows what to expect.

The Network Interface Card

Even though you have a phone line in your house, without a phone to translate your words into electronic signals, there's no way for you to make a call. Likewise, computers need a *Network Interface Card* (also known as a *NIC*) to translate *their* communications into a network-suitable signal. Fortunately, NICs are pretty simple.

Your most likely network setup

Unless you're holding a large party (or have people with special needs), the simplest and easiest networking setup by far to attach all of your computers to a central hub or switch is via *Fast Ethernet* in a *star topology*, connected by *Category 5 twisted-pair cabling* (the medium) attached to a *router/switch* (the central connection) and running *TCP/IP* (the protocol).

In other words, your layout should look like the one shown in Figure 7-1.

- *Star topology* means that you'll be connecting each computer to a central hub or switch (or, in this case, a *router/switch*) via cables. That hub or switch serves as a nerve center that receives the data from each computer and broadcasts it to all the other computers attached to it. In other words, it hooks up all the separate cables and connects them into one big wire so the computers can talk to each other.

  Without a hub or switch, you don't have a network; you have a bunch of computers sitting around idly, unable to talk to each other. Should your hub or switch die, so does your network. (Fortunately, as pieces of hardware go, they're pretty reliable.)

- A *router/switch* (also known as a *broadband router*) is a special form of switch that not only connects the computers together, but also enables those computers to share a DSL or cable modem's Internet connection. If you don't have an Internet connection, a router/switch is still useful because it usually automatically assigns IP addresses for you.

- *Fast Ethernet* is a networking model whereby all the computers on a network are wired into a central hub or switch, as just outlined previously. Each computer broadcasts its data onto the cabling and ignores any broadcasts that aren't addressed to it. If two computers shout at the same time, they both pause for a random period of time and then try to rebroadcast. Most small networks use Ethernet, mainly because it requires practically no configuration; hook a new computer up to an Ethernet network, and it just starts yelling along with everyone else.

- *TCP/IP* is by far the most common networking protocol. It's so common, in fact, that you really need to know how it works before you hold a LAN party, and so we'll explore this in much more detail later in this chapter, when we get to the section "Networking Protocols."

- *Category 5 (also known as 100Base-T) twisted-pair cabling* is what you'll be using to hook the computers into the central hub or switch. It's the standard cabling you associate with computers these days (see Figure 7-2). It's generally blue, black, or gray, it's very flexible, and it ends in small plastic pieces that look a lot like the end of a phone cord. (You can't use phone cord in an Ethernet network, though; the sizing is slightly wrong, and it's not nearly as shielded from electromagnetic resistance as 100Base cables.)

That's the most common setup. Of course, now you need to review the details for each of these five aspects. The following sections describe each of them, and explain how they relate to you and a good game of *Command and Conquer*.

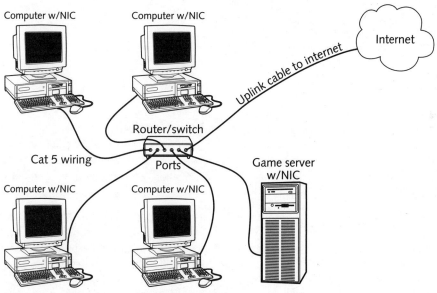

Figure 7-1: A typical network setup for a LAN party

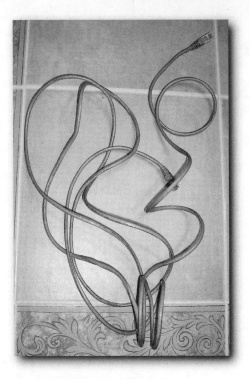

FIGURE 7-2: 100Base-T cable

Adding Consoles to Your Network

Many times, you'll want to hook together a bunch of Xboxes or PlayStation 2s. Because TCP/IP isn't platform-specific, you can feel free to mix PlayStation 2s and computers on the same network!

Unfortunately, thanks to hardware differences, it's usually impossible to hold a deathmatch on mixed platforms—a PlayStation 2 copy of *Jedi Knight II* doesn't know how to talk to a PC, even if the PC is running *Jedi Knight II*. But mixes of Xboxes, PlayStation 2s, and PCs can share the same network backbone to communicate with each other. In other words, hook six PlayStation 2s and six computers up to the same 12-port switch, and all the PlayStations can hear each other, and so can the PCs.

Xboxes are automatically equipped with a NIC card (it's what you plug the cable into), and the PlayStation 2's Network Adaptor is a NIC. Both are predesigned to plug into a TCP/IP Ethernet network, meaning that if you run the configuration described above, you're totally good to go. (Xboxes and PlayStation 2s are configured to request their information from a DHCP server by default, but you can set the addresses manually if you need to. You'll learn what that means in the section "Networking Protocols," later in this chapter.)

How This Book Defines the Term *Network*

For smaller LAN parties with 20 or fewer players, it's likely that you'll all be hooked up to a single switch (or a couple of switches linked together), playing the same game. With so few players, you won't have to worry about traffic overload; despite the fact that your computers are all yelling information back and forth across the same cable, it's still a very small network, and the traffic is still comparatively low.

But at large-scale parties, you can't have everyone sharing the same line; when 60 computers are all screaming information back and forth across the same cable, everything slows to a crawl as the line becomes choked with the babbling of the many different computers.

The only solution? Create smaller *subnetworks* to handle the traffic. Instead of sharing a single wire, you create two separate wires (or more) and put half the computers on Wire Number 1 and the rest on Wire Number 2, thus ensuring that your bandwidth is evenly distributed, as shown in Figure 7-3. That's essentially what routing does, as you'll learn later.

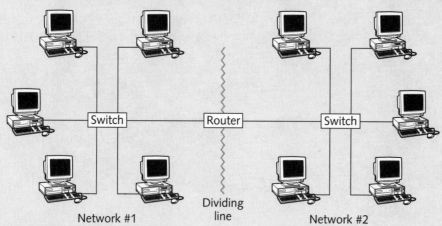

FIGURE 7-3: A network split in half

If I have to keep drawing a distinction between these two terms, I'll be forced to use different terminology throughout this entire book, saying terribly awkward things like "If you have eight or fewer players, this would be your entire network, and for nine or more players, this would be a subnetwork of your full network." That would get boring — and confusing — really fast.

Therefore, for the purposes of this book, a *network* is defined as *several computers that all broadcast across a shared wire* — what network professionals refer to as a *broadcast zone*. That means they're all hooked up to the same hub or switch and effectively are broadcasting messages to each other. Using this definition, a small-scale LAN party can be a single network, but large-scale LAN parties can be five or more smaller networks, separated by *routers* that will only pass on data if they know that a specific computer is on another wire.

Continued

Continued

Technically speaking, once you tie everything together so every computer can speak to each other, the whole thing becomes one network—a large area network. This is technically inaccurate, but it's clearer, so you big geeks bear with me. I'm trying to help out the little guys.

Network Interface Cards

These days, most new computers come pre-installed with *network interface cards*, also known as *NICs* (see Figure 7-4), and that's good. It means that all you have to do is plug a cable into your PC, and it's ready to frag.

FIGURE 7-4: A typical NIC

If you don't know what you have in your computer, the default standard is a *10/100 autoswitch Ethernet card that accepts 100Base-T cable.* (You'll learn what these terms mean in a second.) While some NICs may be configured for fiber-optic cable interfaces or run Token Ring topologies, chances are good you don't have them.

It's important to know that they exist, however, because each network interface card is designed to work with a specific type of cabling and network topology. If you buy some cheapie Token Ring NIC on eBay, it won't work with your Ethernet setup. If you want to hook fiber-optic cable up to a standard NIC, you're out of luck.

Keep in mind that, while topologies and network interface cards are technically two separate items, they are nevertheless closely related. The following sections explain how they work in tandem.

Topologies

So you know now that, thanks to your NIC, your computer can be hooked up to an Ethernet network. What does that mean from a LAN party perspective?

Well, it means it saves you a lot of time. Ethernet is so dirt-common these days that it has become the default; almost all the network hardware you'll see is Ethernet-based. In addition, both Ethernet and NICs are really easy to set up; once you install the NIC and connect all the cables, your work — at least as far as the topologies and network cards go — is pretty much done. (You still have protocol issues to work out, but we'll get to that in a bit.)

Ethernet

Wired Ethernet networks are available in three different speeds, and each is defined in terms of the number of megabytes that can be transmitted per second across the network — a speed also known as *megabytes per second*, or *Mbps*. Even 10 Mbps is pretty fast — it's about 150 times faster than a dialup modem and 15 times faster than a good DSL or cable modem. (Frankly, in my experience, I've found that the difference between 10 Mbps and 100 Mbps at a small, seven-person LAN party isn't all *that* noticeable, except when you're downloading files.)

Fortunately, most networks are going to be running at 100 Mbps or higher — and if it turns out that someone has an ancient 10 Mbps card, it won't slow the rest of the network down.

It used to be that NICs came in one flavor only: You had to buy the 10-Mbps version *or* the 100-Mbps version. If you wanted to hook your 100-Mbps NIC card up to a 10-Mbps network, you were out of luck. Thankfully, most NICs these days (known as *10/100 NICs*) can detect how fast the network is and step up or step down accordingly, a feature known as *autoswitching*. If you've bought your NIC within the past three years or so, chances are good that it can autodetect. (Some older NICs don't autoswitch but can be flipped back and forth between speeds via a toggle on the back of the card.)

Note Even though a Fast Ethernet network may be rated at 100 Mbps, don't expect to see a full 100-megabytes-per-second transfer rate when you start downloading from someone's computer. Some network overhead always prevents the network from running at its full rated capacity. Nonetheless, 70 or 80 Mbps is still pretty darned fast.

The three types of cabled Ethernet available are Fast Ethernet, Gigabit Ethernet, and 10Base-T Ethernet, each of which is described in the following sections.

Fast Ethernet

Also known as a *100Base-TX Ethernet* network, a *Fast Ethernet network* runs at a quick 100 Mbps. These networks require 100Base-T cabling, also known as *Category 5 cabling*, and require NICs that can run at 100 Mbps. A small Ethernet network looks like Figure 7-5.

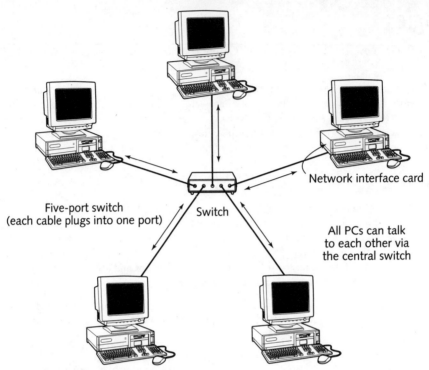

Network interface card

Five-port switch
(each cable plugs into one port)

Switch

All PCs can talk
to each other via
the central switch

FIGURE 7-5: A typical Ethernet setup

Gigabit Ethernet

Gigabit Ethernet supports transfer rates of 1,000 Mbps. Yikes! The great thing about Gigabit Ethernet is that you don't have to upgrade your cabling as long as you're running Category 5 cables; all you have to do is upgrade your hardware. Relatively few computers are installed with network cards that can operate at gigabit speeds, though, and gigabit hubs and switches are still fairly expensive (though they're dropping in price daily). It's unlikely that a casual LAN party will have enough computers with gigabit NIC cards and hardware to form a fully fledged Gigabit Ethernet network. I have yet to see one, but a hard-core party with bleeding-edge computers or a large grouping might be able to. If you do, let me know how fast it feels!

10Base-T Ethernet

10Base-T Ethernet networks can transmit data at 10 Mbps per second. Not surprisingly, they require *10Base-T cabling* (also known as *Category 3 cabling*), and as mentioned before, all the hardware has to run at 10 Mbps — but because 10 Mbps is the low end of networking nowadays, this requirement generally isn't a problem.

What *is* a problem is that you have to use 10Base-T cable, which looks like a phone cord and isn't compatible with the 95 percent of all network cards out there. Therefore, 10Base-T Ethernet is pretty much dead, and I mention it only so you know it exists.

The fourth option: Wireless

There's also a fourth option that eschews wires altogether: *wireless Ethernet* (see Figure 7-6). Basically, you buy a NIC with an antenna that broadcasts and receives radio signals, and all the other wireless computers yell (and hear each other) through open air. Say "Sayonara" to all those hubs, switches, and stupid gray cable!

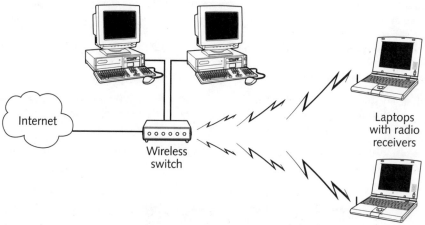

FIGURE 7-6: A typical wireless setup

Wireless-enabled computers can talk to each other easily without the need for a hub or a switch to physically connect them, making it ideal for an impromptu party if you manage to find a couple of people with wireless-enabled computers. As such, wireless Ethernet is becoming increasingly popular among gaming groups and particularly among people who play on laptops; you can simply bring your laptop to the LAN room, set up your little radio wireless beacon, and start playing. It's sinfully easy.

Note Some wireless networks are encrypted using a security protocol called *WEP*, or *Wired Equivalent Privacy*. You will need to type in an access code before you can log onto these networks.

There are technically two flavors of wireless Ethernet—the early 802.11 and 802.11b—but only the 802.11b is commonly used nowadays. The 802.11 was the first wireless standard, but it was both slow (2 Mbps) and unreliable (sometimes its own broadcasts bounced off walls and returned to the antenna, where it was read as an entirely new broadcast). Thankfully, the 802.11b is faster (11 Mbps), more reliable, and pretty much the de facto standard for anything you're likely to buy these days.

(If you're stuck with an old 802.11 wireless interface, it *does* work with 802.11b computers—most of the time. Sometimes, older vendor-specific glitches make it impossible for older interfaces to talk with newer ones.)

The biggest problem you'll run into with wireless is that the weaker the signal is, the slower the data flows. Thus, making sure your wireless computers can all hear each other clearly is critical to wireless Ethernet success. If you have multiple wireless computers in a network, try to put them all close to each other. If you have an access point (discussed), put it up high where all the computers can "see" it.

And, most importantly, *watch your network card*. A lot of wireless NICs have their antenna built right into the card, meaning that, when you actually install it and start playing, your antenna is located at the back of the computer, close to the ground, and possibly shoved underneath a desk. My wireless card is shown in Figure 7-7. Note how my left hand naturally covers my wireless card when I have my fingers on the classic WASD movement keys, blocking the signal. I've acidentally dropped out of a game a few times. Needless to say, this is *not* an ideal receiving location. If you have wireless, raise your antenna as high as you can.

Technically speaking, wireless Ethernet isn't a *separate* Ethernet; you can add wireless Ethernet computers to an existing Ethernet network via a piece of hardware called an *access point*. An access point is simply a hub, switch, or router with an antenna that listens to wireless traffic.

There are two ways to incorporate wireless Ethernet into your network: cable-free and mixed wireless and cable.

FIGURE 7-7: My hand, blocking the signal to my wireless card

The cable-free network

This setup is really simple: You'll need to first make sure that one of the wireless computers is set up to act as a DHCP server so it can hand out IP addresses to anyone who asks for it. Then, ensure that the DHCP server is in a good broadcast zone where everyone can hear it. Assuming you've configured your DHCP properly and that everyone's NICs are working right, you're good to start blasting.

Mixed wireless and cable

In order to get wireless computers and cabled computers to talk to each other, you'll need a broadcast antenna with an Ethernet port, called an *access point*. You connect the access point with cable to your network just as if it were another computer. From that point on, it will broadcast any cable-related data out through its antenna and broadcast any data it picks up through its antenna onto the cable. You can also buy access points that have attached routers and switches for even greater ease of use.

Note that the Internet is most definitely "cabled." If you want Internet access at your party, you will need an access point.

Other options for network topologies

Other options are available to you if you're looking for other network topologies.

One such topology is the *bus topology*, in which all the computers are literally strung together on a cable like Christmas lights (see Figure 7-8). This can only be done if all computers are using coaxial cable, or *thick ethernet* cable, which is rare nowadays, as most Network Interface Cards are 100Base cable-specific. If all the computers do use coaxial cable, you'll have to hook them all up using BNC connectors (small screw-on receptors like the kind you use to hook your TV up to a cable connection) and then make sure the ends are properly terminated so that the signals don't bounce back and forth across the wire.

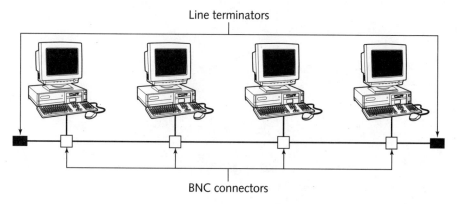

Line terminators

BNC connectors

Note lack of switch or hub

FIGURE 7-8: A typical bus setup

Not only is coaxial cable more difficult to set up, but it's also more inconvenient. Because all the computers rely on each other to keep the chain alive, when one computer is disconnected from the network, the entire network can crash. I strongly recommend that, if you're using coaxial cable to connect all your computers together, spend the extra cash to get proper NICs and a hub — and then get NICs that accept 100Base-T. (Running coaxial cables to connect routers can be okay, though.)

You can also use *Token Ring topology* (see Figure 7-9), but that only works if you're using FDDI or Token Ring networks — not Ethernet. Token Ring networks don't broadcast their signals onto the wire for all to hear; instead, they pass a *token* from computer to computer, which carries a certain amount of data with it. The data passes through each computer in a ring, and, when it gets to its destination, that computer reads the data, strips it off the token, and adds any data that it needs to the token before it passes it on down. Think of the token as the "speaking stick" used around campfires and support groups everywhere.

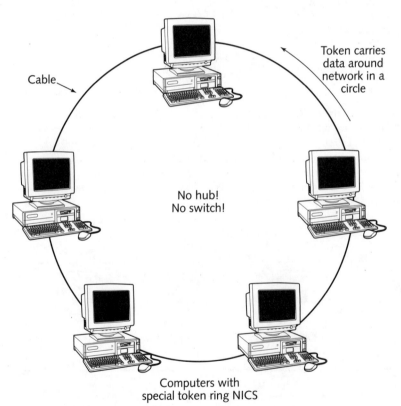

FIGURE 7-9: A typical Token Ring setup

Ring Topologies

Being in a *ring topology* doesn't necessarily mean that the computers are physically laid out in a perfect ring; in fact, they usually aren't. The token is passed from computer to computer in the same order every time, however, so you *could* physically form a ring with the computers in a Token Ring network if you really wanted to (but why would you?).

The problem is that Token Ring networks, which were designed by IBM back when 16 Mbps was blazingly fast thoroughput, never really caught on among the home networking crowd — and it's incompatible with Ethernet. Therefore, even if you're using Token Ring (which is not likely), you'll have to find a significant number of other people who do before you can hold a LAN party using Token Ring.

Fiber Distributed Date Interface (FDDI) is a high-end networking protocol that relies on fiber-optic cable to deliver transfer rates of 1,000 Mbps (and up) across cities, and it also uses tokens to great effect. But FDDI relies on cabling that's difficult to use (as I'll explain in the section "The Medium," later in this chapter), and using FDDI for a LAN party is like using a bazooka to take care of a beehive. It's ridiculously overpowered.

The Medium

The medium we are concerned with in this section is cables. (We've discussed wireless networks, which broadcast radio waves across open air, but if you have to configure the air in your house, you have far deeper problems that I can possibly solve.)

UTP: The most common cable

Because geeks love to make things needlessly complicated, the most popular type of cable goes by three different names: *100 Base-T, Unshielded Twisted Pair,* or *UTP.* They're all the same thing (see Figure 7-10).

Whatever you call it, this kind of cable is popular for three reasons: It's flexible, so it can be laid down pretty much anywhere you want it, it's cheap, and it's easy to make. If you know what you're doing, you can buy UTP cable in huge, 10,000-meter spools and then cut and crimp it to create smaller, computer-ready cables on the fly. (I'll show you how to do that in the next chapter.)

Basically, 100Base-T cable consists of eight small wires, each surrounded by a thin coating of rubber, which are twisted around each other in pairs in order to provide electrical shielding. If they weren't twisted, every time you laid some 100Base-T cable near somebody else's computer, the magnetic field might well scramble the data. It looks a lot like slightly thicker phone wires.

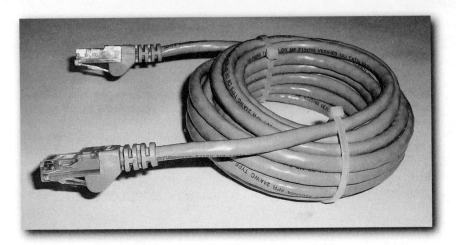

FIGURE 7-10: UTP cable

You need to know two things when purchasing UTP:

- Whether it's *straight-through* (that is, normal) or *crossover* cable
- The *category*, which determines how fast it can carry data

Straight-through versus crossover

Ninety-five percent of the time, you'll be using straight-through cable, which hooks computers up to hubs, switches, and routers — and vice versa.

Occasionally, however, you'll need a hub to talk to another hub or want to string two PCs together directly via their NICs. Then, and *only* then, will you want to use a crossover cable, which enables two devices of the same type to communicate directly. (If you want to know why, you can find out in the next chapter.)

Most of the time, having a crossover cable handy isn't a bad idea, but most small LAN parties can get by without one. (Also, if you're only looking for a head-to-head battle between two players, you can skip the switch and just connect the two PCs together with a crossover.)

Category 3 versus Category 5

UTP is available in two forms: *Category 3* and *Category 5*. Category 3 UTP cable can accept up to 10 Mbps of traffic before it becomes overloaded, and it's incompatible with most network cards currently sold. Category 5 cable can handle up to 1,000 Mbps, and it plugs into just about everything.

They also cost about the same. You do the math.

Category 5e?

I've seen a few stores selling Category 5e cable, which might be confusing if you don't know what it is. In fact, there is no *official* Category 5e; it's a term that cable manufacturers made up to indicate that their Category 5 cable is more resistant to electrical interference and can carry a signal for a longer distance. However, there's no universal standard to tell you how much better Cat 5e cable is.

It's certainly no worse, however.

What else should you know about UTP?

UTP also presents some other smaller problems that probably won't come up for any but the largest LAN parties. 100BaseT can carry data for a practical limit of about 185 meters — string cable out any longer than that, and the signal *attenuates* (or, as normal people would say, "fades into oblivion like a bad radio signal"). Therefore, if you're running cable across an auditorium, you'll have to either use a *repeater*, which takes the signal and amplifies it, or use a cable with a longer signal range, such as coaxial or fiber-optic.

Note Depending on the quality of your cable and the amount of electrical interference in the room, you may be able to go a little bit farther than that 185 meters — or a little less. If you're encountering problems and you're near the maximum length limit for your cable type, you might try using a repeater; switching to a cable that allows for more distance; or moving the hardware closer together.

UTP also is prone to *interference:* In other words, rogue electrical signals can create static on the line, which will prevent the data from reaching its destination. In practical terms, UTP's electrical shielding works fine in all but the most inhospitable environments — factories with large machines, electrical turbines, large gatherings of people purposefully scuffing rubber boots on dry carpets, and so on. Nonetheless, and particularly if you have a lot of computers in one place, sometimes it can be a factor. In a large LAN party with multiple networks, it's generally best to run the cables down central portions of the room, as far away from the hardware as possible.

In general, however, UTP cables are the easiest (and thus, for your purposes, the best) way to link computers together.

Caution If you hold LAN parties on a regular basis, you may want to string cable up through ceilings and under floors in order to get them out of the way. This is a fire code violation in most cities unless you use *plenum* cable — a cable whose plastic sheath is specifically designed to burn with non-toxic smoke.

Other cable types

The next most popular cable is called *coaxial cable*, and it comes in two varieties: 10Base-2 and 10Base-5. If you've ever hooked up a cable television, you have a good idea of what 10Base-2 coaxial cable looks like. It's not particularly popular, since not only is it relatively inflexible, but it also requires special connectors (called BNCs) and terminators to prevent the signal from bouncing back and forth along the wire. Figure 7-11 illustrates a coaxial cable.

FIGURE 7-11: Coaxial cable

However, coaxial cable has two advantages that 10BaseT doesn't have: It can extend out to 500 meters before it loses its signal (as opposed to 10BaseT's slim 100 meters), and it is much better shielded against electrical interference. Because of this, coaxial cable is usually used only at large-scale LAN parties with multiple networks as a *backbone cable* to tie multiple networks together — connecting routers and switches together across large rooms. For small parties, stick to 10BaseT and avoid the hassle.

10Base-2 cable is known as *thinnet*, and it can carry a signal 185 meters before the signal fades away. 10Base-5 cable is called *thicknet*, and it can go a whopping 500 meters — almost a third of a mile!

If you use coaxial cable to connect widespread individual networks, you'll need to buy *terminators* — small electrical resistors that you place at the end of each network to ensure that the signal doesn't bounce back to its originating computer.

The other form of cable that's commonly used in large-scale networks but not in LAN parties is fiber-optic cable. Fiber-optic is as fast as you can get it; it carries a signal for a whopping two kilometers, and it is completely immune to electromagnetic interference. Its drawbacks, however, are almost crippling for a one- or two-day event.

For one thing, you have to have a special fiber-optic interface to use fiber-optic cable; you need special NICs if you want to connect to your fiber-optic line directly, and most hubs, routers, and switches require special hardware to interface with fiber optic. In addition, fiber-optic cable doesn't bend very much, and is extremely fragile compared to other types of cables. If you're planning an event that's large-scale enough to require fiber-optic cable to connect its networks, my advice is to put down this book and go find a real geek to oversee the entire process.

Now that you've waded through all of that, why not just use the handy chart presented in Table 7-1?

Thoughts on cabling

Cables are the lifeblood of your network. Well, actually, they're the veins that *carry* the lifeblood of your network, but it amounts to the same thing. As such, it's worth making sure that you take care of your cables (see Figure 7-12).

Table 7-1 Common Cable Comparisons

Name of Cable	Maximum Throughput	Maximum Length	Notes
Category 5 (thin coaxial)	1,000 Mbps	185 meters	This is what you'll use most of the time. Extremely easy to use.
Category 5 (thick coaxial)	1,000 Mbps	500 meters	Looks like the wire that connects your cable to your television. Doesn't bend as easily. Has strange ends that don't fit into most NICs.
Category 3 (thin coaxial)	10 Mbps	185 meters	Looks a lot like a phone cord. Won't plug into most NICs.
Category 5e	1,000 Mbps	Varies, but longer than Category 5	An unofficial standard available at some stores, Category 5e cable is virtually the same as Category 5 cable except it's more resistant to electrical interference and carries a signal longer.
Fiber-optic	2,000 Mbps and up	2,000 meters	Inflexible and difficult to use for all but the most dedicated of LAN partiers

FIGURE 7-12: **Bundled and tied cables**

To ensure a minimum of confusion at your LAN party, try the following steps:

- **Label your cables.** You can buy small, sticky labels that wrap around the cord itself at almost any office supply shop; *get them.* When a computer arrives, write down the name of the computer and/or its IP address on one of the labels and wrap it around the end of the cord that you're plugging into the hub, switch, or router. Think about it: If you're trying to troubleshoot a single bad connection on a switch with 16 ports, all of which are full, do you really want to guess which cable is which? Take your time, label your cables well, and you will be rewarded with much more convenient troubleshooting.

- **Tie your cables.** You can get official cable wraps made out of gray fabric and Velcro to bundle your cables. You can buy cheap plastic cable twist-ties in megapacks, or you can simply buy a large box of garbage bags at the local Costco and use the plastic ties from that. Regardless of what you use, if you have bundles of cables that are all attached to basically the same place (a hub or a switch), *tie them together.* Having five or six cables lying around like a box of emptied spaghetti is just a hazard waiting to happen. Even if the hapless schlub who trips over them doesn't fall and break his neck, he still might yank a cable out — or worse, pull an expensive piece of hardware off of whatever it's sitting on.

- **Hide your cables.** Here's a quick tip: Before you throw your LAN party, go to a carpet store and try to buy some carpet remnants — often long, slim pieces of carpet that just don't fit into a house. (Those of you with less discerning tastes can often find them in the dumpsters behind the carpet store.) When the day comes and your cables are finally laid out, throw the remnants over the cables that run across aisles and in any other places that people are likely to walk (and trip). If you really want to go pro, get some duct tape and tape the carpets down over the cables so the carpets won't budge.

  If you don't want to get carpet, at least duct tape any cables in high-traffic areas to the floor so they don't move. If you just toss 'em where they lie, cables are a large hazard, both to safety and to your network; it's worth the couple of moments it takes to secure them.

The Central Connection: Hubs, Switches, and Routers

When you connect two or more computers together, you generally don't run a single cable to connect them all. What you do is connect the cables running from the individual computers' NICs into the *ports* on a central piece of hardware that enables the computers to talk to each other.

The number of ports on a hub, router, or switch controls the number of computers that can be attached to it (see Figure 7-13). You can't connect more computers than you have ports! Most hubs and switches come with 6 ports, 8 ports, or 16 ports, although some industrial-sized switches come with 32 or 64 ports.

FIGURE 7-13: A typical switch, front and back

The Mystery of the Dead Port

Occasionally, a hub or switch will be fully functional except for one dead port that refuses to receive or transmit. This is annoying, but it happens. If you find that your connection is dead and all else fails, you might want to try switching the cable to a different port to see if that clears things up.

In addition, most hubs and switches have a tiny green light above each port when they're connected to inform you that they have a live connection; if you don't see that light and the computer on the other end is turned on, *definitely* change that cable to another port.

What Is the Uplink Port?

Hubs, switches, and routers frequently have a special port called an *uplink*. This is used to connect hubs and switches to other hubs and switches, thereby creating a larger network. Do not attach a normal computer to the uplink port.

Switches, hubs, and routers are configured to run at a single speed. Much like NICs, they run at 10 Mbps, 100 Mbps, or 1,000 Mbps (also called *gigabit* speeds).

However, it's becoming increasingly common for routers and switches to autoswitch, just like autoswitching NICs. These central connectors are self-configuring; they'll listen to the traffic that's coming through them and automatically adjust to the slowest speed.

The central hardware comes in four flavors: hubs, switches, routers, and router-switches.

Hubs

Hubs are basically a central point for connecting wires together and creating a network. Hubs pay no attention to whatever's being broadcast; whatever is transmitted into one port is retransmitted out all of the others, even if it's complete garbage. The advantage of hubs is that they're slightly cheaper than switches and maintenance-free.

The hub embodies the same idea as the conference call; it enables all of the computers to talk to each other, and everyone hears everything.

Switches

Like hubs, *switches* are used to connect all the computers on a network together, but switches are slightly more intelligent. They listen to the line to "hear" what computers are connected to them and learn which computer is attached to which port. This process takes seconds, if that. After it has learned the addresses, the switch sends data only to the computer that it's intended for, leaving that information off the other ports.

If a central hub enables computers to have a conference call, the switch enables computers to have private conversations with each other at will, which nobody else can hear. This cuts down on the overhead traffic and ensures that the only traffic a computer hears are the broadcasts that are meant for it, which allows for much greater speed *and* more traffic than a standard hub. (Any signals going out to unknown computers or broadcasts, however, are still transmitted out through all ports.)

Switches are getting cheaper by the day, and the low-end ones require almost no configuration, making them far superior to hubs.

You can use a switch anywhere you'd use a hub, and vice versa. Hubs and switches are completely interchangeable, though switches are vastly superior.

Switches Don't Care about IP Addresses

Switches pay no attention to IP addresses or any other network protocols; they determine which computer is which by a unique identification number embedded in each NIC called the *MAC*, or the Media Access Control number. Thus, unlike routers, switches work independently of software.

Routers

Even with a switch in place, sometimes there's just too much traffic, and it overwhelms the network. (Think of what would happen if 50 mouthy people tried to use a conference call.) In that case, your only choice is to split the network in two.

Routers are put in between two subnetworks in order to segregate them and minimize traffic. They *only* transmit a message if a message from one network is specifically destined for a computer on another network. Otherwise, they stay silent.

It's possible to use multiple routers to split up multiple subnetworks to the point where routers may not even be in direct contact with each other. In fact, the Internet is nothing more than a bunch of tiny subnetworks hooked together by routers!

And speaking of the Internet, a router in Timbuktu may have no idea how to reach Microsoft headquarters in Seattle. If that happens, routers have another job: To figure out a way to transmit packets to a correct subnetwork through the fastest route while preventing unneccessary traffic from reaching other networks.

Routers require a fair amount of configuration to set up. However, they're the only way to host large-scale parties, and they're necessary if you want to connect to the Internet. I can't tell you how to set up your router, as it varies from model to model and is a very complex process, but you should understand that, if your party starts pushing boundaries, you'll need them.

Cross-Reference

For a larger overview of the routing process, see "For Larger Parties Only: Routing," in Chapter 8.

Multihomed Computers

You can actually install more than one NIC in the same computer and have separate IP addresses assigned to each of them. A computer like this is called *multihomed*, and it generally serves as a poor man's router between two subnetworks. Configuring a multihomed computer is outside the scope of this book, but remember that it's an option if you need a router and can't find someone who has a dedicated piece of routing hardware.

Router/switches: The perfect LAN party solution

The rise of DSL and Cable Internet access — and the need for multiple computers to share those superfast connections — has created a hybrid piece of hardware that serves as both a router *and* a switch. Normally, you have three to eight ports available to hook computers into and a WAN port that enables you to connect to outside networks (for example, the Internet) that serves as a mini-router. These are designed mostly to share DSL and cable connections and so are equipped with dumbed-down router interfaces.

Router/switches often serve as the following: a DHCP server to automatically assign IP addresses; a NAT access point to enable everyone to share an Internet connection; and a switch to connect four to eight computers (and did I mention that they require almost no setup?). Therefore, many router/switches are *perfect* for hosting small LAN parties.

Look for a router/switch (some companies also call them *broadband routers*) that has Network Address Translation (which some companies also call *IP sharing*), a built-in firewall, and a little-known feature called *port forwarding*. (You might not ever need port forwarding or Network Address Translation, but it sure comes in handy when you do. You'll learn what it is and when you need it in the next chapter.)

Connecting hubs and switches

You can hook hubs and switches together to effectively create one big hub. If you have an 8-port switch and a 16-port switch, connecting them together with a cable will give you a network that can handle up to 22 computers (see Figure 7-14 for a typical example). (You have 24 ports total on both switches, but one port on each switch will be taken up by the cable that connects the two of them.)

Unfortunately, thanks to cabling restrictions, you need to connect hubs and switches (and routers, if you use them) to each other in a special way. There are two ways to do it: connecting via an *uplink port* and connecting via a *crossover cable*.

You — Yes, YOU! — May Have Already Won the Easiest LAN Party Ever!

If you've paid your ISP $100 or so to buy some weirdo piece of hardware that lets you share an Internet connection, chances are good that you already *have* a router/switch. Moreover, you probably have a NAT access point, as described in the next chapter, which includes a free DHCP server. Furthermore, you most likely have a firewall as well! All you have to do is hook your hub or switch up to that piece of hardware, and you probably have a LAN party that's preconfigured and ready to go.

Be warned, however, that some ISPs have hard-capped the number of computers that can share an Internet connection. For example, on my Earthlink broadband router, I have a maximum of four players allowed at any time. I can get around that if I want, but check your ISP for details.

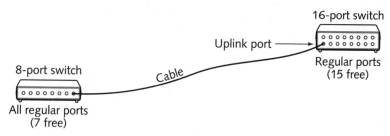

FIGURE **7-14:** Connection between two switches

Connecting via the uplink port

If one of the hubs or switches has a special port, called an *uplink port*, you can use that. Plug the cable into the uplink port on Switch 1, and attach it to a normal port on Switch 2. Don't connect two hubs by running a cable between their two uplink ports.

You can daisychain hubs and switches together with multiple uplinks, using the uplink port on Switch 1 to connect to Switch 2 and then using Switch 2's uplink port to connect to Switch 3 and so on.

Connecting via a crossover cable

A special kind of cable called a *crossover cable* is used to connect PCs directly to PCs or switches to other switches. We've covered that in the section "The Medium," earlier in this chapter, but if you have a crossover cable, you can plug it into regular ports on hubs and switches to connect them, with no uplink required.

Linking four or more switches the smart way

If you're hooking four or more switches together, you'll want to try and avoid creating *bottlenecks*—places where all othe network traffic *has* to go through. What will inevitably happen is that these connections will become overloaded, slowing down your network.

It's much easier to show you this than it is to write about it, so take a look at Figure 7-15, which demonstrates the right and wrong way to hook up four switches.

In the 100 Mpbs network on the top, you can see that, by linking all the switches sequentially, any traffic destined for the opposite side of the network must pass through that central cable. That cable quickly becomes choked as every critical bit of network data tries to pass through it.

But in the network on the bottom, I've hooked three switches into one central switch (which still has a network attached to it). All the computers can talk to each other through the central switch, which is designed to handle large amounts of traffic. The bottleneck is removed, and your network will run faster.

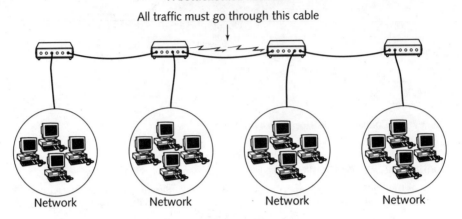

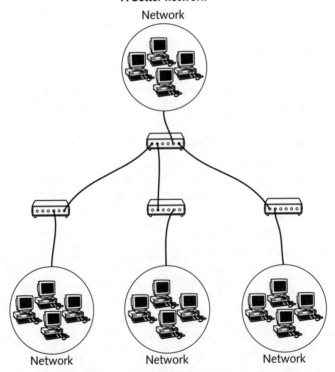

FIGURE 7-15: The network on the top will most likely lead to a network slowdown. The network on the bottom distributes bandwidth more evenly.

For Hub-Only Networks

If you're using all hubs instead of switches (which you shouldn't), there is an obscure rule of networking that arises—the 5/4/3 rule. This states that, if you're setting up a network with hubs (and *only* hubs), an Ethernet signal can travel through only five hubs, with four repeaters, and only three segments can have users. Put more simply, you can have a maximum of five hubs connected to each other, and only three of those hubs can have computers attached to them before the signals fade.

This is yet another reason why hubs are a dying technology.

If you cannot avoid creating a bottleneck, the next best solution is to make sure that the bottle-necked area has enough bandwidth to carry the increased traffic. This is usually done by connecting high-traffic switches or routers with cables that can carry a lot of data—for example, if the bottlenecked Category 5 cable at the top of Figure 7-16 was replaced with a fiber-optic cable that could transmit two gigabits of data per second, the bottleneck would vanish. (You could also make sure that both switches used Gigabit Ethernet hardware so that they would have a 1,000 Mpbs connection. This is the most common solution.)

This central, high-speed line is frequently known as the *backbone* of the network, mostly because, if it is broken, the network cannot run.

The other option is *trunking*. This is a technology that has different names depending on the manufacturer, but the upshot is that you take two or more ports and combine their bandwidth into one logical connection. Say, for example, that you had two 100 Mpbs switches, and you needed to link them via a 300 Mpbs connection. If you ran three cables between the switches and then trunked the three 100 Mbps ports the cables were attached to, you would have one 300 Mpbs connection.

The problem with trunking is twofold. First, it uses a lot of ports and a lot of cable. In the example I just gave, you'd need to dedicate six ports total to the trunk: three on the first switch and three on the second.

Second, all your switches must be from the same manufacturer—or at least follow the same trunking rules. As of the time that I write this chapter, there is no industry standard for trunking. Consult your manual. (Or just use gigabit hardware, as it's easier.)

Networking Protocols

The most common networking protocol you'll encounter is called TCP/IP, and it is by far the most popular for two reasons: It works on every platform, and it's routable. ("Routable" only applies to larger parties or parties with Internet connections, and it's covered in the next chapter if you can't wait.) TCP/IP was developed by the U.S. government to function as a networking protocol even in the event of war, such that, if major portions of the computer network were destroyed, the remaining computers would still be able to communicate. As such, TCP/IP is very flexible and robust; it doesn't care whether you're running a Mac, Windows, Linux, or Unix, and it accomodates large-scale networks with ease.

How large? Well, the entire Internet runs on TCP/IP. Is that large enough for you? (That's also a third reason why TCP/IP is popular — everyone uses it to access their e-mail and their Web pages every day, so most computers have TCP/IP already installed and configured.)

When you hold your first LAN parties, you'll spend what seems an ungodly amount of time looking at TCP/IP addresses, with computers asking you obscure questions about gateways and subnets and whatnot. To run a smooth party, you really should have a rough idea of what IP addresses are and how they work.

So let's get this party started, y'all.

The parts of TCP/IP configuration

When you configure a computer to use TCP/IP, there are generally five things it needs to know, some of which may have been automatically provided for it.

The IP address

The *IP address* is the number that identifies your computer to the world; no two computers on the same network can have the same IP address. (It would be like two people sharing a social security number.) You can either input this address manually, or the computer can receive it automatically from a DHCP server. (A typical IP address looks like this: 206.58.48.73)

The subnet

The *subnet* is the number that separates your IP address into two parts — the *network* and the *host* — which in turn makes it easier to find you when you've broken your LAN party into several separate networks to increase overall speed. If you're using a DHCP server to automatically assign addresses, the subnet is assigned along with the IP address (for example, 255.255.255.0).

The default gateway

A *default gateway* is only really necessary in large networks of 60 people or more or networks that want to access the Internet.

When you have numerous computers in one place, you may have to separate them into smaller subnetworks in order to reduce overhead traffic. (As described earlier, if you have 40 computers all trying to share a line at once, the line may get bogged down; but two separate lines, with 20 computers each, is a lot more manageable.) These smaller networks are connected by *routers*, a specialized piece of hardware whose job is to relay messages back and forth between subnetworks.

If your PC can't contact a computer directly (that is, the computer it wants to talk to is not connected directly to it via a hub or a switch), it will send the data to the IP address listed as the default gateway, which is a router connected directly to that subnetwork. It then becomes that router's job to find a way to get the data to the right place.

If your computer has no default gateway set up, it just throws away any requests for outside data. This doesn't matter on small networks, where all of your computers are attached directly, but it's critical when someone wants to access the Internet. If you don't have a default gateway set up, then your computer immediately sends all of your Internet requests to the garbage can. (It's also very bad in larger networks that *are* routed.)

The DHCP server

The *DHCP server* is used on larger networks and in NAT access points that allow several computers to share a high-speed Internet connection. It's a computer that automatically assigns IP addresses to computers that ask for it. Some older operating systems will require you to input the IP address of the DHCP server; other, smarter systems just yell as loud as they can until a DHCP server answers. If you're given an option that says something like "Obtain an IP address automatically," then you've got a smart computer. Hug it.

DNS server

The *DNS server* is only important if you're accessing the Internet, and even then, it will most likely be the address of a computer outside your network.

IP addressing and the challenges of TCP/IP

The IP address, like a street address, is split into two parts. Think about it: 2907 Ambergate Road *looks* like a single address, but Ambergate Road tells people what street you live on, and 2907 is a specific house on that street.

There's no reason you couldn't number each house sequentially, thus turning "2907 Ambergate Road" into "House Number 46,532" except that mail carriers would have a heck of a time finding your house. Sure, it could be located eventually, but without that subcategory of "Ambergate Road," they would have to count every house in between where they were and your house number of 46,532 to find it. (And you thought mail carriers went postal *now?*)

Furthermore, what happens if someone builds a house between House 46,532 and 46,533? You might have to renumber everything. What a pain. It's far better to subsection everyone's addresses into streets and house numbers.

Network addresses have the same problems; even though computers are faster than people, having a computer flip through a million PC addresses every time it tried to find someone would still be ridiculously slow. Therefore, IP addresses are also split into two parts: the *network number* and the *host number*. The network number tells you what network the computer is located on, and the host number narrows it down to a computer on that network. That way, you can find the address of a PC that's attached to Microsoft or Joe Schmoe's network with equal ease.

Much like the "2907" and the "Ambergate Road," an IP address consists of two parts: the address itself and the subnet:

- An *IP address* is a four-part octet number, separated by dots, where each number is between 1 and 255. For example, the IP address for www.starcitygames.com is **69.50.212.110**, and the IP address for www.wiley.com is **208.215.179.46**.

- The *subnet* is what splits the IP address up into the network and the host number. The subnet is similar to the IP address in that it's also four numbers, separated by dots, except that all of the subnet's numbers are either 255 or 0, such as the following: **255.255.255.0**.

When Subnets Are Assumed

Many programs don't ask you for subnets, mainly because they use IP *Classes*—in other words, these programs assume that any IP address that starts with 209 has a subnet of 255.255.255.0. For the record, the "official" classes of subnets, based on the first number in the IP address, are as follows:

Class A	1-126	255.0.0.0
Class B	128-191	255.255.0.0
Class C	192-223	255.255.255.0

To figure out which is the network (street) number and which is the host (address) number, simply put the IP address over the subnet, as follows:

```
209. 204.  146.   22
255. 255.  255.   0
```

The parts of the address with the "255" under them are the network address—in this case, 209.204.146. The parts without the "255" underneath them are the host address—in this case, 22. In other words, this IP address indicates "computer number 22 on network number 209.204.146."

But what happens if we change the subnet to 255.255.0.0?

```
209. 204.  146.   22
255. 255.  0.     0.
```

Now the network address is 209.204, and the host number is 146.22! In other words, simply by changing the subnet, we have changed this IP address from "computer 206 on network 209.15.176" to "computer 176.206 on network 209.15."

How do computers get these IP addresses?

There are two ways to get an IP address: You can manually set the IP address on your computer, or you can have it assigned to you by a server. (A server whose sole job is to assign IP addresses is called a *DHCP server*.)

Subnetting IP Addresses

It is possible to use subnet masks to increase the number of networks you can use. This involves splitting a subnet into strange half-combinations such as 255.255.255.240 to split a network up into even smaller subsections. Only the largest networks—those with millions of users—ever need to do this, so I'm not going to discuss it beyond telling you it exists. However, if you do happen to look at your IP information, which may have been given to you by a DHCP server that does have millions of users, you might see something odd like this. My advice is not to worry about it.

Setting IP addresses manually

For smaller LAN parties, you can manually set the IP address on each computer—and I'll show you how to do that in Chapter 10, "The Least You Need to Know about Configuring Your Computer." As long as you make sure that all the IP addresses at your party share the same network number, all the computers will be able to talk to each other without a problem.

Caution

Each IP address has to be unique! If you put two identical IP addresses on the same network, you'll start to see some very strange things happening. If you're setting each IP address by hand, make sure you don't double-dip.

Having an IP address assigned to you via DHCP

The manual assignment of IP addresses breaks down once you start networking a large number of computers. For one thing, you have to remember which computer has which IP address—and you just learned what happens if you assign the same IP address to two different computers by mistake. Furthermore, running around and setting up each computer by hand begins to take up serious time—time you'd rather spend partying on the LAN. What should you do for a big party, or even a small one, so that you don't have to waste time?

Enter DHCP. DHCP stands for *Dynamic Host Configuration Protocol*, and it is a computer that assigns IP addresses to computers who need them.

Why Type In Names Instead of Numbers?

All computers running TCP/IP identify and find each other via IP addresses; they don't understand things like www.yahoo.com. However, there is a service called DNS, which acts as a large telephone book for computers. When you type in www.yahoo.com, your computer calls a DNS server and essentially asks it, "Hey, what's the IP address for www.yahoo.com?" and the DNS server returns the IP address so your computer can find it. It's completely irrelevant to the subject of this book, mainly because nobody sane is going to set up his or her own DNS server at a LAN party, but you ought to at least know that it is there.

The Easiest DHCP Server

If you already have multiple computers hooked up to share a broadband Internet connection at home, such as ADSL or cable—which can happen when you've bought a router/switch—there's a pretty good chance that you already have a pre-made DHCP server in place. If you do, you may not have to do anything to configure your IP addresses. Lucky you! For more information, see the section "Sharing A Single Internet Connection via Network Address Translation" in the next chapter to learn how Network Address Translation provides you with a free DHCP server.

Instead of assigning an IP address directly, you simply tell the computer to use the nearest DHCP server. When that computer boots up, it hops online and yells, "Hey! What's my IP address, subnet, and default gateway?"

The DHCP server is configured to hear requests like this and respond. It then looks through its records and says, in effect, "Let me see . . . I've been configured to give out any IP addresses between 169.254.255.01 and 169.254.255.255, and right now, I see that 169.254.255.254 is free. That's your address."

Note

Some older software requires that you input the address of the DHCP server manually.

DHCP will actually save you quite a bit of time when you are assigning IP addresses. Many LAN party diehards consider the DHCP server to be the most important server at the party.

When you should avoid DHCP

Computers that will be game servers should *never* request IP addresses via DHCP (though they're a good bet to set up as a DHCP server). Although it's rare—and generally happens only with badly configured or completely crashed DHCP servers—sometimes computers with DHCP-assigned addresses will change their IP address a few times over the course of a day. If that happens to a game server, suddenly everyone's computers will be pinging the old IP address in a flurry of electronic packets, trying to get information from the wrong computer or a nonexistent one. Always, *always* assign IP addresses manually to game servers.

How do IP addresses work in gaming?

Remember how we had computers shouting back and forth at each other over the line? Now, thanks to TCP/IP and IP addressing, everyone now has a name and a location. Clients shout out their position updates to the server over the wire, and the other computers will check the wire for game updates, realize that a broadcast meant for 209.204.146.22 isn't addressed to them, and promptly ignore it.

IP Addresses for Networks That Don't Talk to the Internet

You may have noted that, for gaming, you'll have to assign individual IP addresses to each computer or Bad Things will happen. You may also note that the Internet runs on the TCP/IP protocol, and as such, every computer on the Internet has to have a unique address.

If you're running a self-contained network, one that isn't connected to the Internet at all, it's no problem; because your computers are isolated, you can call them anything you want. Heck, feel free to give your server an IP address of 207.46.230.220 (that's `Microsoft.com`). What's Bill Gates gonna do—sue? But if you have a computer hooked up to the Internet, your Microsoftian address will cause problems when every request meant for your computer winds up knocking on the behemoth's door.

Fortunately, the people who created the Internet realized that there would be non-Internet networks that would use TCP/IP. Thus, they reserved several IP addresses for that purpose.

If you give your computers addresses between 169.254.0.1 and 169.254.255.254, with a subnet address of 255.255.0.0, you'll be perfectly fine. No computer on the Internet uses those numbers. That's thousands of addresses—more than enough for your average LAN party.

I suggest you get in the habit of always using these IP addresses; it makes things simpler in the long run.

When you're dealing with IP addresses, an arsenal of software tools is bundled with almost every computer that you can use to check your TCP/IP connections and ensure that all the packets are being received:

- **Ping** enables you to send a packet to another computer to verify that you can talk to it. This is handy in all kinds of ways.

- **Ipconfig** tells you what IP address, subnet, and default gateway you're using; allows you to request a new one; and gives you a host of other options.

- **Tracert** enables you to trace a path between your computer and a computer in another network.

Youll learn more about this in Chapter 10, where you'll learn exactly what these are and how they work; and in Chapter 15, where you learn how you can use them to troubleshoot network problems.

TCP/IP Packets

When TCP/IP sends a file (or other information) to another computer, it doesn't send it all at once. Instead, TCP/IP breaks every network broadcast down into tiny bits of data known as *packets* and sends them out separately.

In addition to its precious cargo of data, each packet is tagged with the IP address of the sender, the IP address it's destined for, what other packets need to be reassembled with it, the destination port, a *checksum* number to make sure that it arrives uncorrupted, and a maximum "time to live." (If unreceived packets didn't eventually expire on their own, misrouted traffic would just float around forever, clogging networks like bad cholesterol.)

When a computer receives a valid packet, it stores it, and when it receives all the associated packets, it recombines them into a nice neat file. If a few packets went missing or got mangled along the way, the computer asks the sender to retransmit the missing packets.

This is important because almost all network traffic consists of packets. You can even get programs called *packet sniffers*, which look at the individual packets running through a network to determine what kind of data is being transmitted and analyze where most of it is going.

It's not likely that you'll need to analyze packets at a smaller LAN party, but you should at least know they exist. They are the blood cells of your LAN party; almost invisible to the naked eye, but vital nonetheless.

Binding protocols to network cards

You'll learn all about binding again when we get to Chapter 10, but realize that NICs don't understand TCP/IP (or any other protocol) on their own; a NIC on its own simply listens to the wire and receives packets of data. It's the computer that does the gruntwork, telling the NIC how to interpret TCP/IP data, how to assemble that data into fragments the computer can understand, and how to broadcast signals across the wire so that other computers running TCP/IP will understand it.

This process of teaching a NIC to understand a specific protocol is called *binding*. You can bind more than one protocol to a NIC so that it can understand the TCP/IP protocol *and* the IPX protocol *and* SMB, as well as any other protocol you'd like your computer to understand.

If you have ever accessed the Internet with a computer, then you can be sure that your computer understands TCP/IP. In fact, TCP/IP is so common that most NICs have it automatically bound even if you *haven't* accessed the Net. However, sometimes you'll need to bind some weird protocol like IPX. If that's the case, you can learn how to do it in Chapter 10.

Protocols other than TCP/IP

Protocols other than TCP/IP are currently in use, but unless you're stealing computers from an office network to conduct a late-night LAN stealth party, you probably won't need them. I strongly advise you stick with the Esperanto of the computer world: TCP/IP.

The paragraphs that follow describe a couple of other noteworthy protocols that you may come across.

Netware IPX/SPX

Netware is one of the workhorses of the industry, and their Novell Netware is an operating system used specifically for tying large computer networks together. Earlier versions of Netware used a proprietary protocol called *IPX/SPX* so that Netware servers and clients could talk to each other. But recently, even the mighty Netware has bowed to the pressure of the Internet and started using TCP/IP as the default protocol for their servers, starting with Netware 5.

Still, you might occasionally run into Netware IPX/SPX, especially since a few games still demand you use it. IPX/SPX is a lot easier to configure than TCP/IP — instead of having you assign an address to each computer, Netware uses the unique identification number on the NIC that's installed in each computer. To sort computers into individual networks, IPX uses an *external network number,* which is sort of like the subnet in TCP/IP. (If your IPX network asks you to choose a network number, there's no shame in using 1.)

To make things a little more confusing, IPX/SPX uses several frame types to transmit the data, depending on what kind of Netware server you have. Frames come in four varieties, but the most common are frame types 802.3 or 802.2. For an IPX/SPX network to work properly, all computers must use the same frame type. Most computers know that IPX uses multiple frame types and will automatically choose the frame type for you. Some computers, however, will choose incorrectly. If you're having problems with an IPX network, check the frame type first.

Not all games can run on IPX/SPX! If you're holding a LAN party with a central Netware server that uses IPX/SPX, check the game's manual to see if it's IPX-compatible.

Server Message Block, or Samba

When you're hosting a large LAN party, you want to make sure that everyone has the latest patches and custom maps. Therefore, having a central file server from which everyone can download whatever they need is extremely convenient. The problem is that you'll frequently run into interoperability issues; your Linux box won't talk to the Windows 2000 server, and the lone Mac is left hanging in the dark.

The *Server Message Block,* or *SMB* — commonly known as *Samba* — is very handy for LAN parties. It's a free protocol that enables a Unix server (or Linux, Unix's baby brother) to share files with computers running almost any operating system, as long as they're all running TCP/IP. Samba has the advantage of being an open source program, which means it's created by programmers in their spare time and is available free.

Samba, like almost all open source programs, is something of a pain to set up; because it doesn't cost you anything, it doesn't come with all the easy-install doodads that more expensive programs have. Once you set it up, however, it's fairly easy to administer, and it dodges any Linux/Windows wars. If you're holding a large-scale party, it's worth your time to investigate it.

LocalTalk

LocalTalk is the Macintosh networking protocol you *may* want to use if you have an all-Mac environment — but considering that most Macs built within the last four years (including iMacs) can run TCP/IP Ethernet as well as LocalTalk, even Apple seems to have been slowly shoveling dirt onto LocalTalk. Furthermore, LocalTalk is really slow. I advise you to just skip it.

Summary

That was a lot of information to digest in one chapter, but you should have a basic understanding of the following key points:

- Computers talk to each other by sharing a single wire.
- Cable (and the hardware that allows computers to share a cable) restricts how fast your network can run.
- Most computers use TCP/IP to assign themselves unique identities and to communicate with one another.

Once you've got all of that information firmly fixed in your noggin — and it may require a rereading or two to digest — you can move on to the next chapter, which deals with advanced networking concepts (at least, advanced as far as a LAN party's concerned).

Networking for Large Groups and the Internet

In the last chapter, I gave you the bare minimum of information that you need to know in order to create the backbone for a small LAN party. But networks get exponentially more complex when you add more computers — and if you think dragging another 50 pals into your party will add some complications, what happens when you add 5,000,000? Giving your network access to the Internet is essentially asking for entry into the world's largest computer network, adding, oh, about a billion computers to your network in one shot.

As such, this chapter first explains a part of TCP/IP that comes into play when you add a bunch of computers: routing. Then, later in the chapter, we'll get into an issue that strikes home for many LAN parties: ports and firewalls. The chapter ends with more useful information about UTP cable.

For Larger Parties Only: Routing

Despite the neatness of IP addressing, a problem occurs when you start adding large numbers of people to it — and if you've read the last chapter, I'm sure you can see it.

If you have seven people in a room and they're all shouting at each other, eventually two of them are going to shout at the same time. When that happens, most people will shut up for a moment before yelling again.

That's what many networks do, too, and it's called *Carrier Sense Multiple Access/Collision Detect*, or *CSMA/CD*. When two computers are broadcasting over the same wire at the same time, the signals cross and turn whatever's on the line to gibberish. When that happens, the two computers that were broadcasting will realize they're fouling the wire and back off, retransmitting their position updates a little bit later. It works very well for small networks, as it would for small parties.

However, what if you have seven *hundred* people in a room at the same time? Well, for one thing, it's highly unlikely that any two people *wouldn't* be talking at the same time, and the air would be mostly garbles. Moreover, there stands a good chance that you wouldn't be able to hear someone clearly on the other side of the room, no matter how loudly they shouted.

Thus, we have to resort to what's known as *routing*.

Hooking several networks together via routers

When you're connecting small groups of computers — say, 100 or less — you can generally get away with just hooking them all up and letting it rip. In larger groups, however, routing becomes a necessity because the number of squawking computers slows everyone down.

A computer-free example of routing

To picture routing in a visual sense, think of it this way: You have a huge crowd of seven hundred people who need to talk to each other. Instead of putting seven hundred people in one room, you put 70 people each in ten interconnected rooms; each room is connected to other rooms by four soundproof doors, keeping the noise to a minimum. (Otherwise, much like our squawking computers, nobody could hear each other over the din of everyone talking at once.)

In every room, you have at least one person who stands in the doorway between two rooms and can hear everything said in either room. This guy has a rough idea of where some rooms are, and it's his job to get messages from his assigned room to whoever needs to hear the message. We'll call this guy the "router," and his assigned room is Room 16. (His friends in Room 16 also call him the "default gateway.")

Someone in Room 16 shouts, "This is PHIL! Tell VINNY in ROOM 76 that I HAVE THE FIVE BUCKS I OWE HIM!"

The "router" in this room hears this and realizes two things:

- Because this is Room 16 and Phil needs to get a message to someone in Room 76, this message needs to be handed to someone outside the room.

- He has no idea where Room 76 is.

Now, the router in Room 16 doesn't have a clue where Room 76 is, but he *does* know that even if he has no clue where a given room is, all he has to do is give the message to the router in Room 55 (the room next door), and Room 55's router will pass the message along to someone who knows where Vinny is. Room 16's router passes on Phil's message to the router in Room 55.

The router in Room 55 doesn't know exactly where Room 76 is either — but he knows that the router in Room 38 knows where Room 76 is. He gives the message to the router in Room 38.

Figure 8-1 illustrates how all of this works.

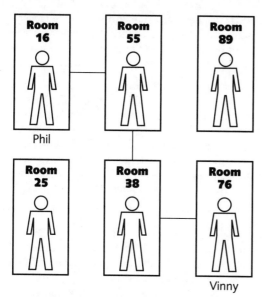

FIGURE 8-1: Phil wants to talk to Vinny, but Vinny's in Room 76 and can't hear him. He has to pass his message off to the router in Room 16, who has the job of getting the message to Vinny.

Therefore, the Router in Room 55 passes on the information — and thankfully, the router in 38 *does* know where Room 76 is. The router in Room 38 takes Phil's message, opens the door to Room 76 (which he is right next to) and shouts the message into the room where Vinny can hear it. At this point, Vinny shouts back:

"TELL PHIL IN ROOM 16 THAT HE OWES ME *TEN* BUCKS!"

Adding routers to networks

Routers work much like Vinny's message — except instead of keeping groups of people in soundproof rooms, you keep groups of computers in their own subnetworks, where they talk quietly amongst themselves. Attached to each of these subnetworks is a piece of hardware called a *router*, which listens to everything that's said in all of the subnetworks that are connected to it.

Physically speaking, you separate computers into these separate rooms (which, in computer terminology, are known as subnetworks), by connecting each set of computers to a different switch, and then linking the various switches together by plugging them into routers.

(However, a router doesn't pay any attention to your physical configuration — all it cares about are the IP addresses of the computers that talk to it.)

A router *only* passes on traffic if it's specifically destined for a subnetwork that is attached directly to the router, or if the traffic needs to pass through that subnetwork to get to its destination. Otherwise, the router refuses to pass it on, serving as the bouncer; unless you have something to say to Subnetwork 1, the router isn't going to pass on the message.

This ensures that the only traffic any given computer will ever hear is traffic specifically intended for that subnetwork, which goes a long way toward making sure that the lines on each subnetwork are kept as clear as possible. If you have four subnetworks all connected to the same router, Subnetwork 1 will not hear anything from Subnetwork 2, Subnetwork 3, or Subnetwork 4 unless a computer on any of those three subnetworks specifically requests to talk to a computer on Subnetwork 1. If all the computers on Subnetwork 2 need to talk to all the computers on Subnetwork 3, the bandwidth on those two subnetworks may become maxed out, but the lines between Subnetwork 1 and Subnetwork 4 will remain blissfully unaffected.

This separation and subdividing is what keeps large networks such as the Internet from becoming overloaded; traffic problems are restricted to local areas.

But how does the router know which computer is on which subnetwork? As indicated earlier, it has nothing to do with what's physically plugged into the router. You might recall from the last chapter that a router determines subnetworks by looking at the *subnet*.

Remember how the subnet (that 255.255.255.0 thing) splits every IP address into two parts — the address and the network? The router looks at the network part of the IP address, as determined by the subnet, to figure out where to send each piece of data. Ideally, all computers on any subnetwork have the same network address.

Therefore, each router generally has at least two IP addresses — one for each network to which it's directly connected. (Large routers may be connected to 20 or 30 subnetworks, and they need an IP address reserved for every subnetwork to which they're connected.)

A Word of Caution

Because routers *only* look at the network portion of an IP address to determine where to send traffic, they don't pay attention to what's physically hooked up to them at all — it's *very* important that the computers attached to a given hub or switch all share a common network address. Otherwise, a misconfigured computer (or a computer attached to the wrong network) might find all of its data being routed elsewhere.

Surprisingly, this happens a lot at LAN parties. People often use a computer to share an Internet connection at home, which works fine at their apartment, but when they bring that PC to your LAN party, it turns into a rogue DHCP server that begins handing out addresses at random. For more details about how this happens and, more important, how you prevent it, see Chapter 15, "Something Just Went Wrong! Fixing Party Problems." For more information on sharing Internet connections, keep reading.

Figure 8-2 illustrates how a router connects the computers in a network.

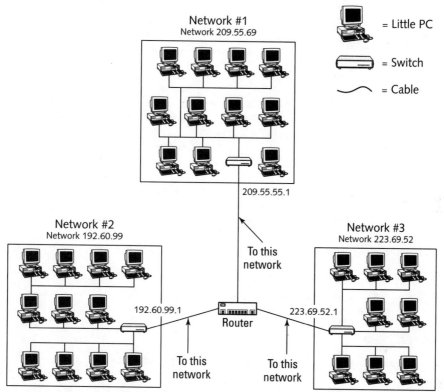

FIGURE 8-2: How your router sees your network

Do-It-Yourself Routers

While hubs and switches are just pieces of hardware, you can either buy a router off the shelf or you can configure a spare computer to serve as a router. All you need is a computer with at least two NICs in it (also known as a *multihomed* computer) and the proper software, and your PC can start doing routing duty.

Configuring a spare computer to serve as a router is moderately complex and well outside the scope of this book, but it can be a cheap alternative if you don't feel like paying Cisco (the most popular maker of routers) a thousand bucks. Just keep it in mind, if your party grows.

There are three basic ways a router directs traffic:

- The router is attached directly to the network and can broadcast information directly to the host computers, like the router in Room 38 of the preceding example.

- The router doesn't know the exact location of the network, but it knows which router can get it to the right place, like the router in Room 55 of our example — this is called a *gateway*.

- The router has no clue at all where this network is, and forwards the information to its go-to person, the way the router in Room 16 asked the router in Room 55. This is called the *default gateway*, and it's the address to which routers (and computers) send all information if the address is not on their network. (Yes, even routers are configured with their own default gateways to which information should be sent when *they* don't know where something goes.)

Now, adding and configuring routers is complex; there are people who are paid full-time salaries to get routers to work, and even *they* don't know everything. As such, this chapter does not attempt to present a comprehensive explanation of how to configure routers.

Cross-Reference For a rough idea of what a routed party looks like, go to Chapter 9, "Sample LAN Party Layouts."

The complete ins and outs of router configuration is clearly beyond the scope of this book. However, if you find that your LAN party network is bogging down and you need a router to help segregate your traffic, check out *Juniper and Cisco Routing* by Walter Goralski (Wiley, 2002) or *The Switch Book: The Complete Guide to LAN Switching Technology* by Rich Siefert (Wiley, 2000).

Even if you don't intend to add a bunch of computers, you may need to connect to the Internet. Every Internet-connected computer needs to talk to at least one router — the one that knows where other Internet routers are. As such, if you're *not* sharing an Internet connection via Network Address Translation (which is unlikely), you'll need to configure all of your computers to point to the IP address of that router, which is called (once again) the *default gateway*.

Managed Switches and VLANs: An Alternative to Routing

If you don't want to use routers, you can use *managed switches*. Managed switches are meant for larger networks, and their main advantage is that you can use them to create *VLANs*.

With VLANs (which stand for *Virtual LANs*), you assign ports on a managed switch to a particular subnetwork. For example, you can tell a managed switch that ports 1 through 4 are on VLAN 1, ports 5 through 8 are on VLAN 2, and ports 9 through 16 are on VLAN 3. VLANs, much like subnetworks in a routed network, do not pass on traffic unless computers in the two VLANs specifically need to talk to each other.

The use of managed switches is of some debate in the world of LAN parties; some people swear by them, while others claim that routers are a lot easier to set up. Personally, I'm more familiar with routers, but I thought you should know that VLANs exist, in case someone mentions them.

Chances are pretty good, however, that you'll be using NAT, and that provides a whole different kettle of fish. Read on.

Ports: The Secret Sixth Part of Every TCP/IP Address and What Computers Do with Them

There is a secret, sixth part used in an IP address — one that isn't discussed much. That's because it normally works without a hitch, but it can be an issue periodically at LAN parties.

When computers send and receive data, they don't want to waste time trying to determine what sort of thing each broadcast is. Is this packet of information a request for a Web page? An AIM message? A *Doom III* packet? If the server had to waste time analyzing each burst of information to determine what it was supposed to do with it, computers would run a lot more slowly.

When clients send information, they generally send it to a specific TCP/IP address and a specific *port* in order to save time. Ports are a number between 0 and 65,536, and they're used to tell the computer what kind of information it's receiving. For example, any TCP/IP request sent to port 80 is automatically considered to be an HTTP request, which is a fancy way of saying that you're asking the server to send you a Web page. Any TCP/IP request sent to port 22 is automatically considered to be a file transfer request. And so on.

The reason you don't know this is because it's mostly transparent. When your Web browser downloads a page, it's smart enough to know to request port 80 automatically — and so you never see it. Most games use their own special port as well, and the games are written so that they only send and receive TCP/IP traffic on their game-specific port. When you connect to a *Battlefield 1942* server, for example, your game sends all game traffic to port 14567 on the server's IP address. You never see this, nor should you most of the time; it's handled for you.

That said, there *are* some times when you'll need to know what port your game uses.

Firewalls, ports, and Internet traffic

Because unscrupulous hackers frequently use unassigned ports to break into computers, using them as a back door, technophiles came up with the idea of creating a *firewall*, something that blocks unknown Internet traffic to keep those nasty hackers at bay.

Firewalls monitor all TCP/IP traffic passing through them and can block or deny any incoming or outgoing traffic based on ports, IP addresses, networks, or any number of other critera. You can, for example, say, "Hey, we don't want the RIAA to see what we're downloading over here; block all Internet traffic coming from IP addresses associated with the RIAA."

The proviso? You'd have to tell the firewall what IP addresses were associated with the RIAA, as there's no universal database of RIAA addresses. Furthermore, there's no guarantee that the RIAA couldn't just borrow an ISP account from a friend, thus getting an entirely *new* IP address, and check in on you. Therefore, as you can already see, firewalls can be penetrated by people who know what they're doing.

Firewalls can be software-based or hardware-based. Furthermore, routers often perform some limited firewalling duties by blocking traffic and denying certain ports. Firewalls can be placed at any point in your network—and *any network that accesses the Internet should have a firewall.*

The best place to have a firewall, if you're installing one, is *at the point of Internet access.* Make sure that anyone who wants to talk to the Internet has to go through the firewall, and any incoming Internet requests have to go back through it. Alternatively, you can ensure that every computer on the network has ZoneAlarm installed. ZoneAlarm is the best free personal firewall around, and can be downloaded at `www.zonelabs.com/store/content/home.jsp`.

Note If you've bought a router/switch to help share an Internet connection, many of them come with firewalls pre-installed. Check your documentation for details, but you may already be hacker-safe. In fact, this hacker-safe nature may prevent you from playing over the Internet! (We'll discuss that in a bit.)

Because hackers frequently subvert unused ports to break into computers, routers and firewalls are generally preconfigured to block traffic coming in on unknown ports—and because most games use their own customized ports, their traffic qualifies as "unknown."

Furthermore, routers and firewalls often use port numbers to block or control *unwanted* traffic. If you know that you don't ever want anyone using FTP on your network, you can simply tell your router to not forward any TCP/IP traffic that's going to port 22. (This is, incidentally, how your boss prevents you from playing *Warcraft III* on your lunch break at work; the router is configured to block any traffic coming in on ports that aren't Web or e-mail-related.)

In other words, sometimes routers and firewalls won't allow traffic past because they don't know what it is. Other times, they won't allow it because they *do* know what it is. The practical upshot of all this is that if you're borrowing someone's router or using a preconfigured router/switch that you bought at a store, you'll occasionally need to tell a router or firewall to allow traffic from port *X*, where *X* is the port number that your favorite shoot-'em-up uses. (Generally you'll find that information buried somewhere deep in the game manual.)

Routers and DHCP

Another occasional problem is that most routers are configured to block DHCP requests by default, which means that a computer in one subnetwork won't be able to request an IP address from a DHCP server in another subnetwork. Generally, it's a good idea to have a separate DHCP server in each subnetwork configured to hand out local IP addresses.

You could be very smart and configure the routers to pass on all DHCP requests to one central DHCP server, which then needs to be smart enough to remember what subnetwork the request came from and hand out an IP address with an appropriate subnet. But that's a lot of work for all but the largest networks.

Alas, I can't tell you how to allow or deny traffic on a firewall, as firewall configuration varies radically depending on who made the program and whether it's software- or hardware-based. If you're running a personal firewall (one that resides on your computer), then you'll usually have to open the icon in your program tray and configure the options, as shown in Figure 8-3.

FIGURE 8-3: Configuring ZoneAlarm to recognize a good game of *Half-Life*

If it's a hardware-based firewall (as is the case with many router/switches, which come pre-installed with firewall software), most of the time you'll have to input an IP address into a Web browser, which will bring up a configuration page, as shown in Figure 8-4. This shouldn't be too complicated if you've read this chapter and the last chapter, as you'll have the network knowledge to know what you want to change. If you run into any problems, you'll have to consult the manual for details.

Remember that if you can't get your routed network to play a certain game, make sure the routers and firewalls are configured to allow the proper port traffic.

Sharing a single Internet connection via Network Address Translation

In these days of high-speed cable and ADSL connections, most folks want to steal some bandwidth off of someone else's Internet connection at one time or another. After you've won the ladder tourney at Phil's Internet party, wouldn't it be nice to hop on IRC via Phil's cable modem to tell people how you totally dominated everyone?

The problem with this is that we have literally run out of Internet addresses. When the Internet was created, four billion or so potential addresses seemed like a lot, but when the Internet caught fire (and remember, each computer and router connected to the Internet needs its own unique IP address), the addresses dried up very quickly.

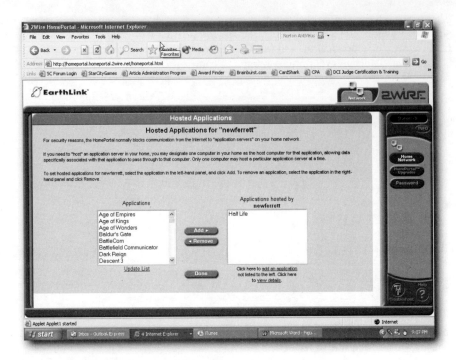

FIGURE 8-4: My EarthLink personal firewall

As such, most Internet Service Providers (ISPs) have a limited number of IP addresses that they can hand out — and they use DHCP servers to recycle unused addresses. When you turn off your computer for the night, chances are pretty good that your ISP takes back the IP address you had been using to surf the Net, and it gives it to someone else. If every ISP assigned seven or ten IP addresses to every paying customer who asked for them, pretty soon your ISP wouldn't have enough to go around.

Seeing that the Internet would break down unless someone managed to free up some room, some very smart people created a way for multiple computers on a small, private network to share a single, public IP address to surf the Internet. They called this NAT, or *Network Address Translation* — and this magic is accomplished with the use of TCP/IP ports.

How Network Address Translation works

Network Address Translation requires a computer called an *access point* that serves as both a DHCP server and a default gateway. That computer can be an actual PC, a router that's configured to perform NAT duties, or a router/switch.

How Unique Does My IP Address Have to Be?

IP addresses only have to be unique *when compared to the other computers on the network*. For example, if you're hooking five computers up to a switch, feel free to give each of them whatever IP address you want; as long as it's not an address shared by any of the other four computers attached to that switch, it won't affect a thing.

But if you want those five computers to be able to communicate with all of the other computers that are connected to the Internet—the largest computer network that exists—then each of those five computers needs to have an IP address that is *not* shared by any of the other four billion computers currently hooked into the Internet. Alternatively, you need to have them share a unique IP address via Network Address Translation, which we'll get to in just a moment.

In any case, the access point is assigned the external IP address that all of the other computers attached to it will use to surf the Net. There is a very big distinction between the "public" external IP address that the NAT provides to the Internet and the "private" Internet IP address that each computer is assigned *by* the NAT. There may be six separate computers on an internal network that's attached to a NAT access point, each with its own separate internal IP addresses and downloading information from different Web sites, but from the Internet's perspective, they're all using the same external IP address.

The access point assigns internal IP addresses to every computer that asks for one, just like a regular DHCP server. However, it assigns addresses only to computers that are directly connected to it—and it only hands out IP addresses between 169.254.0.1 and 169.254.255.254. (If you recall, those are the addresses that have been reserved for internal home networks that will never use the Internet, as discussed in the last chapter—specifically, in the section "IP Addresses for Networks That Don't Talk to the Internet.")

Note The exact range of IP addresses may vary depending on your local implementation of NAT. My EarthLink connection, for example, hands out addresses between 176.16.1.0 and 176.16.1.255. Don't panic if your IP address doesn't start with 169.

The access point also does one other thing: When it assigns an IP address to a computer on the inside, it associates that internal address with a port number on the IP address on the outside, as shown in Figure 8-5.

Whenever a computer on the inside of a NAT network needs information from a server on the Internet, it forwards that request to the NAT access point. The NAT access point then asks the server for information, but it adds a note that says, in effect, "Dear Server: When you send me the information, please send it back to me at this port. Yours in good will, the NAT access point."

Then, whenever the access point gets information sent to, for example, TCP/IP port 38,572, it knows to automatically forward it on to the internal computer it has associated with that port. In this way, many computers can share a single IP address.

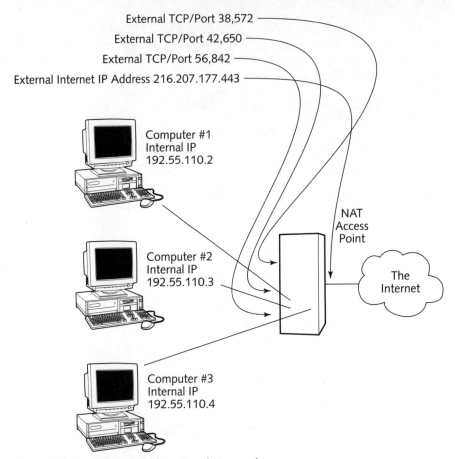

External TCP/Port 38,572

External TCP/Port 42,650

External TCP/Port 56,842

External Internet IP Address 216.207.177.443

Computer #1
Internal IP
192.55.110.2

NAT
Access
Point

The
Internet

Computer #2
Internal IP
192.55.110.3

Computer #3
Internal IP
192.55.110.4

FIGURE 8-5: How Network Address Translation works

This means two things:

- If you've paid extra to a broadband company to get some weird piece of hardware you hook your computers into in order to share your internet connection, you already have a DHCP server. You are *so* good to go. In most cases, all you have to do is to attach your hub or switch to that piece of hardware, and you're all set. (Although some companies have a hard-wired limit on the number of computers that can be hooked up — for example, my Earthlink broadband router allows a maximum of four people to be connected at once. Hey, don't blame me, I got it for free.)

- If you don't have one, you'll either need to buy a router, or configure a computer to serve as a NAT access point. We can show you how to do that with certain styles of Windows in the next chapter, but Linux is a bit too complex to show it. On the plus side, if you set up a NAT access point, you automatically get a DHCP server!

Port Forwarding versus DMZ

Many NAT access points also have a feature called DMZ, which basically says, "Hey! If you get any strange requests, forward them all on to this computer here!" The good thing about this is that it's really easy to configure; all you have to do is provide the internal IP address, and all unrequested traffic from every port will automatically be handed over to your target computer.

The downside to this feature is that it can be dangerous. NAT access points generally ignore strange traffic for a good reason; it's mostly hack attempts or spyware. If you use DMZ, you're basically opening one computer's door to every dimwit with a script kiddie program.

My suggestion is that if you're too lazy to look up the ports (and there's nothing wrong with being lazy) and want to use a DMZ, be sure to install ZoneAlarm or some other firewall on the server so that it's safe from any strange attempts.

Enabling others to dial in to your NAT

Dialing out to the Internet with NAT is a snap. All it does is associate each Internet request with a port on the NAT access point, and it sends the traffic right in. But in all of these cases, *a computer on the inside of the NAT network has acted first*.

What happens when friends want to play over the Internet? They're telling their *Quake III* that the game server is located at the NAT access point's external IP address, but it isn't. That IP address is only a forwarding address for all of the computers on the inside of the NAT network.

So how does the NAT access point know who to give this unrequested information to? Well, the answer is that most of them don't — and they don't bother to find out, either. Most NATs ignore the external request to talk to a *Quake III* server altogether, figuring it's some sort of hack attempt.

What you'll need then, my friend, is a feature called *port forwarding*.

Port forwarding is a feature that many NAT access points have, which basically says, "If you get a request for information at a certain port, forward it straight on to this computer on the inside of the network." Or, to put it another way, "Hey, NAT Access Point, if you get a random request to join a *Quake III* game, send it straight on to the internal *Quake III* server."

Once again, because each router and NAT access point works differently, I can't tell you specifically how to set this up. But you'll need to know both the port that your game uses (some games use a range of ports), and the internal IP address of the game server (use `ipconfig` to see what it is, as I explain in the next chapter). And, once again, this will generally involve plugging some IP address into a Web browser and configuring it manually.

Making your own UTP network cable

You can save a lot of money by buying a large spool of Category 5 cable — generally, it's only between 5 and 12 cents per foot. You can get the cheapest cable, of course, but do you really want to get to The Big Party Day and discover that your cheap cable might as well be a wax string hung between two tin cans for all it transmits?

There are, however, two other things that you need to watch out for when buying cable.

First, you do *not* want solid-wire cable; it's intended to be used inside walls and in formal networks where you rarely (if ever) move it around, and it does not bend well. Stranded-wire cable bends easily and conducts signals better, so that's what you should get.

Second, the cable's internal *color-coding* should be clearly recognizable. Every Category 5 cable has eight smaller wires snuggled inside the insulation sheath; you should be able to tell the difference at a glance between all eight. You'll be stuffing each of those tiny wires into a plastic holder in a very specific pattern, and you don't want to mix them up!

The official color-coding is called the *T-568B* standard, and you'll be able to tell which are which because they'll be intertwined. You should see the following:

- A blue and a striped blue-white cable

- An orange and a striped orange-white cable

- A green and a striped green-white cable

- A brown and a striped brown-white cable

Note Newer cables are supposed to use the T-568A standard, but confusingly, they have the exact same colors as the T-568B, but the pin assignments to each cable are different. As long as you keep the cables consistent, you shouldn't have a problem.

You will also need two other things:

- **A bag of RJ-45 connectors.** These are the little plastic doodads that are attached to the ends of network cable, and they are packaged in bags of 50 or 100. There are two kinds of connectors: solid-wire and stranded-wire. I've already told you to get stranded-wire cable, so buy stranded-wire connectors. (If you have blatantly ignored my advice and bought solid, then you'll have to buy the matching connector; differing connectors and cables are incompatible.)

- **A high-quality crimping tool.** These tools are fairly expensive, about $30 to $60 a pop, but they pay for themselves in short order. You'll want a crimper that has a built-in wire cutter and a blade to strip insulation; if you buy or borrow a crimper without these, you'll need to buy the cutter and the blade separately.

Next, you have to figure out what sort of cable you want to create. You have two options: *crossover* or *straight-through*.

Straight-through cables are what you'll want 90 percent of the time; they're how you hook computers up to hubs and switches, and hubs and switches to each other.

Crossover cables are used to connect two computers directly to each other — or, in some cases, routers to other routers. Unless someone specifically requests a crossover cable, you'll want a straight-through cable.

Creating a straight-through cable

The first thing you do when creating your own cable is to measure it. Carefully. You don't want to go to all the trouble of cutting, stripping, inserting, and crimping a cable, only to discover that it's a foot short.

The next thing you do is cut through the cable on both ends cleanly with the wirecutter. If the blades on your cutter are dull, sharpen them or get a new cutter; squeezing the cable until it smooshes in two is *not* what you want.

Next, strip the outer sheathing back off the cable. You need to be very careful here, as nicking the insulation on the inner wires may well ruin your cable. If you screw it up and nick it, cut further back and lop off the nicked segment, and then try again.

Untwist the wires from one another and arrange them in the order shown in Figure 8-6.

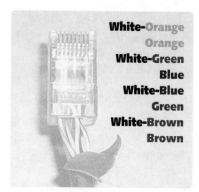

White-Orange
Orange
White-Green
Blue
White-Blue
Green
White-Brown
Brown

FIGURE 8-6: Standard cable wire arrangement

Arrange the wires in a straight line, and then lop off the edges in one clean, straight cut. (As you can see in Figure 8-7, which shows a sample crimping tool, there is a razor blade cutter in the middle.) The idea is to put them in so that the edges all line up neatly when you push them into the RJ-45 connector and the bare copper ends touch the internal connections in the computer. If all eight ends aren't touching simultaneously, it won't work, so make sure you cut like a ruler!

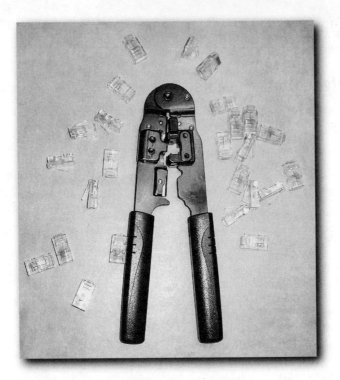

FIGURE 8-7: A crimper and some RJ-45 connectors

Now take the RJ-45 connector and hold it as shown in Figure 8-8, with the plastic release clip facing away from you and the opening for the wires pointed down.

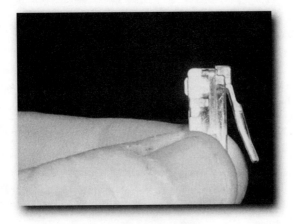

FIGURE 8-8: Holding the RJ-45 connector

Carefully insert the wires, keeping them in the color order listed above, into the connector partway. You'll feel resistance as the wires enter the connector grooves. Sometimes the wires will twist around when you push them in, so make sure they're still in the correct order before you shove them home. Push the cable as far as you can into the connector, as shown in Figure 8-9.

If you do it wrong, one of two things will happen: You'll have cut the insulation off of the cable too long, and the individual inner wires will be hanging out of the end of the cable (as you can see in my clumsy attempt in the figure) or you'll have cut it too short, and the inner wires won't be able to reach the end of the connector.

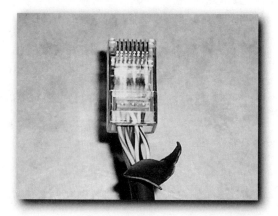

FIGURE 8-9: A hand-made Category 5 cable. Notice how all the wires up top are pushed evenly to the edge of the connector. Also notice how clumsy I am; if I was better at making cables, the wires would still be in the protective outer sheath instead of hanging loosely out of the bottom of the RJ-45 connector.

Double-check that the wires are all in the right order, and then put the connector into the opening of the crimping tool. Squeeze the handle tightly. Repeat for the other end, and you've made your first cable.

Now actually check the cable, either by actually using it and confirming that the two computers can talk to each other, or by using a *cable tester tool*; for about thirty bucks, you can purchase a mechanical doodad whereby you plug both ends of the cable into the tester, and it will light up if the cable has a good connection on both ends.

Don't Assume That It's Easy!

Creating your own cable is tricky at first and requires some practice. I went to a LAN party once where the host had bought the raw cable spool and had his tools all set up, but he was unable to mash out cable for a full hour despite instructions, and he wasted a lot of our time. Do yourself a favor: If you're making your own cable, experiment a couple of times *before* the party to make sure you can do it right.

All right, I'll admit it. That host was me. *I* was the idiot. Just learn from my mistakes, would ya?

Creating a crossover cable

Making a crossover cable is almost exactly the same as creating a straight-through cable, except that you change the order that the wires go in on the second connector. Instead of the standard wire order, they go in as shown in Figure 8-10.

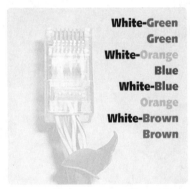

White-Green
Green
White-Orange
Blue
White-Blue
Orange
White-Brown
Brown

FIGURE 8-10: Crossover cable configuration

Set them up as shown in Figure 8-10, and you have a perfect crossover cable.

Summary

In this chapter, you've learned some of the advanced techniques of networking. Routing is the method by which large networks are split up into subnetworks, and game programs use ports to communicate. If you misconfigure a router, you can accidentally send all of your requests into la-la land; if you misconfigure a firewall, you may not be able to play.

Now that you've got all of that exciting theory under your belt, let's head on to Chapter 9, where you can examine three LAN party examples to see how this all works in practice.

Sample LAN Party Layouts

Now that you've examined the ins and outs of networking, you're all probably wondering the same thing: How do you put all of this to good use? To help you out, this chapter lays out three sample networks for some typical LAN parties you might hold:

➤ A 10 Mpbs network for a five-person *Return to Castle Wolfenstein* death match

➤ A 100 Mpbs network for a 17-person get-together at which participants can play either *Battlefield 1942* or *Half-Life 2* and share an Internet connection along the way

➤ A network for 63 people with six different game servers available, plus a wireless connection for those folks with laptops

Between the three of these, you should be able to get a good idea of how things work.

Physical and Network Layouts

When you're designing your LAN party, you need to consider two things:

➤ The network layout

➤ The physical layout

To determine the *network layout*, you need to tally up whatever networking hardware you have available for your party, and then figure out how all of your computers will be hooked together. This gives you a general idea of what your wiring plan is going to look like. To determine the *physical layout*, you need to look at the space you have to work with, and then figure out how you're going to cram all those computers into that space.

The challenge is keeping *both* layouts in mind when designing your LAN party, since they affect each other. For example, if you have a house with two big rooms that are 50 feet apart from each other, it might be a good idea to use a separate switch in each room even if only seven people are showing up. While technically you *could* hook all of the computers up to one eight-port switch, it's a lot easier to run one 50-foot cable between the rooms to connect two switches together, as opposed to running three long, expensive, and potentially hazardous cables down a hallway.

But what if you don't have two switches? In that case, you need to work with what you have on hand. That's why you usually start with the network layout, because the network hardware is your biggest limitation. The number of switches, routers, and cables you have available determines your setup more than anything else.

Note For the three general layouts described here, I'm *not* going to list specific computers — for example: three Windows 98 machines, one Windows 2000 machine, and one Linux machine. If you set the computers up with proper IP addresses and the game running on the server can accept both Linux and Windows connections, the exact number is mostly irrelevant. If your game doesn't accept both connections, then you're going to have problems anyway.

The Five-Person Get-Together

Fred's decided to hold a party in his house. He's not that computer-savvy, but he wants to deathmatch his pals with a minimum of effort. He has a reasonably large house that looks like the one shown in Figure 9-1.

Fred will figure out the network layout first and then move on to the physical layout. Fred is lucky; this is the most common scenario, but it's also the easiest to set up.

The five-person network layout

Fortunately, the network Fred wants to build is about as simple as it gets. The trickiest bit is going to be finding a way to cram all of these people into his house!

What Fred wants to do

- Get five people hooked together and fragging with a minimum of effort.

How Fred will do this

- Hook all six computers (five players and a server) into a central hub with Category 5 cable.
- Manually assign IP addresses.

What Fred has

- Nothing.

What Fred will need

- **A cheap Ethernet hub or switch**
- **Six Category 5 cables**
- **Six computers with NICs**
- **Enough legal copies of the relevant games**

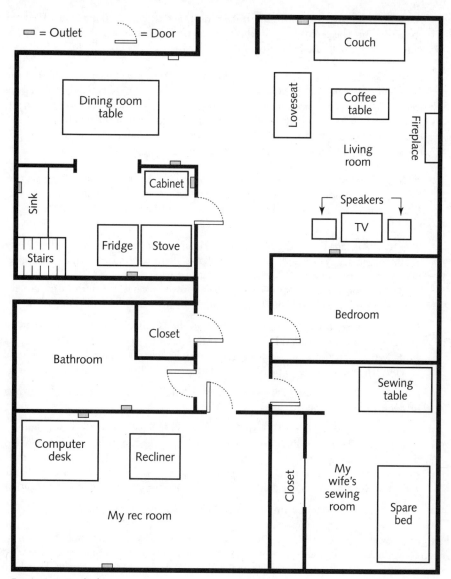

FIGURE 9-1: Fred's house

Why Fred needs this stuff and what Fred does

- **Five computers with network interface cards (NICs).** He checks with his friends to make sure they all have NICs installed on their computers; you can't use a modem to connect to a small network like this.

- **A game server with a network interface card.** Being a good computer geek, Fred has a spare computer he can use to host their games. Unfortunately, it's not his fastest computer — he wants to use his personal PC to play the game — but it'll do.

Do you need to have a dedicated server for a small LAN party? I personally prefer them, but when I asked my friends to review this chapter, they all told me that I was full of it and that a small LAN party does not need a separate server. You do not need to procure a separate computer for your party. If you want to know more about the difference between dedicated game servers and just having people connect to your computer while you play, check out Chapter 12, "Setting Up a Game Server."

- **A cheap Ethernet hub or switch.** Because Fred will be hooking up at least six people, he'll need a minimum of six *ports* on his hub or switch. He does some looking on the Internet and finds something that looks ideal: A 10/100 auto-sensing switch with eight ports for $49.99!

  The 10/100 means that if the NICs on his friends' computers are set up to handle traffic at 100 megabytes per second, the switch will automatically transmit data at that speed; otherwise, it transmits at 10 Mbps. Fred's not sure what each of his friends are running at, and he's not sure he wants to expend the effort to find out. Even if it turns out everyone else is slow, 10 Mpbs is plenty fast enough for what they have planned.

- **Enough cable to link all of the computers together.** Fred knows he'll need to get six Category 5 cables to make this work, but at this point he doesn't know the lengths he's going to need. Furthermore, he won't know until he actually measures his house and figures out where he's going to place the computers. He holds off on buying cable for now.

  He also realizes that even with six computers, it might be cheaper to make his own, but he doesn't want to have to learn how to do it.

- **Enough copies of the game he wants to play to do so legally.** Most games require you to keep a valid CD in each PC's drive, even if you're playing the game on a server. (This is their way of raking in the bucks.) The dedicated server programs, however, are a different story; some require valid game CDs, some don't. Fred doesn't have to buy copies of the game for everyone, of course, but if his friends don't bring them, there won't be a party.

- **Enough tables to set the computers on.** Nobody wants to sit on the floor.

Fred will hook the computers up via cables, using a single central router/switch. He then will assign individual IP addresses to each computer, using the IP addresses and the subnet for home networks outlined in Chapter 7, in the section "IP Addresses for Networks That Don't Talk to the Internet."

There's a much easier way to assign IP addresses. If Fred had bought a router/switch with NAT translation (also known as IP assigning), he could simply have hooked up all of the computers to the router/switch and it would have assigned IP addresses for him. In fact, I'd argue that he should have done that, as router/switches make things *so* much easier.

His network layout looks something like what is shown in Figure 9-2.

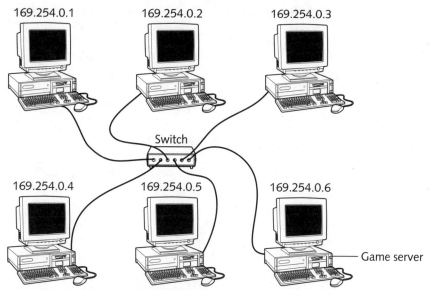

169.254.0.1   169.254.0.2   169.254.0.3

Switch

169.254.0.4   169.254.0.5   169.254.0.6

Game server

FIGURE 9-2: Fred's five-person network layout (plus the game server)

The five-person physical layout

Fred's home, like most homes, is slightly troublesome as far as LAN gaming is concerned. If you look at where his computer is right now, it's very far away from where the other people will be playing. Furthermore, he doesn't have a great deal of space to fit everyone into one location.

Alternative Layouts

Fred had an alternate solution that would have kept him closer to the action; he could have cleared out his girlfriend's sewing room, making space for two players, and moved the recliner out of his room to make room for one other player. Then, he could have left one player stranded in the living room.

However, that involves moving a lot more furniture, which leads to a very important point: *It's okay to be lazy*. The less furniture, books, and other stuff you have to heave around, the better.

(In addition, it would have required stringing a lot of cable through that central hallway, particularly around the bathroom area, which would be a real danger.)

Fred decides that he's going to have to move the coffee table to make room for two players and a game server, and that he will place the switch in the living room. Two other players will be seated at the dining room table. Reluctantly, he runs one very long cable from his computer into the living room switch. Alas, Fred will be slightly isolated from the action, but at least he won't have to move his computer!

Fred then measures out his house, and sees that he will need two 20-foot cables for the computers in the dining room, three 10-foot cables for the computers in the living room, and one 60-foot cable to connect his computer to the switch.

However, Fred has one problem that concerns him: Does he have enough power to run five computers in the living room and dining room area? What if they're all on the same power circuit? Fred maps out his power (as he has read Chapter 6, "Avoiding Power Failures") and discovers what's shown in Figure 9-3.

As it turns out, Fred very well could have blown his power had he plugged the two dining room computers into the outlet on the kitchen circuit. Fortunately, Fred's smart and just switches those two computers over to the other outlet. (There is a very minor danger of overload if Fred's pals turn on the TV in the living room, but Fred decides he can live with that.)

Fred also looks at his house and tries to determine if there are any safety issues. Well, Fred doesn't *formally* check for safety issues; he just looks at the piles of unread books that he's heaped in the corners of the living room until he can afford a new bookcase and thinks, Jeez, somebody could trip on that. He cleans up the messy books and sorts them into boxes, which has the pleasant side effect of making his girlfriend extremely grateful.

The five-person final layout

Fred's final layout, both physical and network, looks like what's shown in Figure 9-4.

When he lays everything out, Fred takes great care to use duct tape to tape down the cables that cross hallways and other areas so nobody trips and takes out the entire network. He also runs the cables along the sides of the walls when he can.

The day arrives, as do his friends, and Fred spends a great day capping Nazi zombies with his pals.

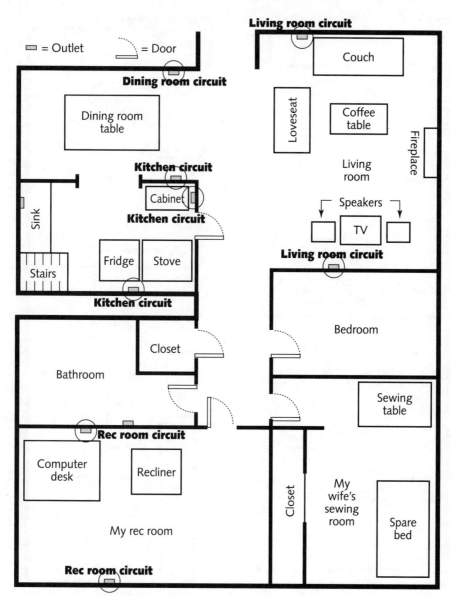

FIGURE 9-3: The power map for Fred's house

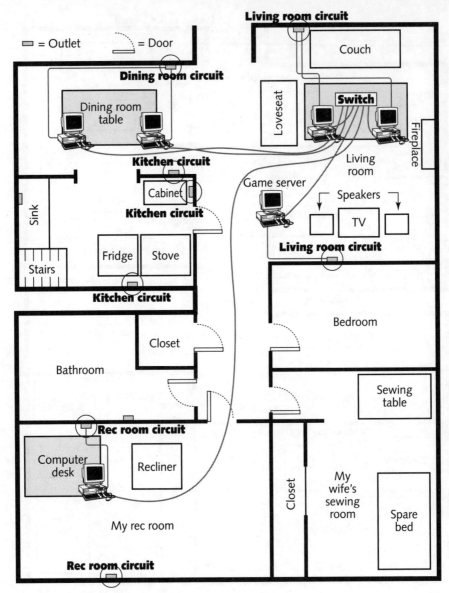

Figure 9-4: Fred's final layout

The 17-Person Deathmatch

Fred's initial six-person LAN party was such a success that he's suddenly found 11 other friends who want to join up! Hey, nothing attracts people like success. This time, he's decided that he's going to move his party out to his garage, which is attached to his house. (Garages are often excellent places to hold mid-sized LAN parties, as they're large and spacious.) His garage looks similar to what is shown in Figure 9-5.

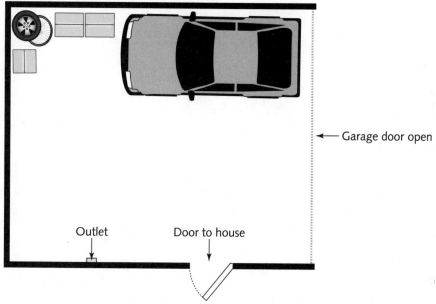

FIGURE 9-5: Fred's garage

This time, Fred wants to get ambitious; he wants to add Internet access to this party. He has a broadband connection at his house and he'd like to share it. In addition, manually configuring the computers for the last party was a huge hassle, and he wants to add a DHCP server this time around. Fortunately, because routers/switches come with NAT, which in turn comes with a bundled DHCP server, he can kill two birds with one stone!

He also wants to have two separate game servers — one for *Battlefield 1942* and one for *Half-Life 2* (which isn't out at the time I write this, but hey, I can dream).

The 17-person network layout

Fred still has the equipment left over from his last party and wants to use it, which is not only natural, it's very smart. Why get new equipment when you can make do with old equipment?

What Fred wants to do

- Create a network that links 17 people together at 100 Mbps.
- Add an additional game server.
- Add a DHCP server so that he doesn't have to manually assign IP addresses.
- Share a DSL Internet connection for outbound traffic, but not have anyone dial in to play externally.

How Fred will do this

- Hook each of the computers into one of three separate switches.
- Daisychain the three switches together to create one large network.
- Use the router/switch to serve as a DHCP server.
- Share the Internet connection with the router/switch.

What Fred has

- A 10/100 eight-port switch
- Two 10-foot lengths of Category 5 cable, two 20-foot lengths of Category 5 cable, and one 60-foot length of Category 5 cable

What Fred will need

- A seven-port 10/100 router/switch (also known as a broadband router) with NAT addressing
- A 10/100 eight-port switch
- A thousand-foot roll of Category 5 cable
- An RJ-45 crimping tool (with built-in wire cutters and insulation strippers)
- A bag of 50 RJ-45 connectors
- Labels to mark which cables are which
- Patches of carpet and/or duct tape to secure the cables
- A second computer that can function as a game server
- A room large enough to hold and power all of these computers

Why Fred needs all of this and what Fred does

- **Create a network that links 17 people together at 100 Mbps.** Fred tells everyone that this is a Fast Ethernet party and everyone's NIC has to be capable of running at 100 Mbps. Fortunately, 100 Mbps is pretty much standard these days.

  In addition, rather than have people bring their own cable, which may or may not be Category 5, he decides to make his own Category 5 cable. That will both ensure that the network is running at 100 Mbps *and* save Fred some money, as buying several custom lengths of pre-made cable can get mighty expensive.

(Fred could also just ask people to bring their own cable, but he's stringing wire across a garage and he's worried that people will show up with cable that's too short for the job.)

■ **Add an additional game server.** Because this will be a gathering of dedicated gamers, Fred's reasonably certain that *someone* attending has held a LAN party in the past, and has a server on hand. As it turns out, yes, one of the players who plans to attend has a custom-made *Battlefield 1942* server, freeing Fred up to use his server for *Half-Life 2*.

Alas, Fred's computer was fine for hosting *Castle Wolfenstein*, but *Half-Life 2* pushes the envelope of gaming, and the slower computer he used as a server last time probably won't work. Fred sighs and realizes that he'll have to use his top-of-the-line personal PC as a server, and resigns himself to playing on the slower computer.

■ **Add a DHCP server so that he doesn't have to manually assign IP addresses.** With that many people, manually configuring everyone's computers and making sure that all the right IP addresses are typed in would be a huge pain. DHCP will automate that process and ensure that nothing goes wrong. Although he could set up one of the two game servers to be a DHCP server, instead he's going to get a router/switch that serves double-duty.

■ **Share a DSL Internet connection for outbound traffic, but not have anyone dial in to play externally.** This is what the router/switch does! Fred will run a cable between the router's uplink port and the DSL box, though that may prove troublesome later because the DSL box is all the way back in his computer room, almost a hundred feet away.

■ **Hook each of the computers into one of three separate switches.** Fred realizes that he could simply buy a 24-port router/switch and connect everyone with no problems, but that poses one large problem for him: He'd have to buy a 24-port router/switch (which is mighty expensive).

As such, Fred buys a seven-port router/switch (because they sell for about $100, he figures it'll come in useful elsewhere) and e-mails the 17 partygoers to see if anyone has an eight-port switch he can borrow. As it turns out, yes, one of them does.

Tip

Borrowing equipment is a time-honored way of saving cash. Just make sure you have a backup plan if the people you are borrowing from don't show. In this case, Fred decides that if his friend with the switch bails out at the last second, he can always bop on down to the local computer store and buy one, and then drive over to his friend's house and bop his friend upside the head.

■ **Daisychain the three switches together to create one large network.** The router/switch and his friend's switch both have uplink ports, enabling Fred to daisychain them together without any special cabling.

Alas, the cheapie eight-port switch that Fred bought for his first LAN party does not have an uplink port. Even more dismaying, the router/switch's uplink port needs to be used to connect to the DSL box. Given that only two uplink ports and four networks need to be connected (the three switches and the big network of the Internet), Fred will have to use a *crossover cable* to connect his friend's switch to the router/switch.

Fred plugs a regular cable into a regular port in his cheapie switch and connects it to the uplink port on his friend's switch. Then he plugs the crossover cable into a normal port on both the router/switch and a normal port on his friend's switch, connecting them together. The resulting setup looks like what is shown in Figure 9-6.

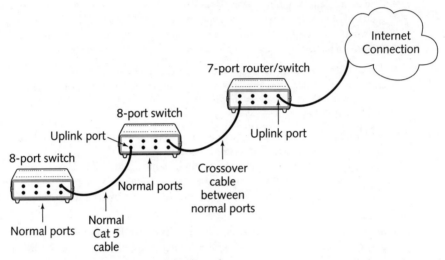

FIGURE 9-6: Connecting three switches together

And voila! All the computers attached to any of the three switches will now be able to talk to one another, and the Internet.

Note

Some routers/switches have both an uplink port and a port specifically designed to connect to the DSL or cable modem. If Fred had bought that kind of router/switch, he could have daisychained them all together without having to use a crossover cable.

To minimize traffic, though, Fred asks people beforehand what game they plan to play all day, and tries to put each game server and its players on the same switch. As such, he labels each of the three switches the *Battlefield 1942* switch, the *Half-Life 2* switch, and the *Internet* switch. No harm will be done if people decide to change to a different game halfway through the day, but it might help things stay speedier.

- **A 1,000-foot roll of Category 5 cable, an RJ-45 crimping tool (with built-in wire cutters and insulation strippers), and a bag of 50 RJ-45 connectors.** This costs Fred about $160, but making his own cables will save him money. Fred spends the night before the party learning how to make cable — and after about an hour and a half of practice, he finally gets it down so he can do it reliably. He does *not* pull the bozo move of waiting until the party to see whether he can make cable or not, like some idiots do (including, um, the author).

- **Labels to mark which cables are which.** With 17 people, plus three switches, there will be a lot of cables hanging about; if something goes wrong, Fred wants to be able to narrow the problem down at a moment's notice. When hooking a computer to a switch, he puts a tag at both ends: The end that's plugged into a switch indicates which computer the line goes to, and the end that's plugged into the NIC indicates which switch the line is connected to.

- **Patches of carpet and/or duct tape.** All those wires will be a real tripping hazard; laying carpet over the wire will help prevent any accidents.

- **A room that's large enough to handle everyone's computers.** Fortunately, Fred has a space that's large enough to put all of his friends in — a two-car garage will be slightly cramped, but it will serve. If Fred didn't have that space — and many people don't — then he would have had to rent a room that was large enough, had a DSL connection, and enough of a power supply to keep everyone online and fraggin'.

If *you* need to rent, I've told you how in Chapter 3, "Choosing a Site for Your Party."

The final network configuration will look something like what is shown in Figure 9-7.

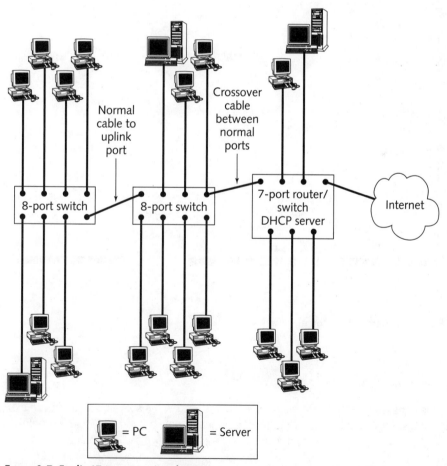

FIGURE 9-7: Fred's 17-person network setup

The 17-person physical layout

Putting the computers in the garage is both easier and harder than putting them in Fred's house. It's easier because it's all in one space; unlike his home, where Fred had to cram computers in between his couches and the television, the garage is a relatively empty space. He can just cram tables in as he sees fit, which means his network is very flexible. He puts them around the rim and throws some tables in the center, for a layout that looks like what is shown in Figure 9-8.

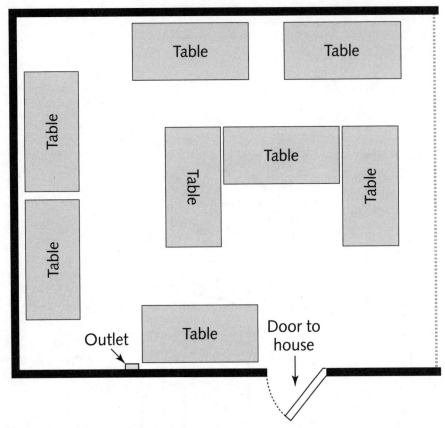

FIGURE 9-8: Fred's 17-person physical layout

But Is It Safe?

Sadly, this configuration has one major problem, as Fred will discover: The aisles are extremely narrow, and toting computers and monitors in when people are already seated is going to be a struggle. It would be nice if he had a roomier garage—but, alas, Fred has to work with what he's got.

Unfortunately, the garage has several potential drawbacks:

- **Lack of power.** Fred has precisely one power circuit in the garage — actually, the entire power wiring of his garage consists of the overhead light and a single outlet.

- **Lack of DSL access.** Strangely enough, Fred does not have his garage wired for Internet access.

- **Potential safety issues.** Like most people, Fred uses his garage as a storage space for all of the junk he doesn't want in the house; the walls and floor are covered with rakes, leaf blowers, and other sorts of equipment. Furthermore, because Fred doesn't spend a whole lot of time in his garage, he's unsure if the roof is watertight; he knows his car doesn't get wet when it rains, but he's not quite sure about the corners.

- **No furniture.** Fred has all sorts of desks and tables in his house, but there's nothing in his garage.

Thankfully, these drawbacks can all be rectified.

First things first: Fred aims a hose at the top of his garage to simulate a rainstorm and has a friend stand inside to see whether there are any leaks. Thankfully, there aren't any. Then he gets his friend to help him clear the miscellaneous debris out from the garage. (Fred's girlfriend isn't a gamer, but she certainly appreciates the way LAN parties make Fred do household chores!)

Next, Fred remembers the LAN partiers' credo: *Beg before you borrow*. Fred has one collapsible table, but after checking with his friends, he is able to scrounge up seven six-foot tables (remember, a six-foot table can generally hold two gamers). Fred's going to have to haul his dining room table out there, but that's better than renting furniture.

Finally, Fred is going to have to run cables — very long cables. He knows he will have to run a very long cable through the garage to hook his router/switch to his DSL connection in his computer room. (He could also move his DSL connection to the kitchen, which has a phone outlet, but Fred doesn't want to have potentially fragile equipment in a heavily trafficked room.)

With 19 computers total (17 players and two servers), Fred will need at least two additional power circuits in the garage, and possibly three for safety's sake. Fred runs two long extension cords from the living room and the dining room into the garage, and then runs several smaller cords to spread the power out among the tables. Needless to say, he tapes these all down thoroughly.

The 17-person final layout

The result looks something like what is shown in Figure 9-9.

When everyone shows up it's a lot of work getting set up, but the day is most excellent. In fact, it's so good that they decide to extend it to *two* days, leaving the computers in place overnight with a space heater so they can play on Sunday, too. Not everyone shows up for Day 2, of course, but those who do are pumped.

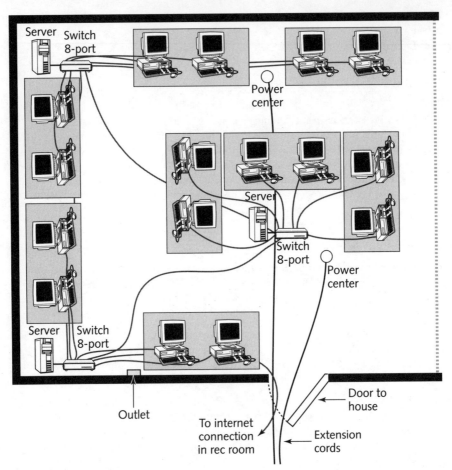

FIGURE 9-9: Fred's 17-person final layout

The 63-Person Megagame

Fred has gone truly bonkers at this point, and he decides that he needs to hold the biggest LAN party his town has ever seen! (Fred lives in a small town.) He's going to have to rent a hall to make this happen, but he decides he wants to pull out all the stops. There are a few snags this time, however:

- **There are a lot of people here.** For the first time, Fred's going to have to separate computers into distinct networks with a router.

- **More games! More!** People are tired of just fragging, so they want to play multiplayer *Civilization 3* and *Command and Conquer* variants. In addition, they want another server to play *Counterstrike,* and one to play *Doom 3.*

- **Someone has a gigabit switch to spare.** About six people have gigabit NICs on their computers, and Fred wants to see what happens if he sets up a gigabit subnetwork.

- **The local laptop user group wants to play, and they have wireless.** Fred figures this isn't a problem; one of them has an access port, so he can add them on.

- **People want to connect to the servers via the Internet.** The last party was such a success that a couple of gamers in other nearby towns want to join in on the fraggin'!

Fred has his work cut out for him! Luckily, he finds an empty hall, which looks something like what is shown in Figure 9-10.

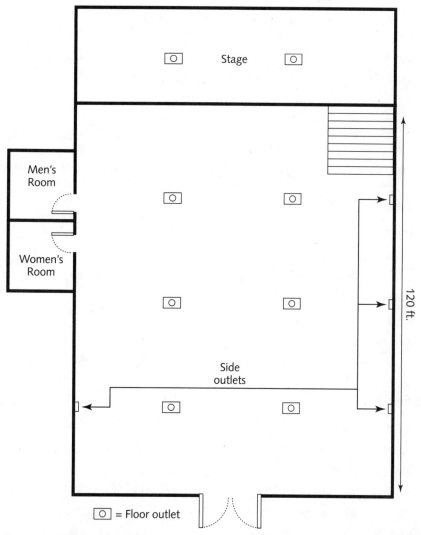

FIGURE 9-10: Fred's rented hall

The 63-person network layout

This one is slightly trickier, because now we're dealing with routing and wireless access, plus a separate DHCP server. But no pain, no gain!

What Fred wants to do

- Have a network that links 63 people together, isolating gamers into three subnetworks.
- Add a DHCP server so that he doesn't have to manually assign IP addresses.
- Share a high-speed Internet connection for outbound traffic and have external Internet users be able to connect and play games on the network.
- Enable wireless laptop users to connect to the network.

How Fred will do this

- Use three switches to create five separate networks.
- Use a router to connect the networks but separate the traffic.
- Connect a wireless access point to the router.
- Use a router to serve as a NAT access point.
- Set up the router to automatically route all outside game requests to each game server.

What Fred has

- Two 10/100 eight-port switches
- At least one thousand-foot roll of Category 5 cable
- An RJ-45 crimping tool (with built-in wire cutters and insulation strippers)
- A bag of 100 RJ-45 connectors
- Labels to mark which cables are which
- Patches of carpet and duct tape
- A room large enough to hold and power all of these computers

What Fred needs

- A five-port router
- A wireless access point
- Two game servers
- Three switches with enough combined ports to connect all of the computers
- Way too much spare time
- Endless patience

Why Fred needs all of this and what Fred does

- **Have a network that links 63 people together.** Fred decides to split up the three Ethernet networks by using a router to separate them — and since Fred has so many people attending, splitting up the traffic probably isn't the worst thing he can do. It'll keep his network very zippy.

  Alas, because he now has to upgrade to a *real* router, Fred has no need for the piddly router/switch he used before. It might even cause conflicts. Fortunately, most router/switches have a setting you can use to turn off the routing, reducing them into a simple switch.

- **Use a router to connect the networks but separate the traffic.** Because Fred realizes that he's going to have to get a router, he decides to ask around (remember, always ask before you buy) and finds that a small, five-port Cisco router is available. With five ports to work with, Fred decides to split his 63-plus computers into five networks:

  - A small gigabit network, with six computers that have gigabit-enabled NICs

  - The wireless network, connected via an access point

  - The Internet connection

  - Two separate 100-Mbps game networks, each with three game servers apiece

Fred also realizes that in addition to reserving IP addresses for six game servers and a DHCP server, he should also include a patch server — a computer from which users can download the latest patches and maps for the six games everyone will be playing during the party. (Most of the games won't accept a new client if it's not running the same version as the server, meaning that if you're not up-to-date, you're not playing.) Fred decides that he'll reserve eight separate IP addresses.

Fred will also need to reserve five additional IP addresses — one for each port on the router. Remember that a router's job is to pass data from one network to another; the router "knows" which networks are attached to it by looking at the network segment of the IP addresses that have been assigned to each of its ports.

Sounds complicated, doesn't it? It isn't. Let's look at it from the router's point of view:

Is Fred Working Too Hard for a Party Like This?

Assuming that everyone was running at 100 Mbps, couldn't Fred simply hook all of his users up via switches? The answer is yes. Realistically speaking, you can probably hook together three or four hundred computers via switches before you start to see any noticeable deterioration in network speed. However, I'm using this odd case as an example of what routers are for and how they're used — and frankly, I didn't feel like mapping out a 700-node LAN party to prove a point.

"Why, look!" says the router. "My third port over here has an IP address of 169.254.0.1, and the subnet address is 255.255.255.0! Hmm. That must mean that if I send some data out via my *third* port, it's going to *network number 169.254.0*!

"Likewise, my first port has an IP address of 169.254.254.1, and the subnet address is also 255.255.255.0. Therefore, my first port must be attached to network 169.254.254!"

The router then thinks some more, as routers are wont to do.

"If I want to send something to network 169.254.0," it reasons, "I'd better broadcast it out port number 3. And if something's destined for network 169.254.254, I need to forward it out to port number 1. Got it."

Having an IP address assigned to each port is important for another reason: If a computer wants to send data to a computer that it knows is on another network, that's the IP address it sends the data to.

Note

Those of you who have been paying attention will remember that this IP address is also called the *default gateway*. If you don't give a PC a default gateway and it has a message intended for another network, it just deletes the data and forgets about it. This can cause some extreme problems.

The computer trusts that the router will know where to send the data—and it trusts it *so* completely, in fact, that once that computer sends the data off properly, it never checks to confirm that it arrived safely.

Therefore, misconfigured routers can be bad news. Fortunately, this is a rather simple setup; there's only one router, and it's connected to all the networks.

Note

If Fred were hooking a couple of thousand people together, he'd need multiple routers to handle the hundreds of networks—and in turn, each of those routers would have a default gateway of its own. After that, Fred would have to worry about things such as *broadcast storms* and the technologies such as *spanning tree protocol* that are designed to quash them. Of course, because large-scale routing projects get ridiculously complicated very quickly and are *way* outside the scope of this book, I'll route any questions *you* have on that subject to your local bookstore or routing guru.

Fred's DHCP server will have to remember which IP addresses are reserved, and be able to assign the rest depending on what network they come from. Fred realizes that for the first time, his DHCP server will have to provide a default gateway address in addition to the IP address and subnet. He makes a note to read up on how to do that, and tests it out the night before.

- **Share a DSL Internet connection for outbound traffic and enable external Internet users to connect and play games on the network.** In order to do this, Fred realizes that he will have to configure his router to perform Network Address Translation, so he reads the router's user manual to figure out how to set that up.

  He also realizes that if he wants people to connect to the game server, he will need to set up port forwarding on his router so that any requests sent to the router's external IP address for a game of *Half-Life 2* are automatically routed to the internal IP address of the *Half-Life 2* server, and the external *Rainbow Six* requests are sent to the internal Rainbow Six server, and so forth.

  Fred creates a chart of the IP addresses he has reserved for each game server, and the TCP/IP ports that each of those games use. He then tells the router that all requests for each game's specific array of ports should be automatically forwarded on to that game's server.

> **Note**
>
> I wish I could tell you *how* Fred configures the router, but that all depends on what kind of router Fred has. A discussion on router configuration is outside the scope of this book; you'll have to consult your router's manual for details.

- **Allow wireless laptop users to connect to the network.** Allowing Wi-Fi users to connect to the network is fairly easy; the leader of the local laptop guild has a wireless access point, or WAP. All Fred has to do is configure the DHCP server to treat any requests from this WAP as a separate network, connect it to the router, and he'll be all set.

His network layout looks similar to what is shown in Figure 9-11.

The 63-person physical layout

Thankfully, much like the garage, Fred's rented hall is a large open space with a lot of power circuits. (Of course, it should be; Fred shopped around until he found a hall that met his needs. He also got the management to throw in rental tables as part of the deal.) Fortunately, with more room, Fred can create comfortable places with aisles—unlike his cramped garage! Fred will need to run some extension cords to get power to the center of the room, but that's not a problem. The only real issue here is where to set up the Check-In Station, and whether there should be an area for people to get together and talk. Fred decides to put the Check-In Station at the front of the room, and creates a gathering place where he'll put the pizza and other items later.

As for the WAP, the space Fred rents has a stage, so he decides to use that. He puts that wireless access point way up high, so it looks something like what is shown in Figure 9-12.

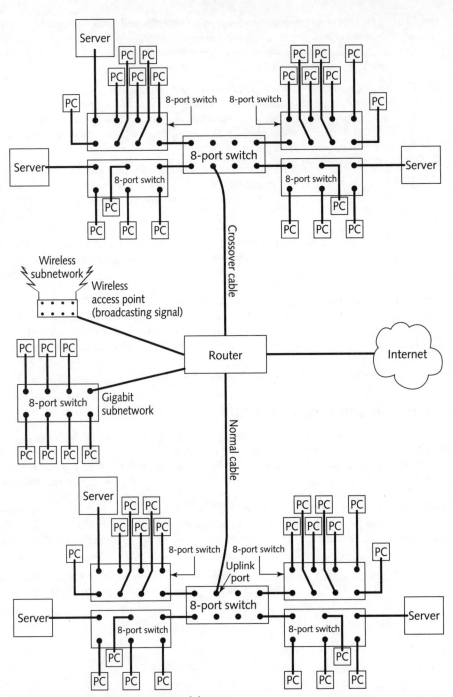

FIGURE 9-11: Fred's 63-person network layout

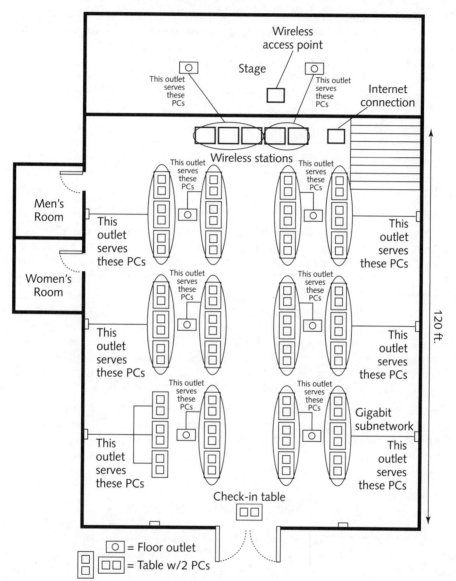

FIGURE 9-12: Fred's 63-person physical layout

The 63-person final layout

Fred puts out the call to all computer geeks in the area and thankfully he winds up with switches and servers to spare.

He then buys a boatload of cable and gets a friend to help him with cable duty the night before; the last thing Fred wants on the day of the party is to be stuck mashing wires. He makes sure to put his Wireless Ethernet access point in a very prominent place, where it can receive all the broadcasts that are sent out. He gets all of the tables, power strips, and wiring laid out the night before, creating numbered access points for all the computers. He even creates a diagram that he posts on the wall, showing the space he's assigned for each person's machine.

Fred knows that for a LAN party of this magnitude, it's important to have contingency plans, so he assigns a friend to be in charge of any last-minute wiring, and another friend to handle any hardware difficulties. (Fred himself will handle any software problems.) The friend who's bringing the Cisco router has agreed to troubleshoot anything that goes wrong from a routing perspective.

In the end, his layout looks something like what is shown in Figure 9-13.

On the day of the party, he starts everything up and—it works only partially. All the computers on the same network as the DHCP server get their IP addresses without a hitch, and some computers in other networks are assigned proper addresses without a hitch. But other computers in other networks get nothing. Depending on their machines, they either assign themselves an IP address or do nothing at all.

A few moments of frantic consultation reveals that the router is not passing on DHCP broadcasts from other networks to the DHCP server. It turns out that the few computers that were able to access the DHCP server and get valid addresses were the ones that actually knew the exact address of the DHCP server; the router forwarded it on like normal data. The rest of the computers just yelled as loud as they could for a DHCP address—and because they didn't have a specific address to which it could be sent, the router ignored them.

After a moment of reconfiguration, the Cisco guy activates the *DHCP relay* function of the router, instructing the router to send all DHCP broadcasts to the DHCP server's address. Everyone who was IP-less reboots their machines and gets a valid address, and everyone is happy once again.

Keep It Simple, Stupid

A note to ward off techno-geeks: Yes, I am aware that you could have instructed each computer to request a new DHCP address by typing **ipconfig /release** and then **ipconfig /renew** on Windows PCs, or **inconfig** on Unix and Linux machines. There is a lesson to be learned here, however: *Sometimes the simplest solution is the best*. Which would you rather do—ask everyone to type in an obscure set of commands that vary depending on the operating system they're running, or just tell everyone to reboot?

By the way, make sure everyone doesn't reboot simultaneously, thereby blowing a fuse.

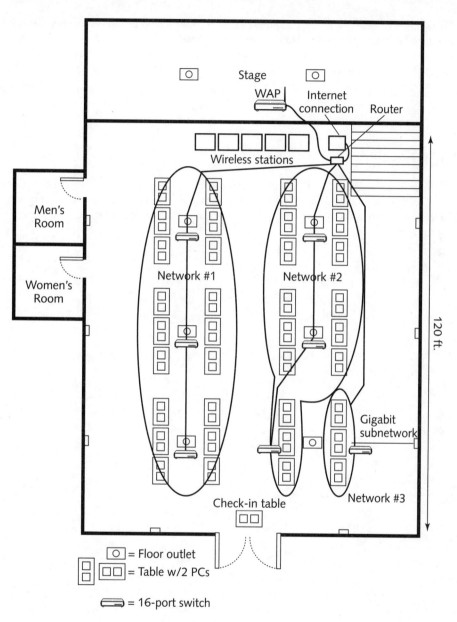

Figure 9-13: Fred's 63-person final layout

Fred's 63-person party goes off stunningly. Actually, another eleven laptop users show up, and at the end of the day he's successfully hosted a 75-person LAN party with only a minor hitch. Fred spends the final hours of the day dismantling all the hardware and returning switches — and then he collapses, secure in the knowledge that He Did It.

Later, he gets a call from someone in the next town over. They have about four hundred people who want to hold a LAN party, but they don't know how.

Summary

All right! I've shown you the thought processes involved in creating LAN parties, and given you a couple of sample layouts. (Feel free to steal them, if you'd like.) Now that you know the issues involved in laying out a party, it's time to move on to the next stage: configuring individual computers!

The Least You Need to Know about Configuring Your Computer

Each computer you'll run into has its own little quirks, and each has its own operating system. Obviously, I can't show you how to do everything on each operating system — space is limited, after all — but I can show you how to do the basics on each.

Configuring Computers

This chapter will show you how to do the following:

➤ Assign an IP address manually

➤ Ask a machine to request a TCP/IP address from a DHCP server

➤ Bind TCP/IP to a network card (if necessary)

At the end of the chapter, I'll also show you where the standard TCP/IP troubleshooting tools (ping, ipconfig, and tracert) can be found for each system, and briefly explain how to use them.

Cross-Reference DHCP? IP address? Network card? If you don't know what any of these terms mean, I *strongly* suggest that you refer back to Chapter 7, "The Least You Need to Know about Networking," and read it to get a basic understanding of computer networking. At the very least, read the section called "The Parts of TCP/IP Configuration."

Note Configuring machines to request DHCP from a specific IP address is not typical. Most computers these days — including Xboxes and PlayStation 2s — are configured by default to request an address from a DHCP server automatically. I'm telling you how to do it here in case it comes up, but don't go out of your way to configure a machine until you have evidence suggesting that it is *not* set to request a DHCP assignment automatically.

Binding

Those of you who read Chapter 7 will no doubt recall that, left unattended, network interface cards (NICs) do nothing but listen to the line. It's the computer that actually has to do all the dirty work, telling the NIC how to translate the signals from a specific network protocol. When you instruct a computer how to understand, for example, TCP/IP, you say that you have *bound* TCP/IP to your network interface.

You can bind more than one protocol to a card, if you'd like; you can bind TCP/IP, IPX/SPX, and even NetBIOS all to the same NIC without any problems whatsoever. The NIC will then listen to the line and check every piece of data it hears to determine whether it's any of the protocols that it knows. Essentially, the card interprets what it's hearing as follows: "Is that TCP/IP? Nope. Is that IPX? Nope. Wait, that's NetBIOS!"

The challenge is properly *ordering* the bindings. You *always* want to bind the protocol that is being used the most first. Why?

Well, let's say that you've bound the protocols to your network interface card in the following order: IPX/SPX, NetBIOS, and TCP/IP. Every time the NIC hears a TCP/IP signal, it will first check to see whether it's IPX, check to see whether it's NetBIOS, and then finally discover that it's TCP/IP. Needless to say, when a computer is doing this several thousand times per minute, it will be wasting a lot of time checking every packet twice before it finally realizes it's good old TCP/IP.

As such, the rule is as follows:

> *Bind as few protocols as you can get away with. If you have to bind more than one, make sure the computer looks at the most commonly used protocol first.*

Is that clear?

Windows 95/98/SE/ME/NT

The most popular flavor of Windows at the moment is Windows 95/98/SE/ME/NT, though Windows XP seems to be surpassing it. Even if your computer isn't a Windows machine and you hate Windows with a passion that could melt linoleum, do yourself a favor and look at this information anyway. Eventually, somebody's going to ask you to help them.

Asking a Windows 95/98/SE/ME/NT machine to request a TCP/IP address from a DHCP server

Follow these steps to request a TCP/IP address from a DHCP server:

1. Double-click My Computer.

2. Double-click Control Panel.

3. Double-click Network. You should see something similar to what is shown in Figure 10-1.

4. Here's where it gets tricky. You should see something that says TCP/IP ->, and something with either NIC or Ethernet in it. Either way, this is your computer's way of telling you that TCP/IP is bound to the card (see Figure 10-2).

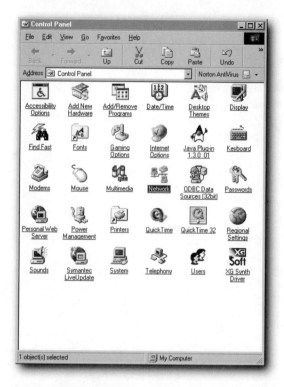

FIGURE 10-1: The Network icon of the Windows 98 Control Panel

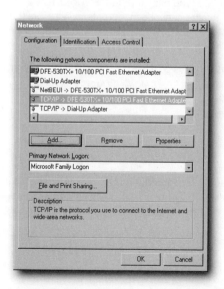

FIGURE 10-2: TCP/IP bound to the 10/100 PCI
Ethernet Adaptor

5. Click Properties and then select the IP Address tab (see Figure 10-3).

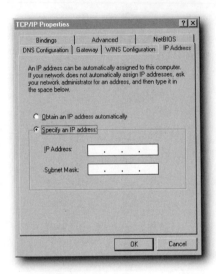

FIGURE 10-3: IP Address tab

6. If it's not already selected, click the Obtain an IP Address Automatically radio button and then click OK.

If you're doing this on a Windows NT machine, you may have to be logged in as an administrator—or at least someone with the power to alter network configurations—before it will let you do this.

Assigning a TCP/IP Address to a Windows 95/98/SE/ME Machine Manually

Follow these steps to assign a TCP/IP address to a Windows 95/98/SE/ME machine manually:

1. Double-click My Computer.

2. Double-click Control Panel.

3. Double-click Network (see Figure 10-4).

4. Here's where it gets tricky; you should see something that says TCP/IP -> and something with either NIC or Ethernet in it. Either way, this is your computer's way of telling you that TCP/IP is bound to the card (see Figure 10-5).

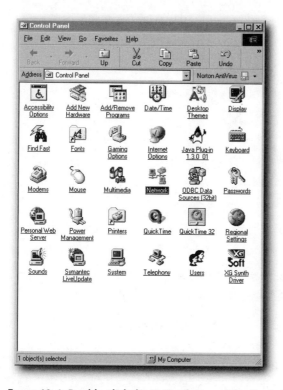

FIGURE 10-4: Double-click the Network icon of the Control Panel

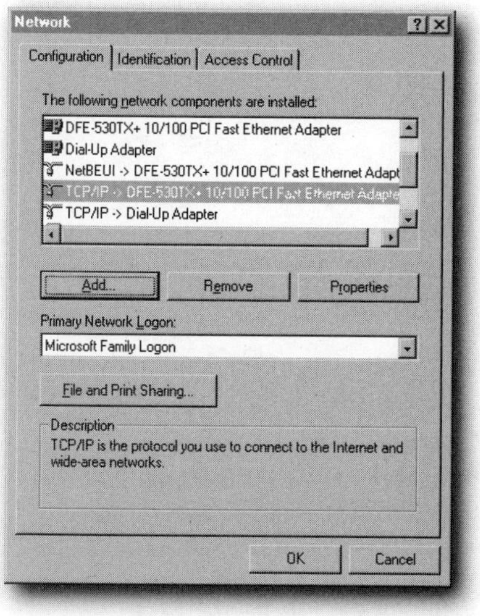

FIGURE 10-5: TCP/IP, still bound to the Ethernet card

5. Click Properties and then select the IP Address tab (see Figure 10-6).

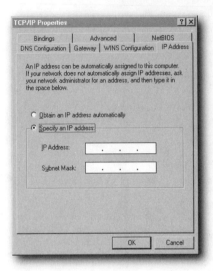

FIGURE 10-6: The IP Address tab of the Properties window

6. Click the Specify an IP Address radio button; the IP Address and Subnet Mask fields will then become available. Type in the IP Address and Subnet Mask that you have been assigned, as shown in Figure 10-7 — but be careful! Remember that, if you mistype a number here, your computer may not be able to talk to other computers at your party.

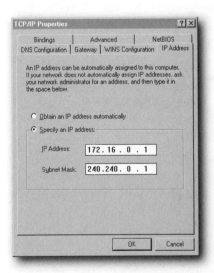

FIGURE 10-7: Typing in an IP address in Windows 98

7. If you're using routers, click the Gateway tab. Type in the IP address of the router that will be forwarding all outside traffic for this network and then click Add.

8. Click OK.

> **Caution**
>
> When your LAN party is done, be sure to reset your computer to request an IP address from a DHCP computer, as described above. Otherwise, because most Internet service providers automatically assign IP addresses via DHCP, you may not be able to access the Internet afterwards.

Binding TCP/IP (or another protocol) to a network card on Windows 95/98/SE/ME

Follow these steps to bind TCP/IP (or any other protocol) to a network card on Windows 95/98/SE/ME:

1. Make sure you have your Windows installation disk handy; you'll need some files off of it.

2. Double-click My Computer.

3. Double-click Control Panel.

4. Double-click Network.

5. Check to see whether TCP/IP is already bound to this NIC (see Figure 10-8). Look for something that says TCP/IP -> and either NIC or Ethernet. If you find something, this is your computer's way of telling you that TCP/IP is already bound to this card. You need go no further.

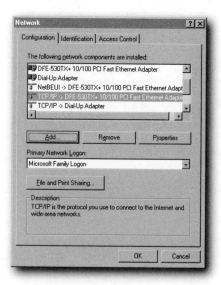

FIGURE 10-8: Changing the IP properties

6. If you don't find anything, click the Add button.

7. Click Protocol and then click the Add button, as shown in Figure 10-9. Windows will update its driver base, which will take a few seconds to a few minutes, depending on your computer.

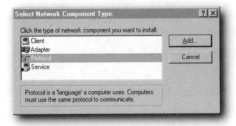

FIGURE 10-9: Click the Protocol network type to install the appropriate network component

8. Under the Manufacturers list, select Microsoft and then select TCP/IP. (Or, if you're installing another protocol, such as IPX, you'll have to click through the selections until you find the one you want—see Figure 10-10.) Click OK. In all probability, you'll be asked to insert an installation disk so it can copy the necessary files.

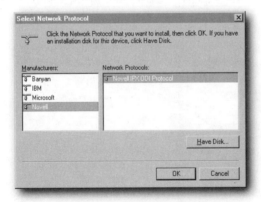

FIGURE 10-10: Selecting a network protocol

9. When your protocol is listed, click the OK button. Your computer will reboot; when it does, that protocol should be bound to all installed NICs.

Windows 2000

Microsoft's current heavy-duty server software, Win2K, is automatically installed with TCP/IP.

Asking a Windows 2000 machine to request a TCP/IP address from a DHCP server

Follow these steps to ask a Windows 2000 machine to request a TCP/IP address from a DHCP server:

1. Make sure you're logged in as Administrator or at least as someone with the rights to change protocol bindings.

2. Right-click the My Network Places icon on the Win2K desktop, and select Properties.

3. You should see an icon that says Local Area Connection. Underneath, it should have a description of the card — something like Intel(R) Pro 10/100 S Desktop Adapter. Double-click that.

4. Click the Obtain an IP Address Automatically radio button and then click OK. Click OK again.

Assigning an IP address to a Windows 2000 machine manually

Follow these steps to manually assign an IP address to a Windows 2000 machine manually:

1. Make sure you're logged in as Administrator or at least as someone with the rights to change protocol bindings.

2. Right-click the My Network Places icon on the Win2K desktop, and select Properties.

3. You should see an icon that says Local Area Connection. Underneath, it should have a description of the card — something like Intel(R) Pro 10/100 S Desktop Adapter. Double-click that.

4. Click the Use the Following IP Address radio button, and enter the IP address and subnet that you have been assigned — but be careful! Remember that, if you mistype a number here, your computer may not be able to talk to other computers at your party.

5. If you're using routers, type in the IP address of the router that will be forwarding all outside traffic for this network into the Default Gateway field. Click OK, and then click OK again.

Caution

When your LAN party is done, be sure to reset your computer to request an IP address from a DHCP computer, as described previously. Otherwise, because most Internet service providers automatically assign IP addresses via DHCP, you may not be able to access the Internet afterwards.

Binding TCP/IP to a Windows 2000 network card

You don't need to bind TCP/IP to a Windows 2000 network card. Windows 2000 comes automatically installed with TCP/IP, and it's bound automatically to all network interfaces. Still, if you need to install some other protocol, such as IPX/SPX, here's how you do it:

1. Make sure you're logged in as Administrator or at least as someone with the rights to change protocol bindings.

2. Right-click the My Network Places icon on the Win2K desktop, and select Properties.

3. You should see an icon that says Local Area Connection. Underneath, it should have a description of the card — something like Intel(R) Pro 10/100 S Desktop Adapter. Double-click that.

4. Click Install.

5. Click Protocol. You'll be shown a list of protocols that are already on Windows 2000 and waiting to be installed. If one of those is your protocol, click it and click OK.

6. If not, click Have Disk, point XP to the disk drive on which your protocol is located, and then click OK.

7. Windows will bind that protocol to your NIC. When it's done, click Close.

Windows XP

The latest Windows operating system, Windows XP, is so easy to use that hard-core techies may throw up their hands in frustration. (Whether from joy or from frustration that they can't get at the internal goodies easily is a question open for debate.) Anyway, the following material describes how to configure Windows XP:

Asking a Windows XP machine to request a TCP/IP address from a DHCP server

Follow these steps to ask a Windows XP machine to request a TCP/IP address from a DHCP server:

1. Select Control Panel from the Start menu.

2. Double-click Network Connections. (Alternatively, if you're using the Category view, click Network and Internet Connections and then click Network Connections.)

3. You should see an icon that says Local Area Connection. Underneath, it should have a description of the card — something like Intel(R) Pro 10/100 S Desktop Adapter," as shown in Figure 10-11. Double-click that.

4. Select Internet Protocol (TCP/IP) and click the Properties button, as shown in Figure 10-12.

5. Click the Obtain an IP Address Automatically radio button and click OK, as shown in Figure 10-13.

6. Click OK again.

FIGURE 10-11: Your Internet connection, as it appears in Windows XP

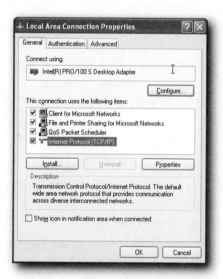

FIGURE 10-12: The properties of your Internet
connections, where you can change TCP/IP

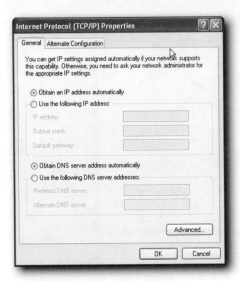

FIGURE 10-13: Telling Windows XP to obtain a DHCP connection automatically

Assigning an IP address manually to a Windows XP machine

Follow these steps to manually assign an IP address to a Windows XP machine:

1. Select Control Panel from the Start menu.

2. Double-click Network Connections. (If you're using the Category view, click Network and Internet Connections and then click Network Connections.)

3. You should see an icon that says Local Area Connection. Underneath, it should have a description of the card — something like Intel(R) Pro 10/100 S Desktop Adapter. Double-click that.

4. Select Internet Protocol (TCP/IP) and click Properties.

5. Click the Use the Following IP Address radio button, as shown in Figure 10-14, and enter the IP address and subnet that you have been assigned — but be careful! Remember that, if you mistype a number here, your computer may not be able to talk to other computers at your party.

6. If you're using routers, type in the IP address of the router that will be forwarding all outside traffic for this network into the Default Gateway field. Click OK and then click OK again.

When your LAN party is done, be sure to reset your computer to request an IP address from a DHCP computer, as described above. Otherwise, because most Internet service providers automatically assign IP addresses via DHCP, you may not be able to access the Internet afterwards.

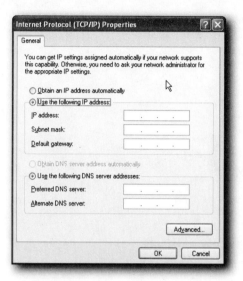

FIGURE 10-14: Setting a Windows XP computer's
IP address manually

Binding TCP/IP (or any other protocol) to a NIC on Windows XP

You don't need to bind TCP/IP to a network card on Windows XP. Windows XP comes automatically installed with TCP/IP, and it's bound automatically to all network interfaces — so unless some psycho deleted TCP/IP from your system, you shouldn't have a problem. Still, if you need to install some other protocol, such as IPX/SPX, here's how you'd do it:

1. Select Control Panel from the Start menu.

2. Double-click Network Connections. (If you're using the Category view, click Network and Internet Connections and then click Network Connections.)

3. You should see an icon that says Local Area Connection. Underneath, it should have a description of the card — something like Intel(R) Pro 10/100 S Desktop Adapter. Double-click that.

4. Click Install and then click Protocol, as shown in Figure 10-15.

5. You'll be shown a list of protocols (see Figure 10-16) that are already on Windows XP and waiting to be installed (generally, Network Monitor Driver and NWLink, Microsoft's version of IPX/SPX). If one of these is your protocol, click it and click OK.

6. If you need a different protocol, click Have Disk, point XP to the disk drive on which your protocol is located, and then click OK.

7. Windows will bind that protocol to your NIC. When it's done, click Close. You will have to reboot your computer.

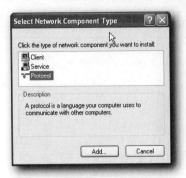

FIGURE 10-15: Installing a protocol

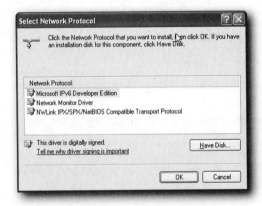

FIGURE 10-16: A list of alternative protocols

Macintosh OS 8.x and 9.x

The standbys of Macintosh operating systems for years, most newer Macintoshes will be running OS X on faster machines (if they belong to gamers). Still, you'll occasionally run into some classic OSs.

Asking a machine to request a TCP/IP address from a DHCP server on a Mac with OS 8.x or 9.x

Follow these steps to ask a machine to request a TCP/IP address from a DHCP server on a Mac with OS 8.x or 9.x:

1. Click the Apple menu in the upper left-hand corner of your screen, and select Control Panels.

2. Double-click TCP/IP.

3. Under the Configure menu, select Using DHCP Server. Leave the DHCP Client ID field blank unless you have a specific DHCP IP address to which you'd like it to connect. (If you don't know what I'm talking about, leave it blank.)

4. Click the Close box; when it asks you to save changes to the current configuration, click Save.

Assigning an IP address manually on a Mac with OS 8.x or 9.x

Follow these steps to manually assign an IP address on a Mac with OS 8.x or 9.x:

1. Click the Apple menu in the upper left-hand corner of your screen, and select Control Panels.

2. Double-click TCP/IP.

3. Under the Configure menu, select Manually.

4. Input the IP address and subnet mask you have been assigned in the IP Address and Subnet Mask fields, respectively.

5. If you're using routers, type the IP address of the router that will be forwarding all outside traffic for this network into the Router Address field.

6. Click the Close box; when it asks you to save changes to the current configuration, click Save.

Caution

When your LAN party is done, be sure to reset your computer to request an IP address from a DHCP computer, as described above. Otherwise, because most Internet service providers automatically assign IP addresses via DHCP, you may not be able to access the Internet afterwards.

Mac OS X

Macintosh's latest and greatest operating system, Mac OS X, works much like the OS 8.x or 9.x.

Asking a machine to request a TCP/IP address from a DHCP server on a Mac with OS X

Follow these steps to ask a machine to request a TCP/IP address from a DHCP server on a Mac with OS X:

1. Launch the System Preferences menu from the Apple menu (see Figure 10-17).

2. Double-click Network and then select the TCP/IP tab.

3. In the Configure IPv4 field, select Using DHCP, as shown in Figure 10-18. Leave the DHCP Client ID field blank unless you have a specific DHCP IP address to which you'd like it to connect. (If you don't know what I'm talking about, leave it blank.)

4. Click the Apply Now box.

FIGURE 10-17: The System Preferences tray in OS X

FIGURE 10-18: Setting the Mac to use DHCP automatically

Assigning an IP address manually on a Mac with OS X

Follow these steps to assign an IP address manually on a Mac with OS X:

1. Launch the System Preferences menu from the Apple menu.

2. Double-click Network and then select the TCP/IP tab.

3. In the Configure IPv4 menu, select Manually, as shown in Figure 10-19.

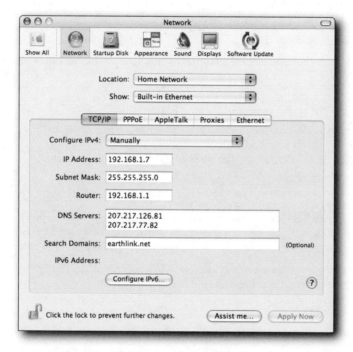

FIGURE 10-19: Setting a Mac's IP address manually

4. Input the IP address and subnet mask you have been assigned in the IP Address and Subnet Mask fields, respectively.

5. If you're using routers, type the IP address of the router that will be forwarding all outside traffic for this network into the Router Address field.

6. Click the Apply Now box.

PlayStation 2

The PlayStation 2 is pretty easy to configure, as it uses only the TCP/IP protocol and asks for a DHCP server by default. The following sections explain how to do both easily.

Asking a machine to request a TCP/IP address from a DHCP server on a PlayStation 2

Follow these steps to ask a machine to request a TCP/IP address from a DHCP server on a PlayStation 2:

1. Select High Speed Connection (Cable or DSL) and press the X button.

2. Select Automatic Settings and press the X button. You will be asked whether your ISP requires a user name and password. If you have a NAT access point established, the answer is no. Select No and press the X button.

3. You will be asked if you need a DHCP Host Name. Select No and press the X button.

4. The PS2 will try to connect to the Internet; if it is successful, it will allow you to press the X button to save this configuration. Do so.

Assigning a TCP/IP address manually to a PlayStation 2

Follow these steps to manually assign a TCP/IP address to a PlayStation 2:

1. Select High Speed Connection (Cable or DSL) and press the X button.

2. Select Manual Settings and press the X button.

3. You will now be at a screen that enables you to input the IP address, the subnet (called the *netmask* here), the default gateway (called the *default router address* here), and two DNS addresses. It will, helpfully, provide you with a calculator-style interface to enter the correct numbers with your game pad. Input them all and press X to confirm.

4. The PS2 will try to connect to the Internet; if it is successful, it will allow you to press the X button to save this configuration. Do so.

Xbox

Like the PlayStation 2, the Xbox is also pretty easy to configure, as it only uses the TCP/IP protocol and asks for a DHCP server by default. As such, you should only need to assign an IP address in the weirdest of circumstances — but again, I'll show you how to it here in case you ever need to.

Assigning a TCP/IP address manually to an Xbox

Follow these steps to assign a TCP/IP address manually to an Xbox:

1. Select High Speed Connection (Cable or DSL) and press the X button.

2. Select Manual Settings and press the X button.

3. You will now be at a screen that enables you to input the IP address, the subnet (called the *netmask* here), the default gateway (called the *default router address* here), and two DNS addresses. It will, helpfully, provide you with a calculator-style interface to enter the correct numbers with your game pad. Input them all and press X to confirm.

4. The Xbox will try to connect to the Internet; if it is successful, it will allow you to press the X button to save this configuration. Do so.

Ping, IPConfig, and Other Tools: How (and When) to Use Them

If your network begins to act erratically, you'll need to use TCP/IP's troubleshooting tools to ferret out the problem. Youll learn much more about these tools in the Chapter 15, "Something Just Went Wrong! Fixing Party Problems," which provides many suggestions for troubleshooting, but here's a quickie overview.

The main tool you'll use is *ping*. Ping sends a small packet to a specified computer via the TCP/IP protocol, asks for a request, and then it tracks the amount of time it takes to hear back. You're probably familiar with pings to some extent, as that's what you use to track the lag time on remote game servers when you're playing at home — and ping time, in turn, is a good indication of whether it's worth connecting.

On smaller networks, however, ping is useful for testing connections to computers — to determine whether you can find it at all.

Finding Ping, IPConfig, and Traceroute on your machine

These three tools are fairly omnipresent by now, and, in all probability, they're already on your machine if you access the Internet.

Linux/Unix

Considering that ping was developed on Unix, almost every build of Linux or Unix has ping built into it these days; you should be able to simply use it from the command line as you would any other utility.

Windows

From the Start menu, select Run and type **Command** when it asks you for the name of the program. A DOS window will open; you should be able to use ping (or anything else) from there.

Macintosh

Unfortunately, there is no native ping utility for the Macintosh — at least not for OS 8.x and 9.x. You'll have to download a ping program from the Internet, such as MacPING or MacTCPWatcher. If you have OS X, you can access the Terminal, which is the Mac equivalent of the command line.

Using Ping

Ping is a pretty simple utility: Simply type **Ping (*ip address*)**, as follows:

```
Ping 127.0.0.1
```

Ping will then send out four packets, and, with luck, you'll see a result that looks something like the following:

```
Pinging 127.0.0.1 with 32 bytes of data
```

```
Reply from 127.0.0.1: bytes=32 time<1ms TTL=128
Reply from 127.0.0.1: bytes=32 time<1ms TTL=128
Reply from 127.0.0.1: bytes=32 time<1ms TTL=128
Reply from 127.0.0.1: bytes=32 time<1ms TTL=128
```

Other information appears in the preceding output as well.

It tells you that you got a reply in less than one millisecond (<1ms), which you really should, considering that 127.0.0.1 is your own network card! If you type, say, **Ping www.yahoo.com,** you'll get something more realistic, such as the following:

```
Reply from 66.218.71.113: bytes=32 time=100ms TTL=52
```

That means it took one hundred milliseconds to get the request and return. However, if the ping request never gets a reply, you'll get this:

```
Request timed out.
Request timed out.
Request timed out.
Request timed out.
```

That means the computer never responded to the ping. This could mean one of four things:

- **The line is down.** Somewhere between your computer and this computer, a cable is broken and isn't transmitting data.

- **The computer is down.** For whatever reason — it's turned off, it's overloaded, it's just having a bad day — the computer is unable to reply.

- **The router is down.** The router may be misconfigured and sending the ping request to the wrong network.

- **The computer is configured not to reply to pings.** You can overload a computer by flooding it with too many pings or with misconfigured pings. Hackers routinely try. Ping www.microsoft.com, for example, and you'll get no response. That doesn't mean Microsoft has collapsed, but that Microsoft has been burned by one too many bad ping attacks. If everything else fails, see if the remote computer has security software (like a firewall), and try to disable it.

You can use ping to track a variety of problems, among which are the following:

- **Ping the server to determine whether this computer can reach it from here.** If it can, then the problem's not in the network.

- **Ping 127.0.0.1 to determine whether the NIC is working properly.**

- **If you're dealing with a single network, ping other computers on that network.** If you can't access any of the computers, chances are good that your cable is bad or the port to which this computer is connected may be dead.

- **If you're dealing with several networks connected via routers, ping the default gateway.** This is to determine whether your router itself is active.

- **Ping some computers on other networks.** If you can ping the router but can't ping a computer elsewhere, the problem is most likely in your router's configuration.

The Most Common Problem When One Computer Can't Ping Another

What is the most common problem? The cable's loose. D'oh! Every technician has at least once spent an hour trying to track down a software problem when the real issue is the hardware. *Always check the cabling.*

Moreover, if you're trying to track down a loose wire and have someone else to watch the screen, ping x.x.x.x -t (where x.x.x.x is the IP address of the computer you're trying to reach) will ping a computer continually until you press Ctrl+C.

Ipconfig

If you're looking for information about your current connection, *ipconfig* tells you everything you need to know about your current setup. Simply type in the following:

```
Ipconfig /all
```

You'll be shown the IP information for every network interface you have, as shown in Figure 10-20, including the IP address, the subnet, whether DHCP is enabled, when it got its address from DHCP, and so on. If you want to know all your local IP details, here's where you go.

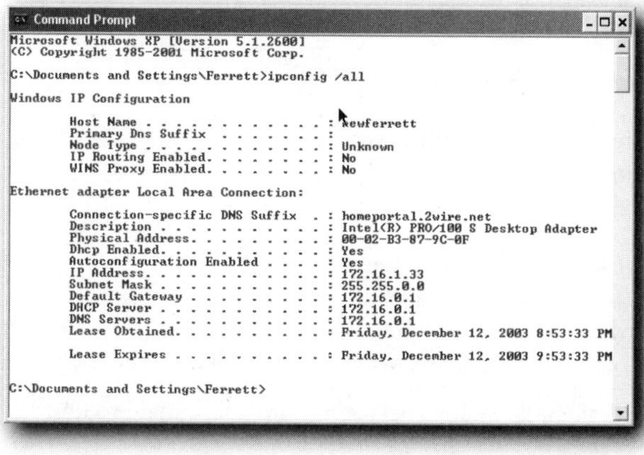

FIGURE 10-20: A complete ipconfig /all screen

You can also type **Ipconfig /renew**, which will re-request a new IP address from a DHCP server. This comes in handy sometimes if the server has accidentally given it the wrong address and you don't want to reboot.

Tracert

If you're having difficulty with your routing, *tracert* (an abbreviation of *trace route*) will provide you with the number of routers that it takes to direct all your network traffic from your computer to the server you're trying to reach.

Tip

If you don't understand what "routing" means, then you may want to read Chapter 8, "Networking for Large Groups and the Internet." However, if routing isn't a concern to you, you may want to just skip this part.

Simply type the following:

```
Tracert 127.0.0.1
```

Here, 127.0.0.1 is the IP address you'd like to reach. Tracert will then generate a list of the IP addresses and host addresses (the Web name), as well as a bunch of ping times. Each list item is the IP address of the next router to which your network traffic is being handed.

For example, Figure 10.21 illustrates how I tracert www.starcitygames.com.

```
CA   Command Prompt                                                       _ □ x

Tracing route to starcitygames.com [69.50.212.110]
over a maximum of 30 hops:

  1     1 ms    <1 ms    <1 ms  homeportal.homeportal.2wire.net [172.16.0.1]
  2    23 ms    23 ms    23 ms  h-69-3-250-1.SFLDMIDN.dynamic.covad.net [69.3.25
0.1]
  3    23 ms    23 ms    23 ms  192.168.7.17
  4    22 ms    23 ms    22 ms  ge-5-1-133.hsa1.Detroit1.Level3.net [63.211.20.1
85]
  5    21 ms    23 ms    23 ms  ge-6-0-0.mp1.Detroit1.Level3.net [64.159.0.201]

  6    28 ms    30 ms    29 ms  so-0-1-0.bbr2.Chicago1.Level3.net [64.159.1.34]

  7    28 ms    29 ms    30 ms  so-9-0.core2.Chicago1.Level3.net [4.68.112.198]

  8    28 ms    29 ms    29 ms  broadwing-level3-oc12.Chicago1.Level3.net [209.0
.225.10]
  9    32 ms    33 ms    32 ms  pi-1-0.c1.gnwd.broadwing.net [216.140.15.1]
 10    47 ms    48 ms    49 ms  p0-3-0.c1.ftwo.broadwing.net [216.140.4.213]
 11    95 ms    95 ms    95 ms  so0-0-0.a1.phnx.broadwing.net [216.140.2.154]
 12    96 ms    93 ms    95 ms  p0-0-0.e0.phnx.broadwing.net [216.140.2.166]
 13   101 ms    96 ms    95 ms  67.96.217.154
 14    84 ms    85 ms    86 ms  fe2-0.br2.phx.cybertrails.com [162.42.149.18]
 15    85 ms    86 ms    86 ms  fe4-0.cr2.phx.cybertrails.com [162.42.149.26]
 16    98 ms    95 ms    94 ms  162.42.145.2
 17    98 ms    95 ms    96 ms  69.50.212.110

Trace complete.
```

FIGURE 10-21: Tracing the route my IP packets take between my home in Ohio and a server in Virginia

The first router my network traffic goes to is homeportal.homeportal.2wire.net, as you can see in the right-hand column. That's the host address of the router/switch in my house that enables me to share my DSL connection with my wife. (The three numbers beforehand are the three ping attempts to that router, which show how quickly that router responds.)

The second router is 69.3.250.1, which is my Internet service provider's main router.

From there, my request is handed off to 15 different routers in various places in America as each router tries to find the quickest possible route between my home in Cleveland, Ohio, and the server, which is located in Roanoke, Virginia. It hands my request off to a couple of routers in Detroit and then to a few routers in Chicago before finally finding a router that can send my network request directly to www.starcitygames.com in Roanoke, Virginia. (Each different router that my request is handed off to is called a *hop*.)

Note

Why Detroit? Geographically astute readers may have noted that Virginia is on the East Coast of America, whereas Detroit and Chicago are *west* of Ohio. Routers try to find the *fastest* path to your destination, not the *shortest*. Chances are good that there was a high-speed connection between Ohio and Chicago that was quicker than any direct route.

This information is useful when you have a broken connection in a routed network, because tracert will show you where the problem lies. It may be that your request is being handed off to a broken router or that your traffic is being routed mistakenly to the wrong network. In either case, tracert can help you locate the problem.

Setting Up a DHCP Server on Windows XP/Windows 2000

You may have noticed that I've mentioned DHCP servers many times. I'm not going to tell you how to set up a fully functional DHCP server, however. There is a good reason for that:

DHCP servers can be fairly complicated. Moreover, they're easy to screw up if you don't know what you're doing. Setting up a client to request a DHCP address is easy, but configuring a server properly can be a royal pain. It's a lot easier to buy (or beg) a router/switch, which does all this automatically for you.

Tip If you're comfortable downloading and installing software, you might try 602 LAN Suite, an almost frighteningly complete LAN management package that not only includes a DHCP server, but also contains just about every other program you'd need to run a medium-sized LAN— including a firewall, NAT services, virus-checking, a Web server and, well . . . a lot more. It's free if you're holding a party of under five users and reasonably inexpensive for larger parties. You can download it at www.software602.com.

However, if you can't get a router/switch, you can take a quickie route and use Windows XP's *Internet connection sharing,* which turns your PC into a Network Address Translation access point,which, if you'll recall, includes a very limited DHCP server. You can do this even if you don't intend to have Internet access at your party; just configure it when you do have access to an Internet connection, even a slow one such as dialup. Your NAT-enabled Windows XP server will continue to provide DHCP service, even if it can't access the Internet.

Tip If you don't know what Network Address Translation is, hie on over to Chapter 8, "Networking for Large Groups and the Internet."

Note, however, that bringing a computer with Internet connection sharing capabilities to a LAN party is bad form, as it will instantly become a rogue DHCP server, handing out IP addresses that may conflict with existing addresses; or, worse yet, it can cause the router to send everyone's server requests into a black hole. Therefore, you'll also want to know how to turn Internet connection sharing *off.*

Tip Remember that if you've set up Windows as a DHCP server, it needs to be up and running before you turn on any of the other computers. Clients can't request IP addresses from a computer that's not online yet!

Setting Up a Server on Linux

Walking you through a radically simplified version of setting up a DHCP server on Linux might do you more harm than good, as many flavors of Linux are out there, and many of them are complex. A complete discussion of this subject is outside the scope of this book. I will say that most flavors of Linux offer both Network Address Translation (which is also called *IP Masquerading*) and DHCP as options and that configuring them varies greatly depending on what version of Linux you have.

Don't worry, however. There are many fine Wiley books out there to choose from; consult www.wiley.com/compbooks or your local bookstore for numerous options. I personally prefer the Bible series (such as the Red Hat 9 Bible), which tend to be pretty comprehensive.

Setting up Internet connection sharing (and a quick DHCP server) in Windows XP/Windows 2000

Here are the steps you need to take to make your Windows box an IP-address-givin' machine:

1. Select Control Panel from the Start menu.

> If you're using Windows 2000, you will most likely need to be logged in as Administrator to do this.

2. Double-click Network Connections. (Or, if you're using the Category view, click Network and Internet Connections and then click Network Connections.)

3. Right-click Network Connections and select Properties. Click the Advanced tab if you're using Windows XP (see Figure 10-22) or the Sharing tab if you're using Windows 2000.

4. Click the Allow Other Network Users to Connect through this Computer's Internet Connection check box.

> If you have a router/switch in place already, this option may not be available. If you do have one available, shouldn't you be using that instead?

5. Click OK.

6. Answer Yes to the dialogue box that appears next, which, when translated from geeks-peak, says, "If you have any computers with manually assigned IP addresses on the network, make sure they've got a network address of 192.168.0 and a default gateway of 192.168.0.1."

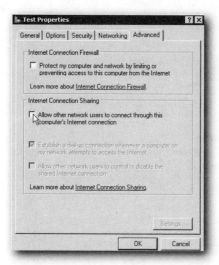

FIGURE 10-22: Sharing an Internet connection
under Windows XP

Configuring client computers to use Windows XP's DHCP server

This is a trick section; you need do nothing. As long as the client is set to automatically request an IP address from a DHCP server, it will automatically connect to the Windows machine and get one.

Turning off Windows XP/Windows 2000 Internet Connection Sharing

As I said earlier, this comes up a lot at parties. Turning it off is fairly simple, though:

1. Select Run from the Start menu.

2. Type **services.msc** and click OK. The Microsoft Management Console will open, as shown in Figure 10-23.

3. Look for Internet Connection Services in the Name column. The name may be partially hidden, as it is in Figure 10-23.

4. Right-click it and select Properties.

5. Change the Startup type from Automatic to Disabled, as shown in Figure 10-24. Click OK.

6. To turn it back on again at the end of the party, repeat Steps 1 through 5, but change it from Disabled to Automatic in Step 5.

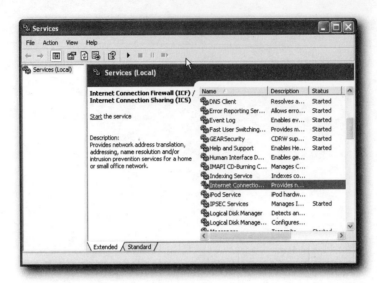

FIGURE 10-23: Services.msc, which enables you to see all Windows processes

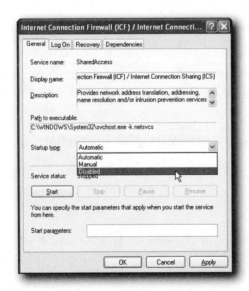

FIGURE 10-24: Disabling Internet connection sharing

Summary

After reading this chapter, you should be able to configure your computer, whatever it is, for the most common LAN party tasks.

In the next chapter, we'll be discussing something that's not quite as easily configured: your staff! Even if you only have four or five people attending your party, knowing what roles staff commonly handle during the course of larger LAN parties can help you understand what *you'll* need to do on the day of the event itself. So let's move 'em out, campers!

Staffing Issues and Common LAN Party Roles

LAN parties are a techie phenomenon, so the concept of *staff* is usually undervalued. Hardware and new games are cool and sexy, and are written up in *Wired* and *PC Magazine,* but there are no dazzling advances in people technology, no articles devoted to new people drivers and upgrades. Therefore, when you ask folks what's needed to hold a LAN party, most people will talk about switches and cables because that's the cool part of the LAN party.

But you can't forget people, not if you're going to run a *good* LAN party.

People set up the cables, show guests to their tables, and make sure the pizza is distributed in an equitable fashion. People are what make LAN parties *happen.* A large part of running a good LAN party comes from looking at what your guests want, and figuring out how to give it to them quickly and quietly with the people you have to work with, even if you are that only person.

This chapter is technically about staffing, but really it's about knowing what your guests will want. So read on. Even if people don't have control panels or water-cooled processors, they're just as important as the hardware or software, maybe even more so.

How Much Staff Do You Need?

The answer to the question of how much staff to get is pretty simple: One person for every eight to 15 people is a good rule of thumb. Therefore, if you're holding a LAN party in your basement, chances are pretty good that you're the staff.

However, that doesn't mean that this chapter is a complete waste of time for you! Although the material in this chapter is obviously geared for larger parties, the various roles that staffers play will give you a good idea of the things you'll need to do during your LAN party. You might not have thought of yourself as "The Party Mom," but if you're the only staffer there, guess what? You're it, whether you chose to be or not.

I do admit, though, that the last half of the chapter, on gathering and retaining staff, is pretty useless for a four-person LAN party. You can blitz right by that section.

Common Staff Roles at LAN Parties

The staff at a LAN party is there to accomplish two things:

- **Ensure that everyone has a good time.** You do this by addressing the fundamentals: Is the network working? Are people comfortable? Do they have enough food to eat?

- **Prevent collateral damage.** Think about it: Everyone shows up to a kegger, but few people offer to wash the dishes at the end of the night. Well, things are no different in the world of LAN parties. Making sure that everything's put away and tidied up at the end of the evening is boring and tedious, especially after all the fun you've had, but it needs to be done, unless you have a *very* sloppy place and don't care.

Given that you're attempting to accomplish specific goals, LAN party staffers can be assigned to address each of these needs. At most LAN parties, the most common roles to fill in answer to specific needs are as follows:

- The Techie
- The Backbone Person
- The Equipment Wrangler
- The Dedicated Server Host
- The Pizza Wizard
- The Receptionist
- The Floor Sweeper
- The Party Mom
- The Muscle Goon

The following sections describe the important functions that each of these people fulfills.

The Techie

In smaller parties, the Techie is the jack-of-all-trades who also serves as Equipment Wrangler and Backbone Person — the person who sets up the LAN in advance and hooks everyone up.

At larger parties, though, you may need to split the positions into two parts. The Backbone Person, as mentioned in the following section, is the person who's in charge of setting up the network the night before; the Techie is the person who handles all the computer tech support on the day of the party itself. This person doesn't set up the network, but every time someone has a problem connecting to it, the Techie is the person who sits down at the computer and gets it working again.

The Techie and Backbone Person positions, incidentally, may bleed into each other. For example, Techies sit down at someone's PC and do everything they can to get it working. After some brief troubleshooting, this person may realize that the problem is with a router that's blocking the wrong type of network traffic; fixing that router is the Backbone Person's job.

The Backbone Person

The *backbone* is the central switch through which most of the network's traffic is directed. The Backbone Person is the individual in charge of designing and laying out the LAN, putting all the cables and routers where they need to be in order to get everyone's computers talking to each other. If Internet access is planned, the Backbone Person sets it up. If there's a wireless network, the Backbone Person sets up the wireless access point. If a cable's not working, the Backbone Person finds a new one, or just crimps the existing one.

When the day of the event arrives, the Backbone Person has it pretty easy. All of the setup work has been done the night before. Now the Techie is the go-to person.

The Equipment Wrangler

At *really* large parties, just getting the routers and cable and such may be a job unto itself. The Equipment Wrangler is the Radar O'Reilly of the big LAN party — the person who procures all the routers and switches, buys cabling supplies at the cheapest possible prices, and is in charge of returning any borrowed equipment in better-than-good condition.

The Dedicated Server Host

Setting up a game server and choosing the appropriate maps can sometimes be a real hassle, depending on the system and game you're playing. The Dedicated Server Host is the person who brings his or her pre-made *CounterStrike* system to the party and makes sure that it's running smoothly.

We love the Dedicated Server Host. You will, too — especially if you read Chapter 13, "The Complete Day-of-the-Party Timeline."

The Pizza Wizard

At smaller parties, the Pizza Wizard has an informal role: making the late-night soda runs to 7-11 and ordering the pizza. Neither are small roles, however. Late-night supermarket runs in particular can be tricky, as everyone wants her or his own brand of food or drink, and no one ever has enough singles to cover the cost. The Pizza Wizard must embody the following qualities and be able to carry out the following tasks: be good with math in order to ensure that everyone gets his or her proper change, be able to provide his or her own transportation so that errands can be run quickly, and be willing to go alone if no one wants to go along for the ride.

At larger parties, the Pizza Wizard is in charge of *selling* food in order to recoup costs. He or she is the one who restocks the fridge, gets more ice when it's necessary, orders the pizza, and in general, plays Apu, the convenience store owner, to your hungry and thirsty Simpsons.

The Pizza Wizards have to be extra-reliable because they're handling cold hard cash, as it's very easy for the Pizza Wizard to give freebies to friends when nobody else is looking, thus eating (literally) into your profit margin. Make someone the Pizza Wizard only if you trust him or her—and as I state later in the chapter, this doesn't mean that you have to *like* the person; you just need to *trust* her or him. If your potential Pizza Wizard can tell a great story but hasn't kept a steady job in the past year, then maybe you want to think about putting someone less likable but more reliable in charge.

It is entirely possible to have multiple Pizza Wizards, who take shifts. Ideally, however, there should be one High Pizza Wizard who tallies up what was sold at the end of the evening and makes a careful note of what to order at future events. Did the pretzels stay on the shelf all night while the Ho-Hos disappeared in three hours? Order more Ho-Hos and less pretzels the next time.

The better you understand the tastes of your local LAN partygoers, the more food you can sell the next time you throw a party.

The Receptionist

The Receptionist (see Figure 11-1) is in charge of checking everyone in, taking their money, and ushering them to their seats. The Receptionist needs to be a people person for two very important reasons.

First, this person is the public face of the event, and a surly or insulting Receptionist will taint your entire party. People will not remember the fun they had; they will remember the gratuitous insult they received upon entering the room: "You're running *Windows 98*? Haw haw!"; or that they spent fifteen minutes trying to find someone to talk to before they could check in.

Second, of all the roles described here, the Receptionist gets to spend the least time fragging. Particularly at the beginning of the party, the Receptionist will be walking people around and therefore miss out on a lot of play time. As such, it's in your best interest to find a person who really likes talking to new people. The best Receptionists are the ones who'd *rather* spend all day discussing movies and upcoming game releases.

Even at smaller parties, however, the Receptionist has an important role: answering the phone when it rings.

Tip

Make sure that whoever you choose for the Receptionist is good with directions and knows the area.

If I take a wrong turn on the way to your house, and I will (I get lost going to the bathroom), then the Receptionist will be the person who guides me to your party. If the Receptionist doesn't know where I am, or how to tell me how to find the party, then I may wander aimlessly through the worst section of town as I try to bushwhack my way to the LAN party site. I may not even be able to get there at all.

So, please, choose someone who can read a map and who knows the neighborhood reasonably well (because I can't, and I don't—and chances are good that someone else coming to the LAN party can't and doesn't either).

FIGURE 11-1: Is this the face you want to present to your friends?

The Floor Sweeper

Face it: LAN party attendees are pigs. It is the Floor Sweeper's job to make sure that the garbage is regularly emptied and to walk the floor periodically to ensure that the area is reasonably clean. This person functions as the Cleanliness Police, and ensures that you do not lose your rental deposit if your LAN party takes place at a location other than your home.

Note that the Floor Sweeper's job is not Janitor. It is *not* the function of Floor Sweepers to wander around the place playing Alice the Maid as they pick up everyone's work area for them. It *is*, however, a fine idea for the Floor Sweeper to wander through once every hour or so with an empty garbage bag, exhorting everyone to throw their trash into it. This person may even demand that someone clean up a particularly filthy station.

One more helpful hint: If someone carrying a bag full of garbage tells you to clean up, *don't argue with him*. While the Floor Sweeper is a vital role, it is not nearly as cool as being the Techie or even the Receptionist. Do not vex Floor Sweepers or they may go ballistic.

The Party Mom

Party Mom is a very special position, but it is usually not an official one. However, as LAN parties reach a critical mass of 15 or more people, having a Party Mom becomes critical.

The Party Mom role is generally filled by older women, but you do not need to be a mom, or even a woman, to be an effective Party Mom. What you have to be is sensitive and good at dealing with upset people, because whenever a nasty argument breaks out or someone's feelings are hurt, it is the Party Mom's job to sit down with everyone and pour oil upon the waters.

The Party Mom is the peacemaker.

Unlike the other positions, you can't appoint someone to be the Party Mom. The Party Mom *has* to be someone who's naturally sensitive and good at calming people down. Psychodrama doesn't break out at every party, of course, but when someone feels slighted, it's good for him to have somewhere to turn. The Party Mom is the one who notices someone's down, takes him aside, and just talks with him for a while until the person feels better.

A Party Mom will often assume this role without you asking. (The best Party Moms are natural cheerleaders.) When that happens, recognize that you have a Party Mom in your midst and treasure her (or him). A good Party Mom is invaluable if you have one.

The Muscle Goon

While most gamer body types are at the extremes — pudgy or skinny — there's always one person who's really into karate, the SCA, or some other form of combat adventures. He (or she) does not take bull from anyone, and may well be a former member of the military or a bouncer.

These people are not the ones who continually brag about their black belts or talk about their fights. They are quiet, reserved, and loath to use violence except as a last resort. If you push them, however, they *will* use violence, and with frightening efficiency.

Should someone act up, having someone who is confident in his abilities as a real-life butt-kicker is excellent, particularly if the unruly person must be escorted from the premises. It is hoped that nobody will ever have to resort to such force, but having someone who radiates that quiet confidence can nip many problems in the bud.

Note Larger LAN parties may require middle management; for example, if you have multiple Techies, you may want a Chief Technical Officer to keep them all in line. Also, larger LAN parties may need full-time positions devoted to nonday-of-the-party things, such as publicity and accounting. If you get large enough that you're turning a profit, keep these ideas firmly in mind.

Getting and Keeping a Good Staff

Once you start expanding into larger LAN parties, you realize that this is too much work for one person to do. This is the point when you start adding people, but how do you get people to do good work consistently?

Well, before we can get to that, we need to look at one of the more common problems that people who hold LAN parties encounter: psychological resistance to asking for help.

The importance of delegating

When a LAN party begins to expand, there is the natural tendency to keep doing everything yourself. After all, this is supposed to be a fun time when everyone gets together and hangs out, plays a few games, trades some files, and goes home again.

What people can forget is that work expands exponentially as a LAN party gains new players. You have to do more setup the night before, you have to clean up more stuff afterwards, you have to gather more equipment and help more people set up, and so on. You can wear yourself out holding LAN parties, spending hours of preparation in isolation — all because you want to hold the best party. You're determined to ensure that the only work anyone has to do is bring a computer to the station. After all, who has a good time when he's working?

Therefore, you do all the work yourself in a noble-but-flawed attempt to ensure that the only thing that anyone does at your party is play. Of course, that work keeps expanding as you make Costco runs and crimp cables and sweep the floor and a thousand other tasks.

As the parties continue, people see your hard work. They respect it. They appreciate what you do and tell you they know how much effort you are expending. How can you ask for help when you're getting such great feedback?

But you're getting exhausted. And it's not fun anymore.

Welcome to burnout!

Furthermore, other people are often reluctant to volunteer, either because they don't realize how much effort this now takes or because they don't want to butt in on "your" party. A strange phenomenon that occurs at LAN parties (and with geek cultures in general) is that the host of the party becomes a very minor celebrity, with his main claim to fame being that he is "the person who holds that great LAN party." After a couple of months of gaming, you may be introduced as something like, "This is Sarah — her monthly *CounterStrike* parties totally rock."

You're probably not one of those people who becomes addicted to this kind of low-level fame; but some do, and they get very offended when others offer to help, because they see it as a take-over attempt. They hear "Can I help out?" as "Can I try to steal some of your spotlight?" Helping them is seen as trying to subvert some of Their Party, and it is met with anger and disdain.

Given that strange geek dynamic, there is often a certain territoriality when it comes to parties, especially when they're held at someone's house. People often want to help, but they don't want to step on anyone's toes.

The two tendencies combine for a very bad dynamic: You don't want to be seen as the "nonfun" guy — after all, everyone's giving you mad credit for holding such great parties — and nobody is actually volunteering. There is a natural reluctance to say, "Hey! Step up to the plate and *help out*, here!" Once you do that, you're not as cool. Suddenly, you're no longer The Cool Party-Holder — you're a boss, and people don't like bosses.

Nonetheless, you have to be. *Remember:* LAN parties are supposed to be fun for *everyone*, and that includes *you*. If you're not having fun, then find someone to whom you can start delegating tasks so you can get your frag on, too. Plus, you'd be surprised at how positively people will respond when you ask for a little pre-game help. That weird pseudo-fame thing works both ways, and often someone will be flattered when asked to be a part of the "inside crowd" that organizes the cool LAN party.

It's generally best to start off with someone as a co-worker, having him work side-by-side with you as you set up the network. That person can do a lot of the gruntwork, such as setting up tables or running cable. If he's a real tech-head, you can have him configure a dedicated server or a router. Then, as time goes by and you're sure that person's competent and dedicated, you can start handing him specific positions.

Someone has to be in charge. Either it's you or you'll need to find someone else who will take over for you. Hopefully, it won't be one of those needy fame-seekers.

The big problem with staffers and how to fix it

When you're holding a LAN party, you are automatically a cool person. After all, LAN parties are hip, cutting-edge things that very few people know about, and you are basically directing the actions of 15 or 20 people at this point. You can become a social nexus around which people gather, like the owner of the comic shop or the director of the school play.

As such, people begin to want to be around you. They will often be happy — nay, *thrilled* — to be a part of the "in" team, to tell their friends that they're helping to run the show. They may well drop your name in conversations.

In other words, getting staffers isn't a problem. They want to be on your team.

The problem is that they aren't actually that interested in working.

LAN parties are fun, but the maintenance can be tedious. What you'll find, more often than not, is that people will volunteer eagerly, do their job well at the first event, do it half-heartedly at the next two or three events, and then drift away from being a staff member altogether.

This is a big problem — and if my interviews with people across the country are any indication, it happens a *lot*. The next section describes what you can do to combat this.

Choosing based on responsibility, not likeability

Any office worker will tell you the problems that nepotism causes. "Can you believe my boss hired his best friend for the VP slot?" they'll say. Usually, such stories are followed by tales of woe as incompetent Friends of the Big Cheese screw up everything. Of course, the Big Cheese never sees what a lousy job his pals are doing.

However, when many people are trying to create what is, essentially, a small organizational structure, where do they start? With their best friends and relatives.

Oops.

As I mentioned earlier, in the section about the Pizza Wizard, your good buddy may not be the brightest choice for your right-hand man. For one thing, most people don't choose their friends on the basis of their ability to stick it out in tedious or frustrating situations. Chances are good you're friends with someone because he's a hell of a person, not because he files paperwork with astounding accuracy. As such, your buddy may be very entertaining but completely unreliable.

Worse yet, it's harder to talk to friends who are slacking, particularly if they're dyed-in-the-wool slackers. Most hardcore slackers tend to share a somewhat bizarre mode of thought that goes something like, "If you were really my friend, you wouldn't get on my case about this."

Of course, the obvious counterpoint to that is, "Well, if you were *my* friend, you wouldn't stick me with all the work," but slackers never think that way. What they *will* do is follow a clear pattern of stalling while they assure you that they're *going* to do it, and get angry at you when you tell them it needs to get done *now*, and eventually there will be a bitter fight where they will accuse you of being a fascist and a jerk.

This is not to say that you can't ask friends to help out, of course. But don't assume that, just because someone is your friend, he or she will be there for you. Take a close look at what your friend does in her or his off-time to see whether that person is reliable. Focus especially on the following:

- Has this person had good relationships with roommates in the past? (Danger signs include getting into fights over doing dishes, laundry, or paying the rent on time.)

- Has this person been moving from job to job over the past year? Has he or she been fired from more than one job?

- Does this friend describe all his or her bosses as big jerks who just bully him or her all the time? (Most people have had one or two bad bosses, but a steady string of them usually indicates that your buddy's the problem, not the bosses.)

- If this person is a student, has she or he been consistently late turning in classroom assignments (or always does them at the last possible minute)?

If the answer to any of these questions is "yes," you may want to think twice about asking this person to help out.

Ideally, what you're looking for is someone who's already doing the work without getting the bennies for it. Find someone who's staying after to help, who cleans things up without being asked, who calls beforehand to ask if there's anything you need. These helpful people tend to be quiet, reserved, and often shy.

Giving them a staff position lets them shine.

Assigning specific roles

If you're doing your LAN parties right, you start out small, filling multiple roles at once — you're not only the Techie, but you're also the Backbone Person and the Pizza Wizard. As your party slowly expands and you gain staff, however, specializing is the way to go.

Assigning specific people to specific tasks serves two purposes: First, it makes everyone else's responsibility a lot clearer. When someone's flailing for help and you're all in the middle of a gigantic push in *Battlefield 1942*, it's very easy for people to shrug and say, "Well, someone else can handle that." What happens is that because it's everyone's responsibility, it's no one's responsibility.

Now, that usually doesn't happen with tech support, because LAN parties are very sympathetic to people who can't play. But you'd be surprised how many staffers will find a way to ignore the garbage that's piling up or to just sort of "not hear" the phone ringing during a hot session. If it's the Receptionist or the Floor Sweeper, however, they will know that nobody else is going to do it for them. Worse yet, they'll know that you know.

The other benefit is that it takes less time overall. When you're the Floor Sweeper, you run around once an hour and pick up stuff. When you're the Receptionist, all you do is pick up the phone and check people in. Assigning specific roles allows people to minimize their time spent staffing, and prevents slackers from sitting on their butts all day.

One of the questions that frequently arises is, "How do you choose who does what task?" The answer is that ideally, you match personality to staffing role.

- If someone's a quiet sort who prefers chats on IRC to chats in real life, you probably want to give that person a position that doesn't involve a lot of person-to-person contact, such as the Backbone Person or the Equipment Wrangler. Conversely, if that person's the gregarious sort, he might be perfect for the Receptionist or the Pizza Wizard positions, which involve a lot of face-to-face time.

Tip

When choosing a position that involves a lot of people time, make sure that you don't choose someone who's *too* chatty. Yes, you want someone who's willing to engage in a lot of small talk and who will make your guests feel at home, but you don't want someone who gets so wrapped up in a conversation that he ignores new people walking through the door. Find someone who will be equally friendly to everyone, and who has a pretty good work ethic.

- When searching for people for the grunt jobs (namely, the Floor Sweeper, though the Equipment Wrangler can also be fairly tedious at times), you want to find someone who takes pride in getting things done. NASA calls this the "gardener personality" — a person who finds satisfaction in checking tasks off of lists . . . someone who enjoys a set routine that never varies.

    These people are rare at LAN parties, as most guests crave excitement, but look for quiet, reserved sorts. They usually have day jobs that most people would consider dull (or they get consistently good grades in school, even in classes they hate), and they tend to stay in jobs for a very long time. If you know someone who has held the same job for three years, chances are good that person would be an excellent Floor Sweeper.

- You can often find excellent Techies and Backbone People from the kibitzers — the people who wander up to you and start asking all sorts of questions about your setup, or who offer advice about how you could do things better.

    One potential problem here is that some of these folk are clueless, and are just looking for an opportunity to show off a technical knowledge that they may not actually have. (You'd be surprised how official someone can sound after reading one or two magazine articles.) But if someone's continually asking questions and can actually give useful advice that solves things (as opposed to discussing other technologies that *would* work well here, if you had them), then you might want to put that person to work for you.

- Party Moms just sort of happen. Look for people who naturally insert themselves into arguments, who go out of their way to soothe people's hurts. If you pay attention, you'll notice when that person finally arrives.

- A great way to handle whiners who continually moan that things aren't to their liking is to give them a position. If someone's always complaining about how lame the games are at your party, give this person the Dedicated Server Host position. Now your moaner can load up maps and tournament structures that *he or she* thinks are fun.

    If you do this, however, be wary of someone's biases. If someone's complaining about things that nobody else cares about ("These maps are too easy!"), then you might be harming the rest of the LAN party by putting this person in charge. Make sure someone has valid complaints before you think about promoting that person; some people just like to gripe.

In that same vein, if you promote a complainer into a position of power, make it very clear that he is responsible for making the party fun for *everyone*. Explain that now he has to consider more than just his own needs — that person has to consider the enjoyment of 15 other people and realize that not everyone loves the high-pressure, sniper-friendly maps that he's craving. Most people will see this as a challenge and go all-out in an attempt to cement their reputation as the greatest LAN party staffer ever.

Being grateful and gentle

It can be difficult to remember that your staffers are volunteers when it comes to getting work done, especially when you see them debating the fine points of Lightsaber battles when there are piles of BAWLS Guarana bottles and pizza boxes they should be cleaning.

But remember: You are not paying them anything (or if you are, chances are good it is a pittance). You must be firm in your request without crossing the line into yelling or ordering them about. It is a fine line to dance, but you must plant your feet upon the rope and tightwalk between "too bossy" and "too wussy."

The trick is to make everything seem like a favor (mostly because, well, it is). Instead of, "Hey, get those boxes!" try, "Can you pick up those pizza boxes for me and do a sweep of the room now? Thanks."

Note It's generally a good idea to provide a reasonable time frame with every request, as in, "Can you do that now?" or "Would you mind doing a room sweep in the next hour?" Not surprisingly, requests with a deadline get a better response than the generic requests.

If someone refuses or says he'll do it later, press firmly: "No, it really needs to be done right away. It'll only take a moment, and then you can get back to your chat."

And if the person *still* refuses? Let it go; make a note to take that person off the staff list for your next party, and then see if someone else will do it. Getting into a fight for control proves nothing, and if someone doesn't want to work you really can't force his hand.

Just make sure you don't have to deal with this again. It's important to send the message that nonprofessional behavior means that you won't be invited back.

On the plus side, you can make it a more pleasurable thing to be a staff member. Start the day with a cheerful introduction of your staffers, telling everyone what it is that each person is supposed to do — which not only tells everyone who to go to when they have a problem, but reminds all your guests that these people have jobs to do — and then ask for a big *hip-hip-hurrah!* to celebrate them. At the end of the party, thank your staffers publicly and ask for another cheer.

When someone does a good job, *compliment them*. You don't have to go overboard, but a pat on the shoulder and a quick "You handled that well" can go a long, long way.

In addition, make sure helpful staffers get free (or at least radically discounted) food. When you help someone move across town, the standard payment is pizza and a beer; the least you can do is give these folks a couple of slices for their trouble.

Standing behind your staff

Giving staffers free pizza and cheers means nothing if you don't back them up in what they do. If one of your staff members says that a guest is acting like an idiot, investigate and then kick the offending person out if they're right. If someone ignores the Floor Sweeper's requests, take immediate action.

Don't waffle, and don't tolerate disrespect to the people who are working for you. Remember: Your LAN party is not a democracy. It is an enlightened tyranny, and *you* are in charge.

Switching roles

People get bored when they do the same thing repeatedly. There are a couple of ways to alleviate that.

For one, you can switch people's jobs and try to rotate the uninteresting ones. The Floor Sweeper and the Pizza Wizard are not glamorous jobs, so giving people a new assignment at every party can help alleviate some of the boredom.

A better idea is to meld jobs, training the Floor Sweeper to become a backup Techie. (Although training a Techie to become a Floor Sweeper might be kind of insulting.) Laying out the LAN is always fascinating for people who don't know much about networking, so explaining how things work is a good hook to get people involved. If you can, arrange it so that they're learning something.

Two, if you have a large pool of people to work with, don't just switch jobs — switch *people*. As mentioned, people tend to work really hard the first time, and then slack off. Therefore, only have someone work a staff shift once every two or three parties, and try to cultivate new members to serve on the Scut Team. Tell them to think of it as their civic duty.

Sucking up to techies effectively

You can get anybody to hand out cans of Red Bull, but finding someone who can rig up an emergency Internet connection out of a cell phone, a ball of waxed string, and two tin cans?

Actually, it's not that difficult. After all, you're running the kind of event that gearheads are drawn to! If you hold a couple of open LAN parties, techies will begin to show up naturally, for LAN parties are a classic techie recreational activity. (If no techies are showing up, perhaps you're not publicizing the event enough to get the attention of your local tech guys. If that's the case, I suggest looking at Chapter 5, "Saving Money on Your LAN Party," which discusses PR.) Actually keeping techies around to consistently do work for you is of the highest priority, because they're the people who can make your LAN party sing.

In addition to all of the preceding ideas for keeping your staff happy, here are a few tricks to keep your hackers working hard:

- Don't abuse their skills
- Encourage experimentation
- Get more techies

The following sections examine each of these hints.

Not abusing their skills

True, techies know more than you do. But chances are good that they work with computers for a living, and they probably don't want to spend their time playing tech support somewhere else. Calling them over every time a problem comes up (which drags them away from their game) is sure to eventually alienate your techies.

If you have a problem, try to handle it yourself first. If you're stumped, *then* go for your big guns, but even then, explain to them what you did to try to fix it first. Never make it seem like you're making them do the work because you're too lazy to figure it out yourself.

Encouraging experimentation

Many hackers share a love for trying out the latest and greatest technical advances — a love that is not usually encouraged at their jobs. Tell your techies to consider your LAN party their experimental laboratory, where they can expand their skills and try out new things. Not all techies want this — some of them just want to play — but many will look upon having their own mini-network to fool around with as a challenge.

The only downside is that sometimes their latest experiment can go down in flames. Remind them that while they can add whatever doo-dads they like around the fringes, the core networking and gaming part of the party has to keep running smoothly. A good compromise is to have one network segment be "the experiment zone" while the rest of it remains unaffected.

Getting more techies

There's a reason why local user groups are so popular; nothing makes a hardcore hacker happier than having someone to debate with. Where else can they carry on a spirited face-to-face debate about the merits of routing protocols?

It sounds silly, but one of the best ways to get and keep techies is to get more of them. Once you achieve critical mass, you may well wind up with all of the hackers in town; everyone loves a party!

Summary

In this chapter, you examined one of the most important parts of hosting LAN parties — getting people (even if that "people" is just you) to pitch in and help everyone have a great time. Dealing with people can be exhausting at times because there's no Ctrl+Alt+Delete, but most of the time it works out just fine.

In the next chapter, you'll be learning about another very important part of many LAN parties: the *dedicated server*, which enables mid- to large-size parties to run smoothly.

Setting Up a Dedicated Game Server

There are two ways you can set up a server to function, although only one works for larger parties:

➤ **Nondedicated (sometimes known as *Listen* mode).** With this type of setup, not only can you host a game, you can play at that computer. This sounds great — until you realize that your PC is most likely maxed out just from running a single-player game. Asking it to keep track of six or seven other players *and* send out constant messages *and* update your screen 30 times a second with fabulous 3D graphics is enough to make almost any machine stutter. And most of them will.

Unfortunately, when computer games become overloaded, they tend to prioritize things so that the local player's game runs smoothly, sometimes waiting hundreds of milliseconds before getting around to tending to requests from remote PCs. This processing delay is, for all intents and purposes, the exact same thing as a bad ping time — the exact thing you're supposed to be *avoiding* when you hold a LAN party! And since one person at your party (the person at that machine) experiences no lag while everyone else is suffering, it can lead to some real bad blood in a competitive environment.

➤ **Dedicated.** With this setup, your computer skips producing any fancy graphics. Instead, it dedicates all of its processing power to keeping track of where everyone is and who's shot who, and broadcasting that information back to all of its clients ASAP.

In other words, dedicated servers are the only way to go.

Am I Biased?

When I sent preliminary copies of this book to my friends to get some feedback, the number one complaint that I heard went something like this:

"Ferrett, I hold small LAN parties all the time. I use servers in Listen mode and I *never* have problems with them. Why are you so hard on nondedicated servers?"

Now, me, I've had bad experiences with nondedicated servers, but I am willing to admit that not every party needs one—especially smaller, first-time parties for which procuring a separate PC may be a real problem. Parties with eight or fewer people can most likely get by with a server in listen mode, assuming the server is a fast one.

However, if you do have a spare computer to use, even at a small party, I think that putting in a dedicated server is never a bad idea.

What Kind of Computer Should You Use As a Server?

Because you want to have fast processing and response, you now know that you want a computer that does nothing but act as a server. The next question is invariably, "So how fast should it be?"

The answer is almost invariably, "As fast as it would take to run the game itself, plus as much extra as you can spare." Dedicated server programs are notorious resource hogs. That said, it still doesn't really answer the core questions: How much RAM and how fast a processor?

Sadly, I can't say. It would be nice if I could give you a hard formula to determine what your players-to-RAM ratio is, but player overhead varies from game to game. Each additional player burns up a few megahertz on your processor and takes up some RAM. However, there are some general rules:

- In general, the more players there are, the more server resources are spent. A top-of-the-line game on a top-of-the-line machine will likely struggle to keep up with 30 players.

- Older games (such as *Counter-Strike*) require fewer resources than a new eye-popping game, such as *Tron 2.0*. Thus, you might be able to get away with an older machine for older games, or host a lot more players on a top-of-the-line machine with an older game. A new game on an older machine can be death.

- Mods and custom maps use up more server resources. Generally, the maps that come with a game are optimized for the game's engine. Custom mods and maps, which are written by fans, either push the envelope of the game's engine or are written without concern for optimization—or sometimes both. As a result, heavily customized maps tend to be more of a drain.

Most of the time, it's safer to just bring out the machine with the best processor and a boatload of RAM. Fortunately, having a top-of-the-line graphics card doesn't matter as much when the game's graphics are reduced to a command-line window, so you can often get away with a lesser rig, but don't ever use the *worst* computer in the room.

Unlike Internet servers, you don't have to worry about running out of bandwidth. The average cable modem can support 20 players max, but even with a puny 10 Mbps hookup, you've got 10 times as much bandwidth to work with.

Dedicated Servers

Though most programs will allow you to start up a game server from within the game itself, that's usually wasteful. When you start up the game in single-player mode and then put it into server mode, you generally load a lot of useless stuff into memory that could be used to host more players — for example, since the server is never going to actually put any graphics on screen, does it need to load all of those graphics routines into memory?

As such, most popular games (but not all) have a *dedicated server program* — a stripped-down and optimized version of the game that is used *only* for hosting. Some games have the dedicated server program installed with the normal game, leaving you with the job of finding it buried in some strange directory, but most of the time you'll have to hunt it down on the Internet.

Tip

While you can Google up the location of a dedicated server, I find www.fileplanet.com to be the quickest one-stop shop for dedicated servers. You may have to wait for half an hour before you can download (at least, that's the case for their non-premium servers; they offer no-wait servers for a fee), but I've never had Fileplanet drop a connection halfway through a 150 MB download. This *has* happened to me, however, when downloading dedicated servers from the official sites — especially right after a hot game has been released and the company's FTP servers are being hammered with requests from all over the world. In addition, Fileplanet always has the latest patches and dedicated servers.

Variations on Dedicated Server Programs Are Practically Endless

Every game's dedicated server program has its own quirks, so it would be impossible to cover them all here. If I made this book 700 pages long, I *might* be able to cram in tutorials on all of the popular games, but then a new wave of releases would come out and this book would be out of date.

Right now, as this chapter is written, the most popular online games are *Counter-Strike*, *Battlefield 1942*, *Castle Wolfenstein*, *America's Army*, and *Unreal Tournament 2003*. That's sure to change as soon as this book is released. Computer games wait for no one. *Doom 3*, *Battlefield Vietnam*, and *Half-Life 2* are sure to be popular, but I obviously can't give you tutorials on games that haven't been released at the time that I write this!

Right now, you can look for the programs described above at the following sites — they're relatively stable sites, but there are no guarantees that these links will always be around:

Continued

Continued

- **Counter-Strike Dedicated Server Tutorial:** `server.counter-strike.net/server.php?cmd=howto`

- **Battlefield 1942 Dedicated Server Tutorial:** `www.planetbattlefield.com/bf1942/game/server/guide.shtml`

- **Castle Wolfenstein Dedicated Server Tutorial:** `www.planetwolfenstein.com/server`

- **America's Army Dedicated Server Tutorial:** `syntechsoftware.com/ST07052002P.php`

- **Unreal Tournament 2003 Dedicated Server Tutorial:** `www.unrealadmin.org/modules.php?name=Sections&op=listarticles&secid=5`

In this chapter, I'll be using the most popular LAN party game, *Counter-Strike* (which, in case you didn't know, is a popular game mod based on the *Half-Life* engine), to demonstrate many of the *principles* of dedicated server configuration. Alas, to know the *specifics* of *your* game's dedicated server program, you'll have to read the documentation.

Changing Settings on Your Dedicated Server Program

There are two ways to change the settings on your dedicated server program: via a *command-line interface* or a *graphical interface*. That's just a fancy way of saying "You can type in commands" (command-line) or "You can use your mouse to change the settings in a Windows dialog box" (graphical). Every server program has a command-line interface that enables you to change the server's setup, but not all of them have a graphical interface, which is a shame, because the graphical programs are much easier to use.

We'll start with the tricky one first: command-line interfaces.

Command-Line interfaces: Nonintuitive, but powerful

A command-line interface does not use the mouse. It provides no pretty graphics, just an old-fashioned terminal screen that looks something like what is shown in Figure 12-1.

So how do you control something that doesn't give you user-friendly graphical menus? You do it the old-fashioned way (and one that Linux users are long used to): You start it from the *command-line interface*, typing in a name at a Windows command prompt instead of choosing it from the Start menu. If you want to run the dedicated server program with certain settings, you type the name of the program (also known as the *command*), and then feed it several *parameters*, which tell your computer how the program should be started.

In very simplistic terms, let's use the analogy of ordering a sandwich from a deli. The order "Give me a ham sandwich" would be the command, and "hold the mayo" would be the parameter that indicates how the sandwich is presented.

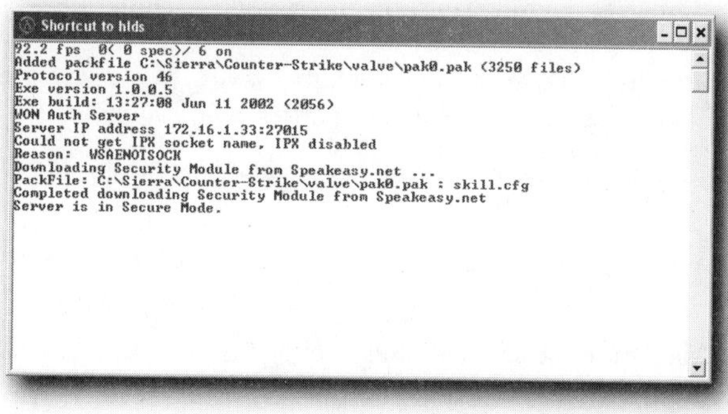

FIGURE 12-1: *Counter-Strike* HLDS.exe, the command-line interface for *Half-Life* and *Counter-Strike*

Note

Where is the command prompt? On Linux, the command prompt is usually your default option. In Windows, you need to select Run from the Start menu and then type **cmd.exe**. On some versions of Windows, you can also find the command prompt on the Start menu under Accessories ⇨ Command Prompt.

This example might be a little *too* simplistic. Therefore, let's use a real-life gaming example to demonstrate. If you wanted to start up the *Counter-Strike* dedicated server program, you might type the following at the Windows command prompt:

```
C:\Program Files\Sierra\Half-Life\hlds.exe -game cstrike +map
weaselhunt +maxplayers 16
```

In one very long line, you have started up the *Half-Life* dedicated server program (hlds.exe); and without selecting a single menu item, you have already told the program that you want to start it up with the *Counter-Strike* mod (-game cstrike), the weaselhunt map (+map weaselhunt), with a maximum number of 16 players (+maxplayers 16).

Command-line interfaces allow for an often staggering array of options; for example, there are 144 parameters you can use to customize the games on your *Counter-Strike Half-Life* dedicated server alone!

For the Technologically Impaired

The C:\Program Files\Sierra\Half-Life\ part of the command is the path to the dedicated server program—the way your computer knows in which folder the program can be found. Paths are a fairly elementary portion of computer configuration, and I'm assuming that you understand how they work. If not, check out the *Windows for Dummies* series, which is excellent for beginners.

Some *Counter-Strike* parameters, such as the following, are obvious and helpful:

- **-nomaster**: Prevents your LAN *Counter-Strike* server from trying to verify its presence with an official *Half-Life* WON server; critical if your party has no Internet access

- **+mp_autocrosshair 1**: Allows the use of autoaim crosshairs (mp_autocrosshair 0 will disallow their use)

- **+mp_falldamage 1**: Activates realistic falling damage (mp_falldamage 0 will deactivate it)

- **+mp_flashlight 1**: Allows the use of the flashlight (mp_flashlight 0 will ensure that players can't use the flashlight)

- **+mp_footsteps 1**: Activates footstep sounds (mp_footsteps 0 will deactivate them)

- **+mp_forcerespawn 1**: Players will automatically respawn when killed (mp_forcerespawn 0 will deactivate this)

- **+mp_fraglimit <number>**: Whenever a player reaches this number of frags, the map will change

- **+mp_timelimit <number>**: Sets the time, in minutes, between map changes

- **+mp_weaponstay 1**: Weapons will remain on the field after a player picks them up (mp_weaponstay 0 will disallow)

- **+hostname <name>**: Enables customization of the name of your server from the default of "Counter-Strike 1.0 server" to, say, "Ferrett's Amazing Lan-O-Matic Frag Machine"

- **+sv_aim 1**: Allows the use of autoaim. (sv_aim 0 will disallow the use of autoaim)

- **+sv_airmove 1**: Allows players to move in midair (sv_airmove 0 will prevent players from moving in midair)

- **+sv_cheats 0**: Disallows cheat codes

- **+sv_friction <number>**: Sets the friction in the games (larger numbers equal more friction)

- **+sv_gravity <number>**: Sets the gravity in the games (larger numbers equal heavier gravity)

Some are less useful, but may occasionally come in handy:

- **+mapcyclefile <name>**: The name refers to a text file that lists the maps this server's games will cycle through. (If you do not enter this parameter, the default file is mapcycle.txt, which is explained in a bit.)

- **+hostport <number>**: Sets the port that players will use to connect to this computer. If you're concerned about security issues, you may wish to change the port number so that unauthorized players won't know where to break in.

Cross-Reference

If you don't know what a port is or why you'd alter it, see Chapter 8, "Networking for Large Groups and the Internet."

- `+mp_decals <number>`: Sets the maximum number of wall spatters (blood, bullet holes, burn marks) visible at any time. Lowering this number may help speed up slower servers.

- `+filterban 1`: Allows you to ban an IP address.

And some are just plain obscure:

- `+decalfrequency <seconds>`: Sets how often a player can display his logo

- `+sv_netsize <number>`: Sets the maximum network packet size

- `+sv_skyname <name>`: Sets the sky texture

- `+sv_stepsize <number>`: Sets how easy it is for a player to climb up slopes

You can mix and match these parameters to create extremely customized games. Again, using *Counter-Strike* as an example, type in the following:

```
C:\Program Files\Sierra\Half-Life\hlds.exe -game cstrike -nomaster
+map weaselhunt +mp_timelimit 10 +mapcyclefile mymaps.txt
+maxplayers 20 +mp_weaponstay 0 +mp_forcerespawn 1 +sv_cheats 0
```

This will start up a LAN-based (-nomaster) *Counter-Strike* game (-game cstrike) that begins with the weaselhunt map (+map weaselhunt), and then switches to another map after 10 minutes (+mp_timelimit 10), getting the next map to use from a custom file I've created (+mapcyclefile mymaps.txt). When players die on this server, they will get back into action immediately (+mp_forcerespawn 1), and when a weapon is picked up, it will remain on the ground for others to use (+mp_weaponstay 0). No more than 20 players will be able to connect to this server (+maxplayers 20), and no cheat codes will be used (+sv_cheats 0)!

Don't Use These Parameters for Other Programs!

Remember that these are all *Counter-Strike*-specific parameters; I'm just using them as an example to show you how parameters work. (It also doesn't hurt that *Counter-Strike* is one of the most popular LAN party games out there, and you'll probably have to learn to configure it sooner or later.) Every game has its own specific parameters for configuring its dedicated server, and you should look them up.

For the record, dedicated server documentation does not usually come with a game, unless the game has an *exceptionally* good manual. You usually have to look up the parameters online. Try Googling "*<Name of Game>* dedicated server tutorial" or "*<Name of Game>* dedicated server options" for help.

Making long commands easier

As you can see, some of these command-line commands can get downright Byzantine when you're inputting a lot of parameters! Typing three-line commands repeatedly can be frustrating, especially when one wrong keystroke can send the entire program into a tizzy. For example, if you mistakenly type +map `waselhunt` instead of +map `weaselhunt`, you will watch the program choke as it tries to load a nonexistent map.

There are four ways to preload your server's configuration:

- Icons
- Configuration files
- Up arrow
- Shell scripts

The following sections examine each of these.

Using icons

Right-click a shortcut on your desktop and you'll see a pop-up menu that looks something like the one shown in Figure 12-2. (Select Properties to see a whole new dialog box, which you can skip ahead to see in Figure 12-3.)

FIGURE 12-2: Selecting properties from a shortcut menu

In the dialog box that appears after you choose Properties from the pop-up menu, you'll see a field called Target. That's actually a command. Shortcuts are just tiny, um, shortcuts to command lines that save you time; in fact, they've been so successful that most people have forgotten that the command line even exists!

Note

Shortcuts are the icons with tiny arrows in the left-hand corner. If an icon doesn't have one of those arrows, it's merely an icon and these tricks won't work.

Double-clicking a shortcut to start a program is *exactly the same* as starting up a command prompt, typing in whatever is in that shortcut's Target field, and pressing Enter. (Obviously, double-clicking is a *lot* quicker.)

Therefore, you can add parameters to a shortcut's Target field to make it start up a program with customized settings. You do it as follows:

1. Right-click the dedicated server program's shortcut and select Copy.

Tip

What do you do if your program has no shortcut? If you have a program on your Start menu, you can drag it off the menu and onto your desktop to create a shortcut. Otherwise, you can right-click on an empty space on your desktop and select New ⇨ Shortcut.

2. Find an empty space on the desktop, right-click, and select Paste Shortcut.

3. Right-click the new shortcut icon and select Properties. (If that doesn't bring it up automatically, you'll need to select the Shortcut tab.)

4. Change the Target field to whatever command you want to enter; for example,
   `C:\Program Files\Sierra\Half-Life\hlds.exe -game cstrike +map weaselhunt +maxplayers 16`.

It should look something like what is shown in Figure 12-3.

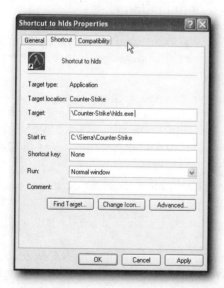

FIGURE 12-3: Shortcut tab of the Properties dialog box

From now on, whenever you double-click this shortcut, it will automatically start up your dedicated server with the appropriate parameters.

Using configuration files

In many games, the default settings for the game are stored in *configuration files,* small text files that the server program reads upon startup. These configuration files are usually little more than lists of parameters, and you can edit them.

Continuing with our amazing lust for *Counter-Strike,* I'll use it to provide you with examples of some of the issues that can arise with configuration files. In *Counter-Strike,* you can alter four files, which offer four lessons that will help you with *any* game that has configuration files:

- `server.cfg`
- `autoexec.cfg`
- `mapcycle.txt`
- `motd.txt`

The following sections examine each of these in turn.

server.cfg

This file is reread automatically whenever the map changes, and it's where you place parameters that affect individual games, such as whether weapons refresh after you've picked them up and whether realistic falling damage is enabled.

The Dangers of Editing Configuration Files

Configuration files are critical to a game program's well-being, and it's fairly easy to mistype something that causes the entire game to crash or act strangely. Therefore, there are three things you always want to do when altering configuration files:

- **Always save configuration files as text**. If you save them in a nontext format, the server program won't be able to read them and Bad Things Will Happen. Don't use Word or WordPad to alter a configuration file, because frequently those programs put in additional formatting that interferes with the game's ability to read it; *only* open and save configuration files with Notebook or Vi or some other text-only program.

- **Always back up the configuration files before you alter them**. This isn't a big deal; just use your operating system's copy command to put copies of your original configuration files in some other directory. Should you accidentally screw up the original files, you have pristine working copies you can put back in.

- **Be careful when typing, and look carefully at your server documentation**. As already noted, sometimes putting a parameter in the wrong place can cause very strange things to happen. Make sure you've read the official documentation, or at the very least have skimmed a good game-specific tutorial.

In order to run a LAN server (*Counter-Strike* defaults to try to run as an Internet server), you'll need to add the lines `sv_lan 1` and `sv_updaterate 100` to server.cfg.

The lesson: Sometimes you have to alter the configuration files (or parameters) to optimize your server for LAN party play. Many games default to starting up as an Internet-based server, which can cause problems at LAN parties without Internet access; an Internet-based dedicated server will often attempt to access a *master server* on the Internet and log in to it, and then fail when it cannot register.

autoexec.cfg

This file is run once upon startup and never looked at again, and it's where you place global commands such as `maxplayers` and the starting `map`.

Be aware, however, that *Counter-Strike* considers the `map` command to be the final line in the `autoexec.cfg` file, regardless of where the `map` command actually is. If other commands appear after the `map` command, the server program will ignore them. Thus, you *must* make the `map` command your final line in `autoexec.cfg`.

The lesson: Actually, there are *three* universal lessons to be learned here:

First, it's often critical to have the parameters in configuration files listed in a very specific order. Read your dedicated server's documentation for details to determine whether you must follow any rules.

Second, `autoexec.cfg` is not created by default. You have to create your own text file, save it as `autoexec.cfg`, and put it in the `cstrike` directory. Some programs function just fine without configuration files, but will use them if you create them.

Third, `autoexec.cfg` isn't very useful. Because all you can put in it are parameters that run once at startup, it's usually easier to just give it the parameters on the command line and be done with it. Just because you *can* do something with a configuration file doesn't necessarily mean that it's a *good* idea.

mapcycle.txt

This file is a list of map files through which the server rotates. Unless it's told otherwise with a specific `map` command, the server's first game starts with the first map listed here, and goes on to the next map listed whenever a new map is called for. When it gets to the end of the list, it cycles back to the top.

Though *Half-Life* maps end in .bsp, you do not list the .bsp suffix when listing maps in `mapcycle.txt`. Therefore, if you wanted to add `weaselhunt.bsp` to your list of maps, you would simply list it as `weaselhunt`. This isn't particularly intuitive.

The lesson: Sometimes configuration files require you to type things in very specific ways; a small typo or extra words can cause the entire configuration to break or act strangely. If you were to type `weaselhunt.bsp` into `mapcycle.txt`, for example, your server would play `hldm1` (the default map) instead of the maps you thought you had chosen.

motd.txt

This is where the *message of the day* is stored — the message that players see whenever they first log on to the server. This message frequently lists the rules of conduct or useful contact information, and the amount of time players are forced to see it is contained in the `motd_display_time` parameter in the server.cfg file.

The lesson: Well, there really isn't one here. Move along.

<table>
<tr><td>**Note**</td><td>Keep in mind that this is just an example from the most popular LAN party game, to show you how it can be done. Many games have only one or two configuration files, and some have none at all. Consult your dedicated server documentation for details.</td></tr>
</table>

Using the up arrow

If you have typed in a lengthy command and screwed it up, you can always press the up arrow. For both the Windows command prompt and most versions of Linux, pressing the up arrow will repeat your last command but will not input it; instead, it stays on the line waiting for you to press enter. This allows you to use the left arrow to go back and edit your botched command.

Incidentally, you can press the up and down arrows repeatedly to cycle through the commands that you've already typed in. This can come in extremely handy when you're doing maintenance work.

Using shell scripts

If you're dealing with an exclusively command-line program such as Linux (or, to be technically correct, Linux without a windowing program), you may not be able to use icons. You can, however, use *shell scripts* — small text files that store larger commands.

The quick-and-dirty procedure is as follows:

1. Use a text editor such as vi, emacs, or pico to write the command as you would like it to be executed.

2. Save the command with a memorable name.

3. Tell your Linux operating system to recognize your script as an executable file by typing **chmod 755** *<script name>*.

4. To execute the script from now on, type *./<script name>*.

Graphical interfaces: Easier, most of the time

Many newer games now come with user-friendly dedicated server programs that have actual windows and pretty screens.

This is a godsend to server admins, because graphical interfaces are intuitive and easy to start up. You simply click the appropriate buttons and things get done. This is as good as it gets — and really, do you need to be told, "Click the right buttons and press OK when you're done"?

Unfortunately, a lot of dedicated servers are still mired in the Land of Command Lines, but the geek community being what it is, someone's always willing to write a shareware program that provides a graphical or a Web-based interface to a dedicated server program. If you hunt around the fan sites, you'll usually be able to find a server administration program you can install to avoid dealing with command lines, as in Figure 12-4.

The Dark Side of Shareware Tools

Shareware administration tools are written and distributed for free, by enthusiasts. As such, they can be buggy—and sometimes the person who's been fixing the bugs will suddenly quit. Furthermore, because they're fan-created, they may not be available until a month or two after a game's release. And last, they're sometimes extremely hard to install.

The lesson: Shareware tools can be tremendously handy, but don't get addicted to them. They might not be there when you need them.

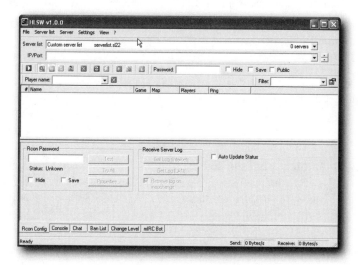

FIGURE 12-4: HLSW, a Counter-Strike server admin tool

Be aware that graphical administration tools don't *replace* the command line; instead, they usually serve as an add-on program that hands off the parameters to the command line and rewrites the configuration files *for* you. Under normal circumstances, a graphical administration tool won't do anything that you can't do on the command line—and they usually do less.

That's not to say that graphical administration programs can't be handy; they are! Assuming that you don't need to configure your server extensively (and most people don't), then they'll do the job just fine. If you ever need to roll up your hands and start really tweaking settings, however, then remember that the command line interface lies underneath it all, waiting patiently for the day you might need it.

Configuring on the fly: Remote administration

All of this is great when the server starts up, but what happens when you start fragging? Sometimes you need to boot some jerk off your server, or want to change the way the game is played, and it's a pain to have to keep moving back and forth between your client computer and your server computer. What you need is some form of remote administration, so that you can control your server from another computer.

Fortunately, this is usually built right into the dedicated server software — after all, these games are meant to be played on the Internet! A lot of games are hosted on servers that are hundreds of miles away, and it would be mighty inconvenient if you had to catch a plane to Detroit just to boot a player.

However, server programs won't let just anyone log on — in fact, for security purposes, most of them are configured to refuse remote administration requests by default. You'll usually have to do one of two things before you can administer a server remotely:

- Start up the server program with a parameter that tells it to allow remote administration requests (and often this parameter requires you to enter an administrator's password).

- Change a configuration file on the server itself so that it accepts remote requests. This is slightly more secure, and it also requires that you set a password.

Exactly like the dedicated server interfaces, remote administration is handled in one of two ways: graphical interfaces and command-line interfaces. But just to make things more complex, it's usually *easier* to use the command-line interface to change a server's settings once a game is in progress.

The following section explains why.

Controlling a server remotely from the command line

To start up a server program, you have to use the Windows or Linux command line. To *administer* a server program, however, you usually have to use the *game's* command-line interface. Most games have a drop-down command line, which is accessed by pressing the tilde (~) key when you're playing the game, as shown in Figure 12-5.

This is handy because it enables you to change the server settings without having to exit the game or switch to a Windows command prompt.

Caution

A game will not stop when you bring up its command-line interface! If you're concerned with boosting your frag count, don't start changing server settings in the middle of a game.

Usually, you have to type in a command that logs you on to the server as an administrator. In *Counter-Strike*, for example, that command is rcon <password>, and in *Battlefield 1942*, that command is admin.enableremoteadmin <password>.

After that, you will generally have to preface each server command with some administrative-sounding junk so that your local machine knows to forward the request to the server. For example, to boot a player off of a *Counter-Strike* server, you would type **rcon kick <playername>**, whereas in *Battlefield 1942*, you'd type **admin.execremotecommand "admin.kickPlayer <player id#>"**.

If you have multiple servers to administer (or if a server is full and you need access without logging in), you can generally connect to each server by typing in its IP address — for example, in *Counter-Strike*, you can type **rcon <IP address>**, then **rcon_port <port #>**, and finally **rcon_password <password>**.

FIGURE 12-5: *Return to Castle Wolfenstein* command-line screen

There are many commands, but most of them are related to keeping track of users, changing maps, and changing game settings.

Caution

Be aware that not all parameters are useful as console commands, and vice versa; for example, using +map <mapname> while you're *starting* a *Counter-Strike* server will start up that server with the named map. Typing **rcon map <mapname>** at the console, however, will kick everyone off the server and then restart it with that map. The command you're probably looking for is changelevel <mapname>.

Graphical programs

Many games come with remote server administration tools you can install, just like any other program. They generally involve a similar process of starting up the remote server manager, inputting the IP address (and sometimes the port number) of the server, and typing in the administrative password. From there on, you'll be able to change settings on your server just as if you had a normal graphical interface.

Summary

Dedicated servers are a useful part of almost every LAN party. They can be a slight pain to set up properly sometimes, but once you get them running, they're usually pain-free—and they make everything so much faster. It is hoped that in the future, more games will be developed with graphical dedicated server programs, but for the time being, the command line still rules.

In the next chapter, you'll learn what to do on the day of the party. Let's go!

The Complete Day-of-the Party Timeline

You've done your planning, you've called your pals to borrow the equipment, and last night you got together with a couple of friends and set up the actual LAN. Today, actual *people* will be showing up, and it's up to you to get them all seated and logged on.

If you've done your homework from Chapter 4, "The Complete Preparty Timeline," you've done all of the prep work that will enable you to hold the party—in fact, Chapter 4 covers everything you need to do, right up until the night before the party. Now it's time to deal with the actual day of the party, and this chapter shows you what happens when a typical LAN party begins—the flow and structure of a good LAN party, what can go wrong, and how you can set up things to make your party flow smoothly.

Unlike Chapter 4, this chapter is mostly intended for larger LAN parties. Although you will be able to find tidbits of information stashed away in this chapter that can prove useful for the small party, most smaller parties consist of "Set up computers, order pizza at some point during the day, and clean up after everyone's gone."

When you start adding more people to a party, however—say, more than 10 people or so—you really do need to start codifying how you do everything. Informal procedures work well for small groups in which you can talk to everyone, but they fall apart at larger levels, seeding parties with ugly delays and miscommunications. This chapter shows you how larger LAN parties work so that you can get an idea of the flow of medium to large LAN parties. Fortunately, wrangling even a large LAN party isn't that hard, though there *are* a lot of niggling details that need to be handled. In this chapter, I'll give you a general timeline of the things you need to do on the day of your party, from the last-minute double-checking and pep rally to the often-tedious breakdown at the end of the day.

Hear that? That's the knock at your door. Your first guest is here, so let's get started!

The Three Types of Parties

I'll be honest: This chapter's not for everyone. Therefore, consider the kind of party you want to hold to see how relevant this information is likely to be for your situation.

You and a few friends (fewer than 10 people)

If you've read this far, chances are good you know what you need to do, and with so few people, there's no need to write up a checklist. Yes, you still need to get your friends seated in the right places, go over the rules, and clean up at the end of the evening (and you probably should clean up once or twice during the event), but that can all be done informally.

Small LAN parties tend to be like any other small party; you spend the morning cleaning up the house and buying potato chips, but the actual party itself doesn't need a whole lot of structure. If you're bored, you just shout out that you want to play *Neverwinter Nights* for a while, and hopefully everyone agrees with you. If you want pizza, you just say, "Hey, can we get some pizza?"

Considering that playing it by ear is a lot easier than everything I'll be discussing later in this chapter, I strongly suggest that you *keep* it informal for as long as you can. A couple of friends hanging out and playing *Warcraft III* is a lot less work than a formalized LAN party.

Inviting the entire neighborhood (10 to 30 people)

In these mid-size groups, chances are good that you still know everyone by name, but at some point, you hit a critical mass where just letting your friends check in becomes inefficient. The tables are all mapped out, but you're only one person, and people are setting up in the wrong places while you're checking someone else in; while you're fixing that, everyone else is waiting for the rest of the party to begin. How soon you hit the wall depends on the overall independence and responsibility of your social group, but you'll know it when it happens. It's signified by multiple power outages, a lot of networking errors, and tedious post-party cleanups.

It's not a bad idea to start formalizing things before you hit that wall, in order to keep everything running smoothly. You don't have to be an iron-fisted dictator, but a couple of light rules and check-in procedures can help keep everyone in line.

The megaparty (30+ people)

This chapter's made for you. You are most likely setting up at an external location and are charging admission, which means that you don't have a lot of control over who shows up. In addition, you have a lot of staff out there, and legal issues become more of a concern.

We're now ready to look at how most LAN parties proceed.

Before People Arrive: The Setup

Ideally, you've laid out the network and secured the physical space the night before, as I suggested in Chapter 4, "The Complete Preparty Timeline." On the big day, you want to arrive about a half hour early just to make sure everything's ready. Specifically, you want to ensure that two critical things are ready.

The last-minute double-check

Look around the party space to make sure your handiwork is still standing. Check the power, the phone lines, the cables, the Internet connection, and anything else you have organized. Make sure the soda's cold, and that nobody has noshed on the chips. Verify that you have change ready if you're charging admission.

If you arrive early, then you have time to fix things if something has gone awry or you've over-looked something. If you leave everything until the last minute, you're doomed.

The preparty staff talk

If you have more than one staffer, have them show up early so you can talk with them, as shown in Figure 13-1. The talk can be informal (as it frequently is at mid-sized parties) or it can be a big speech before a crowd of seven to eight people, but the talk serves two purposes: It gets people excited and it helps them to understand what's expected of them.

Remember that staffing isn't nearly as fun as fragging, so take this time to get your staff excited and thrilled about helping out.

FIGURE 13-1: Ferrett gives the line to his staff. They are, as usual, listening attentively.

Many people, particularly techies, see this sort of jocular enthusiasm as a Dilbertesque mind-lessness, and are loath to actually show excitement lest they be tagged as a marketroid. Their speeches tend to be low-key, glumly accurate, and mostly ineffective. You don't have to take the smiley-faced zombie approach of flight attendants and sales reps, where *everything* is a wonder-ful thing and we're all so *happy*, but the reason why managers try to get people involved in company cheer is because it *works*. If you can get your staff looking forward to the day of the event, you're halfway to a great party.

Pump the fist. Talk about the day as if it were going to be the best ever. You'd be surprised how infectious this approach is.

The speech itself usually involves the following parts:

1. **"Gosh, you folks are great."** These people are helping you out, and you take this moment to tell them how much you appreciate it. (If the party is starting in the morn-ing, this is when someone makes a joke along the lines of, "If you really think we're great, then why did you make us get up early?" Laugh and move on.) Remind them that this party, at which a lot of people are going to be having fun, could not happen without them, and that makes them really great people. (This is, incidentally, 100 percent true.)

2. **"Here's who does what" or "Joe, you'll be handling tech support today."** This is where you discuss who will be filling what roles during the party, and what's expected of them.

For more information on the common roles at LAN parties, refer to Chapter 11, "Staffing Issues and Common LAN Party Roles."

3. **"I expect everyone to follow these procedures . . ."** If you have a specific way that you want people doing things (such as using a checklist to get everyone seated and escorting new visitors to their seats), tell them now.

4. **"The issues I think may come up today are . . ."** If you think there may be problems, spell them out in advance and let everyone know what to do. (Of course, if you *know* there are going to be problems, why not fix them now?)

5. **"This is going to be the best party ever!"** Finish up your talk and set 'em loose! At many parties, this is where people do high-fives and cheer. It's really not a bad idea.

A Law I'd Like to See Enacted

If someone hosting a party requires the staff to come to a morning meeting and does not have coffee and doughnuts waiting when people get there, I personally believe that the death penalty is the only appropriate response. If you're hauling people out of bed, spend the 20 bucks to spring for refreshments, would ya?

They're Heeere! (What to Do When People Arrive)

As your guests begin to trickle in, your LAN party begins. The goal, obviously, is to get everyone set up and fragging ASAP so that you can spend the rest of your time blissfully blasting everything in sight. How do you accomplish that?

Actually, you can get that done in two parts. The *check-in procedures* help your guests to get oriented with a minimum of fuss, and the *party announcements* help your guests to understand what is expected of them at this event, which could prove invaluable in the rare case of any legal issue arising.

Let's start with the point of entry: the check-in.

Check-in procedures

There are few things more embarrassing than wandering into a LAN party and looking around cluelessly, not knowing who you're supposed to talk to. Therefore, *every event* should have a place with a big sign that says "Check-In" so that everyone knows who's in charge of this thing, and with whom they should speak if they have any problems.

At smaller parties, the check-in station can be just a sign over your personal computer, but at larger parties, you should set up a dedicated check-in table with a dedicated staffer present at all times to take people's money, give them the rules of setup, and handle any difficulties that come up.

("Dedicated," incidentally, means that this person is not playing a game, or at the very least is playing a game that he or she can pause at will. A check-in table where someone has to wait 15 minutes to check in is Bad News; your check-in staffer should make eye contact with every person who walks through the door in order to invite them in.)

 Cross-Reference For further musings on LAN party staff roles and the sort of person you want as Receptionist, see Chapter 11, "Staffing Issues and Common LAN Party Roles."

Whatever you decide to use, the check-in station should be the first thing you see when you enter the party site — and it should offer a good line-of-sight to as much of the room as possible.

It should also have the party rules and a party map posted prominently above it, where everyone can see them. At mid- to large-size parties, you'll frequently be telling people where to check in by pointing at the map, which saves you the time of escorting them there.

The check-in checklist

Not all parties need a checklist. Particularly at smaller events, where you can just show guests to their seat and let them set up, they're actually a waste of time. For larger events, however, the check-in process may involve several parts for each person who walks through your door, including the following:

- Taking the person's money

- Getting the person to sign the legal release form

- Handing the person the party disc

- Assigning table space

- Walking first-timers through

- Making party announcements

When you're trying to do all of that for 30 or 40 guests, mistakes are made, and people are waiting. Having a checklist for each person means that you don't risk missing a step; it sounds silly, but studies have shown that the mere act of *having a checklist in hand* makes you run things more methodically, even if you don't actually physically check everything off. Forcing someone to ask, "Well, did I do the full five steps?" helps them avoid the errors that result from repetition.

Whether you formally codify your check-in procedures or not, you will have to deal with each of these steps in one form or another. The following sections describe each of the aforementioned parts of the checklist.

Taking their money

Obviously, this only applies to LAN parties where you're charging admission, but it's arguably the most critical step if you *are* recouping your costs with a fee. There are two ways of taking money:

- **"Thanks."** You put it in your pocket and walk away. This is excellent for smaller venues, even if it's less than satisfying.

- **The cash register.** You can usually buy one relatively cheaply at Costco or another bulk warehouse, or you can remember the LAN partiers' creed and try to borrow one from someone before the event. If you borrow one, however, be sure to get a manual or a tutorial on how to use it, because some cash registers are pretty user-hostile.

In either case, you'll usually want to have a roll of tickets handy, serving as proof that someone has paid in case there's a dispute. The standard method is to tear the ticket in half, keeping half to keep track of how many people have checked in and handing the guest the other half, just like at the movies. (It also comes in handy when it comes time to raffle off any prizes.)

If you sell tickets in advance — and you should — then print out a list of people who have already paid and have it at the check-in counter, marking them off one by one as they check in. Give them a ticket, too, so they can participate in any raffles!

Signing the legal release form

If you have decided to have people sign a release form in order to absolve yourself of legal responsibility, this is when you get them to sign — right after they give you the money. If you have a legal form that people must sign, you almost *certainly* want a checklist; after all, if someone forgets to sign and gets hurt, you could be sued!

Handling Cash

There are two aspects to handling cash that you should be aware of, even at the smallest party:

You need change. My friend Jim calls $20 bills *yuppie food coupons* because ever since the invention of the ATM, that's all anyone ever has to pay with. Before you start any event, you should stop by the bank the day before and get at least 20 singles, 10 five-dollar bills, and 5 ten-dollar bills to break up those 20s. (That's $120, in case you weren't paying attention.)

For larger parties, the standard is 50 singles, 20 five-dollar bills, and 5 ten-dollar bills, and you'll definitely want a cash register. (That's $200.) Of course, if you have a party where the admission is in nice even denominations ($10, $15, or $20), you can probably skip getting singles.

If you have a party where you'll need change, the standard is 4 rolls of pennies, 1 roll of nickels, 2 rolls of dimes, and 3 rolls of quarters.

You need security. I once had a friend who worked at an independent movie theater. The theater was going under because nobody wanted to watch good art films, and my friend frequently moaned about the fact that once this theater went out of business, she wouldn't have any place to watch the latest Quentin Tarantino flick.

To my great surprise, I discovered that she was stealing from the owner. "Why not?" she shrugged, forgetting the fact that she liked the owner personally and she was putting him out of business.

That taught me a very valuable lesson: Anyone can steal, no matter how nice or motivated they may seem.

If you put someone in charge of handling the money, make sure you trust that person absolutely, and then verify the count at the end of the day. It's very easy to stuff an admission fee or two in a pocket, or to let a friend in free. Count up the total earnings, subtract any change money you had in the register at the beginning of the day, and make sure it adds up to the total number of players who should have paid during the party.

In addition, only one person should handle the money. If something *does* go wrong, you'll want to have a good idea of who's responsible, and that's impossible if seven or eight people have been doing check-in duty. Now, I realize that it's almost impossible to keep the same person at the register for an entire LAN party, but do your best to keep it to two or maybe three people. It helps deter shifty money practices.

Cross-Reference If you're wondering whether you need a release form, skip ahead to Chapter 14, "Legal and Safety Issues."

Handing guests the party disc

A *party disc* is a great idea that many LAN parties use, and I strongly suggest that you use it, too. Given that CD burners are so cheap now, you can easily burn a CD that contains everything your partygoers will need to play at your LAN party, including the following:

- **An anti-virus scanner.** You want clean PCs at this party, and there's no excuse for not checking in. This can be as complex as a freely available scanner such as AVG anti-virus (available from www.grisoft.com), or as simple as a bookmark to an online scanner such as the one found at housecall.trendmicro.com/ or www.pcpitstop.com/antivirus/default.asp. If you're going to have a party CD (and especially if you'll be sharing files), a scanner is pretty much mandatory.

- **A firewall, along with the instructions to configure it.** As I have suggested so many times before, the firewall at www.zonealarm.com is freely available and one of the best on the market. Configuring ZoneAlarm to work with your games involves knowing what ports your games of choice use, but it's fairly easy.

- **The latest patches.** Game patches can weigh in at 100 MB or more, and many servers will not allow older versions of games to connect. Having the latest patches burned onto a CD helps protect fragile Internet connections; if four people start downloading gigantic files at once, your cable modem can slow to a crawl.

- **Custom maps or scenarios.** Many parties love playing on custom-designed levels, but not everyone arrives with these levels — or even knows where to find them. If you are going to be holding a match on a particular community-created mod, then why not put the mod on CD and save everyone some time?

- **Any logon IDs or FAQs your guests might need.** Having a readme.txt file on the CD isn't a guarantee that you won't be asked obvious questions, but it does help. If you need a logon ID to access the Internet or a particular server, putting it on the disc saves time.

- **Goony videos, funny Flash animations, and anything else that might amuse.** If you have some space left over, why not fill it with amusement? Lord knows there's an abundance of Strong Bad e-mails and music video parodies out there that are freely available and righteously funny; why not put 'em on the CD and make your party disc the kind of thing that people will want to take home?

  Another idea is to put all of the pictures from the last LAN party on the CD. Everyone will immediately start scanning through it to find the best pictures of themselves and the dorkiest pictures of their friends.

If you have a party disc, when your guests arrive, instead of asking them to download 50 separate files, you simply hand them each a party disc. Then all they have to do is double-click the D: drive to find everything they need! It's very convenient, and an excellent practice for large parties. It's *particularly* relevant if a pre-logon viral scan is required, as you can mandate an industry-standard viral scan that ensures that everyone's definitions are up-to-date.

Assigning table space

At large parties, it's a very good idea to have the map right behind the check-in station, complete with the names of people who registered in advance, as shown in Figure 13-2.

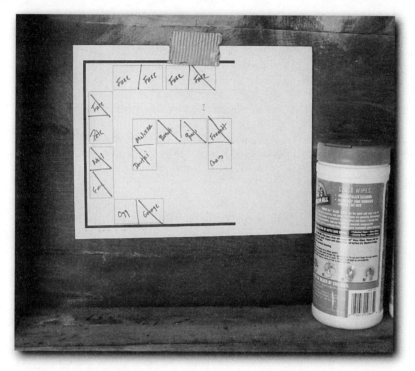

FIGURE 13-2: A crude but effective check-in map hung in the front of my garage

Ideally, people will just look at the map at the Check-In Station and know where they're supposed to set up. In cases where you have open attendance, however, or last-minute stragglers who can't commit, you need to keep tables open. Your best bet for this is to have a Sharpie ready, and as people check in, you just cross the appropriate table off on the map. (I suppose you could write down the name of the person who is seated there, but this is a LAN party, not a restaurant.)

Walking first-timers through

If someone's been to your parties once or twice before, they probably know the routine, but first-time visitors need a little hand-holding to ensure that they plug in where they should, know what intensity of play you folks are used to, and any other party-specific things. It's not a bad idea to walk your first-time guests over to their station and take two or three minutes to go over what they need to do and what's expected of them.

This applies even to first-time guests who have attended other LAN parties. Who knows what sorts of bad habits they've picked up at parties that aren't run as wonderfully as yours are run?

Making party announcements

At the beginning of every party, before anyone starts logging on to any game servers, you need to have a short talk with your guests. As mentioned previously, rules are in place to ensure that everyone knows what's acceptable behavior (and, to a lesser degree, to prevent lawsuits).

For more on LAN party rules, refer to Chapter 2, "Setting Your Party's Parameters."

Your job now is to make sure that *nobody can claim ignorance*.

Make sure everyone is seated (or at least within earshot) and is paying attention. Stand where everyone can see you and speak in a loud, clear voice. *Don't* let people carry on conversations during your speech, *especially* if they're regular attendees or close friends of yours. Letting people talk during your party announcements sends two very unwanted messages:

- It tells your friends (and everyone else, for that matter) that you're willing to make exceptions for them. If they get out of hand later in the party, it's going to be that much harder to play the authority figure, as you've already overlooked their rude behavior at least once.

- As for your first-time guests, they will either assume that you run a very sloppy party or that this is an Old Boys Club, where anyone who is friends with the owner can do whatever they want. In the case of the first assumption, you might as well tell them that they can get away with anything; with the second assumption, you're halfway toward alienating someone before you've even started.

The speech itself should be in three parts:

- **Introduction and announcements.** Start off by saying who you are and welcoming everyone, and then tell your guests about anything special that's going on at this party — any raffles, special events, or unusual formats that you'll be running during the event. Tell people to whom they should speak if they have a problem (which is usually you at a smaller party, although if you've designated a Techie Person, you might want to point that person out now).

- **Thank-yous and acknowledgments.** Thank the staff. If anyone has loaned you equipment, thank that person. If the person actually present at the party, have him or her stand up and take a bow. In particular, if anyone has agreed to sponsor the event, *thank that person as loudly and as graciously as possible.*

For more details on getting a sponsor, see Chapter 5, "Saving Money on Your LAN Party."

- **The party rules.** Go over them, one by one; you don't have to read them exactly as they're written, but you *do* have to get the gist of each rule across. When you're done, take questions to ensure that everyone understands the rules clearly. Then request everyone to raise their hand to indicate that they agree to abide by the rules of your party.

When giving the speech, make it as short as possible. Your half-hour speech may be agonizingly complete, but people are going to fall asleep halfway through unless you're a spoken-word artist like Henry Rollins. Try to keep all speeches under 10 minutes, and preferably under five.

Using Your Guests to Pimp Your Party

If you have a sponsor, it is a *very* good idea to let them know that their advertising and give-aways are having an effect. After all, they're not just giving you keychain USB flash drives out of the goodness of their heart! And there's no better way to show a business that their advertising works than to have your guests show up and say, "You know, I came here because I heard about you at Ferrett's LAN party."

Therefore, during your acknowledgments, it can't hurt to say something like, "If you buy something from our sponsor, be sure to let them know that you heard about them here. That helps us to get better prizes and/or cheaper entry fees." It is hoped that your guests will keep reminding your sponsor that their generosity is helping their bottom line.

The Daily Grind: Things to Do during Your Party

You'll be happy to know that once everything has started up, the party will usually run smoothly until the end. That said, however, you do want to watch for a few ongoing issues and events.

The walk-around

About once every two hours or so, have someone responsible walk around the party and take a fresh look at what's going on. The following are areas of concern:

- **Excitement.** If everyone's off chatting in a corner and few people are actually playing the games you've set up, maybe it's time to start up some kooky game variants just to get people fired up. If you've been playing for a while, it might be time for dinner to get people's blood sugar back up to normal levels. Or, if it's late enough, maybe it's time to call it a night.

- **Safety.** Remember that if someone trips and hurts himself at this party, that person can sue you. It's not likely, but why not take some time to see if any cables have sprung loose, or if any computers are jutting out dangerously into the aisles? Has anything been moved and is now balanced precariously, just waiting for disaster? Fix it now, before it becomes a *real* problem.

- **Refuse.** Garbage piles up at these events like you wouldn't believe. If you want to avoid a particularly hellish end-of-day cleanup, look around now for messes on tables and clean them up before they swell into a mess that only Oscar the Grouch could love. If the garbage cans are full, take them out. If someone's station is stacked high with BAWLS Guarana bottles and pizza crusts, ask them to take a minute to clean it up *now*.

This suggestion applies to big parties only, but it's a good one (if I say so myself). Some gas stations have an hourly schedule posted inside their bathrooms; once an hour, the clerk on duty has to go in, look around, and initial the schedule (actually adding any paper towels or toilet paper is another matter, of course).

If you have a huge party, you might want to adopt this strategy to ensure that someone's out there checking the floor periodically, and to determine the last time that it was done. Post a schedule at the Check-In Station and have your staffers sign off whenever they make the rounds.

Handling tech support

Make sure you have your Techie at the ready in case something happens, and have a backup if he or she goes out on a food run. Most of the time, your problems will occur at start-up, but occasionally you will experience a server crash or an Internet outage that needs to be fixed.

Handling visitors

If you're holding your LAN party in a public space, passers-by will often want to know what's going on. These people might become partygoers at future events, but at the moment they're usually a big pain, asking a lot of questions and wanting to look around. They may actually just want to hang around and talk, which may or may not be a benefit depending on how socially adept they are. They may also decide to steal something when nobody's looking. Therefore, I don't advise that you let them hang about.

Someone needs to greet these people, answer their questions quickly, and shoo them off.

Giving out door prizes

As mentioned previously, the best parties space out the prizes so that they occur at regular intervals, giving out tiny prizes at first and ramping up to the best prize at the end of the day. If you have a giveaway, make an announcement to get everyone's attention, make a big deal about it, hand out the prize, and then get back to fragging.

For more on prizes, refer to Chapter 5, "Saving Money on Your LAN Party."

Taking photos

If you have a Web site, nothing promotes your next LAN party better than your last LAN party. Take photos of all the major events so people can see what a great time you're having!

If you take pictures of nothing else, always, *always* take pictures of winners — both game winners and door prize winners. Players love to see photos of themselves next to a big "Finalist" banner, and sponsors love to see pictures of enthusiastic people holding up their products.

Be sure to send the photos on to your sponsors in case they don't drop by your Web site.

Holding side events

If you have a case-modding contest or a special ladder tourney, you'll have to hold them during the party, and hold them on time. Obvious, but necessary.

Taking meal breaks

Don't forget that at some point, you should probably enforce an "official" break so that everyone can get together and share food. Not only is it a bonding experience, it stops people from getting burned out and serves as a nice change of pace.

If you raid the cash register to get some money for pizza or soda, as many parties are wont to do, get a receipt and leave it with the cash. That way, when the register comes up $30 short at the end of the day, you'll immediately know why.

Finally, when you're ordering out for food, don't forget to ask people what they want! Nothing makes someone feel more invisible than being overlooked when it comes to food.

The End-of-Day Breakdown: Can't We Just Go Home?

Well, your event's over. You've shut down the servers and shooed people out.

Now what?

Breakdown

This is the long, slow slog whereby you dutifully wind up the cables, pack up the tables, and file everything away. The best tip I can give is to do it methodically and with the same care that you took setting everything up; I myself am guilty of more than a few post-party rush jobs, and I've almost always suffered later for it. Roll the cables up neatly and put them all in the same box, label any storage supplies for later use, and stack the chairs neatly.

Above all, make sure that you handle borrowed equipment with care. If you made any changes to something's configuration, restore it to the way you found it. If it came in a box, put it back in the box. Remember: You want to be able to borrow again in the future, so take extra care when it comes to loaner equipment. If you can, return it in *better* condition than when you received it, as I suggested in Chapter 5, "Saving Money on Your LAN Party."

Tip Never leave computers or other valuable equipment in your car for extended periods of time. Not only is it environmentally dangerous (something can freeze or overheat), but the danger of theft is *very* real. If you're moving hardware at the end of the day, put the equipment near the door, but don't put it out in the car until you're ready to leave. You may want to post a guard.

Clean up

Once all of the furniture and chairs are put away, pick up all the loose trash and then take out the garbage. Vacuum the floor, and look for any stains you can clean up now before they set.

This is also where you'll find any lost items. Put them aside where you can find them for the next party, and make an announcement on the Web site in case anyone wants to claim them.

If you're renting a space, take a photo when you're done so there are no questions about the condition you returned it in. Don't take a digital photo, of course; everyone knows those can be manipulated, and they're not particularly solid evidence in court. Take a good old-fashioned paper Kodak or Polaroid shot to prove that you returned your rental space in reasonably-clean condition.

Count the cash

If you've charged an admission fee, keep everyone who was at the cash register around while you tally up the money. If you find any large discrepancies, ask people quietly and calmly what happened. Keep in mind that big cash shortages aren't usually malicious; in fact, the biggest cause of cash discrepancies is "We took some money for needed expenses and forgot to tell you."

A Few Days After: Wrapping Up

The LAN party doesn't end after everyone has left and you're done cleaning up. Hopefully, people have had such a great time that they'll want to relive it, and you're just the person to make that happen.

Update your Web site

What are you going to do with all of those pictures you took? Why, you're going to plaster them all over your LAN party's site, of course! Create a section of your site that shows everyone what happened, complete with small write-ups about who won what tournaments, door prizes, and any other memorable aspects of your party.

Thank your lenders

Call them up and offer a quick thanks for loaning you that cable, or that router, or that server. They'll appreciate it.

Discuss future events

Did it go well? Do you want to hold another party in the future? If the answer is yes, then you want to sit down with some of the guests and solicit their feedback about what you did right and, more important, what you did wrong. Were there too few game servers, and should you think about adding an additional server or two? Were you playing the right kind of games? Should you have had a wider variety of game types, or maybe goofier formats of your existing games? Do you want to add Internet access at the next event or maybe think about *not* having Internet access in the future?

Talk about what you'd like to see at future parties, and start planning now. Incidentally, this is an excellent forum topic to get your discussion boards buzzing.

Summary

This chapter presented you with an idea of how your average LAN party should proceed — you double-check the setup, get your staffers enthused, check everyone in, play like mad, and then clean up and record the event for posterity.

I know, despite all of this preparation, you still have a sinking feeling about the lurking danger of lawsuits. Sure, we're a little lawsuit-crazy in America, but that just means you'd better know where your liabilities are when you invite people over to your house. Not to worry — I'll tell you what they are in the next chapter.

Legal and Safety Issues

True story: A ski resort, worried about potential lawsuits from injured customers, decided to plaster the entire resort with warning signs informing everyone about how safe each slope was.

Someone skied into a sign and was hurt. He sued.

The *Chicago Sun-Times* refers to this era as the Not Me decade, in which everybody else is responsible for everything. Unfortunately, they have a point. It's not likely that someone will sue you, but lawsuits are like plane crashes; the chances of it happening are low, but the consequences if someone *does* sue can be catastrophic.

Thus, it's in your best interests to make sure that you're protected should anything happen. This chapter describes the legal issues confronting anyone wishing to host a LAN party. Armed with the information provided here, you should be able to host an anxiety-free event.

The Legal Issues of LAN Parties

There are generally three areas in which LAN parties can run afoul of the law — liability, copyright infringement, and alcohol:

➤ *Liability* is what happens when someone is hurt or suffers property damage at your LAN party and decides that you should have been able to prevent that injury or damage.

➤ *Copyright infringement* is the trading of illegal warez (which is hacker slang for commercial programs traded illegally), MP3s, or DivX videos, or anything else of the sort.

➤ *Alcohol* covers all the legal issues that come up when you decide to have alcoholic beverages at your party: What happens if you serve alcohol to a minor? What happens if someone drives home drunk from your party and kills someone or is killed?

The problem with all of these issues is that it is very difficult to offer hard-and-fast guidelines, because it depends on both your local, state and county laws and the severity of the infringement. (There's a big difference between someone picking up a virus at your party and an electrical short that fries 10 people's motherboards.) Because this book isn't a legal tome, this chapter deals with all of these issues briefly, and provides some general guidelines about how to handle them.

Liability and the LAN party

Liability is legally defined as "accountability and responsibility to others, enforceable by legal or criminal sanctions." In other words, if someone files a suit against you, that person is claiming that whatever bad thing happened to him or her at your party was your fault, and that you could have prevented it.

In all likelihood, you will claim that it *wasn't* your fault. Ultimately, the court will determine who really was responsible, and how much you could have done to prevent whatever terrible thing it was that occurred.

However, whether you are truly guilty or not, the first rule of liability is that *you never want to go to court*. Not only is defending yourself in a lawsuit an expensive proposition, there are no hard-and-fast guarantees about winning your case. We've all heard ridiculous stories of burglars who injure themselves while breaking into someone's house and then sue for damages. Although some cases should be no-brainers, once a case actually goes to trial, you have no guarantees that the court will rule in your favor.

Therefore, your goal is to prevent anyone from even *thinking* about filing a lawsuit against you, and you do this by making the possibility of a case so difficult that their lawyers will tell them that they can't possibly win. You can help to prevent lawsuits via three methods: prevention, information, and liability waivers. The following sections describe each of these methods.

Liabilities generally fall into one of two categories:

- **Physical injury.** For example, someone might trip over a cable and dislocate an arm, or two kids might get into a fight at your party and get black eyes and bruises.

- **Property damage.** For example, someone might pick up a virus at your party and lose all his data. Theft is also in this category; someone else might have his iPod stolen at your site.

Of the two liabilities, injuries are far more likely to cause lawsuits than property damage. Fortunately, the best way to prevent injury lawsuits is by preventing the injuries from happening in the first place.

Prevention: The best method of stopping lawsuits

Most liability lawsuits are attempting to resolve one particular question: Who is responsible for the problem?

The good news is that, in general, as long as you have posted visible warnings saying "We are not responsible for your property," property damage is generally not taken too seriously by the courts. If your guests went to a lot of trouble to bring thousands of dollars of valuable equipment to a public place that did not guarantee safety, it's hard to argue that they didn't realize it could be dangerous. Therefore, the responsibility and accountability is almost entirely theirs.

The bad news is that as long as the injured party can show negligence, personal injury is *always* a potential liability. If you invite people to come to your party, that invitation suggests a subtle but legally binding implication that you are bringing them to a safe place. You can post 15,000 signs saying, "We're not responsible for injury," but if your cables are lying all over the floor, creating a potential trip hazard for anyone who walks by (as in Figure 14-1), you can still be held responsible if someone falls. You have presented that person with a danger that you could have removed.

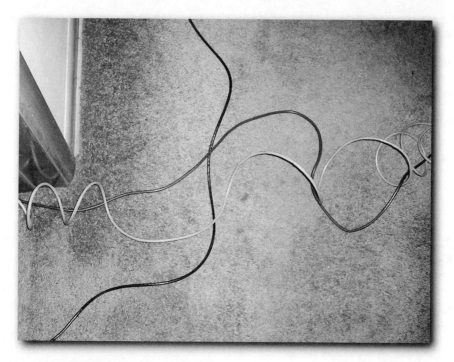

FIGURE 14-1: A lawsuit waiting to happen.

Furthermore, there are limits even to property damage. If you leave guest computers in an unlocked room overnight and someone steals those computers, the owners could argue persuasively that the theft could have been prevented if you had locked the door.

Therefore, the *best* method of forestalling lawsuits is to do everything you can to prevent anything bad from happening in the first place — a legal principle known as *acting in good faith*.

Tip Always keep in mind one overriding rule: If you don't want people to sue, make sure they don't get hurt. This dictum might seem blindingly obvious, but you'd be surprised how often it's forgotten or ignored. Just make sure that *you* don't forget.

You can't prevent anyone from ever getting injured, of course — this is a dangerous world — but if you can show the courts that you went out of your way to tie every bundle of cables together, duct-tape them off to one side, and post warnings about tripping, then you have gone a long way toward showing the court that you did your best to prevent any damages.

Keep in mind that prevention is an ongoing process. Having all the cables tied up at the beginning of the day doesn't count for much if you do some maintenance work at noon and leave them out again. If someone sets up at a station and leaves the computer in the middle of the aisle, you could be responsible. If the aisles become dangerously clogged with garbage at nine at night, you could still be at fault.

Thus, your best bet to prevent lawsuits is to do regular safety checks, walking the floor to make sure everything's in place. It doesn't take that long, and you can have the Floor Sweeper do it.

For more on the Floor Sweeper and other LAN party roles, refer to Chapter 11, "Staffing Issues and Common LAN Party Roles."

Above all, document what you do. You don't necessarily need official records, but having someone who can testify that he or she went on hourly safety patrols is a Good Thing if the lawyers come a-knocking.

Information: Letting your guests know who's responsible

As mentioned in Chapter 2, "Setting Your Party's Parameters," you should read the party ground rules aloud at the beginning of your party. Reading the rules where everyone can hear them removes all possibility of argument — a rude guest can't later say, "Well, *I* didn't know" if he or she is caught doing something shady.

This goes double for liability.

If you set rules of conduct that the guests are supposed to abide by, it becomes very hard for them to prove that anything that happened while they were breaking those rules was your fault. If you told your guests that no horseplay is allowed and someone breaks an arm while playing Tag, you can claim (and legitimately) that you told *everyone* not to do that. That puts the onus on others and makes it fairly clear that they took matters into their own hands.

Furthermore, making sure that everyone knows the rules prevents potential suers from claiming ignorance. If you have posted several copies of the floor rules everywhere and read them aloud at the beginning of the party, the Tag players can't realistically claim that they had no idea that playing that game was a bad idea.

Posting rules doesn't mean that nobody will ever sue, of course. After all, some people are allergic to taking responsibility for their own actions. It does, however, drastically reduce the chances of anyone filing suit, which is your goal.

There are three basic methods of getting the word out:

- **Post your house rules.** Make sure they're prominently displayed. If at all possible, post several copies in different places, including the bathroom. In extreme circumstances, you may even want to have a copy of the rules at every station, or hand them out to people with their welcome packets.

  It's also not a bad idea to have separate signs that announce, in larger font, that you are not responsible for anyone's property.

- **Announce the rules at the beginning of the party.** When everyone is finally settled in, stop the party to read the rules in a loud, clear voice. Ask if anyone has any questions. At the end, ask everyone to raise their hand and say "Aye" to agree that they understand the rules and will abide by them.

- **Make no exceptions.** If it can be proven in court that you knew that people were breaking the rules and you did nothing, you can be held responsible. If you announced that there will be no warez traded at the party and you see someone burning illegal software CDs, *stop them*. If you see somebody running through the aisles, *stop them*.

Furthermore, it's not acceptable to overlook someone's actions; if someone brings a violation of the rules to your attention, you *must* follow up on it. If someone asks you whether it's okay to trade MP3s as long as you don't know about it, your response has to be, "No — I said there will be no trading, period. If I catch you, you'll be out on the street." Be sure to follow up by checking on the person later to make sure that there isn't any trading. Make sure all of your staff knows this, too.

Yes, it's tough to be the disciplinarian, but you must remain firm, or you risk the possibility of a nasty lawsuit.

Liability waivers: Do you need them?

By holding an event, you're opening yourself up to potential legal action. Therefore, why not just insist that people sign a contract stating that they understand everything that could go wrong, thus waiving their rights to sue you, before they can play at your party?

It's not a bad idea, but it has drawbacks.

First of all, getting everyone to sign that much paperwork is a hassle. You have to make sure that everyone signs one, and then you need to keep them all on file for at least two years (or whatever the statute of limitations on tort liability is in your state), just in case someone decides to sue you later. That in itself adds a lot of work.

Second, waivers aren't a catch-all. People can still sue you *even if they signed a waiver*, if it can be proven that you were seriously negligent. If you didn't enforce your ground rules or if your LAN party location can be proven to be dangerously hazardous, then you still might find yourself facing a lawsuit. Waivers make it harder for someone to sue, but they don't absolve you of all responsibility.

Children and LAN Parties

There is one situation for which I strongly encourage you to insist that people sign waivers, and that is when you're dealing with a minor. Children under 18 can get themselves in trouble very easily, particularly when they're left alone with little to no parental supervision for the day — and their parents are the most likely to sue should something go awry with their little bubbeleh.

However, having the minor sign the waiver is useless; one of the things about being a minor is that you can't enter into any legally binding contracts. No, you have to get the minor's *parent* (or legal guardian) to sign the waiver, and you should do so. Sit down with them, face-to-face, and explain what your party will be like, what the potential dangers are (but that you'll take reasonable precautions to ensure that the child will be safe), and have them sign the waiver while you're in the room.

Do not under any circumstances accept a waiver that a minor brings to the party. I know that I forged my mom's signature on a couple of field trip permission slips; unless you know the parents in question personally, trust no one.

A sample waiver

A sample waiver is illustrated in Figure 14-2.

[INSERT YOUR FLOOR RULES HERE]

You must understand these statements and agree to them.

LIMITATION OF LIABILITY: [INSERT NAME OF ORGANIZATION] are not responsible for any damage caused by users or by any of the equipment or programming utilized in the event, or by any technical or human error that may occur. [INSERT NAME OF ORGANIZATION] assumes no liability for any injury, loss, or damage of any kind arising from or in connection with any person's participation in the event — including without limitation, participation in any real life activity.

By participating in the event, each participant agrees to be bound by the official rules, as outlined above. [INSERT NAME OF ORGANIZATION] shall not be liable for punitive, incidental, consequential or special damages, whether or not such damages could have been foreseen and whether or any [INSERT NAME OF ORGANIZATION] received notice of it.

RELEASE: The individual signing below ("Registrant") does hereby release and waive any and all causes of action, claims, losses and damages, whether such causes of action, claims, losses and damages are known or unknown, whether such causes of action, claims, losses, and damages existing in law or in equity, and whether such causes of action, claims, losses, and damages exist under contract, tort, strict liability or other theory, owned by Registrant arising out of, relating to or in connection with the event (collectively, the "claims"). Registrant forever discharges [INSERT NAME OF ORGANIZATION HERE] and their respective directors, officers, employees, agents and representatives from all claims.

INDEMNITY: Registrant does hereby agree to indemnify, defend and hold harmless each [INSERT NAME OF ORGANIZATION HERE] directors, officers, employees, agents and representatives from and against all losses, lawsuits, causes of action, claims and damages which arise from the acts or omissions of registrant in connection with the event.

IF THE REGISTRANT IS A MINOR, THE FOLLOWING MUST COMPLETE BELOW

Registrant's Name (print)   Registrant's Guardian's Name (print)

_____   _____

Registrant's Signature   Registrant's Guardian's Signature

_____   _____

Date   Date

_____   _____

FIGURE 14-2: Waiver of legal responsibility

Alcohol and LAN Parties

Many people enjoy having a couple of beers when they're playing, and I admit that there have been times when I myself have been caught FUI (Fragging Under the Influence). However, adding alcohol to your LAN party adds another layer of complexity—and when you throw minors into the mix, it can get downright dangerous. For larger parties, I don't recommend letting people drink alcohol, because things can spiral out of control very quickly unless you're prepared to do a *lot* of supervising.

The rules on alcohol vary wildly from state to state and town to town, so I can't give you specific laws, but I can provide some general guidelines about how they generally work. If you want to find out the specifics—and you should—you'll need to call your city clerk's office or your county recorder's office for the full skinny.

Most counties have two separate sets of rules—one for public places (read: rental halls) and one for private residences (read: your home). Let's start with your own place.

Private residences

A private residence is anywhere you live, even if it's a rented apartment. The good news is that as a private residence, you do not need a liquor license to serve alcohol (as long as you meet the legal drinking age, of course). What you do in your home is your business, and as long as things don't get out of control, you're golden.

The Designated Driver

Regardless of what size party you're holding, it is *always* a good idea to have a designated driver—someone who picks up and drops off all of the designated drinkers, and who agrees to stay sober for the evening. Ideally, make arrangements in advance, with people deciding beforehand whether they'll be drinking on-site or not; if they'll be drinking, the DD picks them up and drops them off.

It's good policy to enforce a rule whereby people who drive themselves to your party and then wish to drink must first hand over their car keys to you. At the end of the night, the designated driver drives them home—even if they appear perfectly sober.

Having a designated driver and a "nobody who drinks, drives" rule solves two problems: One: Nobody gets hurt. Two: You don't have to argue with people who think they're sober but really aren't. (Or, worse yet, people who *look* sober but turn out to be drunk, usually with tragic consequences.) The rule is that if you drink, you are driven home—*no exceptions*.

Is that a pain? Yes. Is that less of a pain than a drunken car crash that may kill people? You bet.

However, four laws are relevant to your situation:

- **You cannot sell liquor.** You have full permission to give liquor away to guests, or to have guests bring liquor for other people to drink, but the moment you start charging for booze, you need a license.

  Don't think you can get around it, either; traditional dodges to get around the "no sale of alcohol" rule include selling tickets that are exchanged for drinks, charging a flat "all you can drink" fee, or charging an "admission" fee when the primary expense of the party is alcoholic beverages. All are illegal and will get you busted.

  You can share all you like. Just don't try to make a profit.

- **You cannot give liquor to minors or underage drinkers.** You can get into varying degrees of trouble for this, depending on the state. In some states, there is a "gray zone" whereby people who are over 18 (and therefore not minors) but under the legal drinking age are responsible for their own actions. In other states, you're responsible.

  What is common to *all* states, however, is that if a minor gets drunk at your party, it's your fault. You can be charged with a crime, or even sued by the parents.

If the minor is your child, you *are* allowed to decide whether he or she is allowed to drink, as long as the party takes place at your house. It's not illegal to give your kid a glass of wine at Thanksgiving or Hanukkah.

Note that if you aren't of legal drinking age, it's still illegal to drink at home, even if you own the house or rent the apartment yourself.

- **You are responsible for keeping your party under control.** If the neighbors complain or people start spilling out onto the streets and causing a ruckus, the police can (and will) shut your party down.

  If the police are called to your house, they have the legal right to request ID from everyone, to look around for illicit substances, and to generally inquire into your business. Therefore, don't attract their attention in the first place.

- **If a guest at your party becomes intoxicated and injures himself or others, you can be sued.** This is the big one!

  If someone gets loaded at your house, drives home drunk, and crashes into a school bus, every parent who had a child on that bus can (and probably will) sue you. You are responsible for keeping your guests safe — and because you're the one who's going to take the blame if Phil hurts himself, you're the one who has to cut Phil off if he's getting out of control.

  Yes, that means you have to monitor your party, which isn't nearly as fun as getting loaded yourself. Incidentally, this is yet another reason I strongly encourage the use of designated drivers.

Rental properties

Rental properties tend to be finicky when it comes to alcohol, mostly because the property owner is usually the one who bears most of the responsibility should something go wrong. If one of your guests gets out of control and breaks something, or if one of your drunk guests hurts someone, the property owner is the one who is going to bear the costs.

That means there are two steps involved in having alcohol at public places: getting permission from the property owner and enforcing the local drinking laws at the party itself.

Getting alcohol served at your rental property

If you plan to allow alcohol at your off-site party, ask the property owner if he or she has a *liquor license* — a license authorizing the owner to sell alcoholic beverages on the property. Liquor licenses can come in two flavors: one for beer and wine and one for hard liquor. That means you may be able to sell beer on the property, but not rum or vodka.

If the property owner has a license, you may have to purchase alcohol from the owner at ridiculously inflated prices and pay the owner extra for a licensed bartender. This is usually a liability issue and isn't negotiable.

If the owner doesn't have a license, that doesn't mean that you can't drink there — it just means that you can't *sell* alcohol. Bringing your own booze and giving it away for free is fine.

You have to ask the property owner whether it's okay to bring your own booze to a party — and their answer will usually be no. Some smaller places, like churches, may not have a liquor license because they personally don't believe in drinking; others may not want to pay the extra insurance costs that are required of an alcohol-friendly establishment. However, some rental establishments are fine with people bringing their own alcohol in.

If all else fails and the owner forbids alcohol entirely, you can always tell your guests, "We can't stop you if you get drunk elsewhere and come here, but you can't drink on the site." If a legally authorized bar or a guest's private residence is within walking distance, this usually is the safest way to go. However, a lot of people will take this to mean that they can go get drunk in the parking lot, which is illegal for two reasons:

- The parking lot is generally considered "the site" for legal purposes and counts as getting drunk inside.

- Most counties have laws against drinking in public. Should the police catch your pals mixing rum-and-cokes in the backseat of their Honda, they may spend a very exciting night in jail.

The Third Option: Single-Event Permits

If you're desperate to sell booze at your party and the property owner does not have a license, a new option may be to get a *single-event permit*, which allows groups to sell alcoholic beverages at temporary (less than three-day) events. This is how your local crafts festival can sell beer at their booths.

You have to clear this with the property owner first, of course; you can get all the permits you like, but if the owner isn't comfortable with it, it's not going to happen.

In addition, if it can be shown that you've *encouraged* people to get drunk and come to the site, you may well be held responsible for any damage your drunken guests do on the way there. (Read: Drunk driving.) Thus, be very specific in your phrasing, such as "If you want to have a drink, Charlie's Bar is open next door, but you can't bring the drinks back here."

You will also want to find out what the prohibitions on minors and underage drinkers are. It is illegal to give alcohol to minors or underage drinkers under any circumstances — and, yes, it counts if one of your guests is secretly sliding his beer over to his little brother. However, many counties allow minors to be present at events where there is public drinking as long as they are accompanied by a parent or legal guardian. Others, however, may bar them from the premises altogether, or demand a separate "alcohol-free" zone that is strictly enforced by the event holders.

Alcohol laws and enforcement

If you're holding the party, you have to enforce the laws. If you say that you'll create an alcohol-free zone for minors, you *have* to create an effective method of segregating minors, and you *must* monitor it throughout the day to make sure that no one is crossing the lines.

In other words, you can't just post a sign that says "Nobody under 21 drinks" and then turn a blind eye to the high school seniors who are raiding the bar. If you dispense drinks at a public establishment, you must uphold the laws.

What are those laws?

Well, again, the liquor rules for each state and town vary considerably, and you should find out what applies for your local town. However, most places share a core set of rules about liquor; the specifics change, but the general guidelines are fairly standard:

- All states have a rule that you cannot serve liquor to someone who is under the legal drinking age. If you do, you may have your liquor license removed, even for a first-time offense.

- Most states have rules about serving alcohol to blatantly drunk people. Bartenders are required to cut people off if they're dangerously and visibly intoxicated, and may be held liable if someone drinks so heavily that he causes damage to himself (think permanent brain damage or a coma) or others (think drunk driving). Most states have a pamphlet or a free course that will teach you when you should cut people off.

- Most states have a rule about how late you can sell alcohol. If you have a liquor license and are selling booze, you cannot sell alcohol to anyone after that time.

- Most states have laws against *disorderly premises,* which is a way of saying that if the rental property breaks the rules, the police will be called and you may be arrested (or at the very least have your license revoked). The rules about what constitutes disorderly premises vary, but include gambling, lewd and indecent conduct (usually nudity or profanity, but visible pornography might well apply), prostitution, assaults, and illicit drugs being used or sold on the premises.

    Again, if you attract the attention of the local constabulatory, you have given them a free pass to investigate every aspect of your party. Don't attract unwanted attention.

- Almost all states specifically prohibit minors from selling alcohol. No kids behind the bar!

File Sharing, Pirated Music, and LAN Parties

LAN parties are often hotbeds of illegally copied software. In fact, many people look at LAN parties as their local black market — a place where they can exchange all of the latest games, movies, and music at ridiculously high transfer speeds. You bring your collection of music and pirated movies to the party, and you cherry-pick the best parts of everyone else's collection while everyone else makes copies of your best stuff, and everyone goes home with a boatload of free new music, DVDs, and software. Of course, the best part about it is that there's no risk at all of being caught, because you're on a private network.

But is that really true? Is there no danger of being caught?

As of the time of this writing, if you create a private network on which people are illegally trading copyrighted files, you cannot be legally held responsible for what happens on your network (unless, of course, you're one of the people who is pirating software, and this includes owning a server that's hosting illegal files). If a software company or the Recording Industry Association of America (better known as the RIAA) can gather evidence that there *was* illegal trading at your LAN party — for example, by nailing down an IP address that someone was using to trade files over the Internet — then they can subpoena you to get the information, and you have to give it to them.

Note When you see "copyrighted material," think "anything available commercially." If you can buy the latest Matrix movie on DVD or pay to see it in theaters, it's probably not safe to trade.

The result is that you will have to give up your friends to the RIAA's sharklike lawyers, but you yourself will be in the clear — sort of.

The insidious thing about lawsuits is that quite often, the lawyers don't need to *win* the case. If the RIAA can force you to spend $75,000 in legal fees defending yourself, then they can walk away with a sense of triumph. Large companies are notorious for filing suits that they know they have no chance of winning, just to force someone to go broke fighting the charges.

Therefore, although technically speaking you bear no responsibility if your network is a gigantic warez factory, you can still be ruined if some company decides to make an example out of you. (And, might I add, there's no guarantee that the laws won't change between the time I write this and the time you read this.)

So what happens if *you* are found guilty of sharing copyrighted material? That's when the serious trouble begins. The RIAA in particular has been rabid about nailing file sharers, and the rumor at this point is that the next wave of people who get caught will have to pay upwards of $50,000 in penalties and fines. The industry is trying to make an example out of every file sharer they catch.

Is this likely to happen to you? No. I have to be honest here — your chances of getting caught file-sharing at a LAN party are pretty slim, particularly if you don't have Internet access, and they're practically nonexistent if your party is by invitation only.

Note two caveats to that, however:

- **It's wrong.** I'm no fan of the RIAA, but when you pirate music, it's frequently the creators of that music who take it in the shorts. Too many people out there will tell you they're "making a stand" against the industry, but they're actually just cheapskates who don't want to pay for anything. If you like what someone creates — whether it's a game, a movie, or a song — then *reimburse them* so they'll make more.

  The inevitable argument is, "Well, they're already rich. They don't need my money." Usually, that's another way of saying, "I don't think *anyone* needs my money." Furthermore, the royalties paid to artists are much smaller than most people believe, and many artists have kids who need braces, too.

- **It may not always be safe.** Right now, the RIAA is becoming increasingly nasty in their tactics of hunting down file sharers, and eventually they're going to realize that many LAN parties are where all the l33t 4@xx0rz (or, in nonnerd parlance, the most egregious piraters) go to exchange their warez in privacy. If I were an RIAA lawyer, I'd probably be thinking, "Gee, if I send a gamer in undercover to trade some music, I can get 30 or 40 people at once, with physical evidence to prove it."

  Nobody's looking to bust your LAN party right now, but that doesn't mean that nobody ever will. You have been warned!

It's up to you to decide whether it's ethical and worth the risk to share warez. The choice is yours.

Make the right one.

Summary

Liability laws vary from community to community when it comes to LAN parties, but the general rule is to make sure that everyone gets home safe. Your best bet to accomplish that is to take a proactive approach and start thinking about everyone's safety as you plan your party.

In the next chapter, you'll face the worst part of every LAN party: fixing broken things. We all have to do it eventually, so you might as well learn the best ways to tame your wily LAN party.

Something Just Went Wrong! Fixing Party Problems

When I was a young lad, typing away at a DOS prompt in an attempt to get my latest game to run, my mother had to take my phone away from me. Why? Because I'd get so frustrated trying to figure out why my game wasn't working that I would throw things — and one of the nearest objects was the phone.

We went through three broken phones before I realized that destroying electronic equipment wasn't helping me to play my game, and maybe I had better learn how to troubleshoot computer problems effectively. (That, and Mom made me pay to replace the phones, plus a little temper-tantrum fee on the side.)

Sometimes, things will go wrong at your LAN party, and the solution won't be immediately obvious. The secret is to be patient, calm, and methodical. There is a structure you can use to help identify the problem, and I describe it in this chapter. This chapter also discusses some of the more common problems that arise at LAN parties.

For now, one bit of advice: When you call for tech support, make sure your phone is in one piece.

The Basics of Troubleshooting

When something doesn't work at your LAN party, your approach to solving it has to be scientific and studied. Yes, there may be people waiting to play and this is holding them up; yes, the program or equipment may be ridiculously cryptic in its error messages.

Your job is to fix whatever is wrong as quickly as possible, and to do that, you must follow these steps:

1. Assume every problem is nontrivial.

2. Stay calm.

3. Keep people informed.

4. Narrow down the problem.

5. Be methodical.

6. Read the documentation.

7. Call the manufacturer.

Assuming every problem is nontrivial

As a professional techie, I'm as guilty of this as anyone. You see a minor problem crop up and you casually remark, "Oh, I know what that is!" and change a setting that will surely fix it. The problem doesn't go away. Of course, now you're *really* sure you know what the problem is, so you change something *else* that will surely fix it.

Five minutes later, you've changed about 15 things, the problem's still not fixed, and now you can't remember what all the settings were originally.

Use the seven steps outlined above for every problem. Yes, you may think you know what the problem is — and if you're an experienced techie, you may be right 95 percent of the time. But there's always that 5 percent where the problem is deeper than you think it is, and diving head-first into your problem with a bunch of slapdash solutions often makes the problem worse. (It also leads to more frustration, as you've just "fixed" the problem six times and it's *still* broken, which leads you to make more errors.)

Always approach a problem methodically, one step at a time, and take some time after every change to see what's different before moving on to the next fix. After every modification, see if you can ferret out some additional information, which may in turn help you figure out where this glitch is *really* coming from.

Staying calm

As I've already mentioned, there's strong pressure on you to fix any problem at a LAN party *immediately*. People are waiting for you to be done with it so they can get back to the game, but getting angry, or nervous, or frustrated causes you to make mistakes. We've all seen the basketball player who can make a thousand shots on the court but blows it when everyone's watching; getting rattled may cause you to miss some fact that's critical to solving the problem.

You *can* fix this. It *will* get done. Be confident, and don't let the warm breath on the back of your neck get to you.

Keeping people informed

When something that affects everyone breaks down, make an announcement that it's broken, and that you're trying to fix it. If half an hour later it's still broken, announce what progress you've made and who you've called to try to solve the problem. If you've narrowed it down to a specific area, tell the partygoers that. There is no shame in announcing that you haven't figured out the problem yet, but reassure everyone that you're doing everything you can to fix it.

Keeping people in the loop limits their frustration — they may not be playing, but at least they know you're on top of it. Telling them what you have discovered thus far makes them feel like progress is being made. A little sharing makes everyone feel better.

(Of course, if this is just one person's computer, or if it's a networking glitch you're tracking down with a few friends the night before the party, you can ignore this part.)

Narrowing down the problem

Particularly at a LAN party, the problem is generally in one of three areas: the network, the server, or the client.

Quickly finding out which of these areas is affected helps you to focus your efforts on the broken part, and not waste time trying to fix a network connection that may be working just fine.

More important, finding out what area is broken enables you to call the proper person for tech support. Whenever you call a support hotline, the first thing they will attempt to do is convince you that the problem is not really theirs. If they are a router company, they will attempt to convince you that the problem is with the game; if they are a game company, they will tell you that the problem lies in your router. Knowing what is at fault will enable you to properly arm-wrestle a support tech into helping you when you need it, as in, "No, I've checked the router; it's got the proper ports opened up and I can ping the server from every client. *It's the game, punky.*"

Cross-Reference   Narrowing down a problem is *such* an important skill that I've created a separate section to help you learn how to do it. Later in the chapter, in the section "The Common Areas of LAN Party Breakdown," I'll give you an idea of what sorts of problems you tend to see when each of these three areas collapses, and some tests you can perform to check them out.

Being methodical

The scientific process states that when you do an experiment, you only change one thing at a time. If you put sugar and salt on a slug and it dies, what killed it? The sugar or the salt?

Better to pour sugar on the slug, and then salt, and you'll know for sure. (Or, better yet, maybe you shouldn't be so mean to the poor slug.)

When you're fixing a problem, change only one thing at a time, and then see whether the problem is fixed. If it isn't, look at all the available information you have to see if anything changed as a result of *your* change. Don't just start flipping switches and hope for the best; take it slow, and double-check your work.

Reading the documentation

If you have an Internet connection, go online and read the Frequently Asked Questions (FAQs) and search the message boards. Nine times out of 10, you'll find that someone has encountered this problem before, and that there is a solution for it. Check all relevant sites; if you're encountering a problem connecting to a *Quake III* server through a LinkSys router, search the official LinkSys site for *Quake III* references, and the official *Quake III* site for LinkSys references.

If you can't find anyone else who's experiencing your problem, start from the beginning. Crack the manual, and go over the setup step by step to ensure that everything was configured properly in the first place. A lot of the time, the problem boils down to someone skipping a step in the setup process, or inputting something wrong along the way. (This is a particularly common problem on borrowed equipment.) Start from square one and ensure that everything is configured as it's supposed to be, with no surprises.

Calling the manufacturer

When you have given it your best shot and have read the FAQs to make sure that this isn't a common problem, then — and only then — should you call the manufacturer's support hotline. This is your last resort, because you can usually look forward to long wait times and a tedious checklist as the tech support person verifies that you've done your homework. In addition, some large-scale companies charge for tech support.

Be patient, and bear with the support tech as he or she makes sure that you've narrowed down the problem properly. Do *not*, however, allow the tech support person to play ping-pong with you, claiming that it is someone else's problem and sending you off to some other company's tech support; only call when you have definitively narrowed down the problem to a specific piece of hardware or software.

The Value of Computer Manuals

I cannot count the number of times that I have read, from cover to cover, a manual about setting up a program, and then began to install that program, and immediately encountered an error that wasn't mentioned *anywhere* in the book.

The answers you need are *usually* in the official manuals, but not always. Manuals tend to assume an isolated setup, one in which your router is the *only* router and your server program is the *only* program on the machine. A lot of the time, your problem will result from some sort of clash between two separate systems — and there isn't a book or Web site out there that can account for all the weird interplays between thousands of makes of hardware and thousands of different software programs.

This is not your fault. You are not stupid; you are encountering a problem that is rare and strange, and the frustrating thing about computers is that you keep running into rare and strange situations. Stay calm, call the manufacturer, and realize that a lot of the time, you will have to comb through a ridiculously long FAQ and then search a message board to find exactly what's going wrong.

And, yes, the "documentation" includes this book. I am sure that someone will encounter some weirdo networking error that I've never heard of. Don't be frustrated; computers are twitchy, and we must deal with an imperfect world. The best skill you can learn is to stay patient and realize that when it comes to computers, you can never know it all.

A Solution That May Help

In Chapter 16, "Cool Things to Do," I describe a LAN party activity called a *troubleshooting party,* where you get the brightest techies in one place and ask them to spend an hour or two fixing lesser mortals' computers. If you have a troubleshooting party planned, quite often you can get these same people to help you with any problems that come up.

However, do not burden these people with too many requests. Remember: They're there to have fun, too—and if you work them like dogs, they're not going to enjoy it.

In addition, don't settle for subpar service. If it's obvious that the tech support person is reading off of a cue card and doesn't really know what he or she is doing (or worse, assumes you're a total idiot), feel free to ask for another tech or to speak to the manager, particularly if you're paying for the service.

Incidentally, if you're playing with pirated software, you don't get to call tech support. Oh, well.

Narrowing Down the Problem

As already mentioned, when you're trying to track down a problem at a LAN party, quite often the difficulty lies in figuring out *where* the problem is. Is it on the client? The server? The network? The router or switch?

You can use two major techniques to hunt down the source of your issue. The first, using ping to get responses from various computers, can show you what areas of your network a particular computer can reach. The second involves knowing what sorts of things generally happen when a part of your LAN party breaks down.

The following section begins with pinging, as it's usually the first tool you turn to whenever you have any network outages.

Using ping to isolate network breaks

So what do you do when you think you have TCP/IP completely configured on a computer and it still refuses to talk to the other PCs? Well, you can use ping to find out where the problem is, simply by pinging computers until you find a break.

As mentioned in Chapter 10, "The Least You Need to Know about Configuring Your Computer," ping is a very simple command-line prompt. You simply type **Ping** *<ip address>* as follows:

```
Ping 69.50.212.110
```

Ping will then send out four packets to the computer at the designated IP address, which will (you hope) respond to confirm that it received the ping request. In other words, ping says, "Hey! Can you hear me?" and the computer says, "Yeah, I can hear you."

With any luck, you'll see a result that looks something like the following:

```
Pinging 69.50.212.110 with 32 bytes of data

Reply from 69.50.212.110: bytes=32 time=99ms  TTL=128
Reply from 69.50.212.110: bytes=32 time=116ms TTL=128
Reply from 69.50.212.110: bytes=32 time=123ms TTL=128
Reply from 69.50.212.110: bytes=32 time=107ms TTL=128
```

The preceding output tells you that you got a reply, on average, in about a 10th of a second (or, more accurately, somewhere between 99 and 123 milliseconds). If there is no response to the ping request, you'll see something like this:

```
Request timed out.
Request timed out.
Request timed out.
Request timed out.
```

That means the computer never responded to the ping. This could mean one of four things:

- **The line is down.** Somewhere between your computer and this computer, a cable is broken and isn't transmitting data.

- **The computer is down.** For whatever reason — it's turned off, it's overloaded, it's just having a bad day — the computer is unable to reply.

- **The router is down.** The router may be misconfigured and sending the ping request to the wrong network, where there is no computer with that IP address.

- **The computer is configured not to reply to pings.** Hackers routinely use pings to search for hidden computers, and they can overload a computer by flooding it with many (or purposely miswritten) ping requests. Because of that, many computers have personal firewalls that are configured to ignore ping requests.

Two of these circumstances are rare. Generally, at a LAN party, you can walk over to the computer you're trying to ping and see that it's up, so you should hardly ever be pinging a dead computer. In addition, most computers do respond to pings (and if you have personal firewall software on a server, you may want to set it to allow pings when you take it to a party).

That means you can use ping to find broken lines and misconfigured routers, methodically pinging source after source until you find the area that won't ping back. Note the following four rules for using ping to isolate a problem (well, actually, there are six if a network is large enough to warrant the installation of a router):

First Rule: Check the connection.

Second Rule: Ping 127.0.0.1.

Third Rule: Ping a server.

Fourth Rule: Ping another computer on the same subnetwork.

Special Fifth Rule: Ping the router.

Special Sixth Rule: Ping a computer on another subnetwork.

Checking the cable

Always check all the physical connections between the affected computer and the computer it wants to reach. Do this before you start typing out boatloads of obscure commands with your mega-MCSE-networkamondo skills. It'll save you a lot of embarassment in the long run, and you'd be surprised how often the problem is nothing more complex than a loose wire or a dead port on a hub or switch.

Pinging 127.0.0.1

This is the address of your network card, and you're pinging it to see if it responds. If it doesn't, then you have either a dead card or an improperly configured one.

Cross-Reference

If you can't ping 127.0.0.1, the most likely problem is that you haven't bound TCP/IP properly to your NIC. Refer to Chapter 10, "The Least You Need to Know about Configuring Your Computer," for details on binding.

Pinging a server

If a computer can't establish a game with a server, ping the server. If it's successful, then you know that the problem is not in the connection; the two computers can talk to each other just fine.

If this is the only computer that can't log on to the server and you can ping it, then the problem most likely is with the software (and is most likely because of different versions of game software; someone forgot to upgrade!).

If this is one of many computers that can't log on to the server and you can ping it, there is most likely a firewall somewhere that is preventing gaming traffic from going through. You'll have to reconfigure your firewall.

Cross-Reference

For further details on ports, network traffic, and firewalls, refer to Chapter 8, "Networking for Large Groups and the Internet."

Pinging another computer on the same subnetwork

If you can ping your network card and you can't ping the server, check to see whether you can ping other computers on the same subnetwork. "The same subnetwork" is a fancy way of saying *ping the other computers attached directly to the hub or switch.* If you can't get a response from any of those computers, chances are good that your cable is bad or that the port to which this PC is connected may be dead. Try switching to a port that you know is working (usually by switching ports with a computer that can ping other PCs), and verify; and then swap the cable out to see if that fixes the problem.

Alternatively, confirm that all of your computers *are* on the same network — namely, that they have the same subnet and host address. Subtle differences in mistyped IP addresses, particularly if you've entered them by hand or if you have another DHCP server on the network (which can happen — see "The Most Common DHCP Problem" later in the chapter), may cause your computer to believe it's on a different network altogether.

Take a look at the following:

> **Computer #1:** 169.254.0.1, subnet 255.255.255.0
>
> **Computer #2:** 169.254.0.2, subnet 255.255.255.0

Each of these two computers thinks that it is on two separate networks, and they may be sending their data out to a very confused router.

Similarly, look at the following:

> **Computer #1:** 169.254.0.1, subnet 255.255.255.0
>
> **Computer #2:** 192.62.2.10, subnet 255.255.255.0

Because these two addresses were handed out by two different DHCP servers (and again, to see how this can happen, see the section "The Most Common DHCP Problem," later in the chapter), one computer thinks it's on network 169.254.0, and the other computer thinks it's on network 192.62.2. Both computers, when trying to reach each other, will send their requests to the default gateway, which may send them out to the Internet, where they will never be heard from again.

Improperly configured IP addresses can cause many problems, so check a couple of the computers around the network to make sure they're what you think they are!

Tip How do you check a computer's IP address? With the ever-popular ipconfig command, of course! Typing **ipconfig /all** at the command prompt will give you tons of details about the computer's IP address (as shown in Figure 15-1), including when it received its address and subnet mask, its DHCP and DNS server, and what the computer's external host name is (which is useful for Windows file sharing).

```
Command Prompt                                                    _ □ x
Microsoft Windows XP [Version 5.1.2600]
(C) Copyright 1985-2001 Microsoft Corp.

C:\Documents and Settings\Ferrett>ipconfig /all

Windows IP Configuration

        Host Name . . . . . . . . . . . : kewferrett
        Primary Dns Suffix  . . . . . . :
        Node Type . . . . . . . . . . . : Unknown
        IP Routing Enabled. . . . . . . : No
        WINS Proxy Enabled. . . . . . . : No

Ethernet adapter Local Area Connection:

        Connection-specific DNS Suffix  . : homeportal.2wire.net
        Description . . . . . . . . . . . : Intel(R) PRO/100 S Desktop Adapter
        Physical Address. . . . . . . . . : 00-02-B3-87-9C-0F
        Dhcp Enabled. . . . . . . . . . . : Yes
        Autoconfiguration Enabled . . . . : Yes
        IP Address. . . . . . . . . . . . : 172.16.1.33
        Subnet Mask . . . . . . . . . . . : 255.255.0.0
        Default Gateway . . . . . . . . . : 172.16.0.1
        DHCP Server . . . . . . . . . . . : 172.16.0.1
        DNS Servers . . . . . . . . . . . : 172.16.0.1
        Lease Obtained. . . . . . . . . . : Friday, December 12, 2003 8:53:33 PM

        Lease Expires . . . . . . . . . . : Friday, December 12, 2003 9:53:33 PM

C:\Documents and Settings\Ferrett>
```

FIGURE 15-1: A complete ipconfig /all

Pinging the router

Obviously, pinging the router will only work if you *have* a router. What you're doing with this technique is checking to see whether your router itself is active. Generally, you'll know right away when a router is down, as all of the other computers on the network will be affected too, but sometimes only one computer is actually trying to access data that's outside the network. (For example, if six people are all playing *Command and Conquer* on a local server and the seventh is trying to access *Duke Nukem* on a remote server, the *Duke Nukem* gamer may be the only one who notices.) If the router is down, you'll have to fix it; check the wires that connect the router to all of the other networks to make sure they're plugged in. Failing that, try rebooting the router.

Pinging a computer on another subnetwork

Again, this technique will only work if you have a router.

If you can ping the router but can't ping a computer elsewhere, the problem is most likely in your router's tables; your router evidently doesn't know where to send it, or is sending it to the wrong place.

Unfortunately, routers are complex beasties with operating systems that vary wildly depending on who makes them, and troubleshooting routers is outside the scope of this book. My best advice is to tell you to either flush the current routing table and reboot the router so it recreates its routing table from scratch, or, if you have static routing tables that you have manually entered into your router, double-check them to make sure they're correct. You can also use the tracert command, which will show you the IP addresses to which the router is forwarding your data along the way, which may help you isolate the problem.

The common areas of LAN party breakdown

As mentioned earlier, most LAN party problems originate in one of three categories:

- The network
- The server
- The client

The following sections describe the warning signs of a problem in each of these areas.

Network problems

"Network problems" is something of a misnomer, because if you've done the reading thus far, you know that networks are comprised of several parts: the wires that make up the network, the hubs and switches, any routers you may have, the DHCP server, and of course the ever-popular firewall. Regardless of where the problem lies, however, the end result of any network outage is that one or more computers can't talk to each other.

Thankfully, network problems usually boil down to two separate cases: widespread outages and computer-specific outages. Usually, you use a combination of common sense and ping hunting to find out where the problem lies.

Widespread outages

Usually, widespread outages stem from a bad or incorrectly configured hub, switch, or router.

The first question that must be answered is, "Are the affected computers completely isolated from the network, or can they can ping **some** computers (just not all)?" Remember that not every network outage is global, and finding out where the affected PCs are having problems will usually point to where the problem lies.

For example, if the computers hooked up to a switch can ping each other but not the server, you know the problem is most likely somewhere between the switch and the server (and is most likely a loose or dead cable). If the affected computers can ping one server but not another, you can start looking at the connections and routers that lie between the server and the computers in that area. If you can ping any computer on your local network but can't ping a server on the Internet, you definitely want to look at the router that provides Internet access.

The second question is, "What types of traffic can get through?" Many times, you can ping a server, but you can't connect to it with the game. This usually indicates that a firewall of some sort is blocking the appropriate traffic, and you'll want to adjust the settings. (See Chapter 8, "Networking for Large Groups and the Internet," for more information on firewalls and network traffic.)

The final question is, "What do the affected computers have in common?" If the only computers that can't ping a specific server are all hooked up to the same switch, you know the problem is most likely something to do with the switch. If all of the computers on the left side of the room can't ping anything and they're all served by the same DHCP server, chances are good the problem's related to the DHCP server.

If the affected computers have nothing in common — different switches, different DHCP servers, different routers — then it's probably a client-specific issue writ large. Particularly at large LAN parties, you'll find that many clients arrive with their computers incorrectly configured. If the computer outages are all over the map, chances are good that several people showed up with misconfigured computers.

Computer-specific outages

This problem boils down to, "I can't connect to the network but everything else is fine." Usually, you have to ping a few computers to verify that their connection is, in fact, completely dead.

However, I'll reiterate here that *the* most common form of computer outage is a broken connection — and that broken connection is usually a loose cable, a bad cable, or a dead port. Before you start tweaking software settings, *make sure the cable is plugged in.*

Even the best of us have our "D'oh!" moments where we forget to check the plug. Always, *always* check that first.

Server problems

Server problems reflect situations in which several people cannot log on to the game server, but the network connection between the server and the affected computers is fine (that is, you can ping the server from all the clients). This type of problem usually originates from one of the following sources:

The Most Common DHCP Problem

Many times, people have set up their own home network using Windows ME or later, and have installed Network Address Translation on their computer to share a cable connection. Unfortunately, this turns their computer into a DHCP server, which, when it is plugged into your network, will immediately start handing out IP addresses that may conflict with the ones that have already been established.

If you have a weird network problem in which half the computers have an IP address with a different network segment (for example, half of them are 192.68.2.x and the other half are 169.42.2.x), someone most likely has Network Address Translation (NAT) turned on and needs to turn it off.

You can track down the rogue DHCP server by typing ipconfig /all at the command prompt of an affected computer, which will return the IP address of its DHCP server—and, more important, when it obtained an IP address from the server, which should help you determine when the rogue DHCP server came online. Chapter 10, "The Least You Need to Know About Configuring Your Computer," has information on how to disable NAT.

- The server is behind some sort of firewall, either on the machine itself or on one of the routers/switches, which is allowing pings and HTTP traffic, but disallowing game traffic. To fix this problem, you'll need to open up the appropriate ports on your firewall; for more information on firewalls, see Chapter 8, "Networking for Large Groups and the Internet."

- The server is configured with a maximum number of players, and is currently maxed out. Double-check to see how your server started.

- The server itself has crashed. Whoops! Restart.

- (Rarely) You accidentally changed a parameter and the server is attempting to accept connections on a custom port that's not the standard game port.

- (Even more rarely) You have a badly configured DHCP and it has changed the IP address of your server in midgame, causing clients everywhere to look for the server at the wrong address.

Client problems

Client problems involve isolated computers that cannot access the server to play a game. These generally fall into one of four categories:

- Is the network cable plugged in tightly? It isn't? Please, plug it in.

- Is the machine set to request a DHCP address, or was the IP address set to the one requested at the beginning of the party? If not, fix it now. (As I mentioned earlier in "The Most Common DHCP Problem," guests will often bring a machine that is preconfigured to *be* a DHCP server, resulting in multiple DHCP servers on a network. This causes no end of problems.)

- Does the machine have the updated patch, and is it trying to connect to the server with an older version of the game? If a missing patch is the problem, simply install it now.

- Is the machine connecting via the correct port? If not, fix that now. (This only happens at tourneys where you're changing the port for some bizarre security reason.)

Noncomputer Problems

Not all of your problems are going to be computer-related. Sometimes you run into a social problem—people are getting angry, or something other than a computer breaks down. Obviously, I can't go into all of the issues that might crop up when you're playing—I am *not* going to detail how to plunge a toilet—but I will say that two of the biggest issues that come up are the power going out and someone needing to be booted.

Power outages

Power can go out—and does. This topic is discussed in detail in Chapter 6, "Avoiding Power Failures." Refer to the end of that chapter for the full skinny, assuming that you can scrounge up a flashlight so you have enough light to read it!

People outages

There are times when you have to ask someone to leave your party—when someone's causing such a ruckus or inspiring such hatred that nobody can enjoy themselves while this yutz is stinking up the place.

The good (and bad) part about kicking someone out is that it happens so rarely that you will never have a chance to get good at it. Most people will take the hint and calm down; you may have to tell them repeatedly, but it's almost never bad enough that you have to eject them from the building.

However, if you ever do have to remove someone from your party immediately, here are some guidelines:

1. **Remember that this is your party, and your call.** I can't tell you what sorts of behavior should result in someone being booted, because that's up to you. Me, I hate it when people run around screaming vulgarities and doing insulting dances at people they just fragged, and I'm always tempted to boot them, but you might *like* that kind of hard-core party. I know of many parties where it's acceptable to smoke pot behind closed doors (which, may I remind you, is currently illegal), and, conversely, of many parties where any drug use will get you instantly banned. Therefore, *you* have to make the call as to what's unacceptable behavior.

   However, any physical violence, theft, cheating, or equipment trashing *demands* an instant ejection, lest these morons think they can get away with it in the future.

2. **Be absolutely sure that removal is the solution.** Tossing someone should always be the last resort. This isn't some IRC chat room where you can just ban someone for no reason; in this case, you're going to be physically confronting people who will most likely be upset, asking them to pack their stuff up and leave in front of the entire room, and shepherding them out. (If you're ejecting someone from a paid event, be warned that you'll most likely be alienating someone who will badmouth you and your events for a *very* long time.)

Thus, make sure that either the sin is so horrible that it can't be forgiven (such as violence or theft), or you've tried to talk to the player(s) on multiple occasions and they have consistently refused to cooperate. Always do *everything* you can to resolve the situation via other methods before kicking someone out.

3. **Get some friends.** Never attempt to kick someone out on your own. It's usually better to have a group of two or three people behind you, which serves two purposes: The sheer number of people will help to cow an unruly player into submission, and the fact that you have people backing you up helps to establish that this was not solely your decision. You'll do the talking, of course, but having several people behind you — one of whom should be the Muscle Goon, as mentioned in Chapter 11 — helps to establish a consensus. Ideally, your united front should look something like what is shown in Figure 15-2.

Figure 15-2: Correct posture to assume when ejecting an unruly partygoer

In addition, note that if you can't find two people who are willing to back you up, then maybe you want to reconsider your decision. If you're the only one who's offended, maybe you should be more tolerant. (Or maybe you need to be the voice of reason.)

4. **State clearly why you want them to leave, and accept no arguments.** Tell them what they're guilty of, and explain that you want them to pack their equipment right now and get out. Be calm, clear, and authoritative. Do not show anger.

   They will argue with you, telling you that what you're doing is unfair — and worst of all, if you have been too quick on the gun to throw them out, they may even have a valid solution that would have fixed the problem.

   Unfortunately, now you're committed; if you back down at this point, everyone will know that you can be argued into submission, which means that future kick-outs will be met with whining and a *lot* of angry arguments in an attempt to weasel out of it. It's far better to have a reputation as a despot than it is to have a rep as a softie who can be manipulated. Therefore, even if they're absolutely, 100 percent, totally right, just nod and say, "I'm sorry, it's too late, you have to go."

   This is another reason why kicking someone out should be your last option. Make sure you've done everything, because by the time you get the team together and storm over with demands, *you can't go back*. Make sure that you're comfortable with your decision before you commit.

5. **Watch them as they leave.** You'll feel stupid hanging over them as they gather up their stuff, but if you leave them alone, they might decide that, what the heck, they've been caught anyway, why not do something *truly* stupid or harmful on the way out? Do not let them out of your sight once you have told them to leave.

6. **If they refuse to go, call the police.** This is your house (or your party), and you can charge them with trespassing or unruly conduct. Generally, the threat of calling the police will be enough to get someone to scamper, but the truly stubborn will look you in the eye and say, "Make me." (Keep in mind that practically no LAN parties have jerks of this magnitude; I'm covering a total nuclear meltdown-style, absolute worst-case scenario.)

   Don't touch anyone physically, and do not touch anyone's equipment. Not only are you asking to get into a fight, but you may incur legal consequences even if you're trained to handle yourself in physical situations. You are within your rights to let the professionals handle it, and should. Don't let some jerk bully you into making a mistake.

Summary

In this chapter, you've learned the best way to handle problems: calmly, logically, and methodically. Do not get upset, try to isolate your problem, and you should be fine.

We're reaching the end now. In the next chapter, you'll learn about some fun stuff for LAN parties!

Cool Things to Do at Your LAN Party

I f you've read the last 15 chapters, you now know how to run a LAN party. You understand IP addressing, know where to scrounge the best equipment, and know how to structure the day so everything runs smoothly.

But do you know what makes a LAN party *cool*?

This last chapter is devoted to the neat stuff — the touches that make a LAN party memorable. You don't need to have any of these to hold a LAN party, but then again, technically speaking, you don't need salt or side dishes at a meal.

The things you will learn about in this chapter just make a LAN party better, so you might want to consider including them. These items can be roughly divided into two categories:

> **Environmental bonuses.** Isn't it nice to have a big-screen television to sit down at? How about a DJ spinning hardcore techno? These are the kinds of enhancements that it's nice to have around when you are basically sitting in one spot all day.
>
> Actually, I'd call "file sharing" an environmental bonus, but that topic is so big I had to give its own section, "Sharing Files," later on in the chapter.

> **LAN party activities.** "At 12:30, we're holding our case-modding how-to session. At 4:00, it's the Nerf Gun Bug-Hunt. Then, after hours, when the kiddies have gone home, we're going to be busting open the Big Keg O'Frag." This covers all of the events you can hold at a LAN party to fill in the time between the kills.

Note that if you would like to share any cool things you've done at your LAN party, feel free to e-mail me at theferrett@theferrett.com to tell me what they are. Maybe, if this book does well enough, there will be a second edition with all of your tips in it!

Environmental Bonuses

A LAN party should be more than a bunch of people at their computers, staring at a cathode-ray tube while they play a game for eight hours straight. Other distractions should be available, so that when you walk away from the screen, you have something else to look at other than, say, the floor.

This section is devoted to your LAN party's surroundings; when you take away the network, what else can you offer to make things fun for everyone?

Screen excess: Showing the game

You can actually make the game larger than life in a number of ways. Most of them involve utilizing projection technology to put your computer games up where everyone can see them. It's a cool visual hook for your room to have your best and most interesting game zipping along in glowing LCD colors. (Also, it doesn't hurt to have a set of monster speakers hooked up so the windows rattle every time someone uses the rocket launcher.)

Fortunately, hooking a computer up to a television or stereo is pretty easy to do.

Plugging your PC into a television

Most televisions require an *RCA cable* in order to hook up a computer. RCA cables are your standard audio-visual cables; you hook them into Nintendos, PlayStations, and DVD players. Figure 16-1 shows you a picture of an RCA cable.

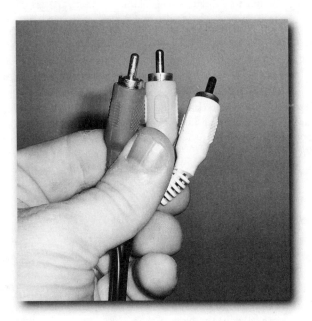

FIGURE 16-1: RCA cable

RCA cables are available in two-plug versions (one is the audio channel and one is the video channel) and three-plug versions (one is the right audio channel, one is the left audio channel, and the last is the video channel).

Computers with top-of-the-line video cards will have "Television Out" or "TV Out" plugs on the back—you can plug in your RCA cable here. This is, needless to say, a snap; just plug the cables into the sockets on your PC and your video card, and you're good to go!

Other computers may not offer this amazing technology, so you'll need to get a pair of *Y-Adaptor cables* — a cable with a small connector on one end that's designed to plug into your computer card. (The other end has two RCA-compatible plugs, enabling you to connect your computer to the TV.) If your computer does not have a TV Out plug, you'll need one cable to plug into your sound card's external audio plug (whatever it's called) and one to plug into your video card's A/V Out socket (or whatever it's called), as shown in Figure 16-2.

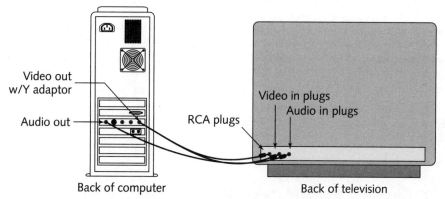

FIGURE 16-2: Hooking a computer *without* a premade RCA "Video Out" plug to a television. This gets a lot easier if you have a video card that's TV-ready!

Note one problem with this setup: A computer monitor, even the worst monitor, offers far better resolution than most TVs. (High-definition television is the sole exception, but even then you can sometimes wind up with some strange blurs and bleeds on a plasma screen.) After you put your image on the television, you may find that it's distorted, unclear, fuzzy, or even radically resized. Moreover, you will almost certainly find that the colors are muddier and that heavy flickering occurs.

If you have a video card with TV Out, chances are good that somewhere in the settings there is a Television setting that enables you to change your display to a high-contrast version designed specifically to look good on televisions. Alas, since its location varies so much by manufacturer and make, I can't tell you exactly where it is, but the information should be somewhere in the manual or online.

Should you have no TV Out (or if you don't want to change your personal display settings to make things look good on an external screen), you have a second option: a *scan converter*. A scan converter is an independent piece of hardware that translates computer video output into a television-friendly signal, and it's used routinely for PowerPoint presentations and the like. High-end scan converters can cost more than four thousand dollars for business-heavy equipment, but you can get a respectable one suitable for LAN parties for under $150 at the time of this writing.

The disadvantage of low-end scan converters is that some of them are *software-aided* — that is, your computer actually lends some horsepower to aid in the conversion process. If you're running a high-end game, you may not have the horsepower to spare, and using it may cause errors as your graphics card competes with the the scan adaptor. In addition, many low-end scan converters have a maximum resolution of 800×600 — fine for business use, but not good for your

UT 2003 deathmatch. Worse yet, some of them will accept input of 1,024×728, but only put out 800×600, and will thus show only part of the action.

The lesson? Check the requirements very closely before you buy (or borrow!).

Plugging your PC into an LCD projector

An LCD projector is what many LAN parties use in lieu of a television. Essentially, it takes a computer input and projects it onto a flat surface in much the same way that a movie projector does. An LCD projector is better than a television (even with a scan adaptor) because it's custom-designed to use computer input. LCD projectors frequently have special features designed specifically to enhance computer presentation, such as multiple computer inputs that you can switch between when someone takes the lead in a match; external jacks into which you can plug high-end speakers; and remote controls that enable you to change the display from across the room. Most LCD projectors also have RCA jacks so you can plug a television in when needed.

LCD projectors are also cool because you can project an image onto any available surface. I've heard of LAN parties that displayed the game on the ceiling so that every gamer could look up and see it at a glance!

The downside to an LCD projector is that, well, it projects. Just as movie theaters turn the lights off before they start showing a movie, you should only use an LCD projector in a dim or dark area. While you *can* use an LCD projector in a well-lit room, the image can appear washed out if you're not careful. LCD projectors track their brightness in lumens, and you'll need a minimum of 500 lumens for a well-lit room. If you're using any sort of spotlights or anything else, figure that you'll need a lot more.

Be aware that LCD projectors are fairly expensive, as they're designed mostly for corporate use. Of course, by now you have memorized the LAN partiers' creed: *Beg before you buy!* You may well know people who can borrow one from their day job for the weekend.

If you do bring in an LCD projector, the good news is that most of them are designed to be carried around. The bad news is that this makes them easy to steal—and did I mention how expensive they are? If you use one, you probably want to consider having some sort of lock-down system (such as a padlock and plastic-coated chain) to attach your projector to something sturdy.

The wall of monitors

Another very impressive idea if you have a lot of free time (or just way too many spare monitors) is to give *every* guest a separate feed to a front-of-the-room monitor. This takes a lot of advance prep work, but you can come up with something that's totally stunning—and something that enables nongamers to sit back and watch literally *all* the action!

Adding console games to a computer network

One of the easiest (and most common) ways of making a LAN party fun is to add extra games from a different system. If you're playing all-PC, someone *always* has a PlayStation 2, a GameCube, or an XBox to spare; ask them to bring them to the party so everyone can play!

Following are some general guidelines for adding consoles to an existing LAN Party:

- **Have them in a separate area.** Stuffing consoles into the middle of a LAN party will annoy both computer and console enthusiasts because, unlike computers, where one person sits at one keyboard, consoles are made for people to gather around. That means you can't use headphones for consoles, and will have to turn the volume up for the TV. This noise level is further exacerbated by the fact that console players usually trash talk a lot, proclaiming their skills to all within earshot.

  This noise bugs the PC players, who have to use their headphones. And furthermore, if you plop a TV into the middle of a LAN party, the console players probably won't have enough space to gather.

  The lesson? Set someplace aside for console gaming only.

- **Have good seating.** Consoles aren't as intense as computers, where you're hunched over a keyboard; with a PlayStation 2, you just lean back on the controller and twiddle your thumbs. The best way to enjoy a console game is on a comfortable couch or recliner, so make sure you have at least one handy (and preferably multiple seats with cushions).

- **Use a good TV with excellent sound.** Since you want this to be a gathering place, get a big TV (preferably a nice widescreen, a yard across) with good speakers. If you have surround sound speakers, hook 'em up! Make it as inviting as possible.

  There are three styles of other games you can play: single-console, multi-console, and DDR.

Single-console games

A single game console can provide a lot of fun, as you can usually have two players going head-to-head. However, you do *not* want to play any long games that require great concentration and a lot of time; usually, that's what you're playing on the computers! You want a quick, relatively mindless game that serves as the sherbet between courses at a fine restaurant; something to cleanse your palate between the salad and the soup.

In other words, what you want is quickie party games that people will be able to complete quickly, not massive role-playing or horror-survival games that take a single person hours to win. Especially good are games suitable for competing in short rounds at which someone wins, so that everyone can take turns. Good games include the following:

- *Mario Party* and any of its variants

- Any sort of fighting game (*Tekken*, *Dead or Alive*, *Soul Calibur*, *Virtua Fighter*, and so forth)

- Any sport-styled racing games, such as *SSX Tricky*, *Tony Hawk*, or *Gran Turismo*

- Puzzle games such as *Super Puzzle Fighter II* (the best head-to-head puzzle game ever invented, for my money!)

- *Grand Theft Auto III*, which breaks all the criteria I gave you before, but it's incredibly fun to watch, even if you're *not* playing.

Multi-console games

As we all know, the PS2 and Xbox are geared to be networked, and you can plug them into your existing network the same way that you can any other computer. That means you have the ability to go head-to-head on a whole range of games, providing even more entertainment!

If you announce that it's an Xbox party, people will bring in their Xboxes. You have not lived until you've played eight-person *Halo* on the Xbox, I promise; it is, in all senses, hellafun.

DDR

DDR stands for *Dance Dance Revolution*, which is by far the most popular side game at LAN parties. In fact, some people spend more time DDRing than they do playing computer games at a LAN party!

Dance Dance Revolution, for those three of you who don't know, is unique among videogames in that it's physical. (You *can* play it on a game pad, but that's kind of missing the point.) Instead of a joystick, you're instead given a three-foot-wide pad with four arrows — up, down, right, and left — that you can step on. DDR plays music and arrows scroll up the screen; you're supposed to step on the pads in syncopated rhythm with the music. Miss too many arrows and you're out of the game. It's hard to sum it up in a picture, but Figure 16-3 makes a valiant attempt.

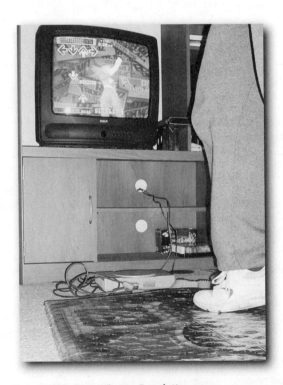

FIGURE 16-3: Dance Dance Revolution

At high levels, your feet become a Flintstone-style blur of toes; advanced players can add spice by hitting the pads with their elbows and doing Michael Jackson–style twirls in between the "official" steps. Watching a DDR master is awesome indeed! (If you want to see some videos of top players in full-out DDR mode, www.DDRfreak.com has some excellent videos of championship battles.)

This combination of exercise, coordination, and music has become an addiction for many — especially given that there are well over two hundred DDR songs to choose from, ranging the gamut from full-on Japanese pop to heavy metal. Most are extremely catchy. (My favorite? A toss-up between "Drop the Bomb" and "Make it Better," but not the So-Real mix.)

DDR started out as an arcade-based phenomenon, but it has spread to the home. At the time of this writing, there are more than twenty-five arcade variants and sequels to the original DDR, each with its own songs, steps, and variations; and over 6.5 million copies of DDR have been sold worldwide for consoles. Needless to say, it's a worldwide phenomenon.

There are two ways to play DDR: as a console game or as an arcade machine. We'll examine both, starting with the coolest and most troublesome.

DDR arcade

The best way to play *Dance Dance Revolution* is in the arcade, because the home pads you can buy are generally substandard. A good solid DDR machine has metal pads that register every step, excellent speakers, and a large metal rail that you can grab to do extra-special stunts if you're a pro. You can rent a DDR machine in some places, but it involves a fair amount of hassle:

- **DDR arcade machines are extremely large and heavy.** You'll be lucky to cram one onto the back of a pickup truck, and three people can't carry one. You won't be able to fit it through a normal door. Getting transportation for a full-fledged DDR machine can be a huge hassle.

  In addition, you'll have to reserve a large footprint space on your floor plan to account for any DDR machine. The exact square footage varies from model to model — they have huge models designed for large arcades and smaller ones designed for bars — but they're all pretty darned big.

- **DDR arcade machines are expensive.** They start at around $18,000 and increase from there. You're not going to buy one, of course, but the price of the unit affects what people will charge to rent them. You're easily going to be looking at a couple of hundred dollars to rent it, plus a very hefty security deposit.

- **DDR arcade machines are in high demand.** When I called around to rent one for one of my parties, nobody had any in stock to rent; they had sold or leased them all to local arcades. Getting one on short notice is likely to be nearly impossible.

However, renting a DDR machine has two advantages that can't be beat:

- **DDR arcade machines are supremely cool.** Having a full-fledged machine at your party is the absolute bomb. I wouldn't advise it for a smaller event, but having a DDR machine for the weekend at a big party gives you mad style points.

■ **DDR arcade machines can give you some return on investment.** Although you can set a DDR machine to free play, you can also keep it in quarter-gobbling mode and get some cash back from it. Just be sure to have tons of quarters on hand to provide spare change for your local DDR maniacs.

If you'd like to rent an arcade machine, you can do a Yahoo! yellow pages search for "arcade" and look for places that have "supply" or "amusement" in their title, and then call around. Many arcade owners do not "rent" per se; they *lease*, with the option to return the machine prematurely for a fee. The difference between leasing and renting is that if you keep your DDR machine for long enough, eventually you'll buy it. The disadvantage is that it's more expensive to rent, and many amusement supply stores won't lease for less than a month.

Furthermore, many of them don't deliver. This can be a real pain.

But it's *so* damn *cool!*

DDR console (The methadone of DDR)

If you can't get a real DDR machine, you'll have to settle for the console version. Versions of DDR are available for the PlayStation 2 and the XBox, although you'll have to buy special controllers to hook up to each of them.

To properly recreate the arcade experience, you need two things: an excellent sound system and a pair of good game pads. (You want two so people can play head-to-head.) The sound system is easy enough to set up: get a good pair of speakers and hook them up to the television — preferably, some sort of surround sound system. (Actually, this is a fine idea for any console game.)

Unfortunately, most of the pads have one of two problems: they're too cheap or they're pricey. The good pads (also known as *hard pads*) are made of metal and plastic, and currently run between $100 and $200. The latter will serve wonderfully for a DDR party, but that's almost $400 for two top-of-the-line pads!

Tip Don't forget the LAN partiers creed: *Beg before you borrow.* See if someone has some hard pads they're willing to bring to the party.

The *soft pads* are made of soft plastic, and they are distinctly substandard. They don't register it well when someone steps on them — and, worse yet, because they're little more than plastic blankets (think of a Twister board), they tend to slip a lot. When the whole point of the game is stepping on four arrows, having those arrows slip two or three inches between steps can ruin a whole game!

Soft pads will run you between $25 and $50, but you can save a lot of money by modding your pads, providing a hard backing to them so that they don't slip. Here's the secret:

1. Buy a 33×36-inch sheet of ½-inch-thick plywood for each pad. (Pressed board will do.)

2. Buy two three-foot segments of hardwood floor covering (a thick clear plastic sheet) for each pad.

3. Place the soft pad on the plywood board. Use duct tape to tape the pad to the plywood, taping along the edges and underneath.

4. Lay the first segment of hardwood covering over the top half of the pad. (It won't be big enough to lay over the entire board.) Staple along the edges of the wood to affix the covering to the wood, *but do not staple through the pad*, lest you accidentally staple through a much-needed wire.

5. Lay the second piece of hardwood covering over the top half. Once again, staple.

6. Turn it over and staple the hardwood covering to the back of the board.

7. Get a piece of clear packaging tape and tape the seam along the center so that nobody trips on it.

Your final result will look like what is shown in Figure 16-4.

FIGURE 16-4: A finished modded pad. You'll want to use *clear* floor covering, instead of being a yutz who uses floor covering with patterns, as I did. (Fortunately, it doesn't affect the game play.)

DVD breaks

When you have a big whoppin' television, nothing's better than taking a break to watch some obscure movie such as *Glen or Glenda* — or even a comfort movie like *Fellowship of the Ring*. Offering scheduled movies and television shows can provide a nice rhythm and flow to the entire day.

In fact, many larger parties wall off a section of their floor and create a 24-hour "movie room," in which they show continual loops of the latest imported anime episodes, Buffy episodes, and rare science-fiction films like *Zardoz*. An area like this demands a comfortable couch, a couple of throw chairs, reasonable darkness, and preferably a projection screen. Popcorn and jujubes extra.

Music, both canned and DJ'd

What's better than grooving to some crazy beat while you're dismantling your enemy's power base, one unit at a time? If your location has a good speaker system (or you can borrow a good loud system), burn a mix CD to blister people's ears and bring the noise at your jam.

Just make sure you know what your players' musical tastes are. I'm partial to hard rock and hip-grinding electronica, but many players prefer the lyrical styles of O.G. gangsta music or Japanime pop. You don't have to play something that *everyone* loves, but make sure you're not playing *The Best of Barbra Streisand* or the soundtrack to *The Lion King* when everyone would rather be listening to Kid Rock. And be sure to change the CD occasionally, or have a multi-CD setup so that the tunes don't become repetitive. Remember: You're trying to keep the energy level up, not have everyone muttering, "Lordy, *that* song again?"

As a matter of fact, if you've got an outside location with a lot of players, hire the hottest DJ from the local club to spin some beats for your party. Usually, most nightclub DJs don't work during the day, and you can get them to work day parties for a reasonable price because it doesn't conflict with their night job and gives them extra exposure. If you're willing to lay out moderate bucks (or happen to know a hungry DJ who needs the publicity), you can often get someone to spin discs for an entire evening.

Be sure to tell the DJ that you're not interested in getting people to dance — you want excitement. Most DJs enjoy the challenge of trying to put together a custom playlist that keeps the energy up when nobody's actually moving.

If you *get* a DJ, promote them to the high heavens — and ask them to push your LAN party when they're playing their nightly gig, too. A DJ, particularly a popular underground one, adds a level of hipness to your party that really lends a lot of excitement to your event.

Tip Live music isn't quite as good. Not only do the amps and microphones of a rock band demand valuable power that you may need for your LAN party, but they tend to be too loud and abrasive. DJs can learn to play for the background, but most live bands demand an audience.

Add a party to your LAN

The best way to hold a LAN party is in conjunction with some other celebration. Making a LAN party–themed celebration for some other event makes both better! Why not have a LAN party barbecue, or a LAN party birthday party, or a LAN party Fourth of July?

Having a LAN party as an adjunct, and not the main event, allows significant others, children, and nongamers to come along for the ride, which makes it far more of a group activity. (The only caveat is that if you hold a nongamer party, you want to offer some nongamer activities to keep people interested, such as *Dance Dance Revolution*, Twister, or a barbecue.)

Having LAN parties as adjuncts presents some challenges, mainly related to having small children or strangers around expensive computer equipment. My suggestion is that if you hold a LAN party on the side, be sure to put someone on security duty the entire time, and have someone keep an eye out for potentially damaging shenanigans.

Room decorations

Just because you're in a big empty space or a cluttered apartment is no reason not to spruce it up a bit. No, I'm not talking about Martha Stewart–style floral arrangements; I'm talking kick-butt-cool decorations that lend a theme to a party, things like the following:

- **The military look.** Hang camouflage nets over the playing area, and have all of the staffers wear military uniforms. It certainly helps in enforcing good behavior.

- **The sci-fi look.** You're already using neon piping and chrome inlays for your case mods — why not utilize that for the party? Use black lights overhead to give it a dimly lit *Enterprise* mood, and leave a lot of monitors on with weird glowing images, preferably lifted from exterior shots of old science-fiction TV shows.

- **The medieval look.** Put a lot of garlands around, hang swords on the wall, and have everyone haul out their Society for Creative Anachronism and RenFaire outfits. This is especially good after the release of the latest computer role-playing game, such as *Neverwinter Nights* or *Temple of Elemental Evil*.

Do these sound dorky? Well, that's because they *are* dorky — and in a major way. But if you have the right kind of party, you can take pride in your rampant geekery.

Most people will never go to these outlandish efforts, and rightfully so, but sometimes they pay off in spades. I wouldn't advise using these for a first-time party — you have enough to do — but these sorts of extra efforts are great for an annual event, or for livening up a routine get-together that's starting to feel a little dull.

Sharing Files

Actually, this information should be in the "Environmental Bonuses" section, because having a nice place to trade files, cool hacks, and (legal) MP3s at 100 megabytes per second is a luxury that every LAN party should enjoy. Back in the days of free Napster, a lot of my friends went out of their way to set up their own Kazaa-style file-sharing networks in order to make our LAN parties sing. Alas, those days are over, and the companies that made the appropriate software have gone out of business. What we have left is Windows file shares, FTP, and Samba.

Windows file sharing allows you to create what's known as a *file server* — a place where people can download the latest patches and software. All you have to do is take a folder on your PC and *share* it with the network, which makes that folder accessible to any computer that asks. Users can also, depending on how you set up the shared folder, upload their own files there so everyone can access them.

Tip

As a general rule, it's a lot easier to have one computer designated as the file server, to which everyone uploads their files, as opposed to a lot of shared folders scattered across everyone's computers. This also allows for greater security, as you can configure the file server's antivirus program to scan all new files and disinfect them if necessary.

The downside is that sharing files can be a potential security breach (a lot of hackers access Windows computers via the file-sharing protocols), and that it radically increases the potential of a network-aware virus or worm spreading catastrophically through your LAN party, taking every computer down with it. Unlike the Internet, networks are very small places, and a virus or a worm can spread at lightning speed. I've heard horror stories of twenty-person LAN parties brought to a screaming halt in under three minutes.

That brings up two extremely important points:

- **If you're going to allow file sharing, demand a check-in virus scan.** Don't allow people to scan with whatever virus checker they have around. A lot of people don't update their virus definitions on a regular basis, and usually it's the new viruses that cause the biggest problems. Make sure everyone is using an up-to-date checker.

- **Do not disable your firewall software entirely when playing.** In an effort to conserve precious CPU cycles, many gamers turn off their firewall so that their PC can devote its full power to gaming. This is a mistake, as many viruses and worms can detect that they're on a network and quietly infiltrate other computers via some obscure port or back door. Having firewall software helps you to avoid this awful fate.

Your best personal firewall software, as I've mentioned before, is ZoneAlarm (which can be downloaded at www.ZoneAlarm.com), and the most common free virus scanner is AVG anti-virus (which can be downloaded at www.grisoft.com). Both have free or single-user versions that allow for unlimited use. But like all software, even if you *can* get it for free, you should pay to register it if you use it enough!

However, there is a catch: Most personal firewalls (that is, the ones installed directly on your computer, as opposed to hardware-based firewalls on routers and router/switches) will completely shut down any ping attempts or shared folders by default. (I myself once spent an embarrassing afternoon chasing down a problem with sharing files on my laptop before finally remembering: *Oh yeah, my laptop has a firewall on it, doesn't it?* I spent fifteen minutes reading up on how to reconfigure my firewall, and the problem was solved.) Therefore, make sure that you read your firewall's documentation to find out how to allow file sharing.

Tip

In many personal firewalls, you may be able to establish a *trust zone*—a range of IP addresses for which the firewall's standards are low enough to allow things such as file sharing and ping attempts, but are still strong enough to disallow viral infiltration. Check your firewall's manual for details.

File sharing, at least for Windows, is fairly simple: You designate a folder or a hard drive that will be made available to outside computers on the same network. Computers on the same network (also called a *workgroup* in Windows parlance) can then see each other and download and/or change any files in those folders or drives.

Though you *can* do it, *never* share a hard drive that contains operating system files. If you have a separate drive that's just for file sharing, wonderful—otherwise, sharing an entire drive leaves you vulnerable to hackers, who can delete or maliciously alter your system files. Instead, only share folders that you know contain nothing that can compromise or damage your computer if they are deleted or altered.

Sharing folders under Windows XP/2000

Windows XP/2000 is the most popular operating system, and will probably be where most of your sharing takes place. Fortunately, sharing folders and finding them is very simple in Windows XP/2000.

Finding a shared folder on Windows XP/2000

Hunting down the shared folders available is pretty simple:

1. Select My Network Places. My Network Places is available from the Start menu on many machines, but you may have to look on the side of My Documents to get to it, as shown in Figure 16-5.

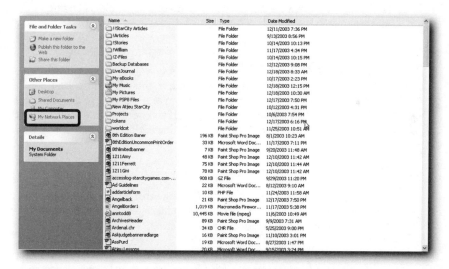

FIGURE 16-5: Where you might find My Network Places if it's not immediately evident

In any case, once you find My Network Places (wherever it is), it looks very much like Figure 16-6.

2. Double-click a folder to access its contents.

You should be able to make copies of any files in the shared folders in the same way you can copy files in local folders on your own PC. You may also, depending on how the person shared their folder, be able to upload your own files to the shared folder or even alter the files that are in there.

FIGURE 16-6: My Network Places, with a bunch of shared folders on three other computers

Sharing a folder in Windows XP/2000

Sharing a folder in Windows XP/2000 is fairly simple, though there is a catch: Most home versions of Windows XP will only allow a maximum of ten people to download at once. (That's why it's a *home* version, not a *professional* version.) If you need more than ten people Hoovering files off of your computer at once, you'll need Windows 2000 or some other professional server operating system.

To share a folder, follow these steps:

1. Find a folder that you'd like to share. Make sure that it's not a folder that contains anything valuable, either itself or any of its subfolders. Remember: People may be able to access and delete these files, so don't take chances.

Never share a drive that has operating system files on it. If you give anyone access to the Program Files folder or your Windows folder, I do not take any responsibility for what happens to you when some idiot gets bored.

If you have any files you want to share, why not put them in that folder now?

2. Right-click the folder and select Properties.
3. Click the Sharing tab, as shown in Figure 16-7.
4. Check the Share This Folder on the Network box.

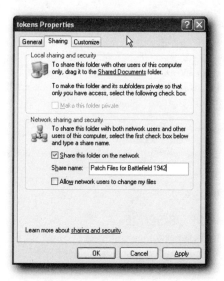

FIGURE 16-7: The Sharing tab of the Properties
dialog box

5. Give your shared folder a descriptive name, such as "Patch files" or "MP3s from Artists Not On RIAA Labels" so that, when people go browsing for shared folders, they'll know what each one is at a glance.

If you use a name longer than 12 characters, computers running older versions of Windows (such as Windows 98 or Windows ME) will not be able to see the shares. If there are no Windows 98 or ME computers on your network, name it whatever you want!

6. If you'd like people to be able to upload their own files to your shared folder, check the Allow Network Users to Change My Files box. Unfortunately, this means that people will be able to delete and alter files at will. Oh, well. Make sure you have backup copies of your files elsewhere on your computer!

Unsharing a folder in Windows XP/2000

When the LAN party is done, you don't want to leave these folders open for anyone who asks; they're a potential security risk. Better to close them now:

1. Right-click the shared folder and select Properties.

2. Choose the Sharing tab.

3. Uncheck the Share This Folder on the Network box. Click OK.

Windows 95/98/SE/ME

The earlier versions of Windows are slightly clunky, because their file sharing wasn't truly integrated. Unlike newer versions of Microsoft's latest cash cow, which just asks for all shared folders and puts them in one place for you, under Windows 95/98/ME, you need to know the network name of the computer before you can find the shared folder, and then navigate your way to that specific computer and find the shared file.

This is further made troublesome by the fact that on many Windows 95/98/ME computers, you need to install a protocol in order to give people access to your shared files. Needless to say, asking the average computer user to install a networking protocol in order to share files goes over like a lead balloon.

It can be done, however, and I'll show you how.

Finding a shared folder on Windows 95/98/SE/ME

As already mentioned, before you can find a shared folder, you need to know the name of the computer on which the shared folder resides. Every Windows computer has a name, even if it's a name assigned by default — I'll show you how to find that name in the section "Troubleshooting File Sharing," later in the chapter. Use the following steps to find a computer and its trove of precious, precious files:

1. On the desktop, double-click the Network Neighborhood icon (or My Network Places in Windows ME). Figure 16-8 illustrates the resulting screen.

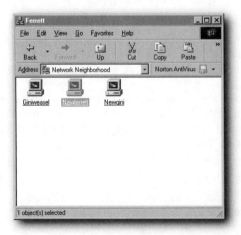

FIGURE 16-8: The author's Network Neighborhood —
take a look around!

2. Double-click the name of the computer containing the shared folder. You'll see a listing of the folders available, as shown in Figure 16-9.

**FIGURE 16-9: Shared folders on a specific computer
(in this case, Newferrett)**

3. Double-click on the folder to access its contents. (You may have to enter a password, in which case you should ask the owner of the computer what the password is.)

You should be able to make copies of any files in the shared folders in the same way you can copy files in local folders on your own PC. You may also, depending how the person shared their folder, be able to upload your own files to the shared folder or even alter the files that are there.

Sharing a folder in Windows 95/98/ME

1. Find a folder that you'd like to share. Make sure that it's not a folder that contains anything valuable, including any of the subfolders. Remember: People may be able to access and delete these files, so don't take chances.

As mentioned earlier, *never share a drive with operating system files on it*. If you give anyone access to your Program Files folder or your Windows folder, you're leaving the door wide open to major systems crashes.

If you have any files you want to share, why not put them in that folder now?

2. Right-click the folder and select Sharing. The Sharing tab of the Folder Properties dialog box will appear, as shown in Figure 16-10.

Tip

If you don't see Sharing as an option, your computer does not have the file-sharing protocols installed. I'll show you how to do that in the next section.

3. Click the Shared As radio button, and enter a short, descriptive name for the folder. (Said descriptive name must be 12 or fewer characters, so be creative.)

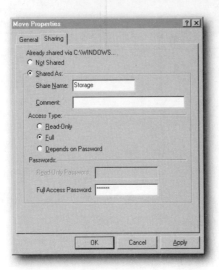

FIGURE **16-10: The Sharing tab of the Folder Properties dialog box**

4. Select the type of folder access you want. You have three options: Read-only, Full, and Depends on Password. Read-only will prevent people from changing or uploading files, while Full will let remote users do whatever they want.

   Depends on Password allows you to set two separate passwords: one that will give remote users read-only access, and another that will give them full access.

5. If you'd like people to enter a password before they can access this folder, put in a password here. (If you chose Depends on Password, you can put in both passwords now.)

Note

Strangely enough, Windows XP does not allow you to put a password on a shared folder. Theoretically, this is because Windows XP has greater *security granularity*, which is a fancy way of saying that WinXP enables you to fine-tune your access so that you don't need crude passwords-by-folder methods. Unfortunately, the lengths you have to go to in order to access that extra security are such a royal pain that I'm not even bothering to go into them here. Suffice it to say that you expend a lot of effort to get very little return in most circumstances.

6. Click OK.

To install the Windows 95/98/ME file-sharing protocol

As already mentioned, some early versions of Windows didn't come with the protocol installed. Ideally, yours has it — but if not, here's how you do it!

1. Click the Start button and select Settings ⇨ Control Panel.

2. Double-click the Network icon. The Network dialog box appears, as shown in Figure 16-11.

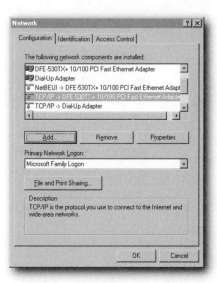

FIGURE **16-11: The Network dialog box**

3. Click the Add button. The Select Network Component Type dialog box appears, as shown in Figure 16-12.

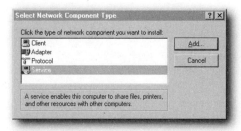

FIGURE **16-12: Select Network Component Type dialog box**

4. Select Service, and then click the Add button. The Select Network Service dialog box will appear, fresh as the morning sunrise, as shown in Figure 16-13.

5. Select File and Printer Sharing for Microsoft Networks. Click OK. Windows will install the appropriate protocols; it may ask you for your installation disc, though hopefully not. (Me, I never remember where I left my Windows installation discs.)

6. When it's done, click the File and Print Sharing button.

7. Check the I Want to Be Able to Give Others Access to My Files button. Click OK.

8. Click OK again. A dialogue box will appear, informing you that you're going to have to restart your computer. Restart and start sharing.

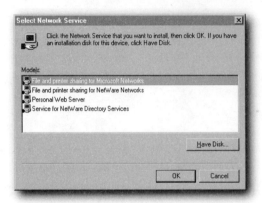

FIGURE 16-13: The Select Network Service dialog box

Unsharing a folder on Windows 95/98/SE/ME

Shared folders are a particular danger on older versions of Windows, as the hacks to get past them are well-known, and you may not have all of the latest patches. If that's the case, you don't want to leave these folders open when you get back home and access your usual Internet connection.

1. Right-click the shared folder and select Sharing.

2. Select the Not Shared radio button at the top.

3. Click OK.

Troubleshooting shared folders

You may encounter one of two problems when a Windows user can't get to a shared folder or folders: firewalls and workgroups/domains.

Firewalls

If there is a firewall on the computer with the shared folder, that firewall is usually set to reject access to shared folders by default. As I said, shared folders are a security risk, and most firewalls figure that it's better safe than sorry.

For more information on firewalls and how they work, refer to Chapter 8, "Networking for Large Groups and the Internet."

However, Microsoft made a truly colossal blunder when it comes to sharing files on Windows XP: Whenever you set up a file share using the Networking Wizard, or whenever you share an Internet connection using Internet connection sharing, *it turns on the firewall by default,* sometimes without even asking you.

Yes, you read that right: Whenever you use the Networking Wizard to set up a shared folder, it then turns on an option that prevents anyone from accessing your shared folders. I can't make this kind of stuff up, folks.

Microsoft's firewall is a good idea, but it has one problem: it's not very customizable (at least, not on most home versions of Windows XP). Unfortunately, in order to grant people access to your folders, you have to turn it off. The following steps show you how:

1. Select Control Panel from your Start menu.

2. Select Network and Internet Connections if you're using the Category View. (If you're not using the Category View, then it won't be an option.)

3. Select Network Connections.

4. If you have the firewall enabled on any of your Internet connections, your connection will indicate that it has a firewall, as shown in Figure 16-14.

FIGURE 16-14: Your Internet connection will look like this if you have a firewall enabled.

Right-click it and select Properties.

5. Select the Advanced tab, and uncheck the box that says Protect My Computer and Network by Limiting or Preventing Access to this Computer from the Internet, as shown in Figure 16-15.

6. Click OK. Click Yes in response to the "Are you sure?" dialogue box.

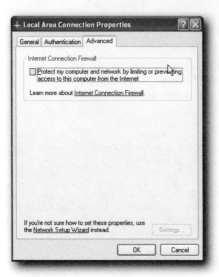

FIGURE 16-15: The Advanced tab, where you can disable your firewall — but don't do this unless you have some other firewall in place!

7. Go to www.zonealarm.com and download a free and customizable personal firewall so you're not completely vulnerable. (Unlike Windows' native firewall, in ZoneAlarm you can set a *Trust zone* that allows people to access your shared folders as long as they're from a specified range of IP addresses — and remember, most small LAN parties consist of a small range of IP addresses.)

Workgroups

In some cases, you'll need to join a *workgroup* or a *domain* in order to access a file. Workgroups and domains are essentially the same thing: They're groups that your computer must join before it can access the shared folders on a specific computer. (Domains are more secure versions of workgroups.) This is required for security purposes.

Think of workgroups and domains as the computer equivalent of gangs; before you can be friends with the Sharks and hang out on their stoop, you have to prove that you are a Shark. Likewise, before you can download files from a shared folder on a computer in the WEASELPCS workgroup, you have to prove that you're a WEASELPCS computer.

Fortunately, proving that you're a member of a workgroup or domain is pretty simple — as long as you know the name of the workgroup or domain you need to access!

Finding the name of your workgroup on a Windows XP/2000 computer

1. Choose My Computer from the Start menu.

2. Click the up arrow button at the top of the screen, as shown in Figure 16-16.

FIGURE 16-16: The up arrow that you must click to go to the right place

Tip

Alternatively, if you're feeling dexterous, you can select My Computer from the Start menu and then right-click it from there.

3. Right-click My Computer and select Properties. Select the Computer Name tab, as shown in Figure 16-17.

FIGURE 16-17: Changing your computer name in the System Properties dialog box

Adding your computer to a workgroup or domain on a Windows XP/2000 computer

Note that a workgroup can consist of one computer. If you're going to be hosting the file server, you can set up your own computer as a workgroup of one, and then have others join your workgroup as they hook up to your network.

1. Repeat steps 1 through 3 as described in the section "Finding the name of your workgroup on a Windows XP/2000 computer," earlier in this chapter.

2. Click the Change button. You will see the dialog box shown in Figure 16-18.

FIGURE 16-18: Changing the name of your workgroup

If your computer does not have a unique name like "newferrett" or "joeyspc," give it one; every computer on a workgroup or a domain must have a unique name.

3. Enter the exact name of the workgroup or domain you'd like to join (or create). Click OK.

4. If you're joining a domain (which you should only need to do at the largest of LAN parties), you need to click the Change button (which will only appear if a domain is available) to request to join the domain. You will probably be asked to log on to the domain as an additional security measure; your network host should be able to provide your logon ID and password.

5. Reboot your computer.

Finding the name of your workgroup and computer on a Windows 95/98/SE/ME computer

1. Select Control Panel from your Start menu.

2. Double-click the Network icon.

3. Select the Identification tab, as shown in Figure 16-19.

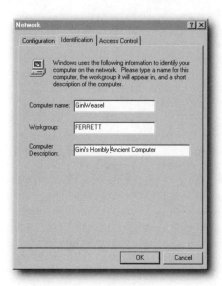

FIGURE **16-19: The Identification tab**

As you can see, the name of your computer is here — in this case, GiniWeasel. (My wife hates my nicknames, but I'm in charge of the home network, so I get to name her computers whatever I want.)

The workgroup is also added here, as is a descriptive name that you can enter to keep track of your PC.

Adding your computer to a workgroup on a Windows 95/98/SE computer

As I mentioned in the Windows XP section, remember that a workgroup can consist of one computer. If you're hosting a file server, you can set up your own computer as a workgroup of one, and then have others join your workgroup as they hook up to your network.

1. Repeat steps 1 through 3, as described in the section " Finding the name of your workgroup and computer on a Windows 95/98/SE/ME computer," earlier in this chapter.

2. If your computer does not have a unique name like "newferrett" or "joeyspc," give it one; all computers on a workgroup or a domain must have a unique name. You can give it one by simply typing in a new name in the Computer Name field. (If you're not sure whether your name is already in use, you can look it up in the Network Neighborhood, as described previously.)

Note

The maximum number of characters in a computer name is 15. Don't go over that.

3. Enter the exact name of the workgroup you'd like to join (or create). Click OK.

4. Reboot your computer or the changes will not take effect.

Accessing an FTP server via Internet Explorer or Netscape Navigator

FTP stands for *File Transfer Protocol*, and it's the Internet standard for passing files back and forth across the Internet. FTP has one major advantage that Windows' shared folders doesn't; every computer knows how to use FTP, whereas many operating systems (such as Linux and OS 8.x and 9.x) need special add-on programs in order to recognize Windows folders.

Alas, the home versions of Windows (Windows 95/98/ME/SE/XP) have no native FTP server support, which means that you have to download an FTP server program and install it if you'd like to run an FTP server on your box. However, Macintosh OS X and most flavors of Linux come with FTP servers ready and waiting to go, making an FTP server a good choice for a party. (You'll learn about FTP servers in the sections for each operating system, a little later in this chapter.)

Unless you have a dedicated FTP program such as WS_FTP, you'll have to use Internet Explorer's or Netscape Navigator's native FTP support to download files. Fortunately, this isn't terribly hard.

To do so, you need to know the IP address of the FTP server, any subdirectories of that server (sometimes people keep the root directory locked out for security purposes), and a logon name and password. (Most FTP servers are configured so that everyone can access them, but some are set up so you need a specific logon name and password to get in.)

Tip If you're accessing an FTP server and it unexpectedly asks you for a logon ID and password, try "anonymous" as the logon ID, and use your e-mail address as the password. Many FTP servers use these as the default logon.

When you're ready to go, type in **ftp://** and then the IP address of the server, as well as any subdirectories needed:

```
ftp://172.16.1.34/~theferrett
```

If you need to supply a logon name and password, you will be asked for them.

From here on, you'll be able to navigate through the files just as you would any other Web page, even if that page is devoid of pretty graphics. Click through the folders, and then click a file to download it to your computer. The window will look like the one shown in Figure 16-20.

Sharing files with Mac OS X

Fortunately, because Windows is the Big Doggie in the world of operating systems, the Macintosh has a lot of built-in support in order to enable Windows-based PCs to connect to it, and to connect to Windows-based PCs.

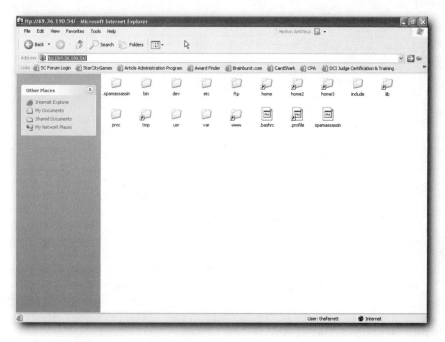

FIGURE 16-20: FTPing files via a browser

To connect to a Windows shared folder with a Macintosh

Fortunately, connecting to a Windows shared folder with a Macintosh is very simple:

1. Select Go from the Finder menu.

2. Click Connect to Server. A dialog box will pop up, showing the names of PCs with shared folders on them (see Figure 16-21).

3. Choose the computer you'd like to use and click Connect. (If you don't see any Windows shared folders, you may need to click Browse first.) You may have to enter a password, either for the folder (Windows 95/98/ME/SE) or for the workgroup or domain (Windows XP/2000).

4. You may now browse the folder as if it were a local drive.

FIGURE 16-21: Viewing Windows shared folders on a Macintosh

Sharing files with a Macintosh

There are two ways to share files with a Mac, one trickier than the other:

- **You can set up an FTP server.** FTP, or File Transfer Protocol, is the Internet standard for getting files from one place to another. If you set your Macintosh up to serve as an FTP server, then any computer will be able to download files from it.

  The downside to this is that while you can technically access FTP from Windows' command prompt, it's tricky to do so for a novice. Most professionals use some sort of FTP program, such as WS_FTP, in order to simplify the procedure. Alternatively, both Internet Explorer and Netscape Navigator have native FTP support built in.

- **You can set up a Samba server.** Samba (recently renamed to the far less-interesting sounding CIFS, or Common Internet File System) enables computers in a small network to exchange files. Macintosh OS 10.1 has a Samba client, which is what enables you to browse through Windows' Shared Folders with aplomb; Macintosh 10.2 (and presumably all later versions) has a Samba *server*, which enables you to set up a shared folder that will look just like a Windows Shared Folder to a Windows machine.

  Alas, installing and setting up the Samba protocol is outside the scope of this book, as it involves getting into the Unix roots of the Macintosh OS. May I suggest taking a look at the *Mac OS X Bible, Jaguar Edition*, by Lon Poole (Wiley Publishing)?

I can, however, tell you how to set up a Mac as an FTP server, as it's sinfully easy:

1. Open System Preferences.

2. Click the Sharing icon. The Sharing Services pane will appear, as shown in Figure 16-22.

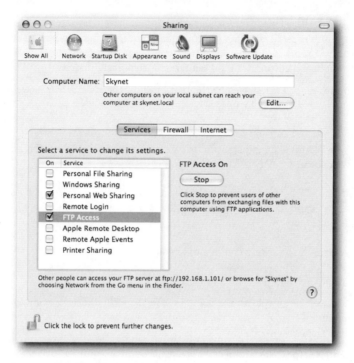

FIGURE 16-22: The Sharing Services pane

3. Check the FTP Access box under the Services tab. Click OK. You're done!

Caution

Remote users can upload files and delete files from your FTP server—and the default directory for that server is your home directory as a user, meaning that anyone can browse through (and download!) your personal files. If you don't want people snooping through your personal files, you might want to create a separate user when you're acting as an FTP server—for example, "FTPDude"—and use that when you're serving up files.

Sharing files with Linux

Alas, transferring files back and forth between Linux servers and Windows is tricky, and fraught with a lot of technical details that are, again, outside the scope of this book.

While Linux technically can access Windows' Shared Folders if it has a Samba client installed, I've heard a lot of horror stories about getting Samba working properly—and let's face it, Linux is not the most user-friendly operating system. Unless you're a real Linux guru, my suggestion is to not try to access Windows shared folders and instead rely on FTP, which works regardless of what platform you're running.

Is that problematic if you're a Linux user at a Windows party? Yes. Your best bet in that case is to offer to *be* the file server, because you have native FTP support built right into your operating system.

Getting FTP files with Linux

As a Linux user, you're most likely using the command prompt. That's good, because the bare-bones FTP client is command-line-based. You'll have to type to browse through, as opposed to clicking, unless you have a custom FTP program that's graphically-based.

To use FTP, simply type **FTP** followed by the IP address of the FTP server, as well as any subdirectories, as shown by the following:

```
ftp 172.16.1.34/~theferrett
```

You may then be asked for a logon name and password, if you're logging onto an FTP server that has security enabled. Type them in at the prompt.

> **Tip** If you're accessing an FTP server and it unexpectedly asks you for a logon ID and password, try "anonymous" as the logon ID, and use your email address as the password. Many FTP servers use this as the default logon.

To use FTP, you have the following commands at your disposal:

- **ls** lists all files on the FTP server, just like Linux' native `ls` command.

- **get** *<filename>* downloads the named file to the local directory you were in when you started up FTP.

- **put** *<filename>* uploads a named file from the local directory you were in when you first started FTP to whatever directory you're currently in on the FTP server.

> **Tip** Many servers allow you to download files, but will not allow you to upload new files or delete existing files. Don't be surprised if you try to delete something and are told that your permissions are insufficient.

- **pwd** shows you the current directory on the FTP server.

- **mget** *<filename1> <filename2> <filename3>*.... allows you to download multiple files at once. There is no real limit to the number of files you can download at once via the command line, though forty-line `mget` commands tend to cause problems.

- **mput** *<filename1> <filename2> <filename3>*.... allows you to upload multiple files at once.

- **cd** *<directoryname>* moves you to the named directory. This is useful for navigating through a server.

- **cdup** moves you back one directory on the tree.

- **delete** *<filename>* deletes a file.

- **rename** *<filename> <new filename>* renames the file.

- **mkdir** creates a directory on the server, if your permissions allow this.

- **rmdir** removes a directory on the server, if your permissions and the server settings allow this. (Many Linux servers don't allow you to delete a directory that has files in it.)

- ! allows you to return temporarily to your command-line shell, usually to change directories. Type exit to return to FTP.

- **bye** exits FTP.

Sharing files with Linux

As mentioned earlier, the easiest way to do this is to start an FTP server. Of course, "easy" is a relative term when it comes to Linux — not only are FTP servers comparatively complex to configure under Linux, but there are so many flavors of Linux that telling you how to set up an FTP server under one flavor of Linux might not work on others.

As such, I must again regretfully say that if you're using Linux and want to be an FTP server, pick up the appropriate Wiley Bible (such as the *Red Hat Linux 9 Bible*, by Christopher Negus, or the *Debian/GNU Linux Bible*, by Steve Hunger (both published by the fantabulous Wiley) and go from there.

LAN Party Activities

I hate to sound like your parent, but do you intend to spend all day plopped in front of that PC? Aren't there better things for you to do?

Not that continual destruction isn't fun, but you can make a LAN party even more fun by providing alternatives — scheduled events that create a nice little breather. In addition to just being plain fun, some events appeal to subsections of the local techie community; the local case-modders might not be motivated to go to a LAN party across town, but they will go if there's a case-modding beauty contest. If you're interested in increasing your attendance, you could do worse than to think about including a couple of the fun events I'll describe in the following sections.

And, as I said before, if you have held a cool event that you want to share with the world, e-mail it to me at theferrett@theferrett.com. I might be able to use your idea in a future edition of this book (with credit, of course).

Charity Events

If you have a LAN party at which you've been turning a profit for the past couple of events, why not hold a raffle or contest and offer the proceeds to a local charity?

All you have to do in most cases is charge an entry fee to participate, and the charity gets some much-needed moolah. You'll feel really good, and it offers other benefits: Not only will your party gain respect in the eyes of the community (thus making it easier to find outside locations and ensure better cooperation with the local law), you get free publicity that may alert new people to your LAN party's existence. (Also, it's a lot easier to get cool freebies when your sponsors know it's for charity.)

There's nothing better than giving back to the community. Any of the following ideas can be turned into some sort of charity-benefiting event; maybe you should think about it.

Mod parties

Visually, most computers are boring. The gray-and-white molded case is the industry standard, and who wants to look at a dull, gray box like the one shown in Figure 16-23?

But human nature being what it is, if a bunch of people show up in the same place with something, they're eventually going to compete to see who has the *prettiest* something. It doesn't matter what that item is; whether it's a doting pet owner walking a purebred poodle or Jimmy Fontino down at the bowling alley showing off his Predator Pursuit opalescent bowling ball, *someone's* going to find a way to show off. Check out Figure 16-24.

FIGURE 16-23: A boring, boring, boring PC

FIGURE 16-24: Now *this* is a cool computer.

As you can see, computers are no exception. Thus began the trend of case-modding.

Case-modding is taking that metal case that holds your chips and drives and modifying it heavily to make it look cool. Of course, not all case-mods are purely decorative; particularly for overclocked PCs, cutting a hole in the case and adding another fan is the only way to prevent it from overheating.

There are several classic modifications, including the following:

- **Painting and stickers.** This is the simplest modification, and usually where people begin. You can do all sorts of interesting things with the outside of a metal case, including custom art and all manner of writing (using wax lettering transfers). Let your imagination run wild! (Just be careful not to paint over any buttons or fans that require access; if you paint your On button, you may wind up with an On button that sticks.)

- **Plastic dying.** Painting plastic isn't nearly as effective as painting sheet metal, so people figured out a way to dye the plastic used for the fronts of disk drives and the plastic parts of monitors. This is done using a special type of spray paint called vinyl dye, which is thin enough to seep into the plastic and color it. This is a time-consuming process that usually requires three or four coats to work, but the results are suitably impressive.

- **Powdercoating.** If regular ol' painting isn't enough for you, you can use powdercoating—the exact same painting process that gives hotrods their unique glossy sheen. You can only powdercoat conductive metals, and you need to bake the paint on at temperatures of about 400 degrees, but the results are *extremely* nice.

- **Chroming.** Usually, you don't do this yourself—you go to the phone book and flip to "Plating" to find someone who chromes items for a living. Bring them your dull, gray case, and walk out with a shiny computer that looks like the tailpipe of a brand-new Harley. Extremely cool.

- **The blowhole.** This involves cutting a hole in the top of the case and installing a fan, usually with some fancy chrome ring on top. Not the prettiest of mods, but it's extremely useful in hot PCs. However, I wouldn't advise doing this until you've had a couple of practice rounds with a jigsaw to make sure that you can cut evenly...

- **Windows.** You can cut a hole in the side of your PC, and then install a plastic or glass window (usually with a rubber inlay to assure a tight fit) so everyone can see the insides of your PC busily whirring away while you frag. (Most gamers with PC windows have gone to some length to spruce up their wires, bundling them away neatly or in some sort of eye-striking arrangement.) For an extra-cool factor, you usually put some sort of clear sticker on the window, like the ones used on the rear windows of cars.

- **Stained-glass or etched windows.** If a regular window isn't enough for you, how about some sort of cool window that looks like a church window or an etched-glass setting— something like the computer shown in Figure 16-25?

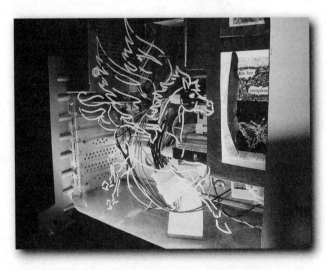

FIGURE 16-25: A very pretty unicorn-themed case-mod

- **Neon piping.** To ensure that your window offers something cool to look at, you can get neon strips in various colors to highlight the inside of your PC. A PC with a window and neon piping looks *extremely* cool, and will make all of the other gamers envious.

- **LEDs.** You can put a lot of cool-looking displays on the outside of your case. Many people have made their computers look like ticking bombs in old "Mission Impossible" shows, which I think is pretty darned neat.

- **Quieter computers.** High-end computers are relatively noisy, with buzzing fans galore. You can alter your computer's case in a number of ways to reduce noise, either by isolation-mounting your hard disk (suspending it via rubber grommets), replacing your noisy fans with quieter ones, moving components around to change their noise level, or applying sound-absorbent padding,

- **Liquid cooling systems.** Want the continual buzzing of that fan gone altogether? Well, not only does water carry away heat 72 times as efficiently as air, it's completely silent! With water-cooling, you use a Peltier Junction (a physical device that chills the water on one side of a tube and transfers the excess heat to the other), and circulate the water to carry heat away. The only problem with this system is that unless you're careful when sealing up the system, water can condense on the cool side (just like it condenses on a cold can of soda) and drip onto the CPU. Therefore, take great pains to ensure that you have the ability to install something according to directions!

- **Three-dimensional add-ons.** People love to go nuts. I've seen *Alien*-modded cases with H. R. Giger-inspired piping, *Matrix* cases with custom displays on the front that have that cool *Matrix*-style display screen (the ones in which the almost-English letters drop to the bottom of the screen), and *Doom*-inspired cases with screaming skulls on the front.

That's not all, though. I've seen fishtank PCs, the "nonexistent" PCs (cases with carefully placed mirrors that create the illusion that you're looking at an empty case), PCs with working toaster slots and a refrigerator, and PCs put into the bottom of a La-Z-Boy recliner. The sky's the limit!

Now, obviously, once the case-modding bug hits your group, there's no turning back. The case-modding community is fiercely competitive, always looking around to see who can come up with the coolest, most radical mod. Therefore, given that they're hungry to top one another, why not offer a contest?

If you live in a reasonably large city and are trying to get more people involved in your community, announce that you'll be offering a prize for the coolest case-mod. (You can learn how to get prizes in Chapter 5, "Saving Money on Your LAN Party.") You'd be surprised by how many people will pop out of the woodwork to show off their phenomenal creation! (Be warned, however, that case-modders tend to want different prizes than normal computer folks; a good upscale handheld jigsaw or a water-cooled system is a much bigger draw to them than a new video card. Fortunately, most case-modders are in it for the fame and ego-stroking of winning the contest, not the goods.)

At the end of the day, put the computers where everyone can see them, and then have everyone in the room vote for the one they think is the most creative. If you have a lot of case-modders, you might want to consider adding extra prizes for categories such as "Most Impressive Technical Accomplishment" and "Best First-Timer's Attempt."

Another good idea is to have a "Case-Modder's Workshop," to which someone brings all of their case-modding equipment and does some on-the-spot computer hacking (literally!) to show people how it's done. Be sure to keep power circuits in mind, though, as many power tools really burn up the amps.

Map design parties

With the advent of the first-person shooter, one of the most interesting developments has been the rise of the design community — the people who create customized levels using their favorite game engine. Some of these levels are relatively simple, being nothing more than maps, but others — like the now famous Counter-Strike — started out as fan-based modifications and became fully-fledged, separate games that pushed the envelope of what the game engine could deliver.

You name it: custom graphics, custom sounds, custom weapons, entire redesigns of core portions of the game. Much like case-modding, the sky's the limit when it comes to level design. And if you have one or two regular attendees who can look under the hood and design a level or two, you can utilize their talent. Chances are good that if they play with you every other weekend, they know what kind of game you enjoy playing, and can design a map that fits your style like a glove, so why not draw upon that talent and ask them to create a map for you?

I've heard many tales of gamers who have created excellent maps, based on feedback. One of the main challenges that level designers face is learning to spot the trouble areas of their level — a sniper area that's just too easily defended, a narrow bridge that's just too hard to cross, a confusing level that gets people lost — and it's often helpful for a designer to get real-time advice about what works and what doesn't. That way, they can show up for the next party with a new level that has been modified according to useful feedback, and then people can make more suggestions. Next thing you know, you have a map that you can't live without!

Again, geeks are competitive. If you have a large party with multiple designers, hold a contest for prizes! Have your level designers submit their own game modification a week in advance (so you can burn it onto discs or put it on a server), and then have everyone play each level. At the end of the evening, vote to see who won. (If you have two prizes, split them into two categories: Most Fun and Best Technical Accomplishment.)

Real-life fragging

One activity that can add a huge level of fun to your event, particularly during warm summer days, is a real-life hunt. Most first-person shooters involve running around a field or a maze and shooting your competitors with some kind of weapon, so why not recreate that run-and-gun experience in real life?

No, *not* with real guns. As I said at the beginning of the book, this isn't Columbine! You can create the feel of a hunt without the violence and bloodshed. You can use the following three gun substitutes to have a good solid chase:

- **Nerf guns.** These are great fun. If you're not familiar with Nerf guns (and if you're not, I pity you), they're bright plastic guns that shoot foam darts or light plastic balls. Some of the latest Nerf designs are extremely creative — you can get bazooka-style guns that use gigantic foam darts, Nerf machine guns, or tiny handguns that can fit under a long sleeve. Most of them are surprisingly accurate at short distances.

Note   You can scan Nerf's catalog at www.nerf.com, although it only represents their current products; they tend to cycle through models relatively quickly, and older versions of Nerf guns abound.

The downside to Nerf guns is that while they're great for a casual game, they're awful for formalized events. Aside from your own honesty, there's no proof that you've been hit by a Nerf gun! Therefore, if you're keeping score, you probably want another style of fake gun.

- **Paintball guns.** This requires a lot of equipment. Not only are paintball guns relatively expensive (starting at about $80 and going way up for a top-of-the-line model — and that's not including the paintballs and air canisters), they're fairly dangerous. You can be potentially blinded by a paintball to the eyes, and even a direct hit on clothing can leave a stinging welt. (I don't even want to talk about the horror stories I've heard from guys who were hit in the crotch.) Therefore, you definitely need goggles and protective padding in order to play safely.

  However, the advantage of paintball is that it offers the closest approximation to actual combat. If you're a hard-core historian, the opportunity to play with guns that have a real weight and feel to them and to hear the "oof!" as you nail someone at long range is priceless.

  In addition, paintball enables you to play in teams very easily, as each team or player can use a different colored ink. There is rarely an argument as to who nailed who when it comes to paintball.

- **Water pistols.** You may have grown up with the cheesy little plastic pistols that leaked water out of a plug in the back. But when you weren't looking, water pistol technology took a major leap forward. Today's water pistols are sleek aquatic combat machines that can hold gallons of water and use pump-action hydraulics to push a painfully strong jet of liquid straight at an unsuspecting enemy. The best part about these pistols is that most of them still cost less than $30.

  The premiere manufacturer of water pistols is Super Soaker (check their site at www.supersoaker.com), and they create some excellent models. Water fights are great for cooling off after a hot day in a computer room (especially if you have no air conditioning), and there's usually incontrovertible evidence that you've been tagged.

Tip

If you're playing teams and are concerned about who shot who, you can use food coloring to tint your water and create (mostly) washable dyes.

The only real disadvantage to a water gun fight is that you need towels afterwards, and probably a change of clothes. But if you're not a hydrophobe, water guns kick serious butt.

Holding a real-life frag can be a major hoot, but you should observe the following guidelines if you want to have a successful side event:

- **Provide equipment.** Most people don't have a good water pistol or a top-of-the-line Nerf gun. (More's the pity, I know.) Therefore, if you want a lot of people to play — and you do — provide guns that they can borrow for the event. It's horrible to have people sitting on the sidelines, wanting to play, but locked out of the event, and more than one potential real-life frag has been scotched because only two people showed up with equipment.

Tip

If you're dealing with paintball guns, which tend to be expensive and easily broken by amateurs, feel free to charge a rental fee. You may want to hook up with the local paintball field to see if they'll provide instruction and rental guns; after all, most paintball fields are eager to recruit new players, and what better way to reach fresh faces than a LAN party?

- **Have a wide-open space outdoors.** Real-life fragging indoors is sure to lead to all sorts of complications; in small spaces, someone's sure to trip and hurt themselves, and in large spaces like hotels and conference rooms, chances are pretty good that some other guest is going to see your roughhousing shenanigans and call in the management.

  (Has this happened to me personally? No comment.)

  Therefore, you want an outdoor space — and it had better be either property you own (or at least rented for the weekend), or a public space with very few people. Running around on someone else's property can lead to trespassing charges, no matter how harmless you may be.

- **Be respectful of other people.** Remember that you're going to be running around with guns clutched in your fists, and that may freak people out. Don't play in a heavily populated area, and don't harass anyone.

  If you're playing in a public arena, the police may show up to investigate; be understanding, and show them that you're playing with toy weapons. Of course, even if it's a fake gun, if the police ask you to drop it, *drop it instantly*.

- **Add some landmarks.** A great game for large-scale events is a Capture the Flag variant, wherein two teams defend their bases (which contain a flag) while trying to get the other team's flag back to their base. Adding some bases, or a prisoner zone in which shot players can be "rescued" or "revived" by living teammates, can make a wide-open field more interesting.

- **Add a hands-off refill area.** Whether it's Nerf guns, water pistols, or paintballs, every faux gun has one thing in common: They all need to be reloaded. Having a no-kill zone where people can rest a bit and refill their ammo makes for a more enjoyable game. (Of course, cutthroat competitors may decide — and quite rightfully — that this makes things too easy, and eliminate the refill zone.)

- **Keep an eye on safety.** Remember: These people will be running around outside, and it's very easy to get hurt when you're running through unfamiliar territory. Before you hold an event, do a thorough walkthrough to remove any hazards like broken glass, and fill in any holes where someone might break an ankle. If the weather is rainy or there are large patches of mud, postpone or call off the event.

Tip

If you're very concerned about lawsuits, you might want to have people sign a release form, as described in Chapter 14, "Legal and Safety Issues." However, remember that a release form only limits your liability; it doesn't remove it altogether. If it can be shown that you knowingly sent people into a dangerous area, you can still be sued.

- **Set a time limit.** It may seem like it would be more fun to let it go on forever, but what usually happens is that people play way past the point where it's fun and get exhausted, which drains their energy for the rest of the day. Play for an hour or so, and then get back to the computers while you're still fresh!

- **Ignore everything I say, except the safety stuff.** Sometimes it's great just to run around like idiots and shoot everything in sight. If people seem to be having more fun just shooting everything that moves, what the heck; go with the flow, baby.

Troubleshooting parties

Inevitably, at any party, someone has some sort of hardware flaw they can't figure out, or a weird bug crops up from time to time, or a program won't work correctly. When you're inviting a bunch of computer-savvy people to an event, why not utilize that collective noggin-power to solve some people's difficulties?

Having a *troubleshooting party* is a long-standing tradition at many LAN parties.Simply set aside an hour during which the brightest brains at the party try to hunt down the problems in glitchy computers that people have brought in to be fixed. Don't force anyone into trouble-shooting duty, but do ask in advance; you'd be surprised how many hardware gurus actually enjoy using their skills for the greater good. (Most of them work for companies where they don't get effusive thanks whenever they fix a problem.)

For many people, the challenge of standing around with a bunch of like-minded companions, debating what the source of the problem could be, is more of a draw than the LAN party itself!

Then, if you can't solve the problem, you can kill two birds with one stone by subjecting the offending computer to the horrific *PC Destruction Event*, as described later. Oh, revenge *is* a dish best served cold.

The LAN party drinking game

A popular drinking game at some parties is called The Big Keg of Frag, and it is indeed a great party game. Essentially, every time you frag someone in a game, you drink a shotglass full of beer. (A can of beer will provide between ten and sixteen shotglasses.) Each game lasts twenty minutes, and you cannot drink more than one can of beer per game.

However, in the course of two hours, your best players will have had six beers, which is sure to slow their reflexes a bit. The brilliant part of this is that while the best players are happily drunk, the worst players will finally have a chance to catch up with the big dogs! (Talk about your self-correcting systems.)

This is a very fun game. Big props to former LANParty.com editor Olivier Adam for this one!

 Drinking to excess is bad. Drinking when you're going to drive is bad. Drinking when you're underage is excessively bad. For a comprehensive look at the legal liabilities that can occur when you add alcohol to a party, see Chapter 14, "Legal and Safety Issues."

Triathlon

AsylumLAN has an interesting idea: the Office Triathalon! They have several goofy contests that include activities such as the office chair race (seeing how fast someone can spin around the room in their chair), the keyboard toss, the AOL CD discus throw, the extension cord wrapping contest (to see how tightly and quickly you can wrap a fifty-foot extension cord), and so on. Points are awarded for first, second, and third place, and the person with the most points at the end of the event wins.

Note   See www.asylumlan.com for some highly entertaining videos. Be prepared for long load times, though.

PC destruction

If you've ever seen *Office Space*, you know how everyone always cheers when the protagonists destroy the copier machine with a baseball bat. And why not? We've all felt that frustration when a PC freezes up for no apparent reason.

At LAN parties, however, you have people with a lot of computers — often more than they need. (I myself have two dead boxes in my basement that I'm *sure* I'll get to one day.) Why not sponsor the art of creative destruction?

You can sell tickets to take a shot at a computer — whether that's via a sledgehammer, a rifle, a welding tool, or just running over it with some sufficiently large construction vehicle. People love watching computer equipment get totalled, and the more creatively the better. Let 'em watch.

Caution   Obviously, safety is paramount for this kind of event. Do *not* ever allow anyone to destroy a monitor at close range; they contain electrical charges that can potentially kill someone, even when unplugged. Always have someone wear safety goggles. Don't destroy a computer anywhere a passerby could get hurt. And if you're going to use a rifle or some other form of explosive destruction, clear it with the local officials in advance and make sure you plan it out very carefully.

Last, you should consider having people sign a legal release form before they can participate; check Chapter 14 for legal liabilities.

Embarrassing contests

One of the more amusing contests you can have is one in which you see how low people will go for a prize. If you can obtain a really good prize to offer, often it's far more amusing to ask, "So what will you do for it?" and put your players through a *Fear Factor*-style contest to see exactly what they're willing to do. Ryan Masanz (who gave me the idea for this one) had everyone hold an "ugly underwear" contest, and then got the female employees from the local Hooters to judge it.

At Lanwar, there is a tradition where people bid on how much duct tape they're willing to have ripped off of their arms in order to get a really cool piece of hardware. On at least one occasion, someone was later duct-taped and bound and then carried around the party like a trophy.

You can probably get your players to do something even more humiliating. Just be sure to observe the following guidelines:

- **Keep it all in good fun.** Remember that you want your players to walk away laughing from this, not emotionally scarred.

- **Don't make them do anything illegal or harmful.** A scavenger hunt for prizes can be fun, but not when one of the items is the siren rack of a police car. (Yes, someone actually did this. Yes, someone else won the prize just before they were hauled off to jail.) Make sure that whatever you ask people to do is within the bounds of the law, and won't get them seriously injured.

Other party games

When you're dealing with computer games and console games, and then go in for a little geekery outside, it's often easy to forget about the real-life face-to-face games you can have. They're not something you want to play extensively — after all, you can play Twister any time, but how often can you play Neverwinter Nights with no lag? — but they do serve as a good change-up.

Excellent games for multiplayer consumption are *Trivial Pursuit*, *Twister*, *Apples to Apples* (my personal favorite), *RoboRally*, *Lunch Money*, Chess, and classic card games such as Texas Hold 'Em and Bridge.

Summary

At last, we come to the end of this book. You have learned about the staff. You have learned about the technical issues. You have learned how to save money.

You now know everything you need to know in order to host a truly phenomenal LAN party. Remember: With great power comes great responsibility, and with great power mapping comes great LAN parties.

Get out there and truly frag 'em all!

The Party Checklists

This appendix contains all the planning questions from Chapter 2 and Chapter 4, assembled into one handy-dandy checklist for your convenience. Feel free to copy these pages and mark them up to your heart's content.

If you're wondering what the issues are behind any of these questions, refer to the original chapters, where I cover the ramifications of each question in great detail.

The Party Parameter Checklist (from Chapter 2)

What day(s) will you be holding this party?

_____

How many people will attend this party? ___

Tip

Remember that many people will *say* they will attend, but then fail to show up on the day of the party. Considering that you may need to move the party to an external location if it's big enough, trying to get an accurate preparty count is critical. Chapter 5 gives you some tips for getting an accurate head count.

Where will this party be held?

_____

Is this party open, closed, or capped?

❑ Open   ❑ Closed   ❑ Capped (___ players maximum)

Is this party hard-core (any tactic that wins is legitimate) or casual (some tactics provide wins that are too easy to pull off)?

❑ Hard core   ❑ Casual

If casual, what tactics are not allowed at this party?

_____

_____

Will this party offer prizes?

❑ Yes   ❑ No

What games will you be playing at this party?

_____

_____

What game variations will you be offering?

❑ Single-Elimination Deathmatch

❑ Ladder Tournaments

❑ Capture the Flag

❑ Cooperative Play

❑ Alternate-Win Matches

❑ Severe Handicapping

❑ Psychotic Locales

❑ Other (please specify): _____

Will you be using custom maps/scenarios (that is, maps or scenarios that do not come with the original game)?

❑ Yes   ❑ No

If you will be using custom maps and scenarios, what maps/scenarios will you be using? (Specify a name and a Web site from which the map(s) can be downloaded.)

_____

Do you want to mandate the use of headphones?

❑ Yes   ❑ No

Tip

Unless you have a really good reason not to, the answer is "Yes, everyone must use headphones instead of speakers."

Will this party include Internet access?

❑ Yes   ❑ No

What equipment should each guest bring to the party?

☑ A computer with a TCP/IP Ethernet NIC

❑ A keyboard and mouse

❑ A mouse pad

❑ A power strip

Tip

Power strips should always come with surge suppressors, just in case there's an electrical surge; unprotected strips could allow surges to damage someone's computer. You may want to mandate that power strips *must* have surge suppressors.

❑ A monitor

❑ Headphones

❑ Software (Specify what software guests should bring, including valid game CDs or any other custom antiviral software):

_____

❑ Other

_____

_____

Will guests have to perform a viral scan before they can log on at this party?

❑ Yes   ❑ No

If so, will you be requiring your guests to use a party-standard scan program, or can they use their own virus scanner?

❑ Your program (please specify):_____   ❑ Their Own

Will guests be allowed to drink at this party?

❑ Yes   ❑ No

Caution

Allowing drinking at a party can have serious legal consequences. See Chapter 14 for the full details of your responsibility if guests will be drinking alcohol.

Will guests be allowed to smoke at this party?

❑ Yes   ❑ No   ❑ Only outside the play area

Will you be serving food and drink at this party?

❑ Yes   ❑ No

If yes, what kind?

_____

Will minors be allowed at this party?

❑ Yes   ❑ No

Caution

Minors can sometimes pose additional legal hazards for your party, particularly if their parents don't know you well. See Chapter 14 for details.

Will guests be required to sign a legal waiver before they can play at this party?

❑ Yes ❑ No

Will you allow nonparticipants to hang around this party and watch?

❑ Yes ❑ No

Will you be charging an admission fee for this party?

❑ Yes ❑ No

If yes, how much?

_____

Note

If you're not sure how much to charge, Chapter 5 discusses setting party admission fees.

What side events (noncomputer game activities) will you hold?

_____

Tip

Chapter 16 has many, many ideas for fun side events that you can hold at your party!

Will you have a lost and found at this party?

❑ Yes ❑ No

The Preparty Checklist (from Chapter 4)

One to six months before the party

❑ Set the parameters and house rules for the party.

❑ Find a place to play that will hold all participants.

❑ Set a date.

❑ Make a list of everything (computer equipment and otherwise) you'll need for the party.

❑ Compare that list against what you currently have.

❑ Send a list of everything you need to all reliable participants, asking them what equipment they're willing to chip in/lend to the party.

❑ Choose staff members.

❑ Send out e-mail announcements.

❑ Put up a Web page.

Tip Even if it's a small party, a Web site where everyone can go for details is very easy to put up in this day of free GeoCities Web page accounts. Put *something* up.

❑ (If necessary) Look for sponsors.

❑ (If open party) Submit party to www.lanparty.com, www.bluesnews.com, and any other local computer sites to let people know the party exists.

❑ Draw up a party map, showing power outlets and where you'll put the tables and other equipment.

The week before the party

❑ Follow up with potential lenders.

❑ Set up pick-up times with lenders.

❑ Burn party discs and print out any welcome materials.

❑ Make and test cables.

❑ (If necessary) Buy any needed equipment.

Tip Remember the LAN Partiers' Creed: *Beg before you buy*. Don't purchase anything without asking first.

❑ (If necessary) Post fliers.

❑ (If necessary) Pick up prizes.

The night before the party

❑ Pick up the equipment.

❑ (If external rented location) Check into your party location.

❑ (If external rented location) Take a picture of the location as it is presented to you for legal purposes.

❑ Set up the furniture.

❑ Lay out the LAN.

❑ Lay out the power.

❑ Test the equipment.

❑ Clean up the area.

❑ Check for loose cables and other safety hazards.

❑ Lock up tightly.

Index

Continued